Understanding Globalization

Understanding Globalization

The Social Consequences of Political, Economic, and Environmental Change

2nd Edition

Robert K. Schaeffer

ROWMAN & LITTLEFIELD PUBLISHERS, INC.
Lanham • Boulder • New York • Oxford

ROWMAN & LITTLEFIELD PUBLISHERS, INC.

Published in the United States of America
by Rowman & Littlefield Publishers, Inc.
An Imprint of the Rowman & Littlefield Publishing Group
4720 Boston Way, Lanham, Maryland 20706
www.rowmanlittlefield.com

12 Hid's Copse Road, Cumnor Hill, Oxford OX2 9JJ, England

British Library Cataloguing in Publication Information Available

Library of Congress Cataloging-in-Publication Data

Schaeffer, Robert K.
    Understanding globalization : the social consequences of political, economic, and
environmental change / Robert K. Schaeffer—2nd ed.
        p. cm.
    Includes bibliographical references and index.
    ISBN 0-7425-1997-X (cloth : alk. paper)—ISBN 0-7425-1998-8 (pbk : alk. paper)
    1. Globalization.   2. Social history—1945–   3. World politics—1945–
    4. Economic history—1945–   5. Global environmental change.   I. Title.
JZ1318 .S33 2003
306'.09—dc21   2002003676

Printed in the United States of America

∞ ™ The paper used in this publication meets the minimum requirements of American
National Standard for Information Sciences—Permanence of Paper for Printed Library
Materials, ANSI/NISO Z39.48-1992.

To my students, one and all

Contents

contributed to rising homelessness in U.S. cities. These developments affected men and women in different ways. The U.S. battle against inflation also triggered a massive debt crisis for countries around the world, a crisis that persists today.

Many poor, "developing" countries borrowed heavily in the 1970s, tapping the financial pools in Eurocurrency markets to promote economic growth. But rising U.S. interest rates and falling commodity prices forced them into bankruptcy and triggered a massive debt crisis. Despite an arduous, two-decade effort to repay their loans, many poor countries remain mired in debt. Moreover, the imposition of "structural adjustment programs" on indebted governments has contributed to poverty, environmental destruction, and a decline in government services, developments that have been particularly hard on women.

Since 1980, commodity prices have fallen for farmers, miners, and oil producers around the world, making it hard for them to repay loans or develop economically. In many regions, globalization has contributed not to prosperity, but to poverty. This chapter examines the role that new technology and consumer behavior has played in these developments. It explains why poor countries have tried to develop manufacturing and tourist industries to increase their incomes, and why this strategy has largely been unsuccessful. It also examines the "traffic in women" associated with the growth of tourist and sex industries in poor countries.

Agricultural revolutions have vastly increased food supplies. But they have also displaced U.S. farmers and contributed to hunger in poor countries around the world. This chapter explains how agricultural technologies can simultaneously increase world food supplies *and* contribute to hunger, a serious problem for women and girls.

In the mid-1980s, scientists warned that the release of heat-trapping gases could trigger global warming, with disastrous results. This chapter explores the debate about contemporary climate change, examines the roles that different heat-trapping gases play, and discusses some of the political and economic strategies that might reduce the threat of global warming.

U.S. officials promoted the adoption of global and regional free trade agreements to promote the export of U.S. goods. Open markets have expanded the volume of world trade, but the benefits of trade have not been equally shared. This chapter examines the winners and losers of new free trade agreements, explains why the globalization of trade has led to widespread protest, and explores the consequences of free trade for producers and consumers around the world.

Acknowledgments

A number of people and organizations contributed to the development of different chapters. My colleagues at Friends of the Earth and Greenpeace supported initial work on dollar devaluations, free trade agreements, population growth, and global climate change. The Office of Appropriate Technology sponsored my initial work on housing and homelessness. Bill Friedland and participants in the globalization of the fresh fruit and vegetable industry working group helped me develop my ideas about food and hunger. My colleagues in Pugwash Conferences on Science and World Affairs, particularly Metta Spencer and Joseph Rotblat, encouraged my research on Yugoslavia. And participants in meetings sponsored by the American Sociological Association and the Political Economy of the World-System reviewed and commented on papers on democratization, free trade agreements, and job loss. Immanuel Wallerstein, Phil McMichael, Ravi Palat, Giovanni Arrighi, and Metta Spencer have my thanks for their work as organizers and editors.

Dean Birkenkamp provided crucial support for this book. His editorial suggestions and advice were important and welcome.

Torry Dickinson, my friend, colleague, and collaborator, deserves special mention for her intellectual contribution to my work. Her interest in history and her appreciation of the social consequences of global change helped shape my ideas and direct my research.

To all of you, my sincere thanks.

1

Theories of Globalization

For social scientists, a "theory" is a set of assumptions or expectations about the world. Social analysts use theory to describe how the world works, explain why it changes, and outline what they expect to occur in the future. This chapter examines "theories" of "globalization," the assumptions and expectations used by social scientists to understand the diverse set of contemporary economic, environmental, and political developments that affect people around the world.

Of course, social analysts have different theories or expectations about globalization. Some theorize that globalization is a positive development for most people around the world, while others argue that it has adverse consequences for many. Some analysts argue that globalization is a "new" development, while others maintain that it is not new but "old," or at least familiar. Some analysts argue that globalization is inevitable or unstoppable, while others insist that it is not.

Policymakers and social scientists not only advance different theories but also use the term *globalization* to mean different things. Most analysts use *globalization* to describe the growth and spread of investment, trade, and production, the introduction of new technology, and the spread of democracy around the world. But others argue that *globalization* should also refer to other contemporary developments such as the spread of environmental pollution, the commercialization of culture and languages, the cross-border migration of people, the spread of drugs and narcotics, and the emergence of social and political protest movements opposed to globalization.

To understand the theories of change and appreciate what is meant by "globalization," it is important first to ask, "*What* is being globalized?" An appreciation of what theorists mean by globalization will make it easier to sort through their different assumptions and expectations.

WHAT IS BEING GLOBALIZED?

Although analysts argue that different things are being globalized, there is a consensus that globalization, at a minimum, refers to the following five developments.

- *Investment*. The growth and spread of investment, capital, money, and financial services are counted by virtually all scholars as an important feature of globalization. The globalization of investment is assisted by a variety of economic institutions: government agencies such as the Federal Reserve in the United States and the Bundesbank in Germany; individual investment banks and financial services corporations such as Citigroup and Barclay's; collective financial institutions such as stock markets, commodity and bond markets, and the Eurocurrency market; and global financial institutions such as the World Bank and International Monetary Fund (IMF).[1]

  Not only have these institutions assisted the growth and spread of investment around the world, but they have also "liberalized" it. The reduction or elimination of laws, barriers, and restrictions on the movement of finance, capital, and monetary flows, which is seen as having "liberalized" investment, has made it easier to move money across national borders.

- *Trade*. A second important feature of contemporary globalization has been the expansion of trade. The growing volume of manufactured goods and raw materials that are traded around the world has been promoted by private, transnational corporations (TNCs); by government policy makers, primarily in Western Europe, Japan, and the United States; and by collective institutions such as the World Trade Organization (WTO) and the Group of Seven (G-7).[2] These institutions have also sought to "liberalize" trade, which has meant reducing the tariffs, taxes, regulations, and barriers that restrict, inhibit, or block the trade between countries around the world.

- *Production*. The migration, relocation, and reorganization of private businesses, and the farms and factories controlled by them, have been a third feature of globalization.[3] The globalization of production has been promoted primarily by private entrepreneurs and TNCs, though it has been assisted by financial institutions and government officials in the advanced Western countries, which have allowed firms to merge and migrate around the world.[4]

- *Technology*. The invention and diffusion of new technologies, particularly of high-tech electronic and biochemical tools, techniques, and services, are a fourth feature of contemporary globalization. These inventions were assisted by government funding and research; developed by scholars, inventors, and entrepreneurs in government, university, and industrial settings; adopted by businesses that produce goods and services; and embraced by consumers who purchased new technologies for their personal use. Technological innovation, in turn, is generally said to assist the expansion of investment, trade, and production and encourage the spread of democracy.

- *Democracy*. In recent years, dozens of nation-states around the world have "democratized." The collapse of dictatorships (in both capitalist and communist countries), and the subsequent adoption of constitutional and representative forms of government, has increased political participation by the citizenry and provided greater individual freedoms and political choice. The "liberalization" of politics is the fifth important feature of globalization. Some analysts have argued that democratization was assisted by the globalization of investment, trade, production, and technology.

Most of the analysts who contribute to the literature agree that these five developments, taken together, are the central features of contemporary globalization. But these are not the only developments that have affected people around the world in recent years. Some scholars have argued that a discussion of globalization should also include at least some of the following developments:

- *Culture*. The commercialization and spread of "Western," particularly American culture by electronic media, fashion, and fast food—symbolized by MTV, Levi's, and McDonald's—is identified by some analysts as an important aspect of globalization.
- *Language*. The adoption of English as the *lingua franca* by people around the world, and the associated decline of national languages, regional dialects, and indigenous languages, is seen by some as another cultural expression of globalization.
- *Migration*. Some treat the cross-border migration of people seeking jobs, particularly from poor to rich countries, and the flight of political refugees as an important aspect of globalization. Many observers argue that migration is prompted, in large part, by the first five kinds of globalization.
- *Environment*. The global spread of pollution and waste, perhaps best illustrated by global warming, the destruction of natural habitats, animal species, resources, and indigenous peoples, and the high rates of energy and resource consumption, are frequently identified as corollaries of globalization.
- *Trafficking of women*. The spread of U.S. military bases overseas, the spread of manufacturing enclaves that produce goods for exports, the growth of the tourist industry, which is now said to be the largest "service" industry in the world, and the growth of the sex industry are seen by feminist theorists as important features of globalization. Feminists argue that the expansion of these industries, which rely heavily on female labor, has contributed to the voluntary and involuntary migration of women into these industries, a development they describe as "trafficking in women."
- *Declining state sovereignty*. The number of independent nation-states has

increased as a result of decolonization and, more recently, democratization. But while most analysts associate the proliferation of states with globalization, some argue that this development is also related to a decline of "sovereignty" for most independent states. States have less sovereignty or real political authority because globalization has shifted power to its institutional sponsors: "stateless" TNCs, the World Bank and IMF, and stock, bond, commodity, and money markets.

- *Drug trafficking.* The expansion and spread of drugs and narcotics, which are sponsored by international drug cartels and mafias based in different countries, are seen by some as a component of globalization, even though they involve the production and trade of illegal goods by criminal organizations.
- *Protest.* The expansion and spread of feminist movements and values, environmental organizations, labor unions, and grassroots protest movements against the institutions that sponsor globalization—particularly the IMF, World Bank, and WTO—are seen by some analysts as a global response to globalization.
- *Ethnic and religious conflict.* Some observers see the outbreak of war in countries that have been partitioned and the eruption of violence between rival ethnic and religious groups around the world as an aspect of globalization. But there is considerable disagreement here. Some scholars argue that ethnic conflict and war are not associated with globalization but are instead an expression of developments that *preceded* it. In this view, ethnic conflict is a *pre*globalization phenomenon. Others argue that it is a reaction against globalization, a kind of *post*globalization development.

Of course, it would be difficult to review all of these developments in this book. But I will discuss many of them, though not in the order they are presented here. Instead of grouping them by subject (investment, trade), this book will examine contemporary developments using a historical, narrative approach.

WHAT IS NOT GLOBALIZED?

For most theorists, globalization refers to important, central developments in the world today. But some analysts disagree, arguing that globalization is so much "globaloney" because it hypes these developments and ignores the fact that globalization does not meaningfully affect most people.[5]

Most of the people around the world have little money to save or invest in global financial markets. Most of the food that they grow, most of the goods that they make, and most of the services they provide are purchased and consumed within the country where they originate. Few of the goods produced are actually traded on "global" markets. In the United States, for example, only 18 percent of the goods and services produced ever enter global trading markets.[6] Most people do not work for TNCs, which migrate and merge, but work instead for themselves—raising families, growing food, and making goods that sustain their households—or work for small businesses, nonprofit organizations, and local or national governments. Most people around the world do not own telephones, computers, fax machines, or even televisions or refrigerators, so the technologies said to be globalizing the planet have had minimal impact on their lives. Most migration occurs *within* countries, so it is primarily a local not global phenomenon. And while many states have democratized, many people around the world still live under dictators or warlords.

Moreover, globalization is a partial, not all-encompassing development. While people in some parts of the world are being integrated and globalized, people in other parts are being distanced and marginalized. I think globalization is a "selective," not "inclusive," development, which bypasses large populations and geographies, particularly people living in sub-Saharan Africa and the interiors of India, China, and the former Soviet Union.

Investment is a good way to indicate the partial character of globalization. Although it is true that cross-border investment is a force for globalization, most investment circulates in the rich countries, not the poor. The rich countries received 83 percent of all direct investment in 1989.[7] Of the remaining 17 percent, China received about half, leaving very little investment to "globalize" the rest of the planet. Consider the fact that in 1996 China (with one billion people) received $42 billion in investment but that India (with nearly one billion people) received only $3 billion.[8] Given this disparity, it is hard to argue that investment is doing very much to globalize India. Moreover, when a country like India does receive a small influx of investment, most of it is concentrated in enclave manufacturing industries, which employ relatively small numbers of people.

The investment that has been available globally has not been distributed widely. It has instead been doled out selectively. As such, it is more appropriate to describe the globalization associated with investment as "selective" rather than "universal."[9] The same holds true for trade, production, technology, and democracy. None of these are universal developments. They are all partial and selective in important ways.

WHO WANTS GLOBALIZATION?

Globalization did not just happen. It occurred because some people wanted it to happen and made sure that it did. But there is a debate about *who* wanted globalization to occur. Proponents of globalization have argued that "everyone" wants globalization—or would if they understood it. Critics of globalization have disagreed, arguing that it is economic and political "elites" who want globalization. These elites, critics state, assume that because globalization is good for themselves, it must therefore also be good for everyone else. This effort by elites to generalize or universalize their self-interest is mistaken, critics argue, because globalization is not good for most people.

The idea that globalization is good for "everybody" has powerful institutional support. It is advocated by most mainstream economists and the award committee for the Nobel Prize in economics, by public policy research institutes, government officials, and policymakers in North America, Western Europe, and Japan. It is supported by op-ed columnists in daily newspapers, business magazines, and television media and by transnational corporations and trade industry associations. It is promoted by central banks and United Nations (UN) institutions: the World Bank, IMF, and WTO.

"Almost all economists and other proponents of free markets believe that globalization promises a world of increasing prosperity and international cooperation [for everyone,]" Princeton economist Robert Gilpin has written.[10] UN officials agree: "This era of globalization is opening many opportunities for millions of people around the world. . . .We have more wealth and technology—and more commitment to a global community—than ever before."[11] The view that everyone stands to gain from globalization was perhaps best expressed by Peter Sutherland, the director of the General Agreement on Tariffs and Trade, the organization that preceded the WTO. He has argued simply that globalization produced "only winners, no losers."[12]

As proof that "everyone" wants globalization, or would want it if they knew what it really was and were in a position to "choose" it, proponents note that people now clamor for foreign investment, rush to purchase imported goods, line up for jobs in export-processing zones, embrace new technologies, and vote for greater democracy. Harvard economist Jeffrey Sachs has argued, "My worry is not that there are too many sweatshops, but too few."[13] Where people are denied an opportunity to choose, they migrate or flee to places where these goods and opportunities are available, proponents argue. From this perspective, globalization is simply a response to a growing "demand" from workers and consumers around the world who "want" the economic and political goods that it provides.

Still, proponents have sometimes been puzzled by a lack of popular enthusiasm and public support for globalization. "Globalization is 'tolerated,' but it is not loved," economist Paul Krugman complained.[14] *BusinessWeek* began a special report on globalization by saying, "It's hard to figure out how a term [*globalization*] that once connoted so much good for the world has fallen into such disrepute."[15]

Proponents argue that indifference or hostility to globalization is due primarily to a lack of understanding about it. People simply do not fully appreciate the benefits of globalization: "It has created millions of jobs from Malaysia to Mexico and a cornucopia of affordable goods to Western consumers. It has brought phone service to 300 million households in developing countries and a transfer of nearly $2 trillion from rich countries to poor through equity, bond invest-

Not an accurate system
but functional

ments, and commercial loans. It has helped topple dictators by making information freely available in once-sheltered societies."[16]

Proponents argue too that many people do not appreciate globalization because it is a difficult process, one that may result in things getting worse, at least for a while, before conditions improve and its benefits become widely available. "The transition would be painful," *BusinessWeek* writers argue, "but inevitably, prosperity would result."[17] Proponents say they warned people that this would occur but that many people did not head their admonitions.

Critics of globalization disagree with the contention that "everybody" wants it, or should. The critics are a diverse lot. They include academic scholars outside economics, labor unions, and the public policy research institutes associated with them, religious groups that participated in Jubilee 2000 (they argue for Third World debt relief), consumer groups like Ralph Nader's Public Citizen, environmental organizations, feminist groups, representatives of some farmers and small business groups, populist politicians such as Ross Perot, and Green parties in the United States and Western Europe.[18] Outside the rich countries, many of the reformed communist parties that came to power in Eastern Europe and the former Soviet Union are critical of globalization (ironically, *un*reformed communist parties in China and Vietnam now support globalization), as do leaders of some small countries, such as Malaysian prime minister Mohamad Mahathir.

The critics argue that it is the economic and political elites in rich countries, assisted by global economic institutions they control—TNCs, IMF, World Bank, WTO—that "want" globalization and drive it forward.[19] These elites, who belong to what is often described as the "Washington Consensus," have promoted globalization because they stand to benefit from it. Their argument that globalization benefits "everyone" is, from the critics' perspective, "a convenient myth which, in part, helps justify and legitimize the neo-liberal global project, that is the creation of a global free market and the consolidation of Anglo-American capitalism within the world's major economic regions."[20]

Except for elites, no one else really wants the economic features of globalization, its critics argue, though they admit that many people *do* want new technologies and democracy. Because there is little popular "demand" for economic globalization, it must be imposed on people by the global institutions that elites control. As proof that everyone does not want globalization, critics point to the protests against IMF and World Bank structural adjustment programs and against WTO negotiating rounds in Seattle. They argue that economic crises in countries that had recently been globalized—Mexico, Russia, Thailand, Indonesia, South Korea—have demonstrated to people in those countries, and to people around the world, that globalization is something they do not want.

I would answer the question "Who wants globalization?" in a somewhat different way. It is a mistake to argue, as proponents do, that everyone wants globalization or stands to benefit from it, that it produces "only winners, no losers."

Nor is globalization always a choice that people voluntarily make. In my view, many of the developments associated with globalization were imposed by institutions seeking to solve immediate problems. The unilateral U.S. decisions to abandon the global monetary system established at Bretton Woods and devalue the dollar (chapter 3), or later raise interest rates (chapter 4), were imposed on others. No one else had any say or choice in the matter. These decisions were taken without consideration for their impact on others, much less their implications for everyone. They were self-interested and particularistic, not altruistic and universalistic. Globalization is often advanced by officials who imagine that their institutional needs and problems are widely shared and that the solutions they propose will benefit not only themselves but everyone else as well. But this is hubris. U.S. dollar devaluations, as we will see, did not benefit all. Nor did the decision to raise interest rates. The needs and goals of globalization's institutional proponents are not synonymous with the needs and goals of many people around the world. There are winners *and* losers, in both rich countries and poor ones. This book will describe who they are and explain why their fortunes diverge.

Moreover, the critics are mistaken when they argue that globalization is always imposed by global institutions and only for the benefit of elites. Elites are not the only people who want globalization or benefit from it. People around the world want change, demanding goods (imported foods, manufactured goods, new technologies, but also drugs) and political opportunities (democracy) that globalization provides. People choose to learn English, a difficult second language, and choose to make arduous journeys across borders to obtain political and economic opportunities. Elected governments in the Czech Republic, Canada, and Mexico have voluntarily introduced globalization, without being forced to do so by global institutions. More than one hundred countries around the world participated in the trade negotiations that resulted in the creation of the WTO, though they may have had their arms twisted by rich countries and may have expressed unhappiness with the outcome. Although the decision to support globalization may have been problematic—not only for poor countries but for rich ones as well—its forward momentum has been assisted by people outside elite institutions based in the rich countries.

THEORIES OF GLOBALIZATION

In general, analysts who study various kinds of globalization share three theoretical assumptions or expectations. First, they assume that globalization is "new," that it is a novel historical development. Second, they argue that globalization makes the world a more "homogeneous" or "singular" place. Third, they maintain that it is an "inevitable," "relentless," or "irreversible" process. Of course, some observers demur from these views, but proponents and critics generally subscribe to these theoretical propositions.

Globalization Is "New"

Most observers assume that globalization is a new development, dating back only to the mid-1980s or early 1990s. Perhaps surprisingly, the proponents and critics of globalization agree that globalization is a radical departure from what preceded it. Until recently (1989 or so), the world was divided into political blocs defined by the cold war. Countries within these blocs typically restricted the flow of investment, goods, ideas, and people, though their efforts to impose restrictions increasingly became unmanageable, obsolete, or foolish. The introduction of new technologies and the end of the cold war broke down the decades-long restrictions on economic behavior and political thought and made possible the adoption of a new set of economic and political relations, what we call globalization, around the world. Neoliberal and postmodernist scholars alike agree that this was a new, even unique development in human history.[21]

A few scholars disagreed, challenging the theoretical assumption that globalization is new. They offered two kinds of rebuttals. From the very beginning of discussions about globalization, world system analysts such as Immanuel Wallerstein have argued that globalization is "old," that the developments associated with it date back to the sixteenth century, and that globalization is just the most contemporary expression of familiar processes.[22]

In the last few years, another group of scholars, both world system and neoliberal, have argued that globalization is not entirely new, that it closely resembles a similar period of globalization at the beginning of the twentieth century. They note that investment and trade in the early twentieth century were more widely distributed, or "globalized," than they are today, that cross-border migration flows were heavier then, and that the new technologies introduced in that era (steamships, underseas telegraphs, breakthroughs in metallurgy, chemistry, and electricity) were as revolutionary then as many technologies are today.[23] This argument, which has received considerable attention of late, has qualified the theoretical assumption that current events are *entirely* new.

I take a somewhat different view on the dating used to define contemporary globalization and take issue with some of the arguments made about its novelty.

Contemporary globalization begins earlier, I think, than most scholars allow. Many of the developments analyzed in this book begin in the early 1970s, not the late 1980s or early 1990s. The discussion of some developments begins even earlier. Change is not neatly contained by bracketed dating systems. Some developments occur on different time lines. So I do not use a rigid, bracketed, dating system (1970–2000) but instead use dates and time lines appropriate to the study of particular kinds of contemporary change.

Moreover, contemporary globalization is similar to, and different from, the era that "previewed" it (early twentieth-century globalization) and the period that immediately "preceded" it (the cold war).

During the early twentieth century, globalization occurred in a world dominated by a handful of "empires." Globalization today occurs in a world where decolonization has eliminated empires and created scores of independent states. The earlier period was characterized by intense inter-imperial rivalry, which led in 1914 to the outbreak of world war *and* an end to globalization as an economic practice. The current period is characterized by an *end* to conflict between rival superpowers (the United States and Soviet Union) and the increasing cooperation of rich countries, which were at each other's throats a hundred years ago. One could say that globalization in the earlier period was associated with rivalry and world war, while globalization in the current era is associated with growing cooperation and a declining risk of world war. These are large and significant differences.

The current era differs from the cold war period that preceded it in important respects. Today, economic practices are less "restricted" and political behavior is less "isolationist" than during the previous period, which was dominated by closed cold war political blocs and restrictive economic practices within them.

But the current era is *not* as different as some people imagine. It is easy to forget that the United States and Soviet Union *together* created the global economic and political institutions that figure so prominently in discussions of globalization today (UN, IMF, World Bank, WTO); that they together supported decolonization and the dissolution of empires, which resulted in a growing number of independent states around the world (192 countries today, up from only 50 or so in 1945); that they both promoted "modernization" and "development," not only for themselves but also for the old empires and postcolonial states, and used the economic tools and political strategies available to them. Of course, many of those strategies are today discredited, and new ones—those associated with globalization—have been adopted in their place. But the idea that powerful states could and should promote development for themselves and others is an old idea that remains alive today.

Contemporary change has not been so abrupt or dramatic that it has created an entirely new or unique world. Continuity with the past is an important element in all the developments described in this book.

Globalization Creates a More Homogeneous World

Most observers argue that the spread of investment, trade, production, technology, and democracy has made the world a more "homogeneous" or singular place. William Grieder's book *One World, Ready or Not* aptly summarizes the common theoretical expectation that globalization will affect people in similar ways and create a more homogeneous, integrated, and "smaller" world.[24] "The world," David Held and Anthony McGrew maintain, is "fast becoming a shared social and economic space."[25] For many analysts, Marshall McLuhan's prediction in the mid-1960s that the world would become a "global village" is now coming to pass as a result of globalization.[26]

But observers disagree as to whether greater integration, uniformity, and homogeneity comprise a positive or negative development. Proponents of neoliberalism and globalization argue that it is a positive development, providing capital, job opportunities, consumer choice, and political freedom. "The injection of U.S. capital and Technology . . . creates jobs and a better standard of living for both [the United States and the recipient country]," George Munoz, head of the Overseas Private Investment Corporation, has argued.[27]

Lawrence Summers, who served as chief economist for the World Bank, then as treasury secretary for the Clinton administration, and then as president of Harvard, has argued that globalization is a universal good. "The laws of economics, it's often forgotten, are like laws of engineering. There's only one set of laws, and they work everywhere."[28] Summers, like other proponents, is confident that the application of these "laws" will provide social and economic benefits for all.

Critics of globalization agree that it creates a more homogeneous world but dispute the assertion that this is a positive development. They argue instead that the spread of investment, trade, production, and technology adversely affects families, local communities, and whole countries, eliminating real diversity and undermining choice. So, for example, they argue that foreign investment can introduce new retail monopolies that disadvantage small businesses, that imported goods can replace local manufacturers, that the growth of sweatshop export industries exploits workers, and that new agricultural technologies undermine subsistence farmers. Globalization has uniform consequences, they argue, but they are largely negative, producing inequality and poverty. The destruction of local languages, diets, species, and culture, they argue, is not a universal good but a global wrong. So they argue that laws of globalization should not everywhere be applied and that local considerations be taken into account.

I take a different view. Globalization does *not* have uniform consequences or create a more "homogeneous" world. Instead, globalization has had *diverse* consequences that were not anticipated in advance. Lawrence Summers may insist on the application of a single set of economic "laws," but they do not "everywhere" apply. They do not even work in ways that economists like Summers expect. Moreover, the diverse consequences are not uniformly positive or negative but simultaneously good for some *and* bad for others. Even *Business-Week* now agrees that this might be true: "The real question isn't whether free markets are good or bad. It is why they are producing such wildly *different* results in different countries [emphasis added]."[29]

The attempt to generalize or universalize about globalization is mistaken. Only by taking a careful, historical analysis of its implementation in particular settings can any assessment be made of its benefits and disadvantages. My answer to the question "Is globalization good or bad?" will be complex. And it will always be accompanied by the answer to a second, related question: "For whom?"

Globalization Is "Inevitable"

Finally, many analysts theorize that globalization is an "inevitable" or "relentless" process, which will be difficult or impossible to reverse. Globalization, Anthony Giddens has written, "has now a speed, inevitability, and force that it has not had before."[30] Proponents of globalization argue that the liberalization of invest-ment, trade, production, and democracy is not a cyclical process (one that comes and goes) but a secular process (one that grows stronger and endures). During the twentieth century, capitalism and democracy were tested by imperial rivalry, world wars and the Great Depression, the threat of fascism, and the spread of communism. But those challenges have all evaporated. Capitalism and democracy have not only survived but endured, strengthened, and spread. In a rejoinder to the Marxist view that the fall of capitalism and the rise of socialism were "inevitable," proponents of globalization retort that Marx had his determin-istic "laws of motion" reversed: it was the fall of socialism and rise of capitalism/democracy that were inevitable.[31]

Critics of globalization often share this view. Thomas Friedman describes globalization as a "brakeless train wreaking havoc," while William Grieder says globalization is a "revolution [that] runs itself."[32] The idea that globalization is a brakeless train suggests it has a relentless force, which is difficult to slow, stop, or reverse.

A smaller group argues that globalization is not inevitable, either because it is prone to "failure" or because it is "unsustainable." Wealthy financier George Soros, a proponent of the idea that it is prone to failure, has warned, "I now fear that the untrammeled intensification of laissez-faire capitalism . . . is endanger-ing our democratic society. Unless it is tempered by the recognition of a com-mon interest . . . our present system is liable to break down."[33] The collapse in the 1990s of economies in Mexico, Thailand, Indonesia, and Russia, which threatened to spread economic disaster around the world, was proof that global-ization is prone to failure, critics contend.

In a similar vein, environmental critics have argued that globalization is not in the long-run "sustainable" because it will run up against ecological limits (e.g., global warming) or encounter social limits because the inequality it produces will trigger protest against it. Demonstrations against the WTO in Seattle are cited as proof that a "mounting backlash" against globalization is setting social limits to its spread.[34]

I do not view globalization as an inevitable or relentless process. What we call globalization was really an ad hoc set of solutions that were advanced by differ-ent institutions to address a series of problems that emerged in the 1970s and 1980s. The ability of these institutions to "solve" these problems was "contingent" not inevitable. By *contingent* I mean that success depended on a particular set of circumstances that varied from one setting to the next. Even when globalization was counted a success, it created a new set of problems that would subsequently have to be addressed. Some solutions, like the devaluation of the dollar, were tried several times without appreciable success. Globalization was neither inevitable nor assured.

It is true that globalization has powerful institutional support, which has given it weight, momentum, and authority. But these institutions—TNCs, the North Atlantic Treaty Organization (NATO), IMF, WTO—were unable to anticipate, fully appreciate, or successfully manage the course of globalization in many respects. This was due in part to their own institutional constraints. Remember that these institutions were created in an earlier period, designed to address a particular set of problems, many of which no longer exist. They were shaped by ideologies that express the views of some, but not all social groups. These ideologies do not easily accommodate the views and needs of groups that are important stakeholders in any durable solution to problems associated with globalization. Even when these institutions are proactive, open-minded, and willing to address change in a collective, democratic manner, as they did when they negotiated a global warming accord in Kyoto, Japan, they have been, as yet, unable to accommodate divergent interests (North vs. South; U.S. vs. European) and implement real solutions.

GLOBALIZATION AND GENDER

Feminist scholars have criticized contemporary theories of globalization for a number of reasons. Feminists argue that accounts of globalization typically neglect the role of women in development, dismiss the adverse impacts of globalization on women, and demonstrate little appreciation of women in theoretical or practical terms. "There is a lot of talk about globalization," Christa Wichterich writes, "but women do not feature very much in it."[35]

The reason why theories of globalization ignore women is easy to explain, feminists argue. The institutions that promote globalization are "gendered." By that feminists mean that these institutions are male-oriented expressions of capitalist "patriarchy." These gender-specific institutions create, maintain, and defend male power in society. This is not a "new" development, according to most feminist theorists but an "old," familiar pattern. "What is called globalization . . . is not a totally new and extraordinary feature but . . . the continuing colonization . . . that has been part and parcel of capitalist patriarchy right from its beginning," Maria Mies and Veronika Bennholdt-Thomsen argue.[36]

Because feminist theorists view the institutions of globalization as gendered—as instruments primarily of white, Western, male elites—they oppose the "universalism" associated with globalization. They argue that globalization is not a universal good (or bad) but an effort by a particular group to shape the world in their own image, to suit their own particular needs. Because globalization was designed by men to serve patriarchy, it should not be surprising that it neglects women, fails to assign them an important role in the globalization project, and dismisses adverse impacts on women as inconsequential.

Most feminist scholars agree that globalization is detrimental to women, thought they concede that globalization does create some employment for women in settings along the "global assembly line": export manufacturing "sweatshops," service industries, tourism, and the sex trade.[37] Many scholars argue that more attention should be paid not only to the impact of globalization on women's employment but also to women's work *outside* the labor force, what Mies and Bennholdt-Thomsen call the "invisible economy" of housework, work in the informal sector, and subsistence production.[38] For many women, entry into the wage-based globalized economy means they have to do "double duty," because they are still expected to do the unpaid work that keeps worker households going.

Although feminists view globalization as detrimental to women, they do not regard it as inevitable. They devote considerable attention to the myriad ways that women oppose globalization through grassroots political efforts and local institutions designed to provide economic alternatives for women. Collective self-help movements, such as the Grameen Bank in Bangladesh, are frequently cited as models for local, nonglobalized institutions that can benefit women.[39] These local political movements and economic institutions are seen by most feminists as vehicles that can simultaneously challenge patriarchal globalization and empower women.[40]

I also think the feminist critique of globalization is sound. Women have been neglected by the globalization literature in general. The institutions that support globalization are gendered, though I would add that they not only express a gender-based view of the world but also one rooted in the class, race, and age-based perspective of Western economic and political elites. Although these institutions imagine that their needs are universal, they are mistaken. The benefits associated with globalization are not universally shared. Globalization has generally meant that most people work harder for less, and this is particularly true for women who are asked to participate in the formal, wage-based economy and continue laboring in informal, nonwage economies.

I agree with feminist scholars that globalization is not inevitable. But the argument that it can be stopped primarily by local, grassroots political and economic movements is, I think, less persuasive. In my view, grassroots political efforts can be successful if they confront "decentralized" institutions (see chapter 10). But they are less likely to succeed if they confront "centralized" institutions directly. Challenges to these are more effectively mounted by movements that are also "centrally" organized. Although much attention has been paid to the centralized institutions that promote globalization, it is important to remember that globalization is sponsored also by decentralized institutions. Against the latter, feminist and other grassroots movements can be effective.

PROCESSES OF GLOBALIZATION

We live in a time of global change. By that I mean that people around the world are affected by common economic, political, and environmental developments: increased competition, fluctuating interest rates, the introduction of new technologies, a changing climate, the fall of communism, and the scourge of violence and drug use. But people experience change in different ways. Global change is not ubiquitous, nor is it a uniform process. It affects some people more than others, in often unexpected and surprising ways. And it can have very different consequences—good and bad—for people in different settings.

This book describes some of the important *processes* of globalization. It uses a historical, narrative approach to answer these questions: How does globalization occur? Whom does it affect, and how? What are its different social consequences?

The book treats global change as a complex, variegated process that rarely proceeds in a direct line, from A to Z, without interruption or deflection. It examines economic, political, and environmental change in much the way that television journalists analyze the weather. When TV journalists report on the weather, they display satellite images of the Earth to identify the global pressure systems that shape the weather in different regions, then use Doppler radar to track the movement of a weather system front across the landscape. As a low-pressure system moves off the Pacific and tracks east across North America, it can have very different consequences for people living along its path. The same storm system may bring fog to people living along the coast, rain to people living in inland valleys, snow to people in the mountains, and clear skies to people living in the plains beyond. The storm might unexpectedly inflict flood, hail, or avalanche on the people in its path, upsetting forecast predictions and weekend plans. People visited by the *same* weather system may experience changing weather in very *different* ways.

Like a weatherman following a series of storms, I will narrate the history of some important global problems that have recently swept across the economic, environmental, and political landscape. These accounts will pay particular attention to the different and sometimes unexpected consequences of change for people, women and men, living in its path.

Global change has recently resulted from efforts to solve particular problems. During the 1970s, 1980s, and 1990s, a series of problems emerged around the world. To solve these problems, international institutions, government officials, private corporations, and social movements adopted policies, practices, or protests that resulted in dramatic social change. These efforts, of course, did not always succeed in addressing the problems people initially confronted. And when they did, they frequently created new problems that demanded further attention. So, as we will see, U.S. policymakers successfully used high interest rates to slow galloping inflation, but this led to the collapse of the domestic savings and loan industry and contributed to rising homelessness in the United States, and it triggered a debt crisis for countries, most of them ruled by dictators, around the world (chapters 4, 5, and 11). Farmers used new technologies to increase food production, but burgeoning food supplies led to falling commodity prices that drove many small farmers out of business (chapter 6). Corporations in the rich countries invented and deployed new agricultural and electronic technologies, but these inventions displaced farmers and miners who had long relied on the export of commodities to earn a living (chapter 7). Political movements overthrew capitalist and communist dictators, but the new democratic governments that replaced them were burdened by the debt incurred by their predecessors, making it difficult for them to promote development or defend democratic political gains (chapter 11). This book will measure the success and assess the failure of efforts to address contemporary problems and the changes associated with them.

Of course, many of the global changes examined here are interconnected. But the stories about change will be told separately. The idea is to provide readers with accounts of change that can be studied individually or read collectively. Where story lines intersect, reference will be made to related developments in other chapters. Some of the early chapters focus on changes that originated in the United States. This was done because the United States is a central actor in the world, and its initiatives are widely felt. It was also done to help U.S. readers appreciate from the outset their relation to global change. As we examine contemporary global processes, keep in mind that shared global developments may have a different meaning for people living in different places.

NOTES

1. Saskia Sassen, "The State and the New Geography of Power," in *The Ends of Globalization: Bringing Society Back In*, ed. Don Kalb, Marco van der Land, Richard Staring, Bart van Steenbergen, and Nico Wilterdink (Lanham, Md.: Rowman & Littlefield, 2000), 54; Giovanni Arrighi, "Globalization, State Sovereignty, and the 'Endless' Accumulation of Capital," in *The Ends of Globalization*, 138; Ryszard Kapuscinaski, *The Shadow of the Sun* (New York: Knopf, 2001), 261–62; Giovanni Arrighi and Beverly Silver, *Chaos and Governance in the Modern World System* (Minneapolis: University of Minnesota Press, 1999), 140; John Schmitt, "Inequality and Globalization: Some Evidence from the United States," in *The Ends of Globalization*, 191.

2. Paul Hirst, "The Global Economy: Myths or Reality," in *The Ends of Globalization*, 25.

3. William Greider, *One World, Ready or Not: The Manic Logic of Global Capitalism* (New York: Simon & Schuster, 1997), 22.

4. Robert Went, *Globalization: Neoliberal Challenge, Radical Responses* (London: Pluto, 2000), 18; David Held and Anthony McGrew, "The Great Globalization Debate: An Introduction," in *The Global Transformations Reader: An Introduction to the Globalization Debate*, ed. David Held and Anthony McGrew (Cambridge: Polity, 2000), 25; Arrighi and Silver, *Chaos and Governance*, 145; Greider, *One World, Ready or Not*, 21; Robert Gilpin, *The Challenge of Global Capitalism: The World Economy in the 21st Century* (Princeton, N.J.: Princeton University Press, 2000), 170.

5. Michael Hanagen, "States and Capital: Globalizations Past and Present," in *The Ends of Globalization*, 249.

6. Went, *Globalization*, 11–12.

7. Torry D. Dickinson, "Selective Globalization: The Relocation of Industrial Production and the Shaping of Women's Work," in *Research in the Sociology of Work*, vol. 6, *The Globalization of Work*, ed. Randy Hodson (Greenwich, Conn.: JAI, 1997), 61.

8. Satoshi Ikeda, "World Production," in *The Age of Transition: Trajectory of the World-System, 1945–2025*, ed. Terence K. Hopkins and Immanuel Wallerstein (London: Zed, 1996), 46; David E. Sanger, "Study Shows Jump in Investing in China and Revival in Mexico," *New York Times*, March 24, 1997; John F. Burns, "India's Five Decades of Progress and Pain," *New York Times*, August 14, 1997.

9. Dickinson, "Selective Globalization,"124.

10. Gilpin, *The Challenge of Global Capitalism*, 293.

11. United Nations Development Program Report 1999, "Globalization with a Human Face," in *The Global Transformations Reader*, 341; Anne Sisson Runyan, "Women in the Neoliberal Frame," in *Gender Politics in Global Governance*, ed. Mary K. Meyer and Elisabeth Prugl (Lanham, Md.: Rowman & Littlefield, 1999), 217–18.

12. Crista Wichterich, *The Globalized Woman: Reports from a Future of Inequality* (London: Zed, 2000), ix.

13. Sarah Anderson, John Cavanagh, and Thea Lee, *Field Guide to the Global Economy* (New York: New Press, 2000), 57.

14. Went, *Globalization*, 1; Vandana Shiva, "The World on the Edge," in *Global Capitalism*, ed. Will Hutton and Anthony Giddens Anthony (New York: New Press, 2000), 18.

15. Engardo, "Global Capitalism," *BusinessWeek*, November 6, 2000, 72.

16. Engardo, "Global Capitalism."

17. Engardo, "Global Capitalism," 75.

18. Joseph Kahn, "Globalization Unites a Many-Striped Multitude of Foes," *New York Times*, April 15, 2000.

19. Philip McMichael, *Development and Social Change: A Global Perspective* (Thousand Oaks, Calif.: Pine Forge, 1996), 177.

20. Held and McGrew, "The Great Globalization Debate," in *The Global Transformations Reader*, 5.

21. Manuel Castells, "Information Technology and Global Capitalism," in *Global Capitalism*, 53; Hanagan, "States and Capital," in *The Ends of Globalization*, 67; Hirst, "The Global Economy," in *The Ends of Globalization*, 3; David Harvey, "Time-Space Compression and the Postmodern Condition," in *The Global Transformations Reader*, 82.

22. Arrighi, "Globalization, State Sovereignty," 125, 272; Maria Mies and Veronika Bennholdt-Thomsen, *The Subsistence Perspective: Beyond the Globalized Economy* (London: Zed, 1999).

23. Alexander Stille, "Globalization Now, a Sequel of Sorts," *New York Times*, August 11, 2001; Niall Ferguson, *The Cash Nexus: Money and Power in the Modern World, 1700–2000* (New York: Basic Books, 2001), 290–93; Paul Hirst and Grahame Thompson, "Globalization and the History of the International Economy," in *The Global Transformation Reader,* 275–78.

24. Meyer and Prugl, *Gender Politics in Global Governance,* 16–17; John Walton and David Seddon, *Free Markets and Food Riots: The Politics of Global Adjustment* (Oxford: Blackwell, 1994), 7.

25. Held and McGrew, "The Great Globalization Debate," in *The Global Transformations Reader,* 1.

26. Harvey, "Time-Space Compression," in *The Global Transformations Reader,* 84.

27. Anderson et al., *Field Guide to the Global Economy,* 47.

28. Duncan Green, *Silent Revolution: The Rise of Market Economies in Latin America* (London: Cassell, 1995), 27.

29. Engardo, "Global Capitalism," 74.

30. Hutton and Giddens, *Global Capitalism,* vii; Ulrich Beck, "What Is Globalization?" in *The Global Transformations Reader,* 102.

31. Francis Fukuyama, "The End of History?" *National Interest* 16 (1989): 3–18.

32. Arrighi, "Globalization, State Sovereignty," in *The Ends of Globalization,* 129; Greider, *One World, Ready or Not,* 26.

33. Arrighi, "Globalization, State Sovereignty," in *The Ends of Globalization,* 129.

34. Arrighi, "Globalization, State Sovereignty," in *The Ends of Globalization.*

35. Wichterich, *The Globalized Woman,* 1.

36. Mies and Bennholdt-Thomsen, *The Subsistence Perspective,* 6.

37. Elisabeth Prugl, "What Is a Worker?" in *Gender Politics in Global Governance,* 200.

38. Mies and Bennholdt-Thomsen, *The Subsistence Perspective,* 31.

39. Naila Kabeer, *Reversed Realities: Gender Hierarchies in Development Thought* (London: Verso, 1994).

40. See Meyer and Prugl, *Gender Politics in Global Governance*; Mies and Bennholdt-Thomsen, *The Subsistence Perspective*; Wichterich, *The Globalized Woman.*

2

Globalizing Production in the United States, Western Europe, and Japan

During the past fifty-five years, two economic developments have altered the way people work in the United States, Western Europe, and Japan. First, the production of goods and services in these three regions has been *redistributed*. Second, the production of goods and services in these regions has been *reorganized*. The redistribution and reorganization of production has contributed to the "globalization" of production.

Between 1945 and 1970, the *redistribution* of production generally promoted economic development in the United States, Western Europe, and Japan, the group of countries described for many years as the "First World" or the "West" and now referred to as the "Triad" or the "North." But after 1970, the redistribution of production generally came at U.S. expense, a process economists in the 1970s called "deindustrialization," because U.S. industries lost business and jobs to firms based in Western Europe and Japan. This development contributed to changing gender relations in the United States because men lost jobs in manufacturing industries at a time when women found work in increasing numbers in the service sector.

Then in the 1980s and 1990s, U.S. firms began *reorganizing* production. Rising stock prices on Wall Street encouraged corporations to buy up other firms and introduce new technologies in the newly merged firms. The resulting reorganization of production made U.S. firms more competitive with businesses in

Western Europe and Japan in the 1990s. But this reorganization also led to "downsizing" or job loss for many workers in the United States.

To appreciate the causes and consequences of these two developments, we will return to the 1950s, when the process of redistributing production among businesses in the United States, Western Europe, and Japan began.

REDISTRIBUTING WORK, 1945–1970

After World War II, male wage workers in the United States produced most of the manufactured goods consumed in the United States, Western Europe, and Japan. Male and female farm households in the United States also produced most of the food consumed in the United States, Western Europe, and Japan. But that changed during the next twenty-five years. By 1973, the United States produced only one-fifth (21.9 percent) of the world's manufactured goods, down from more than half (56.7 percent) in 1948. Meanwhile, businesses in Western Europe and Japan doubled their share of world manufacturing, from 15 to more than 30 percent.[1] By the mid-1970s, Western Europe had also become self-sufficient in food production, so their consumption of food grown in the United States declined substantially. Essentially, a significant share of manufacturing and agricultural production had shifted from the United States to Western Europe and Japan. This redistribution of production, what may be called the globalization of production, began early in the postwar period. Significantly, production was redistributed primarily from the United States to Western Europe and Japan, not to other poor countries. So the globalization of production was a partial and limited process, not a universal development.

Why was production redistributed during this period? Because governments, businesses, and consumers all adopted policies and practices that shifted the location of jobs in manufacturing and agriculture from the United States to other locations.

U.S. policies played a crucial role, helping redistribute production during the postwar period. Although U.S. policies were designed to promote political and military cooperation and foster economic growth within the core, they also contributed to the redistribution of wage work. Here's how.

First, the U.S. government provided public aid worth billions of dollars to its allies through the Marshall Plan and related programs.[2] It also directed vast quantities of military aid to Western Europe and Japan, aid amounting to as much as $2 trillion between 1950 and 1970.[3]

Public aid provided capital that Allied governments used to rebuild wrecked infrastructure and rebuild industries destroyed by war, creating jobs for demobilized soldiers in construction and manufacturing. Without this aid, Western Europeans would have been unable to rebuild.[4] U.S. military spending in Western Europe and Japan provided numerous economic benefits (it also created some social problems; see chapter 4). Because the military purchased goods for overseas U.S. bases from local suppliers, U.S. defense spending created jobs in defense-related industries. U.S. purchases of French aircraft for NATO, for example, created jobs in an industry that would later compete with U.S. aircraft manufacturers.[5] The hundreds of thousands of U.S. troops stationed in Western Europe and Japan spent their wages there, creating jobs for local businesses and injecting dollars, a scarce and important commodity, into local economies. These practices provided capital and cash that were used to create national and local manufacturing and service industries in Western Europe and Japan. And by serving abroad, U.S. soldiers released young men in Western Europe and Japan from military obligations, so they could take jobs producing goods rather than standing guard.

Second, the U.S. government allowed its allies to levy high tariffs (taxes on goods they imported from the United States) and establish strict controls on capital movements. These policies encouraged U.S. firms to invest heavily in Western Europe. General Electric, for example, quadrupled the number of factories it operated in Western Europe between 1949 and 1969.[6] The $78 billion that U.S. firms invested in Western Europe during the 1950s and 1960s was used to create jobs and produce goods there, so that European consumers could purchase goods made by Europeans rather than buying imported goods made by Americans.[7] Private U.S. investments in this period may have resulted in the loss of two million jobs in the United States.[8] This practice, which was encouraged by government policies in the United States and Western Europe, contributed to the redistribution of production in manufacturing industries.

Third, U.S. officials established a global system of fixed exchange rates during the war. The Bretton Woods agreement, as it was called, allowed Western European and Japanese firms to compete as equals in U.S. markets, even though they were not yet competitive with U.S. firms (see chapter 3).[9] Generous postwar exchange rates, which made Western European and Japanese goods seem cheap in U.S. markets, and low U.S. tariffs on imported goods encouraged worker-consumers in the United States to purchase toys, sewing machines, radios, and alcohol from Western Europe and Japan. Exchange rates also persuaded U.S. workers to travel abroad. The $4.8 billion that U.S. worker-tourists spent overseas, most of it in Western Europe, created jobs in service and tourist industries and injected dollars into local economies.[10]

For their part, governments in Western Europe and Japan made the most of opportunities provided by U.S. policies, business practices, and consumer behavior. U.S. public aid, military assistance, private investment, and consumer spending provided them with capital, cash, and markets that they used to create jobs and rebuild industries. Governments in Western Europe and Japan also adopted policies that tapped another important resource: their own domestic workers.

Generally speaking, governments in Western Europe and Japan adopted monetary, trade, and tax policies designed to *discourage* consumption by domestic workers, encouraging them instead to save. By making it difficult for them to purchase imported goods or buy big-ticket items such as houses or cars, they forced workers to save a high percentage of their income. Japanese worker households, for example, put aside nearly 20 percent of their income in the 1950s and 1960s.[11] The money workers deposited in banks and postal accounts were then collected by banks and the government and used to finance the growth of domestic manufacturing industries.[12]

To compensate workers for working hard and saving money, governments in Western Europe provided generous social welfare benefits to workers: pensions, health care, unemployment compensation, and vacations. The "welfare states" established in Western Europe after World War II created electoral support for conservative governments. In Japan, the government took a rather different approach, offering workers few social benefits. But the government did provide generous financing to industries, which then paid benefits to male workers in manufacturing, promising them "lifetime employment" (*shushin koyo*) and a seniority-based wage system (*nenko joretsu seido*).[13] Women employed by large firms in Japan were typically hired only on a "temporary" basis, so they were largely excluded from the benefits designed to compensate worker households for their thrift. The rewards offered male workers were nevertheless sufficient to persuade households to support conservative government throughout the postwar period.

Policymakers in the United States could encourage and permit a redistribution of production, a process that resulted in the distribution of U.S. jobs to manufacturing industries located elsewhere, because a considerable amount of work needed to be done. Workers were needed to rebuild whole economies in Western Europe and Japan, wage wars in Korea and Vietnam, fashion weapons and vehicles for arms and space races with the Soviet Union, build houses and supply durable goods for baby boom households that had scrimped during the Depression and saved during the war, and supply newly independent countries with goods financed by the World Bank and foreign-aid programs. There was *so* much work to be done that the United States could surrender a significant share of production to its allies and *still* provide work for most male workers in the United States. So much work was available that industries could, for the first time, even offer jobs to large numbers of minorities, women, and immigrants.

- *Minorities.* During World War II, the lure of paid work in the North and West, and the pain of institutional racism in the segregated, "Jim Crow" South, persuaded five million African American workers to leave southern farms for jobs in big cities in the North and West, where many found jobs in manufacturing and service industries.[14]
- *Women.* At war's end, many women were forced out of manufacturing industries to make room for returning servicemen. But while the percent-

age of women in the labor force dropped from 34.7 percent in 1944 to 31.1 percent in 1954, the decline was small and women retained a claim on a significant share of the available jobs.[15]

• *Immigrants.* U.S. industries even provided work for a large number of immigrants, one million in the late 1940s, 2.5 million more in the 1950s, and another 3.3 million in the 1960s. Agricultural firms also annually recruited another 300,000 to 445,000 workers from Mexico through the government's Bracero Program.[16]

Western Europe experienced such a large demand for workers that industries could provide virtually full employment for domestic males, offer jobs to eight million ethnic Germans who were forced to immigrate from Eastern Europe and the Soviet Union after the war, and provide work for another three million Germans who fled East Germany before the Berlin Wall was built in 1961. It had so much work available that Western European countries could also recruit millions of other workers from Spain, Portugal, southern Italy, Yugoslavia, Greece, and Turkey (each donated about one million workers to the labor force in Western Europe) through various "guest worker" programs during the 1950s and 1960s.[17]

In Japan, meanwhile, industry provided full employment for men, jobs for many women, though on unequal terms, and found jobs for another 2.6 million Japanese "immigrants," who had immigrated from areas occupied by Japan during the war, much as ethnic Germans in Eastern Europe had done.[18]

Because the demand for workers was so strong, and because many workers belonged to trade unions, which used strikes to demand higher salaries, wages rose in all three regions, though at different rates. In the United States, wages doubled between 1950 and 1970. Wages rose at an even faster rate in Western Europe and Japan. By 1970, they had become comparable to wage levels in the United States.[19]

But while wages rose more rapidly for workers in Western Europe and Japan, their standards of living did not measure up to the living standard of U.S. workers. Policies that discouraged consumption and promoted savings in Western Europe and Japan forced workers to pay high taxes, spend more of their income on food, and made it difficult for them to purchase cars or homes that were comparable to those available, at a lower cost, to workers in the United States. One striking measure of different living standards is this. In 1970, 96 percent of U.S. worker households had flush toilets in their homes. But only 9.2 percent of worker households in Japan had flush toilets in their apartments.[20]

During the twenty-five years after the war, work was widely available, salaries rose, wage differentials narrowed, and standards of living improved for most workers in the United States, Western Europe, and Japan. Under these conditions, the redistribution of production in manufacturing industries was regarded as unproblematic, even beneficial. For U.S. policymakers, the provision of "U.S.

jobs" to industries in Western Europe and Japan was a relatively small price to pay for military unity, political cooperation, and economic growth in the core. But this would change after 1970, when the price of redistributive policies became apparent to businesses and workers in the United States.

REDISTRIBUTION AND DEINDUSTRIALIZATION, 1970–1979

In 1971, the United States posted a modest trade deficit, its first since 1893. Though small, the $2.3 billion trade deficit signaled that the United States had already lost a significant share of production to industries located in Western Europe and Japan. During the next twenty years, U.S. job losses and trade deficits would mount, and much of the production previously performed in U.S. manufacturing industries would be redistributed abroad, a rapid globalization process known in the United States as "deindustrialization." The redistribution of production accelerated in the 1970s because economic conditions had changed. In the early 1970s, the *demand* for manufactured goods fell because the United States withdrew from the war in Vietnam and slowed the pace of the arms and space races with the Soviet Union. It fell too because the OPEC (Organization of Petroleum-Exporting Countries) oil embargo forced up energy prices, and poor Soviet grain harvests raised food prices. As energy and food prices rose, consumers cut back, and demand for manufactured and agricultural goods weakened, triggering a global recession.

Meanwhile, the global *supply* of manufactured goods had steadily increased. The recovery and growth of manufacturing industries in Western Europe and Japan increased supplies of goods from these regions. As a result, the battle for a share of global markets and a claim to a share of production in manufacturing industries intensified. As it did, many important manufacturing industries in the United States lost markets, and the jobs they provided were redistributed to industries located in Western Europe and Japan.

Why was production in U.S. manufacturing industries redistributed during the 1970s? There is no single answer. The reasons varied from one industry to the next. A brief look at government policies, industry practices, and consumer behavior in three important manufacturing industries—steel, autos, and aircraft—illustrates *some* of the different reasons why production was redistributed.

Steel

According to Benjamin Fairless, head of U.S. Steel in 1950, the U.S. steel industry was "bigger than those of *all* other nations on the earth put together."[21]

But the steel industry declined slowly in the 1960s and then rapidly in the 1970s, victimized by U.S. government policy and its own business practices.

During the postwar period, successive U.S. presidents worked hard to keep steel prices low. They did so to prevent steel price increases from triggering inflation and to ensure that the *other* U.S. industries that used steel—automakers, appliance manufacturers—paid low prices for it. When U.S. steel companies announced price hikes, Presidents Kennedy, Johnson, and Nixon attacked the steel industry, lobbied its leaders to rescind price increases, and ordered federal agencies to purchase steel from low-price competitors.[22] But government efforts to keep down prices lowered profit rates and made it difficult for the steel industry to use its earnings to modernize tired, aging plants.[23] The government also used antitrust suits to prevent mergers and promote competition. This helped keep prices low, though mergers might have helped the industry reorganize and increase its efficiency. Ironically, this policy led officials to reject proposed mergers among U.S. firms but allowed them to be acquired by *foreign* firms.[24] When steel industry firms asked the government to levy tariffs on steel imports or prosecute foreign firms producers that illegally "dumped" cheap steel in U.S. markets, officials repeatedly refused.[25]

For their part, industry leaders were slow to adopt new, energy-efficient technology, relying instead on aging plants and outmoded technologies because they wanted to pay for these before investing in new capacity. In 1978, 45 percent of U.S. plate mills were more than twenty-five years old, while only 5 percent of comparable Japanese mills were this old.[26] The industry's acrimonious relations with labor unions also triggered a series of long strikes in the 1950s, forcing the industry to raise worker pay. The industry might have afforded wage increases if it had invested in new technology and increased productivity, but the government's low-price policies made this difficult to do.[27]

Business customers also played a role in the steel industry's decline. U.S. businesses that used steel wanted cheap supplies, so they lobbied hard against steel industry efforts to raise prices or secure government protection against unfair foreign competition. General Motors, for instance, argued that actions against countries that dumped low-price steel in the United States "will have a negative effect on the prices [General Motors pays] for finished products with high steel content."[28] Then in the 1970s, as inflation pushed up steel prices, businesses began using plastic and aluminum materials to replace steel in cars and appliances.[29] This reduced the demand for steel, both foreign and domestic.

The U.S. steel industry was among the first U.S. industries to experience deindustrialization. As early as 1959, the United States imported more steel than it exported. By 1970, the U.S. share of world steel production had plummeted to 20 percent, down from 50 percent in 1945. Steel production then fell from 130 million tons in 1970 and then to 88 million tons in 1985. Today, the industry does not produce enough steel to meet domestic demand, and the

United States is "the only major industrial nation that is not self-sufficient in steel."[30]

Autos

The decline of the U.S. auto industry in the 1970s was due less to government policy than it was to business practices and consumer habits. Its decline was significant because 7.5 million people build, sell, or repair cars and trucks in the United States.[31]

The Volkswagen Beetle was the first import to make inroads in the U.S. market in the 1960s, largely because its size, price, and durability were unmatched by models made in Detroit. By 1970, it had captured 15 percent of the U.S. market.[32] During the 1970s, it was superseded by Japanese models. Japanese cars captured U.S. markets for a variety of reasons. Carmakers in Japan adopted new technologies like the system of "just-in-time production" or "*kanban*," which reduced inventory costs, and made cars that were stronger and used less steel. They developed amicable relations with workers in Japan, enabling them to increase production and improve quality. So when oil prices rose in the 1970s, cost-conscious consumers in the United States turned to high-mileage, inexpensive, durable cars made in Japan. They bought only four million Japanese cars in 1970 but purchased twelve million in 1980.

For their part, U.S. automakers were slow to adopt new technologies and develop cheap, high-quality, fuel-efficient models that could compete with imports. Their acrimonious relations with workers and their unions prevented the industry from significantly improving productivity or quality in the 1960s and 1970s.[33] In 1980, the four major U.S. automakers lost $4 billion and Chrysler was on the verge of bankruptcy.[34]

Still, unlike the steel industry, U.S. automakers were not without resources. In the 1950s and 1960s, Ford had opened factories in Western Europe, building cars and employing workers there. In the 1970s and 1980s, other U.S. carmakers followed suit, opening factories overseas, many in Latin America. By 1980, the industry had *itself* moved 37.2 percent of its production abroad. Production in the U.S. auto industry was redistributed both because other core firms captured U.S. markets and because U.S. firms *themselves* redistributed work to other settings.

Aircraft

Unlike steel or autos, U.S. policymakers provided massive aid to the aircraft industry, which they viewed as essential to national defense. In the 1940s, the government built dams that provided cheap electricity to smelt aluminum, the essential raw material for modern aircraft, and purchased hundreds of thousands of planes from private manufacturers during the war.[35] After the war, the military poured billions of dollars into the industry, financing new technology and designs and providing demand for the development of new military and commercial aircraft. The government's purchase of a transport plane from Boeing enabled it to launch its first successful commercial aircraft, the 707.[36] As a result, the industry captured 90 percent of the world market, a position it held well into the 1970s.

But U.S. dominance did not go unchallenged. In 1965, aircraft firms in Western Europe organized Airbus, a consortium that used government aid to develop commercial aircraft. Government subsidies and private investment from European and American banks enabled Airbus to develop its first plane (with wings from Britain, cockpit from France, tail from Spain, edge flaps from Belgium, body from West Germany, and, importantly, engines from the United States).[37] Unlike its U.S. competitors, the plane ran on two engines rather than three and required two pilots, not three, which saved fuel and lowered operating costs. These were important considerations for Eastern Airlines, which made the first significant purchases of the new plane.[38] By 1988, Airbus had captured 23 percent of the world market. It wrested markets and jobs first from weak U.S. firms such as Lockheed and McDonnell Douglas. During the next decade, Airbus challenged Boeing, the world leader. In 1999, for the first time ever, Airbus received more orders for new planes than Boeing.[39] And in 2000, Airbus announced plans to build a new behemoth jet that could compete with Boeing for the lucrative long-haul business. The Boeing 747, which has long monopolized this business, has been Boeing's most successful plane, accounting for roughly half of its annual profits.[40] The development of a successful challenge by Airbus could have a huge impact on the distribution of aircraft production.

Although the deindustrialization of the U.S. aircraft industry came later than it did to the steel and auto industries, the effect was much the same. "Every time a $50 million airplane is sold by Airbus instead of Boeing," one expert observed, "America loses about 3,500 high-paying jobs for one year."[41]

THE REDISTRIBUTION OF PRODUCTION AND CHANGING GENDER ROLES

The redistribution of production generally resulted in job loss and falling wages for males in U.S. manufacturing industries. By eliminating jobs long reserved for men, the redistribution of production helped transform gender roles in the United States. When the steel, auto, and aircraft industries surrendered markets and ceded jobs to overseas competitors, they laid off the men who smelted steel, assembled cars, and fabricated aircraft. Except for a brief time during World War II, few women worked in these industries. During the postwar period—indeed, for most of this century—work in manufacturing had given men economic power in the labor force (largely through labor unions), political power in public life (primarily through the Democratic Party), and social authority in households (based largely on their role as breadwinners). The loss of wage work in manufacturing undermined male power in public life and male authority in private life.

Of course, job loss has not always resulted in the erosion of male power and authority. During the Great Depression, men lost manufacturing jobs in droves. But because few women were employed in manufacturing or service industries, and those who were lost their jobs, too, *male job loss* did not significantly alter gender roles. In the 1970s, however, male job loss was accompanied by the *entry* of women into service industries. It was the combination of these two, simultaneous developments—the *exit* of men from manufacturing and the *entry* of women into service industries—that transformed gender relations.

During the 1970s, a growing number of women secured work in service industries. This is somewhat surprising. One might think that the end of the war in Vietnam, the demobilization of troops, and the recession triggered by rising oil and food prices would have resulted in the expulsion of women from the labor force, just as it had done after World War II. But women were not expelled because the number of returning soldiers was small, because few women worked in manufacturing industries, and because the service industries where women were employed in large number were actually *growing* in this period.

Women entered the labor force in large numbers during the 1970s for two reasons. First, women needed to secure wage work to maintain household incomes in an inflationary-recessionary, job-and-income-loss environment. In a sense, deindustrialization *pushed* women into the labor force. Second, the service industry, which historically had reserved jobs for women, needed workers as the demand for its goods and services increased. Growing demand was the product of several related developments. Massive advertising and widely available credit encouraged U.S. workers to spend, not save. Workers spent an increasing percentage of their disposable income on consumer goods and services, raising the demand for services from the private sector. Increased government spending on social service–welfare programs also increased the demand for public service sector workers, and women found jobs as teachers, health care workers, and social service administrators.[42] Moreover, as women left home to take private and public sector service jobs, worker households began buying services that women could no longer or easily provide as housewives. This further stimulated the demand for women workers and also teenagers in service industries.[43] In 1964, for example, only 1.7 million Americans worked in restaurants and bars. But 7.1 million did so in 1994.[44] So the expansion of the service industry helped *pull* women into the labor force.

As a result of economic push and pull, the percentage of women in the paid workforce increased from 38 percent in 1970 to 43 percent in 1980. This increase was comparable to the gains made by women during World War II.

After 1980, women continued to enter the labor force, though at a slower rate, rising to 45 percent by 1990.[45]

Of course, women who took paid jobs did not stop working at home. They still shouldered substantial work loads as housewives.[46] So women's *total* work (unpaid household work plus wage work) increased substantially in this period, from an average of about 1,400 hours in 1969 to 1,700 hours in 1987.[47]

As women assumed more prominent economic roles, they also began playing a larger role in public and private life. Feminism and the emergence of the women's movement in the 1970s encouraged women to play more visible roles in politics and public life. The social status given women by wage income, and the autonomy provided by new reproductive technologies and legal rights (the Pill, divorce law reform, abortion rights), made it possible for many women to assume new roles in worker households. Of course, changing economic, political, and social roles for women and men frequently increased tensions between women and men, resulting in high divorce rates and the rise of female-headed households.

This development was perhaps first apparent for poor African American worker households. During the 1950s and 1960s, black men and women had migrated from the South to northern cities, and men found wage work in heavy industries. Because black men were heavily "concentrated in industries like steel" and in cities where manufacturing industries made their home, deindustrialization in the 1970s had a catastrophic impact on jobs and employment for African American males.[48]

The exit of black men from manufacturing, and the entry of black women into service industries and government assistance programs such as Aid to Families with Dependent Children, transformed gender relations and contributed to the rise of female-headed households. But while this development has often been portrayed as symptomatic of problems unique to African American households, it can be more usefully understood as the early expression of problems common to many white and Hispanic households in the United States. The problems evident in African American households were not an aberration but a harbinger. As it turned out, the exit of men from manufacturing and the entry of women into service industries transformed gender relations not only for African American households but also for other ethnic groups as well.

The ongoing redistribution of production in the United States, Western Europe, and Japan was joined in the 1980s and 1990s by another development: the *reorganization* of production.

REORGANIZING PRODUCTION IN THE UNITED STATES, 1980–2000

The redistribution of production, which generally came at the expense of male manufacturing workers in the United States, did not go unnoticed or unchallenged. In the 1980s, U.S. officials, alarmed about the loss of U.S. hegemony, adopted monetary and trade policies designed to reassert U.S. control over the redistributive process, stem manufacturing losses, and reclaim a share of production.

As a first step, U.S. policymakers devalued the dollar, first in 1971 and again in 1985 (a more extensive discussion of this development follows in chapter 3). As a second step in 1979, they raised interest rates (discussed at greater length in chapter 4). Third, in 1986 they initiated a series of trade negotiations with members of the General Agreement on Tariffs and Trade (GATT) and with neighboring states in North America (see chapter 9).[49]

U.S. dollar devaluations encouraged investors from Western Europe and Japan to buy U.S. assets and open factories of their own in the United States. For example, in 1987, Japanese firms built or acquired 239 factories in the United States, up from only 43 in 1984. Total foreign investment in the United States, most of it from Western Europe and Japan, increased from $184 billion in 1985 to $304 billion in 1988.[50]

High U.S. interest rates in the early 1980s persuaded investors in Western Europe, Japan, and Latin America to purchase U.S. treasury bonds. In 1980, for example, foreign investors bought $71 billion worth of U.S. bonds, with two-thirds of the money coming from Western Europe and Japan, and most of the rest from Latin America.[51] These developments encouraged European and Japanese investors to invest, for the first time, in the United States.

Prior to 1980, public resources and private investment had generally traveled in *one* direction, from the United States to Western Europe and Japan. But U.S. monetary policies in the 1980s altered investment traffic patterns. As Western European and Japanese investment in the United States increased (first buying public and then purchasing private assets), investment became *multi*lateral, not unilateral. The emergence of multilateral or "globalized" investment, however, was generally restricted to these three central regions.[52]

Much the same was true of trade. U.S. trade negotiations in the late 1980s and early 1990s were designed to reduce core barriers to U.S. exports. By persuading Western Europe and Japan to reduce trade and other barriers, U.S. officials hoped to increase U.S. exports and change the direction of trade flows. In the 1970s and 1980s, trade goods had been moving *from* Western Europe and Japan *to* the United States. The trade agreement adopted by GATT members in 1994 helped stimulate the flow of U.S. goods to its main trading partners, thereby multilateralizing or globalizing trade, along with investment.

Taken together, U.S. monetary and trade policies helped attract Western European and Japanese investment to the United States and open their doors to some U.S. goods. Essentially, these measures rescinded the economic advantages that U.S. policymakers had given Western Europe and Japan in the late 1940s, when generous monetary and trade policies were used to promote economic recovery and political cooperation during the cold war. But while these steps helped level the economic playing field, they did not greatly improve U.S. performance on the field. The redistribution of production continued in the 1980s, though at a slower pace than it had in the 1970s.

THE STOCK MARKET AND THE
REORGANIZATION OF PRODUCTION
IN THE UNITED STATES

Although U.S. monetary and trade policies helped level the playing field, they did not improve U.S. performance on it. But when U.S. officials amended social security, income tax, and antitrust programs in the early 1980s, they made it possible for U.S. corporations to undertake a vast reorganization of production in manufacturing and service industries. This reorganization helped U.S. industries regain markets in the 1990s, when industries in Japan and Western Europe slumped. For U.S. workers, however, this reorganization also resulted in job loss or downsizing and declining incomes.

The massive reorganization of production in the United States during the 1990s was propelled by obscure but important policy changes in the early 1980s. In 1981, the Reagan administration passed legislation to reform Social Security. As part of the package, officials made Individual Retirement Accounts (IRAs) more widely available to worker households. At the time, officials regarded this as a minor change to the Social Security program. They had little idea that it would have a huge impact on the stock market or trigger a massive reorganization of production.

As a result of changes to IRAs, workers rushed to take advantage of the tax breaks given to IRA accounts, and deposits in IRAs increased from $30 billion in 1980 to $370 billion in 1990. Much of the money deposited in IRA and 401(k) accounts, which also grew rapidly as a result of legislation adopted in 1978, was invested in the stock market, typically through mutual funds.[53] In 1982, less than 10 percent of U.S. households owned stocks. But tax-free accounts encouraged millions to invest in the stock market, and by 1998, nearly 49 percent of U.S. households owned stocks.[54]

In the mid-1980s, wealthy households and foreign investors also began investing heavily in the stock market. Wealthy Americans used money given them by tax cuts (the Reagan administration cut taxes on wealthy households from 70 percent to 28 percent in the early 1980s) to invest in the stock market. Foreign investors rushed to purchase U.S. stocks after the dollar was devalued in 1985 (the devaluation cut the price of U.S. assets for foreign buyers), and foreign investment in the stock market totaled $176 billion in 1986 (see chapter 3).

Investment from these sources poured rivers of money into the stock market. Think of them as downpours that filled the Mississippi (IRAs), the Tennessee (401ks), the Ohio (wealthy individuals), and the Missouri (foreign investors), which swelled the rivers and raised the barges and boats (stocks and bonds) that floated downstream. This flood of investment into the stock market essentially bid up stock prices and lifted the market into a long bull run.

Although government policies pushed investors toward the stock market, Wall Street exerted its own pull. The market was able to attract investors from worker, wealthy, and foreign households because stock prices were rising for the first time in a decade. The market's initial rise was given a jump start by two new government policies. First, the Reagan administration cut corporate taxes. Corporate income tax cuts allowed businesses to increase their dividends to shareholders, making them more attractive to investors. Second, and more important, the Reagan administration stopped enforcing antitrust laws (the 1890 Sherman Act and the 1914 Clayton Act), which had long prevented corporations from merging and monopolizing the production of goods and services. This allowed businesses to merge with other firms, cut costs, increase profits, and raise dividends, making them even more attractive to investors.

As new investment was pushed and pulled into Wall Street, stock prices rose, bid up by growing demand. Rising stock prices in turn put enormous pressure on U.S. corporations to boost profits and increase their payouts to investors, who expected dividends to keep pace with rising stock prices. To keep up with the Dow Joneses, corporate managers *reorganized* production. They merged with other firms, rearranged production, introduced new technology, and laid off or downsized workers in an unrelenting effort to raise productivity, cut costs, and increase profits. Higher profits could then be used to increase shareholder dividends, which in turn helped boost stock prices.

Between 1982 and 1987, the Dow Jones Industrial Average rose from 777 to 2,722, a threefold increase. This bull market came to an end on October 19, 1987, when prices fell 508 points, a 22 percent decline that resulted in a $1 trillion loss for investors. But the market soon recovered because the demand for stocks did not evaporate, as it had after the 1929 crash. Demand remained strong because worker-investors who held stocks in IRAs and 401(k)s could not easily withdraw their money without incurring stiff tax penalties, and because they had invested for the long term, using IRAs to provide for their retirement. Worker investors were, in effect, forced by the tax code to *stay* in the market and prop up prices. When other investors realized that the government and worker households had built a floor under the stock market, below which prices could not easily fall, investment resumed. By 1990, investment had returned to precrash levels, and prices began to rise again. Stock prices then surged upward, and the Dow climbed from 3,000 in 1990 to more than 11,000 in 1999, the longest bull market in U.S. history. As stock prices rose, the reorganization of production accelerated.

For businesses, rising stock prices put enormous pressure on managers to increase their profits so they could pay higher dividends to investors.[55] Firms that failed to do so were punished by investors, who sold off stock and drove down its price. When that happened, managers were fired and the firm became prey to others. To prevent this and survive in an inflationary stock price environment, managers have adopted two strategies to increase profits, payouts, and share prices. Both strategies typically resulted in job loss for workers.

The first strategy has been for managers to reorganize production by merging with other firms, sometimes divesting parts to relieve themselves of unprofitable burdens or to raise cash for other parts. By merging with other firms, managers tried to create economies of scale or obtain control of markets that would enable them to increase profits. Of course, this strategy only became feasible because the federal government stopped enforcing antitrust law.[56]

In 1980, the year before the current merger wave began, corporations announced mergers worth $33 billion. Since then, businesses have merged and merged again. On just one *day* in 1998 (November 23), corporate managers announced mergers worth $40 billion, a sum greater than the value of all mergers in 1980.[57] Between 1981 and 1996, firms arranged mergers worth $2 trillion. And the pace has since accelerated, with mergers worth $1 trillion recorded in 1997 and $1.6 trillion in 1998.[58] All told, there were 151,374 mergers worth $13 trillion between 1980 and 2000. "We're in the greatest merger wave in history," said John Shepard Wiley, a professor of antitrust law at UCLA. "There has been a sea change in [public] attitudes toward large mergers."[59]

A second strategy has been for managers to introduce new technology, lay off workers, and cut costs to increase productivity. For example, managers at Caterpillar, a heavy equipment manufacturer, closed nine plants and spent $1.8 billion to modernize its remaining factories. As new technology was introduced, the firm cut its workforce from ninety thousand to fifty-four thousand and increased production. "We've almost doubled our productivity since the mid-1980s," Caterpillar executive James Owens enthused.[60]

Business efforts to increase productivity have not been limited to manufacturing industries. Computer, phone, fax, and other electronic technologies—scanners, automatic tellers, and so on—have enabled managers to reorganize service sector firms, where it had long been difficult to deploy technology as a way of increasing productivity. The demand for technology that can improve productivity has spawned the growth of the computer industry, which in turn has transformed service industries. In 1995, experts predicted that "half of the nation's 59,000 branch banks will close and 450,000 of the 2.8 million jobs in the banking industry will disappear [by the year 2000]" as a result of new bank technologies like automated tellers.[61] As Carl Thur, president of the American Productivity Center, put it, "The trick [for U.S. business] is to get more output without a surge in employment."[62]

In the 1970s and early 1980s, productivity in U.S. firms increased slowly. But by merging with other firms, reorganizing business, introducing new technologies, laying off workers, and cutting costs, managers were able to increase the productivity of their firms. Between 1982 and 1994, "productivity increased about 19.5 percent."[63] Since then it has recently increased at high annual rates: 2.8 percent in 1996, 2.5 percent in 1997, and 3.0 percent in 1998. These rates are significantly higher than the 1.1 percent annual increases reported from 1973 to 1989.[64]

Increased productivity helped U.S. firms raise profits. Between 1983 and 1996, annual corporate profits nearly quadrupled, from less than $200 billion to $736 billion.[65] Higher profits made it possible to increase dividends to shareholders. This in turn has increased the value of corporate stock, drawn new money into the stock market, and driven stock prices higher, and higher still.

For workers, the reorganization of production, which has been driven by the stock market, has resulted in massive job loss or, as it came to be known, downsizing. Like other phrases used in the 1980s and 1990s—"involuntary force reductions," "rightsizing," "repositioning," "deselection," "reducing head count," "separated," "severed," "unassigned," and "reductions in force"—downsizing has meant one thing: "You're fired."

Mergers resulted in job loss because some jobs in combined firms overlapped. Merged banks did not need two branches on the same street; merged manufacturing firms did not need two sets of accountants to keep the books, much less two assembly lines making the same goods under different brand names.

Between 1981 and 1991, four million workers at Fortune 500 companies lost their jobs, and total employment in these large firms fell from sixteen to twelve million workers.[66] By 1998, the eight hundred largest U.S. firms employed only 17 percent of the workforce, down from nearly 26 percent in 1978.[67] Firms throughout the economy accelerated the pace of layoffs: 1.42 million workers were laid off in 1980, 3.26 million in 1995.[68] Of course, new jobs were also created, but many of them were on a part-time, temporary, or contractual basis. Some firms even "leased" their workers to other firms to cut costs and evade labor law restrictions.[69] As many as thirty million workers are now employed on a part-time, temporary, or contractual basis.[70]

Previous waves of change affected male workers in manufacturing: steel, autos, aircraft, construction. But contemporary downsizing has affected men *and* women, in manufacturing *and* service industries. It has affected skilled workers and college graduates, not just workers with high school diplomas.[71] It has affected white workers, not just African Americans and Hispanics. It has affected managers in offices and assembly line workers in factories. It has created two-tier workplaces, where permanent employees work alongside temporary or "permatemp" workers, who do the same jobs but receive very different salaries and benefits.[72] The only group of workers that has been relatively immune from downsizing has been government workers and public sector employees such as teachers.

Ongoing job loss and the rise of temporary and part-time employment has made it extremely difficult for workers to raise wages, *even though* their productivity has increased and profits have grown. This contrasts sharply with the early postwar period, when productivity gains enabled firms to increase profits.

In the earlier period, corporations raised wages both because they could afford to do so and because widespread union membership helped workers insist that productivity gains be shared. But this has changed. The reorganization of production has *dis*organized workers and weakened unions. Today, the percentage of unionized workers in private industry (only 9.4 percent) is what it was in 1929.[73] Unions would have to recruit fifteen million new members to regain their postwar strength.[74]

Although the reorganization of production has *weakened* worker claims on the profits created by productivity increases, it has *strengthened* investor claims on corporate profits. As a result, profits have been redistributed from workers to managers and shareholders. Because the reorganization of production is now being driven largely by the stock market, investors can now insist that any gains be shared with stockholders and managers, not with workers. As a result, workers have not been able to increase wages, despite the fact that corporations could afford to do so.

There is serious irony here. Workers who invested in the stock market to provide for their retirement helped fuel the stock price inflation that forced corporations to reorganize and, in the process, downsize workers. As *investors*, many workers benefited from rising stock prices and the corporate distribution of profits to shareholders. But as *workers*, many investors experienced job and income loss, which resulted from the reorganization of production and redistribution of profits. One *New York Times* writer captured this irony for workers in a headline that read, "You're Fired! (But Your Stock Is Way Up)."[75]

The reorganization of production led to job loss and declining wages. Labor's share of the national income declined, and the wealth it once claimed has been redistributed upward.[76] The richest 2.7 million Americans now claim as much wealth as the bottom 100 million Americans. The average income of the top 20 percent of American households increased from $109,500 in 1979 to $167,000 in 1997. The richest 1 percent saw their average income skyrocket from $420,000 in 1979 to $1.2 million in 1997, largely because their incomes from stock dividends and rising prices grew enormously.[77] But for the majority of workers during this period, wages actually declined, despite working harder, longer, and more productively. The average income for the bottom 20 percent of American households declined from $11,890 in 1979 to $11,400 in 1997.[78] In 1999, 215 million American workers took "home a thinner slice of the economic pie than [they did] in 1977."[79]

Moreover, men and women are working longer hours. Juliet Schor, author of *The Overworked American*, estimates that the hours worked by wage workers in the United States increased to 1,966 in 1999, surpassing the Japanese by 70 hours and Europeans by 320 hours (or almost nine full work weeks). "Excessive working time is a major problem," she concluded.[80]

Because men and women are working longer, many workers have less time for family, friends, or vacations. Working parents today spend "40 percent less time with their children than they did 30 years ago," MIT economist Lester Thurow reports.[81] Friendships also suffer from heavy work loads. Kim Sibley, who juggles two jobs in Flint, Michigan, was asked by a reporter whether her friends also had dual careers. "I don't have time for friends," she replied.[82]

Vacations are also a disappearing entity. In 1996, 38 percent of all worker families in the United States did *not* take any vacation, an increase from the 34 percent that did not vacation in 1995. And the average length of vacations for those who do manage to enjoy time off has declined from five days to four days in the last ten years.[83]

Increased work loads can sometimes be fatal. The number of workers asked to work evening or night shifts has increased 30 percent since 1985, and fifteen million workers now work nondaytime shifts. As a result, the number of fatigue-related auto accidents has increased. Government highway safety officials estimate that 1,500 traffic deaths and 40,000 injuries are annually caused by fatigued workers, particularly those with late shifts.[84]

LONG-TERM PROBLEMS WITH THE STOCK MARKET

There are two long-term problems with the emergence of the stock market as the institution that drives economic change in the United States. First, the stock market, which has relied on a steady infusion of cash to push stock prices up, may have difficulty obtaining the money it needs to continue growing in the future. Second, the stock market may not be able to sustain stock prices when baby boomers retire and begin withdrawing money from their IRAs and 401(k)s.

During the past twenty years, the stock market has relied on a steady flow of cash from different sources. The flood of cash from IRAs and 401(k)s and pension funds have been critical to its success, helping drive up prices during the longest bull market in history. But the supply of cash from these sources is not unlimited, in part because the amount of money people can contribute to IRAs is restricted by law and by their ability to save.

To encourage a new flood of cash into the stock market, the U.S. Congress in 2001 passed legislation to increase the amount that individuals can contribute to their IRAs, from $2,000 to $5,000 by 2008.[85] But while this step may encourage a new wave of investment, it will come primarily from rich households who can afford to set aside $10,000 (per couple) each year for their retirement. Working- and middle-class households, who now have substantial debts and little savings, will not be able to contribute the full amount. This source of investment is largely tapped out. In the long run, this means that the level of investment that assisted the growth of the stock market in the 1980s and 1990s may no longer be forthcoming. And without new infusions of cash, the market may not be as robust as it has been.

Of course, policymakers have proposed privatizing part of Social Security to make more money available to the stock market. They propose that workers be allowed to take one-half of the money withheld each month from their pay-checks and invest it themselves for their retirement. This would vastly increase the amount of money flowing toward Wall Street. But this plan has several inherent problems. Because the stock market is volatile—it goes up *and* down— workers will assume greater risk than they now do under Social Security, which promises fixed benefits after retirement.[86] Some workers will invest more wisely than others, so workers earning the same amount may end up with very different amounts of money available to them when they retire. Women earn less than men (about 30 percent less on average), so men will have more money available to invest. This could reinforce gender inequality when women and men retire.

A second, long-term problem is this: Many of the working- and middle-class workers who invested in the stock market did so to provide for their retirement. When stock prices declined in 1987 and 2001, they stayed *in* the market, help-ing prop up prices and avert a more serious collapse. They did not sell because they would have been penalized if they withdraw money from IRAs and because they were investing, long-term, for their retirement. Their steadfast support was good for the market and for the economy that depends on its health.

But eventually these worker investors will retire and begin withdrawing money from the market. They will do so in significant numbers because the baby boom generation to which they belong is *large*. As they begin to pull cash out of the market, stock prices could weaken. Remember that money flowing into the market helps create a bull market, while money taken out of the market contri-butes to a bear market. "If demography has played a part in driving the market up," Niall Ferguson has argued, "it can only have the reverse effect as the 'Baby Boomers' retire and begin to live off their accumulated assets."[87]

The decline in stock prices during 2001, particularly after the September 11 disasters at the World Trade Center towers and the Pentagon, illustrated the problems with relying on the stock market to provide money for people's retire-ment. People with 401(k) accounts saw the value of the investments decline, on average, from $46,740 to $41,919.[88] This was the first time in twenty years that "the average account lost money, even after thousands of dollars of new contri-butions."[89] People who retire during a periodic market downturn face a very dif-ferent financial future than people who retire during an upturn. Jim Dellinger, a baker who has a 401(k) through his employer, Giant Foods, saw his two mutual funds decline by 12 and 16 percent during the first six months of 2001. "I think about it every day. I have basically my life savings in there," he said.[90]

BOOM IN THE UNITED STATES, BUST IN
WESTERN EUROPE AND JAPAN, 1990–2000

The reorganization of production resulted in job and income loss for both women and men in the United States. But it also helped manufacturing and service industries increase productivity and profitability, which helped industry increase investment in research and development.[91] These developments improved the performance of U.S. industries in the 1990s in redistributive battles with industries based in Western Europe and Japan. The gains made by U.S. businesses in the 1990s promoted overall economic growth, providing jobs for downsized wage workers, at least for a time, though on a more casual and lower-paid basis.

U.S. businesses expanded and unemployment rates fell after 1992 as a result of several developments. Slumping economies in Western Europe and Japan weakened manufacturing and service industries based there, providing reorganized U.S. industries with the opportunity to make redistributive gains. U.S. businesses did well in the 1990s because businesses in Japan and Western Europe did not.

In the early 1990s, Japan and Western Europe both experienced economic crises. Although the crisis had different origins in each, it confronted both regions with their first real setbacks since World War II, problems that persisted throughout the decade.

Japan

In Japan, problems began in 1985. The devaluation of the dollar eventually doubled the value of the yen, increasing the value of assets held by Japanese banks (see chapter 3). Banks and workers invested this newfound wealth in the stock market and in real estate. The flood of new investment bid up stock and real estate prices. The Nikkei Index (the Japanese stock market) rose from 12,000 in 1986 to 38,916 in 1990, a threefold increase.[92] The price of residential and commercial real estate quadrupled between 1985 and 1990.[93] It was said in 1990 that the value of land in Tokyo alone was worth more than all the land in the United States. Japanese consumers had so much money to burn that they even poured money into the market for pet insects, particularly for rare beetles called *ohkuwagata*. In 1990, single bugs sold for $7,000 at department stores, and one huge specimen sold for $30,000.[94]

But too much money can cause problems. The money pouring into the stock and real estate markets drove prices to unsustainably high levels. In the stock market, prices soared while dividend yields fell.[95] The "bubble" of high stock prices burst in 1990. Prices fell one-half by 1991 and continued falling. Between 1990 and 1992, the Nikkei Index registered a 61 percent decline.[96] Stock prices did not recover from the crash in Japan, as they had in the United States after the 1987 crash, because investors fled the market and did not return.

The Japanese real estate market soon followed. In 1990, many households in Japan found they would need to use the wages of a lifetime just to buy one *tsubo* (six feet by six feet) of land in Tokyo.[97] When owners discovered they could not sell high-priced property, the residential and commercial real estate markets collapsed and prices plummeted, bankrupting individuals, businesses, and banks that had used land as collateral for other loans. The pet insect market also collapsed. Bugs that sold for $7,000 during the beetle mania of the 1980s were marked down to only $300 in 1999.[98]

For workers, the recession led to widespread layoffs and rising unemployment rates, which doubled in the 1990s. This came as a great shock to workers in a country where businesses routinely provided lifetime employment and regular wage increases to their male workers. Corporations began laying off workers, hiring "temporary" workers, eliminating seniority-based pay systems, and introducing "merit pay."[99] "For years, everyone's pay increased as they got older," observed Shoji Hiraide, general manager of a Tokyo department store. "It made everyone think that we are all in the middle class. But lifetime employment is crumbling and salaries are based more on merit and performance. In seven or eight years, Japanese society will look much more like Western society, with gaps between rich and poor that can be clearly seen."[100]

The recession fell most heavily on female workers, who were long treated as "temporary workers" by corporations that guaranteed lifetime employment only to men. Women in temporary jobs were dismissed first. The government disguised rising employment for women by recording them as "housewives," not "unemployed workers." This practice understated real unemployment rates. The fact that Japanese businesses downsized even men in lifetime positions meant that they had already laid off a great many women. "Somehow, although I've done nothing wrong, I feel like a criminal," Kimiko Kauda said after being fired from her job of thirty years. "I have never heard of people being fired in my neighborhood or among my friends."[101]

Western Europe

During the 1990s, Western Europe also became mired in recession, though for different reasons than Japan. Problems began in Germany. The 1989 collapse of the communist government in East Germany led to German unification. The German government then spent $600 billion to rebuild the region's economic infrastructure, provide benefits to workers, purchase voter loyalty, and prevent a "widespread social explosion" by workers laid off as the East deindustrialized.[102] Because spending on this scale—$600 billion for a small region with the population of New York state—can trigger inflation, the government raised taxes, and the Bundesbank, which controls monetary policy, raised interest rates to reduce inflationary pressures. These measures triggered a sharp recession and widespread job loss.[103] In the early 1990s, unemployment rates doubled from 6 percent to 12 percent in Germany, and they were twice this rate in the East, where deindustrialization and recession were joined. Faced with high unemployment rates, German unions agreed to substantial pay cuts (10 percent in 1997), benefit reductions, shorter vacations, and work rule concessions. "Corporations want to abolish the social consensus in Germany," union negotiator Peter Blechschmidt said of the 1997 wage cuts. "They are trying to change this into a different country."[104] A country more like the United States.

The situation in Germany was not unique. Countries throughout Western Europe also experienced recession and rising unemployment, partly due to the cost of European unification. In 1991, most Western European states agreed at Maastricht, in the Netherlands, to adopt a common currency (the United Kingdom did not do so). To prepare for the introduction of a single currency in 1999, governments in the European Union set a number of common economic goals: reducing budget deficits, stabilizing exchange rates, and, most important, reducing inflation. To meet this last goal, member governments raised interest rates. As in Germany, high interest rates triggered a regional recession, and unemployment soared throughout Europe. Unemployment rose to 12 percent in France and Italy, 13 percent in Ireland, 22 percent in Spain, and even more in regions like southern Italy.[105]

Although recession and job loss affected workers throughout Western Europe, women were the big losers, particularly in eastern Germany. Nearly 60 percent of the four million who had been employed in 1989 lost their jobs during the next four years.[106] Only half as many men lost their jobs in the same period. Young people have also been affected in disproportionate numbers. Like Japan, Western European industries had strong seniority systems. So when recession hit, they laid off younger workers. In general, young people were unemployed at twice the rate (21.8 percent) as workers over twenty-five years old.[107]

Of course, by the late 1990s, governments and industries in Western Europe and Japan responded to renewed U.S. competitiveness by reorganizing production. They did so by adopting measures pioneered in the United States. For a start, governments and businesses have tried to increase the role played by investors and stock markets. In Germany, for instance, worker-consumers are being encouraged to adopt an *Aktienkultur,* or "stock culture," and invest their substantial savings in the stock market.[108] To facilitate this, the government plans to cut capital gains taxes on German corporations, which would make it easier for them to reorganize and consolidate industry.[109] And business has increased advertising expenditures to encourage stock market investment. Deutsche Telekom recently spent $150 million on a campaign to advertise a $10 billion stock offering, which was then used to purchase Telecom Italia, one of the first big cross-border mergers in Western Europe.[110] These policies and practices are helping jump-start the Aktienkultur, not only in Germany but across Europe.[111]

Mergers have played a growing role in the reorganization of production in Europe. The value of annual mergers in Western Europe jumped dramatically in the second half of the 1990s, growing from about $150 billion in 1994 to more than $600 billion in 1999.[112] As businesses merged and modernized, they typically downsized workers, just like their corporate counterparts in the United States. This has helped keep unemployment rates high. Downsizing, together with efforts to curb seniority-based pay systems and exact wage concessions from unionized workers, has kept wages from rising.

The spreading merger wave in the United States and Western Europe has itself begun to alter the redistributive process and reorganize production in new ways. Initially, the redistribution of production was managed largely by government policies—exchange rates, tariff barriers, defense spending, and foreign aid. But today, the redistribution of production is directed increasingly by the cross-border corporations that formed when industries reorganized: Mercedes–Chrysler, Ford–Volvo, Renault–Nissan, Aegon TransAmerica–Deutsche Telekom–Telecom Italia, Volkswagen–Rolls Royce, and MCI–Worldcom. These cross-border corporations (XBCs) differ from their transnational corporation (TNC) predecessors. TNCs were firms based in one country, which conducted businesses through subsidiaries in other states. XBCs, by contrast, are firms with origins in more than one state, usually formed by mergers, which conduct business in other states. Because XBCs now redistribute production as a process *internal* to a corporation that spans multiple states, government policies that used to shape the redistributive process now play a less significant role in determining who gets what jobs.

It is important to note that the redistribution of wage work, managed first by governments and more recently by XBCs, generally resulted in the redistribution of production in the United States, Western Europe, and Japan. Jobs in U.S. industries were redistributed to industries in Western Europe and Japan, *not* to industries in poor countries. Ford workers in Detroit lost jobs to Toyota workers in Yokohama and Volkswagen workers in Munich; Boeing workers in Seattle lost jobs to Airbus workers in London, Paris, Milan, and Hamburg. Of course, *some* production was redistributed to industries in Latin America and East Asia, but not much. With a few exceptions, the redistribution and reorganization of production, two processes that define contemporary globalization, have been generally confined in the rich countries. As such, globalization should be understood as a selective, not ubiquitous, process, which best characterizes developments in the United States, Western Europe, and Japan.

Of course, as industries in Western Europe and Japan reorganize along U.S. lines (the process is more advanced in Western Europe than it is in Japan), their ability to compete in redistributive battles with the United States will increase, and they may reclaim some of the production obtained by U.S. industries in the 1990s.

The redistribution and reorganization of production have resulted in job and income loss for workers in all three regions. But while workers in the United States, Western Europe, and Japan face many of the same problems, they do so with different resources at their disposal.

In the United States, worker households are heavily indebted. To maintain their standards of living, they have spent down their savings. During the 1990s, workers in the United States used their savings and borrowed money to shop and buy. "The American consumer has taken the globe from deep contraction back to flatness to recovery," one investment analyst observed.[113] But 1998 was a turning point. This was the first year since the Great Depression that U.S. workers did not acquire *any* net savings.[114] As savings declined, household debts increased. The average consumer debt per household nearly doubled in the last decade, rising from nearly $39,000 in 1990 to $66,000 in 2000. And since 1973, debt has grown as a percentage of income from 58 percent to 85 percent.[115]

Although much of the $5.5 trillion in total household debt is in the form of home loans, worker households now owe $350 billion on their credit cards.[116] Not surprisingly, bankruptcies are at record levels: one in one hundred households annually declare bankruptcy.[117] "There is a lid on earnings, but meanwhile, people's cost of living and their desire for fancier lifestyles go unabated," observed A. Stevens Quigley, a Seattle bankruptcy lawyer.[118] Student debt also grew from $18 billion to $33 billion between 1991 and 1997, and graduates owe $18,000 on average when they leave college.[119]

Although worker households are up to their ears in debt, some can tap other resources that are not typically counted in savings rate/debt burden ledgers. The generation of workers who accumulated savings, pensions, and houses during the 1950s and 1960s has transferred important assets to their children, the heavily indebted baby boomers. Some economists estimate that as much as 25 percent of worker household income comes from parents and relatives.[120] Essentially, the postwar generation has helped the current generation of wage workers survive. In addition to income from this source, worker households who used IRAs to invest in the stock market have generally seen the value of their stocks rise, which would boost their real savings.[121] But even after adjusting for income from these two sources, which are not available to most households, U.S. workers are still heavily indebted.

Compare the condition of worker households in the United States with households in Japan and Western Europe. Although savings rates in Japan and Western Europe have recently declined, as workers used up some savings during the recession and retired workers spent their accumulated savings, they still save a large percentage of their income.[122] In Japan, households saved, on average,

12 percent of their disposable income in 1999 and had deposited $100,000 in the bank.[123]

In the United States, workers are heavily indebted and household account balances are in the red. But in Japan and Western Europe, where workers have substantial savings and few debts, household account balances are in the black. As a consequence, households in Japan and Western Europe are in a much better position to weather changes associated with the redistribution and reorganization of production than their peers in the United States. So while workers in all three regions now have comparable incomes and face similar problems, they confront economic change with different resources. So when new economic storms emerge, their fortunes may diverge.

To understand some of these developments in greater detail, we will now return to the early 1970s, when U.S. policymakers first confronted two important problems: (1) rising competition with businesses in Western Europe and Japan and (2) rising inflation. The solutions U.S. officials advanced to solve these two problems had a huge impact on people in the United States and around the world. Moreover, the consequences of decisions made then are still being felt today.

NOTES

1. Bertrand Bellon and Jorge Niosi, *The Decline of the American Economy* (Montreal: Black Rose Books, 1988), 29.

2. T. E. Vadney, *The World since 1945* (London: Penguin, 1992), 73.

3. Ruth Sivard, *World Military and Social Expenditures, 1987–88* (Washington, D.C.: World Priorities, 1987), 37.

4. Eric Helleiner, *States and the Reemergence of Global Finance: From Bretton Woods to the 1990s* (Ithaca, N.Y.: Cornell University Press, 1994), 58–59.

5. Henry C. Dethloff, *The United States and the Global Economy since 1945* (New York: Harcourt Brace, 1997), 72.

6. Richard J. Barnet and John Cavanah, *Global Dreams: Imperial Corporations and the New World Order* (New York: Touchstone, 1994), 113; Peter Dicken, *Global Shift: The Internationalization of Economic Activity* (New York: Guilford, 1992), 67.

7. Ikeda Satoshi, "World Production," in *The Age of Transition: Trajectory of the World-System, 1945–2025*, ed. Terence K. Hopkins and Immanuel Wallerstein (London: Zed, 1996), 48; A. G. Kenwood and A. L. Lougheed, *The Growth of the International Economy, 1820–1990* (London: Routledge, 1992), 250; Ernst Mandel, *Europe vs. America: Contradictions of Imperialism* (New York: Monthly Review Press, 1970), 13; Cynthia Day Wallace and John M. Kline, *EC 92 and Changing Global Investment Patterns: Implications for the U.S.–EC Relationship* (Washington, D.C.: Center for Strategic and International Studies, 1992), 2; Barnet and Cavanah, *Global Dreams*, 42.

8. This is a rough estimate. Economists calculate that $1 billion of U.S. investment overseas results in the loss of 26,500 domestic jobs. So investments worth $78 billion

would result in the loss of more than two million jobs in the United States, the number of people living in Boston, Kansas City, Miami, and San Francisco.

9. Shigeto Tsru, *Japan's Capitalism: Creative Defeat and Beyond* (Cambridge: Cambridge University Press, 1993), 49–51, 78.

10. Saskia Sassen, *Globalization and Its Discontents* (New York: Harcourt Brace, 1997), 39, 79.

11. Jon Halliday, *A Political History of Japanese Capitalism* (New York: Pantheon, 1975), 279.

12. Shigeto, *Japan's Capitalism*, 109; Halliday, *A Political History of Japanese Capitalism*, 273; Michael J. Piore and Charles F. Sabel, *The Second Industrial Divide: Possibilities for Prosperity* (New York: Basic Books, 1984), 161.

13. Halliday, *A Political History of Japanese Capitalism*, 224–27. In 2000, one woman successfully sued her employer for job discrimination because managers denied her a pay raise for twenty-one years. Howard W. French, "Women Win a Battle, but Job Bias Still Rules Japan," *New York Times*, February 26, 2000.

14. Nicholas Lehman, *The Promised Land: The Great Black Migration and How It Changed America* (New York: Knopf, 1991), 6.

15. Ruth Milkman, "Union Responses to Workforce Feminization in the United States," in *The Challenge of Restructuring: North American Labor Movements Respond*, eds. Jane Jenson and Rianne Mahon (Philadelphia: Temple University Press, 1993), 229.

16. Lawrence Mishel, Jared Bernstein, and John Schmitt, *The State of Working America, 1998–99* (Ithaca, N.Y.: Economic Policy Institute, Cornell University Press, 1999), 182; Paul Hirst and Grahame Thompson, *Globalization in Question: The International Economy and the Possibilities of Governance* (Cambridge: Polity, 1996), 26; Sassen, *Globalization and Its Discontents*, 35; Richard B. Craig, *The Bracero Program: Interest Groups and Foreign Policy* (Austin: University of Texas Press, 1971), 102–3.

17. Saskia Sassen, *Losing Control? Sovereignty in an Age of Globalization* (New York: Columbia University Press, 1996), 81; Faruk Tabak, "The World Labour Force," in *The Age of Transition*, 94; Robert K. Schaeffer, *Power to the People: Democratization around the World* (Boulder, Colo.: Westview, 1997), 66–67, 189.

18. Shigeto, *Japan's Capitalism*, 68.

19. B. J. McCormick, *The World Economy: Patterns of Growth and Change* (Oxford: Allan, 1988), 188.

20. Juliet B. Schor, *The Overworked American: The Unexpected Decline of Leisure* (New York: Basic Books, 1991), 111; Lehman, *The Promised Land*, 111; Halliday, *A Political History of Japanese Capitalism*, 231.

21. Judith Stein, *Running Steel, Running America: Race, Economic Policy, and the Decline of Liberalism* (Chapel Hill: University of North Carolina Press, 1998), 7.

22. Paul R. Lawrence and Davis Dyer, *Renewing American Industry* (New York: Free Press, 1983), 72; Stein, *Running Steel*, 209, 223.

23. Stein, *Running Steel*, 210.

24. Stein, *Running Steel*, 290.

25. In 1967, for example, the Japanese steel industry charged Japanese customers $116 a ton for steel but charged U.S. customers only $96 a ton, a clear case of illegal dumping. Stein, *Running Steel*, 218, 257. Despite evidence that foreign producers were dumping steel and seizing U.S. markets, officials refused to take action, arguing that

doing so would increase domestic prices or undermine political relations with its allies. President Clinton rejected tariffs on cheap steel imports from Russia, despite obvious dumping, because, he said, it would jeopardize U.S.-Soviet political relations and deprive them of the earnings they needed to repay their debts to the West. "It's extremely important that we not cut off one of the few sources of raising hard currency that the Russians have right now," one adviser said. David E. Sanger, "U.S. Says Japan, Brazil Dumped Steel," *New York Times*, February 13, 1999.

26. Ira C. Magaziner and Mark Patinkin, *The Silent War: Inside the Global Business Battles Shaping America's Future* (New York: Vintage, 1990), 309.

27. Stein, *Running Steel*, 16.

28. Leslie Wayne, "American Steel at the Barricades," *New York Times*, December 10, 1998.

29. Lawrence and Dyer, *Renewing American Industry*, 72.

30. Stein, *Running Steel*, 295, 303; Frank Levy, *Dollars and Dreams: The Changing American Income Distribution* (New York: Russell Sage Foundation, 1987), 91; Dethloff, *The United States and the Global Economy since 1945*, 124.

31. Tom Redburn, "A Revolution Built in Mr. Ford's Factory," *New York Times*, January 2, 2000.

32. William J. Abernathy, Kim B. Clark, and Alan M. Kantrow, *Industrial Renaissance: Producing a Competitive Future for America* (New York: Basic Books, 1983), 47, 54; Magaziner and Patinkin, *The Silent War*, 5–7.

33. James A. Geschwender, *Racial Stratification in America* (Dubuque, Iowa: Brown, 1978), 224, 236–37.

34. Lawrence and Dyer, *Renewing American Industry*, 18; Kim Moody, "Labor Giverbacks and Labor Fightbacks," in *The Imperiled Economy. Book II. Through the Safety Net*, ed. Robert Cherry (New York: Union for Radical Economics, 1988), 161.

35. Dethloff, *The United States and the Global Economy since 1945*, 44.

36. William Greider, *One World, Ready or Not: The Manic Logic of Global Capitalism* (New York: Simon & Schuster, 1997), 125; Ian McIntyre, *Dogfight: The Transatlantic Battle over Airbus* (Westport, Conn.: Praeger, 1992), 2.

37. McIntyre, *Dogfight*, 44–45; Magaziner and Patinkin, *The Silent War*, 230, 244, 251–52.

38. McIntyre, *Dogfight*, xx, 44; Magaziner and Patinkin, *The Silent War*, 255.

39. John Tagliabue, "A Yankee in Europe's Court," *New York Times*, February 11, 2000; Magaziner and Patinkin, *The Silent War*, 232.

40. John Tagliabue, "Airbus Industries Is Considering a Very Big Jet," *New York Times*, February 3, 2001.

41. Magaziner and Patinkin, *The Silent War*, 257.

42. Wilson, 1996, 32–33. Many of the women who found public sector jobs were organized by unions. The growth of public sector unions, representing predominantly female workers, prevented unions from declining more sharply than they did. Indeed, unions were much more successful organizing women than men after 1970. Milkman, "Union Responses," 237, 239.

43. Schor, *The Overworked American*, 26.

44. David Cay Johnston, "The Servant Class Is at the Counter," *New York Times*, August 27, 1995.

45. Milkman, "Union Responses," 229.

46. Schor, *The Overworked American,* 87–88.

47. Schor, *The Overworked American,* 29.

48. Stein, *Running Steel,* 306, 316; Barnet and Cavanah, *Global Dreams,* 54.

49. Stock price inflation is a discriminatory economic process. See also the discussion in chapter 4.

50. Edward M. Graham and Paul R. Krugman, *Foreign Direct Investment in the United States* (Washington, D.C.: Institute for International Economics, 1991), 14, 21; Neil Reid, "Japanese Direct Investment in the U.S. Manufacturing Sector," in *The Internationalization of Japan,* eds. Glenn D. Hook and Michael A. Weiner (London: Routledge, 1992), 66; Alan Scott, ed., *The Limits of Globalization: Cases and Arguments* (London: Routledge, 1997), 141.

51. Bill Orr, *The Global Economy in the 90s: A User's Guide* (New York: New York University Press, 1992), 287.

52. Arthur A. Alderson, "Globalization and Deindustrialization: Direct Investment and the Decline of Manufacturing Employment in 17 OECD Nations," *Journal of World-Systems Research* 3, no. 1 (1997): 5.

53. Danny Hakim, "Controlling 401(k) Assets," *New York Times,* November 17, 2000.

54. Richard W. Stevenson, "Fed Says Economy Increased Net Worth of Most Families," *New York Times,* January 19, 2000; Mishel et al., *The State of Working America, 1998–99,* 268.

55. Floyd Norris, "Dividends Rise, but Not as Fast as Stocks," *New York Times,* January 3, 1997.

56. In the 1980s, Republican administrators abandoned antitrust because they believed mergers would increase business efficiency and make U.S. companies stronger and more competitive with megafirms in Western Europe, where antitrust laws are weak, and in Japan, where they are virtually nonexistent.

57. Laura M. Holson, "A Day for Mergers, with $40 Billion in Play," *New York Times,* November 24, 1998.

58. Stephen Labaton, "Merger Wave Spurs a New Scrutiny," *New York Times,* December 13, 1998; Laura M. Holson, "The Deal Still Rules," *New York Times,* February 14, 1999. Bankers and lawyers received more than $2 billion in fees for arranging the Exxon–Mobil merger in 1998. *New York Times,* "Costs of Exxon-Mobil Deal to Top $2 billion," *New York Times,* April 6, 1999.

59. Stephen Labaton, "Despite a Tough Stance or Two, White House Is Still Consolidation Friendly," *New York Times,* November 8, 1999.

60. James Sterngold, "Facing the Next Recession without Fear," *New York Times,* May 9, 1995.

61. Saul Hansell, "Wave of Mergers Is Transforming American Banking," *New York Times,* August 21, 1995.

62. Stanley Aronowitz and William DiFazio, *The Jobless Future: Sci-Tech and the Dogma of Work* (Minneapolis: University of Minnesota Press, 1994), 3.

63. John Judis, "Should an Economist Be in Charge of the Economy?" *The New Republic,* June 7, 1999.

64. Michael Wallace, "Downsizing the American Dream: Work and Family at Centu-

ry's End," in *Challenges for Work and Family in the Twenty-First Century*, eds. Dana Vannoy and Paula J. Dubeck (New York: Aldine de Gruyter, 1998), 23; Mishel et al., *The State of Working America, 1998–99*, 29.

65. Robert J. Samuelson, "Economic Mythmaking," *Newsweek*, September 8, 1997; Mishel et al., *The State of Working America, 1998–99*, 69.

66. Robert D. Hershey, Jr., "Survey Finds 6 Million, Fewer Than Thought, in Impermanent Jobs," *New York Times*, August 19, 1995.

67. Hershey, "Survey Finds."

68. Louis Uchitelle and N. R. Kleinfield, "On the Battlefields of Business, Millions of Casualties," *New York Times*, March 3, 1996. See the critique of this in John Cassidy, "All Worked Up," *New Yorker*, April 22, 1996, 52–53; Davil L. Birch, "The Hidden Economy," *Wall Street Journal*, June 10, 1998, 23, and the *Times'* s response: Louis Uchitelle, "Despite Drop, Rate of Layoffs Remains High," *New York Times*, August 23, 1996.

69. Christopher D. Cook, "Workers for Rent," *In These Times*, July 22, 1996; Barry Meier, "Some 'Worker Leasing' Programs Defraud Insurers and Employers," *New York Times*, March 20, 1992.

70. Chris Tilly, "Short Hours, Short Shrift: The Causes and Consequences of Part-Time Employment," in *New Policies for the Part-Time and Contingent Workforce*, ed. Virgnia L. DuRivage (Armonk, N.Y.: Sharpe, 1992), 15, 17; Hershey, "Survey Finds."

71. One in five college graduates now works in a low-wage job that does *not* require a college degree. Sylvia Nasar, "More College Graduates Taking Low-Wage Jobs," *New York Times*, August 7, 1992.

72. Steven Greenhouse, "Equal Work, Less-Equal Perks," *New York Times*, March 30, 1998.

73. Steven Greenhouse, "Growth in Unions' Membership in 1999 Was the Best in Two Decades," *New York Times*, January 20, 2000.

74. Andrew Hacker, "Who's Sticking to the Union?" *New York Review of Books*, February 18, 1999; Steven Greenhouse, "Union Membership Slides Despite Increased Organizing," *New York Times*, March 22, 1998.

75. Floyd Norris, "You're Fired! (But Your Stock Is Way Up)," *New York Times*, September 3, 1995.

76. Louis Uchitelle, "As Class Struggle Subsides, Less Pie for the Workers," *New York Times*, December 5, 1999.

77. Richard W. Stevenson, "Study Details Income Gap between Rich and Poor," *New York Times*, May 31, 2001.

78. Stevenson, "Study Details"; Jeff Faux and Larry Mishel, "Inequality and the Global Economy," in *Global Capitalism*, eds. Will Hutton and Anthony Giddens (New York: New Press, 2000), 10.

79. David Cay Johnston, "Gap between Rich and Poor Found Substantially Wider," *New York Times*, December 5, 1999.

80. Steven Greenhouse, "So Much Work, So Little Time," *New York Times*, September 5, 1999. Median-income worker households with two wage earners together worked 20 percent more hours in 1997 than they did in 1979.

81. Lester Thurow, "Companies Merge; Families Break Up," *New York Times*, September 3, 1995.

82. John Foren, "Spotlight on Moonlighters," *San Francisco Chronicle*, May 31, 1992.

83. Edwin McDowell, "The Abbreviated Tourist," *New York Times*, July 31, 1997; Edwin McDowell, "More Work or Less Work Can Equal No Time Off," *New York Times*, July 6, 1996.

84. "Sleep-Depriving Jobs Linked to Accidents," *New York Times*, June 4, 1999.

85. David Cay Johnston, "Tax Bill Expands Limits on Retirement Savings," *New York Times*, May 28, 2001.

86. Hal R. Varian, "With Privatization, Market Risks Could Put a Hole in the Social Security Safety Net," *New York Times*, May 31, 2001.

87. Niall Ferguson, *The Cash Nexus: Money and Power in the Modern World, 1700–2000* (New York: Basic Books, 2001), 302.

88. Danny Hakim, "401(k) Accounts Are Losing Money for the First Time," *New York Times*, July 9, 2001.

89. Hakim, "401(k) Accounts."

90. Peter T. Kilborn, "Stock Slide Sinks Hopes in Industrial City," *New York Times*, March 16, 2001.

91. From 1994 to 1999, research and development (R&D) spending increased from $97.1 billion to $166 billion, far more than R&D outlays in Japan, which totaled $95 billion in 1998. William J. Broad, "U.S. Back on Top in Industrial Research," *New York Times*, December 28, 1999; Louis Uchitelle, "The $1.2 Trillion Spigot," *New York Times*, December 30, 1999.

92. Sheryl WuDunn, "The Heavy Burden of Low Rates," *New York Times*, October 11, 1996; Gretchen Morgenson, "Beware of Japanese Bearing Promises," *New York Times*, June 21, 1998; Charles P. Kindleberger, *World Economic Primacy 1500 to 1900* (Oxford: Oxford University Press, 1996), 206–7.

93. Sheryl WuDunn and Nicholas D. Kristof, "Crisis in Banking Is Japanese, but Implications Are Global," *New York Times*, June 27, 1998; Kevin Phillips, *The Politics of Rich and Poor: Wealth and the American Electorate in the Reagan Aftermath* (New York: Random House, 1990), 151.

94. Nicholas D. Kristof, "Long Mandibles, Sleek Carapace. A Steal at $300," *New York Times*, April 10, 1999.

95. Kindleberger, *World Economic Primacy 1500 to 1900*, 207.

96. Kindleberger, *World Economic Primacy 1500 to 1900*.

97. Shigeto, *Japan's Capitalism*, 169; Rob Steven, "Structural Origins of Japan's Direct Foreign Investment," in *The Internationalization of Japan*, 52.

98. Kristof, "Long Mandibles."

99. Stephanie Strom, "Japan's New 'Temp' Workers," *New York Times*, June 17, 1998; Andrew Pollack, "Japanese Starting to Link Pay to Performance, Not Tenure," *New York Times*, October 2, 1993; Sheryl WuDunn, "When Lifetime Jobs Die Prematurely," *New York Times*, June 12, 1996; Stephanie Strom, "Toyota Is Seeking to Stop Use of Seniority to Set Pay," *New York Times*, July 8, 1999; Howard W. French, "Economy's Ebb in Japan Spurs Temporary Jobs," *New York Times*, August 12, 1999; David E. Sanger, "Look Who's Carping about Capitalism," *New York Times*, April 6, 1997.

100. Stephanie Strom, "Tradition of Equality Fading in New Japan," *New York Times*, January 4, 2000.

101. Andrew Pollack, "Jobless in Japan: A Special Kind of Anguish," *New York Times*, May 21, 1993.

102. Stephen Kinzer, "Help Wanted: One Mayor, Please," *New York Times*, March 13, 1995.

103. John Judis, "Germany Dispatch: Middle of Nowhere," *New Republic*, November 29, 1999.

104. Alan Cowell, "German Workers Fear the Miracle Is Over," *New York Times*, July 30, 1997; Nathaniel C. Nash, "In Germany, Downsizing Means 10.3% Jobless," *New York Times*, March 7, 1996; Ferdinand Protzman, "VW Offers Its Workers 4-Day Week or Layoffs," *New York Times*, October 29, 1993.

105. Sylvia Nasar, "Where Joblessness Is a Way of Making a Living," *New York Times*, May 9, 1999; Roger Cohen, "Europeans Consider Shortening Workweek to Relieve Joblessness," *New York Times*, November 22, 1993; Mishel et al., *The State of Working America, 1998–99*, 386; Celestine Bohlen, "Italy's North–South Gap Widens, Posing Problem for Europe, Too," *New York Times*, November 15, 1996.

106. Sabine Lang, "The NGOization of Feminism: Institutionalization and Institution Building within the German Women's Movement," in *Transitions, Environments, Translations: Feminisms in International Politics*, ed. Joan W. Scott, Cora Kaplan, and Debra Keates (New York: Routledge, 1997), 104.

107. Niels Thygesen, Yutaka Kosia, and Robert Z. Lawrence, *Globalization and Trilateral Labor Markets: Evidence and Implications* (New York: Trilateral Commission, 1996), 94–95; Edmund L. Andrews, "The Jobless Are Snared In Europe's Safety Net," *New York Times*, November 9, 1997. Ethnic groups and workers in particular regions have also suffered. North African immigrants in France, for example, have extremely high rates of unemployment. Workers in southern Italy are unemployed at twice the national rate. Bohlen, "Italy's North–South Gap Widens."

108. Edmund L. Andrews, "Making Stock Buyers of Wary Germans," *New York Times*, October 17, 1996; John Tagliabue, "European Giants Set to Close Deal," *New York Times*, April 20, 1999.

109. Edmund L. Andrews, "Germany Proposes Some Tax-Free Stock Sales, Lifting the Market," *New York Times*, December 24, 1999.

110. Andrews, "Making Stock Buyers of Wary Germans"; Tagliabue, "European Giants."

111. John Tagliabue, "Resisting Those Ugly Americans," *New York Times*, January 9, 2000.

112. Rich Miller, "Euro Forces Europe Into Industrial Transformation," *USA Today*, July 19, 1999; Suzanne Kapner and Andrew Ross Sorkin, "American Bankers Invade Europe," *New York Times*, February 3, 2001.

113. Gretchen Morgenson, "U.S. Shoppers Shoulder the Weight of the World," *New York Times*, June 20, 1999.

114. Sylvia Nasar, "Economists Shrug as Savings Rate Declines," *New York Times*, December 21, 1998.

115. Saul Hansell, "We Like You. We Care about You. Now Pay Up," *New York Times*, January 26, 1997; Mishel et al., *The State of Working America, 1998–99*, 275; David Leonhardt, "Belt Tightening Seen as Threat to the Economy," *New York Times*, July 15, 2001.

116. Juliet B. Schor, *The Overspent American: Upscaling, Downshifting, and the New Consumer* (New York: Basic Books, 1998), 72; Maria Fiorini Ramirez, "Americans at Debt's Door," *New York Times*, October 14, 1997.

117. Saul Hansell, "Personal Bankruptcies Surging as Economy Hums," *New York Times*, August 25, 1999.

118. Hansell, "Personal Bankruptices Surging."

119. "Debt-Load Growing for College Graduates," *New York Times*, October 24, 1997; Ethan Bronner, "College Tuition Rises 4%, Outpacing Inflation," *New York Times*, October 8, 1998; Robert D. Hershey, Jr., "Graduating with Credit Problems," *New York Times*, November 10, 1996.

120. Marilyn Fernandez and Kwang Chun Kim, "Dominant and Minority Couples: An Analysis of Family Economic Well-Being," in *Challenges for Work and Family*, 76–77. Some economists estimate that older generations may transfer $10 trillion to younger generations during the next fifty years. But estimates about the size of intergenerational transfers are the subject of considerable dispute. One study estimated that the older generation may transfer a much greater amount, between $41 trillion and $136 trillion. See David Cay Johnston, "A Larger Legacy May Await Generations X, Y and Z," *New York Times*, October 20, 1999.

121. Klaus Friedrich, "The Real American Savings Rate," *New York Times*, May 4, 1999.

122. Kindleberger, *World Economic Primacy 1500 to 1900*, 205.

123. Stephanie Strom, "Japan's Investors Become Bullish on Merrill Lynch," *New York Times*, January 6, 2000; Stephanie Strom, "Shopping for Recovery," *New York Times*, May 29, 1998.

3

Dollar Devaluations

At the beginning of the 1970s, Americans faced two economic problems: declining competitiveness and rising inflation. The postwar economic recovery of Western Europe and Japan had enabled businesses there to become more competitive with U.S. firms. As a result, U.S. businesses found it increasingly difficult to sell their goods in foreign and domestic markets. In 1971, for the first time in the twentieth century, the United States posted a trade deficit, meaning that Americans purchased more goods from other countries than they sold to people living in those countries. U.S. policymakers worried about the trade deficit because it signaled that the competitiveness of U.S. firms had declined, that production in the United States was being redistributed to other countries, and that U.S. workers were losing jobs to foreigners.

At the same time, U.S. military spending on the war in Vietnam had pushed up wages and prices, leading to inflation. Policymakers worried about inflation because it is a discriminatory economic process. Some workers can keep up with inflation because they can demand and get higher wages. But other workers cannot easily obtain higher wages, so their real income declines in an inflationary environment. The same is true of businesses. Some firms can raise prices and pass higher costs along to consumers. Oil companies can do this because people have to buy gas to get to work. But other businesses cannot easily do so because consumers will stop buying their goods if the price goes up. If they cannot pass along higher costs, they lose money and face bankruptcy. Because inflation is a discriminatory process, policymakers worked to fight inflation.

On August 15, 1971, President Richard Nixon confronted both problems simultaneously. To improve U.S. competitiveness, he took steps to devalue the dollar in relation to currencies in Western Europe and Japan. And to fight inflation, he introduced wage and price controls, which were designed to limit wage raises and price increases. The "Nixon Shocks," or *shokku* (shocks) as these were called in Japan, marked the beginning of U.S. efforts to solve two serious economic problems.[1] As we will see, the economic "solutions" devised by Nixon and subsequent U.S. presidents had mixed success. Dollar devaluations in 1971 and again in 1985 did not greatly improve competitiveness, redistribute production, or stem job loss in the United States. Moreover, they created some serious, unanticipated economic problems in the United States and around the world.

In the United States, dollar devaluations led to the purchase of U.S. businesses, real estate, and natural resources by foreigners, with important consequences for U.S. workers. Overseas, dollar devaluations contributed to declining incomes for oil-producing countries, which contributed to war in the Persian Gulf. U.S. dollar devaluations also wrecked the international system of fixed exchange rates, which had been established by the United States at Bretton Woods during World War II. The system that replaced it led to global monetary instability, which created serious problems for countries around the world during the 1990s.

Wage and price controls did not curb inflation in the 1970s. But during the 1980s, government economists successfully used high interest rates to curb inflation. But high interest rates contributed to a host of other economic problems. In Latin America, Eastern Europe, and Africa, high U.S. interest rates triggered a massive debt crisis that crippled economies and triggered massive political change (see chapters 5 and 11). In the United States, high interest rates wrecked the savings and loan industry and led to increasing homelessness. The effects of high interest rates are still being felt, in the United States and around the world, today.

To explain these developments in detail, we will look first at currency devaluations and at efforts to improve U.S. competitiveness. In the next chapter, we will examine efforts to curb inflation. Both stories begin in 1971 with Nixon's August 15 speech. Both stories have two parts. The dollar is devalued twice, first in 1971 and again in 1985. And there are two anti-inflationary campaigns, the first in 1971 and the second beginning in 1979. By focusing on successive "solutions" to economic problems, we will discuss the problems with macroeconomic management. U.S. attempts to improve competitiveness and fight inflation have had significant consequences for people across the globe.

Although the story of government efforts to improve U.S. competitiveness and the story about the government's fight against inflation will be told separately, they are joined in important ways. For example, high interest rates in the early 1980s strengthened the value of the dollar, creating problems that led to a second, deeper devaluation of the dollar in 1985. We will note these connections as the stories unfold. Both stories are also about the social "costs" and unanticipated "problems" associated with the macroeconomic decisions made by policymakers in the United States, Western Europe, and Japan. In this regard, it is useful to describe how powerful economic institutions can create global changes that affect people's lives. The Group of Five, for instance, played an important role in the 1985 decision to devalue the dollar; the Federal Reserve system was a central actor in the anti-inflationary campaigns of the early 1980s. These institutions are relatively obscure to most people, though their decisions have important impacts on people living in different parts of the world.

1971 DOLLAR DEVALUATION

"At the end of World War II, the economies of the major industrial nations of Europe and Asia were shattered," President Nixon told his television audience on August 15, 1971. "Today, largely with our help, they have regained their vitality. They have become our strong competitors. . . . But now that [they] have become economically strong . . . the time has come for exchange rates to be set straight, and for the major nations to compete as equals."[2]

In this speech, Nixon recognized that the ability of U.S. firms to compete with businesses in Western Europe and Japan had eroded during the postwar period (see chapter 2). To improve U.S. competitiveness and redistribute production from Western Europe and Japan "back" to the United States, Nixon devalued the dollar and altered the relations among currencies in all three regions. By changing exchange rates, Nixon hoped to change consumer behavior in all three regions and persuade U.S. consumers to "Buy American." If consumers could be persuaded to purchase domestic, not foreign goods, U.S. trade deficits would shrink and U.S. jobs would be saved.

Nixon's devaluation of the dollar opened a two-decade campaign to improve the competitiveness of U.S. firms and save jobs by changing global monetary relations. But the monetary policies of Nixon and, later, President Ronald Reagan did not greatly improve the ability of U.S. firms to compete with other foreign businesses, failed to persuade consumers to buy American, and did little to save jobs. Moreover, successive dollar devaluations, the first in 1971 and a second in 1985, created other problems that policymakers did not expect or appreciate.

As Nixon noted, businesses in Western Europe and Japan became "strong competitors" during the postwar period for a variety of reasons. They "regained their vitality" because they adopted policies designed to develop economically and received substantial U.S. economic aid amounting to $14.3 billion, according to Nixon's calculations. They also benefited from favorable exchange rates that were set by the Bretton Woods agreement, an international monetary treaty named after the New Hampshire town where negotiations were held in 1944.

The Bretton Woods agreement made the U.S. dollar the world's monetary standard and fixed the value of other currencies in relation to the dollar. For example, the value of the yen, Japan's currency, was fixed at a rate of 360 yen to the dollar between 1949 and 1971. This low rate made it easy for Japanese firms to sell their "cheap" goods in the United States, while making it difficult for Japanese consumers to buy "expensive" American goods in Japan. In effect, exchange rates set at Bretton Woods helped Japanese and Western European businesses sell their goods at home (where U.S. goods were relatively expensive) and abroad, particularly in the United States (where their goods were relatively cheap). The exchange rates fixed after World War II acted somewhat like a golfer's handicap, making the price or "score" of Japanese and Western European firms lower than they would be otherwise.

In golf, the handicapping system is designed to let poor players compete as equals with more skilled players. By allowing poor players to deduct a given number of strokes (their handicap) from their actual score, an unskilled player could compete with a PGA professional playing without a handicap. Likewise, the exchange rates set in the 1940s enabled less productive businesses in Western Europe and Japan to compete as equals with more productive U.S. firms in American markets. The difference between the fixed exchange rate system established at Bretton Woods and the golf handicapping system is that, in golf, players' handicaps *decline* as their skills improve. But the Bretton Woods system did not do this because exchange rates were fixed. So while businesses in Western Europe and Japan improved their "game" during the postwar period, their currency handicap remained the same. By analogy, the result was like giving a handicap to a skilled professional who had just joined the PGA tour. Given an exchange rate "handicap" and their much-improved skills, firms in Western Europe and Japan were able beat U.S. firms in American markets.[3]

The sale of Volkswagen Beetles and Sony transistor radios to U.S. consumers in the 1960s helped West German and Japanese economies recover and grow. While they grew stronger, producing goods that were of increasing quality, the exchange rates did not change, which kept their products cheap. By the late 1960s, they had begun to compete successfully with American firms in both domestic and U.S. markets, where consumers purchased their goods in increasing volume. Also, in 1971, the United States imported more goods than it exported, posting a $2.3 billion trade deficit, the first in decades.[4]

Government officials viewed the trade deficit as a sign that the ability of U.S. firms to compete with businesses in Western Europe and Japan had declined. They blamed the redistribution of production, and the job loss associated with it, on the monetary system, which assigned favorable exchange rates to U.S. competitors. But it was difficult for officials to alter long-standing exchange rates because the values of other currencies were fixed in relation to the dollar. In effect, they could not alter exchange rates unless they were prepared to abandon the dollar's role as the monetary standard for currencies around the world.

By 1971, officials decided to eliminate the dollar as a monetary standard and destroy the Bretton Woods system for two reasons. First, the value of the dollar was weakening. When the dollar became the global monetary standard, the United States agreed to supply dollars to people around the world so they could pay for the imports they needed to rebuild their shattered economies. The United States used the Marshall Plan, foreign aid, and overseas military spending to provide dollars to countries that needed "hard currency" to pay for imports. By providing liquidity and easing cash flow problems, the dollars supplied by the United States helped countries in Western Europe and East Asia grow and prosper. But while U.S. overseas spending helped provide much-needed cash, continued military spending on NATO and the war in Vietnam pumped too many dollars into the world economy. Dollars piled up in central banks around the world. To reduce their stocks of dollars, which they found increasingly difficult to use, some governments decided to return them to the United States and cash them in for gold, at the rate of $35 to the ounce, a rate set by the Bretton Woods agreement.

By the late 1960s and early 1970s, it became clear that the number of dollars in global circulation far outstripped the amount of gold stored at Fort Knox. If too many countries had asked to redeem dollars for gold, the U.S. government would soon exhaust its gold reserves and the dollar would lose its value as a standard.

The fact that the world economy needed the United States to pump dollars into the monetary system to maintain liquidity, but the fact that doing so undermined the value of the dollar and its role as a global monetary standard, was know to economists as the Trifflin Dilemma because it was first identified by Robert Trifflin, an economist who published a book on this subject, *Gold and the Dollar Crisis*, in 1960.[5]

To address this problem, Nixon administration officials decided to stop redeeming gold for dollars and force a devaluation of the dollar vis-à-vis other currencies in Western Europe and Japan. By lowering the value of the dollar and raising the value of other "hard" currencies, U.S. firms could sell more of the (now-cheaper) goods overseas, and U.S. consumers would be discouraged from buying (now more expensive) products from Western Europe and Japan. By exporting more and importing less, Nixon administration officials reasoned that they could eliminate the trade deficit, restore the competitiveness of U.S. firms, and save jobs in the United States. By abandoning the Bretton Woods system of fixed exchange rates (and the promise to convert dollars for gold at $35 an ounce), and devaluing the dollar—by making "exchange rates to be set straight," as Nixon put it—U.S. businesses could again "compete as equals."

Although Nixon's 1971 policy was designed to devalue the dollar, he was reluctant to describe it that way. He argued that his actions would not result in "the bugaboo of . . . what is called 'devaluation.'" And he told viewers that "if you want to buy a foreign car or take a trip abroad, market conditions may cause your dollar to buy slightly less. But if . . . you buy American-made products, in America, your dollar will be worth just as much tomorrow as it is today." Nixon and Treasury Secretary John Connally argued that this new policy was not a "devaluation" because Nixon administration officials in previous months had proclaimed they would not devalue the dollar to improve U.S. competitiveness.[6]

But this, and Connally's subsequent press conference statement that the dollar had not been devalued "by Presidential action," was misleading. As Paul Volcker, a Treasury Department official who helped draft Nixon's speech, later recalled, a dollar devaluation "was exactly what we had decided was essential."[7] Nixon was reluctant to call it a devaluation because this term was politically charged. But if one looks at his own example, Nixon describes precisely what a devaluation is all about. The dollar devaluation did not mean that a dollar could buy fewer *American* goods. But it *did* mean that Americans could not purchase as many *foreign* goods, either in the United States or abroad, as they could previously. As a result of changing exchange rates, which weakened the dollar and strengthened first world currencies (franc, yen, deutsche mark), an American tourist in Paris could buy fewer croissants and a shopper in Des Moines could buy fewer Christmas toys labeled "Made in Japan."

As a result of Nixon's 1971 policy, the dollar's value fell and other hard currencies rose during the next few months. By December 1971, the dollar had fallen between 8 and 17 percent, depending on the currency. The yen, for example, rose 16.9 percent, to 308 yen to the dollar.[8] After this initial change, the dollar overall slowly declined to about 25 percent of its August 1971 value by the end of the decade (275 yen to the dollar).

One might have expected Nixon's dollar devaluation, and the collapse of the Bretton Woods system (the values of different currencies were no longer fixed and instead began to float in relation to the dollar and to other currencies), to improve U.S. competitiveness, reduce its trade deficit, and save jobs. After all, that was the administration's intent. But it did not. The modest $2.3 billion trade deficit in 1971 grew to $25.5 billion by 1980, a tenfold increase.[9]

U.S. trade deficits increased in part because Americans spent more on imported oil and high-mileage foreign cars. Rising oil prices, which tripled between 1973 and 1974, also increased the cost of imported oil.[10] In 1973, for instance, the United States spent $23.9 billion for imported oil.[11]

Climbing gas prices, which were the product of the 1973 OPEC oil embargo, persuaded U.S. consumers to buy high-mileage Toyotas and Hondas. During the 1970s, U.S. demand for reliable high-mileage Japanese cars grew dramatically (see chapter 2). In 1970, Japanese automakers sold about four million cars in the United States. By 1975, Nissan had surpassed Volkswagen as the leading foreign car manufacturer, and by the end of the decade, Japanese manufacturers had sold nearly twelve million cars.[12]

Rising oil prices contributed to a growing U.S. trade deficit in two ways, first by increasing the cost of imported oil and second by increasing U.S. demand for foreign autos. Another oil embargo in 1978 tripled prices again. So whatever gains the 1971 dollar devaluation might have been achieved were undermined by rising oil prices and increasing consumer demand for imported goods.

While the value of the dollar fell during the 1970s as a result of Nixon's policies, the dollar actually increased in value during the first half of the 1980s, largely as a result of efforts to curb inflation. As we will see in chapter 4, former

Nixon aide Paul Volcker, who became head of the Federal Reserve System in 1979, took steps to raise interest rates as a way to slow inflation. As a result, interest rates on government bonds (savings bonds, Treasury bills) rose to very high levels, as high as 20 percent. Attracted by rates that were higher than they could earn on their savings in other countries, investors from around the world bought U.S. bonds. By 1986, the Japanese had purchased $186 billion in U.S. Treasury Bonds.[13]

This massive purchase of U.S. bonds, which was stimulated by high interest rates, increased the value of the dollar. The increasing value of the dollar undermined whatever gains had been achieved by Nixon's devaluation. Volcker observed that, by the end of 1984, "the yen and the mark, relative to the dollar, had been driven back . . . to their 1973 levels or below, and their car, machinery, and electronics manufacturers were finding the lush American market easy pickings."[14]

U.S. firms found it more difficult to sell their (now more expensive) goods abroad, while (now-cheaper) foreign products flooded U.S. markets. As a result, U.S. trade deficits exploded from $25.3 billion in 1980 to $122 billion in 1985.[15] And nearly one-third of this deficit, $50 billion, was with Japan.[16] Princeton economist Robert Gilpin observed, "In the first part of 1986, the United States had achieved the impossible: it had a deficit with almost every one of its trading partners. Not since 1864 had the U.S. trade balance been so negative."[17]

Whereas a $2.3 billion trade deficit had seemed a major problem requiring dramatic solutions in 1971, U.S. officials in 1985 faced a trade deficit sixty times bigger. To deal with declining competitiveness and soaring trade deficits, officials again turned to a dollar devaluation as the cure for economic ills.

1985 DEVALUATION: THE PLAZA ACCORDS

As U.S. trade deficits rose to unprecedented levels in the mid-1980s, government officials once again sought to devalue the dollar to improve the competitiveness of U.S. firms in foreign and domestic markets. But this time, they could not act alone, as they had in 1971. Because exchange rates were no longer fixed, and because world currency markets played a larger role in setting the value of different currencies, the Reagan administration had to secure the cooperation of other governments in Western Europe and Japan to successfully devalue the dollar. In September 1985, the Reagan administration asked the financial representatives of the five leading economic powers, then known as the Group of Five (G-5), to meet at the Plaza Hotel in New York City and hammer out an agreement to devalue the dollar in relation to other hard currencies.

When they convened in the White and Gold Room of the Plaza Hotel on September 22, representatives from the United States, Japan, West Germany, France, and the United Kingdom agreed to devalue the dollar. They issued an ɪɴ..ɔcuous statement saying that "some orderly appreciation of the main non-dollar currencies against the dollar is desirable. They [the Group of Five] stand ready to cooperate more closely to encourage this when to do so would be helpful."[18]

Reagan administration officials, like Nixon, were reluctant to describe their decision as a "dollar devaluation." Instead, they called it an "appreciation" of "nondollar currencies," which is the same thing. They insisted that "it does not represent a fundamental change in the exchange rate intervention policy," though that is exactly what it was, since the agreement made by G-5 members specified interventionary steps to be taken. As one Reagan official later said, "No country ever likes to say that their currency will depreciate. . . . A government does not make statements that imply weakness."[19]

Although the G-5 ministers said they wanted to see the dollar depreciate, they refused to say how much it should be devalued. They kept this decision secret from the public.

In private, G-5 ministers agreed to devalue the dollar substantially. Over the next two years, the dollar would fall to one-half its 1985 value against the yen and the deutsche mark. And it would continue to fall, to only one-third its 1985 value by the early 1990s. So in 1993, for example, the yen traded for 105 to the dollar, down from 250 in 1985.[20]

The decision to devalue the dollar was made by an institution—the G-5—that was largely unknown to the public prior to its 1985 meeting in New York. But the decisions made by this secretive and select group had important global consequences.

SUMMITS AND SHERPAS

Although the 1985 Plaza Accords would have profound consequences for people around the world, the meeting was not widely noticed. On the day it was announced, the *New York Times* gave more attention to an earthquake in Mexico City. Except for financial experts, the economic tremors produced by the Plaza Accords went unregistered by the public. This was because first world economic summits were typically secret and select. As Volcker, one of two U.S. representatives at the meeting, said, "Until that day, [the G-5] had been a secret organization. Nobody outside a very tight official circle knew exactly where and when the five ministers met, what they discussed, and what they agreed. This was the first time a G-5 meeting was announced in advance [it was announced the day before] and a communique was issued afterward."[21]

The meeting was so secret that Japanese finance minister Noboru Takeshita "arranged to play golf at a course near Narita airport . . . but then, without playing the back nine," he slipped off to the airport and boarded a Pan Am jet to New York so that the press would not notice his departure from Japan.[22]

The secretive G-5 grew out of a meeting first held in the White House library in April 1973. The "Library Group" consisted of the finance ministers and sometimes central bank governors of the United States, West Germany, France, and the United Kingdom. They added the minister from Japan the following year.[23] In 1975, French president Valery Giscard d'Estaing called a summit meeting of ministers from the United States, France, West Germany, Japan, the United Kingdom, and also Italy. They added Canada the following year. At these Group of Seven (G-7) summits, the finance ministers played important roles, crafting the economic agenda for political leaders. Because they worked to prepare presidents and prime ministers for these "summits," insiders referred to them as "sherpas." A British official is said to have coined the phrase because sherpas are the native porters who help mountaineers scale "summits" in the Himalayas.[24]

After the Plaza Accords were announced, Canadian and Italian officials complained that they were excluded, and the following year they were added, so that in 1986 the G-5 and G-7 became officially known as the G-7.[25]

Not only has the G-5/7 been secretive, but it has been a selective group as well. Most of the world's 190-plus countries have been excluded from its meetings. Some of them have since formed the Group of 77, which has 120 members and convenes an "alternative economic summit" when the G-7 holds its annual meeting. G-7 members have not opened the door to participation by others because, as Prime Minister Helmut Schmidt of West Germany explained, "We want a private, informal meeting of those who *really* matter in the world."[26]

The first world countries had other reasons for maintaining secrecy among a select group. If they had announced how much they intended to devalue the dollar after the Plaza meeting, people would have rushed to sell dollars and buy other currencies, which could have caused financial chaos. Because they did not disclose their plans, currency traders reacted "cautiously" to the announcement, according to the *New York Times*.[27]

IMPACT OF THE PLAZA ACCORDS

Although the Plaza Accords initiated a substantial devaluation of the dollar, they created a host of new problems. First and foremost, the dollar devaluation did *not* reduce the U.S. trade deficit. In 1985, the United States recorded a $122 billion trade deficit. By raising the prices of imported goods, G-5 ministers expected U.S. consumers to buy fewer foreign goods; by lowering the value of the dollar, they expected consumers in other countries to buy more U.S.-made goods. But despite a substantial devaluation, the U.S. trade deficit actually *increased* to $155 billion in 1986 and $170 billion in 1987. It then decreased slowly, though it remained at pre-1985 levels in 1988 ($137 billion) and 1989 ($129 billion), before falling to $122 billion in 1990.[28] It would rise again in the 1990s. Volcker said of this development, "One of the ironies of [this] story . . .

is that, after repeated depreciation of the dollar since 1971 to the point where it is 60 percent lower against the yen and 53 percent lower against the deutsche mark, the American trade and current account deficits are nonetheless much higher than anything imagined in the 1960s."[29]

What went wrong? Why didn't the dollar devaluation accomplish the goals of U.S. policymakers? The reason is that manufacturers and consumers did not respond to macroeconomic changes in the way policymakers expected.

The devaluation of the dollar and the appreciation of the yen should have *doubled* the price of Japanese imports. But Japanese automakers did not double their prices after the Plaza Accords. As economist Daniel Burstein explained, "A Nissan automobile that sold in the United States for $9,000 in 1984, and should have sold for $18,000 in 1987 according to changes in yen/dollar exchange rates, actually sold for only $11,000. If it had really sold for $18,000, it might well have been priced out of the market. At $11,000 . . . it was still highly competitive. In fact, Nissan's total U.S. car sales for 1987 fell only 3 percent from the prior year."[30]

Rather than raise prices to conform with post-Plaza exchange rates, Japanese firms kept price increases modest, squeezed costs, and accepted lower profits to retain their share of U.S. markets. U.S. manufacturers, meanwhile, actually *increased* their prices to keep up with Japanese price increases. "Studies by auto market research firm J. D. Power confirm that while Japanese manufacturers were raising U.S. prices an average of 9–13 percent from 1985 to 1988, General Motors, Ford and Chrysler were raising prices by . . . 12–15 percent."[31]

Essentially, U.S. firms refused to take advantage of changing exchange rates. Rather than keep prices steady, which would have given U.S. automakers a price advantage vis-à-vis foreign carmakers, U.S. firms *raised* their prices so they could make more money per car (rather than expand their production of cars) and swell profits, not increase their market share. U.S. firms emphasized short-term profits rather than increased market share because they wanted to increase stock prices and shareholder dividends (see chapter 2). They did this because the U.S. stock market plays a much greater role in corporate decision making than it does in Japan, where firms do not seek to reward stockholders with dividends and instead concentrate on long-term investment strategies.

Faced with only modest price differentials between imported and domestic goods, differences that often disappeared when quality and brand loyalty were considered, U.S. consumers kept purchasing imported goods from Western Europe and Japan. Given a choice between a Honda Accord and a Chrysler K-car, cars close in price despite the dollar devaluation, American consumers kept buying Hondas.

Because foreign and domestic producers and U.S. consumers did not behave as policymakers expected, U.S. trade deficits increased and the Plaza Accords did not achieve their objectives. As this became apparent in the late 1980s, economists sought to explain the failure of macroeconomic policy. They used the term *hysteresis,* which means a "resistance to change," to describe the unwillingness of producers and consumers to act as economic theory predicted and monetary officials expected.[32] But this abstract term, which is drawn from physics, is simply a way of saying that people don't always act as economic theory says they should. Manufacturers and consumers did not do as they were "told," refusing to sell aggressively or "Buy American."

The Plaza Accords resulted in problems in the United States and other countries that G-5 representatives did not anticipate. In the United States, the decline of the dollar reduced the value of U.S. assets, while the appreciation of currencies in Western Europe and Japan provided investors there with the means to purchase U.S. assets at bargain prices. "In 1974, the three largest banks in the world were American while only two of the top ten were Japanese," notes one economist. But by 1988, largely as a result of devaluation, "of the 25 largest banks in the world . . . 17 were Japanese (nine of them were in the top ten), 7 were Western European and 1 was from the United States."[33]

The growth of Japanese and Western European banks was due in part to the dollar devaluation, which increased their assets. Assets rose because Japanese and European banks are larger, on average, than their U.S. counterparts, so they were able to use size to their advantage. Japan has only 158 commercial banks; the United States has 14,000.[34]

As a result of the dollar devaluation, Japanese and Western European investors could buy U.S. banks and businesses, real estate, and natural resources for half price. At post-Plaza prices, foreign businesses rushed to invest in the United States. In the three years after 1985, Japanese firms invested $235 billion in the United States, purchasing government bonds ($30 billion in 1988), U.S. corporations (Sony purchased Columbia Records in 1988), real estate (Rockefeller Center in New York City and Pebble Beach in California), and natural resources (timber from the Pacific Northwest).[35] This development altered postwar investment patterns. Until 1985, investment generally flowed outward from the United States to Western Europe and Japan. After 1985, it began to flow in as well, a process that multilaterized or "globalized" investment substantially (see chapter 2).

Of course, the sale of U.S. assets to foreign investors may have little or no impact on jobs. Japanese investors did not fire Hollywood actors and filmmakers when they purchased entertainment companies, nor did they fire greenskeepers at Pebble Beach or ski instructors at Heavenly Valley. The impact of investment on jobs varies from industry to industry. In one industry, however, the dollar devaluation did contribute to substantial job loss: the Pacific Northwest timber industry.

FALLING DOLLAR, FALLING TREES

The Plaza Accords had a dramatic impact on timber and jobs in the Pacific Northwest, the heavily forested region west of the Cascade Mountains in Washington, Oregon, and northern California. The dollar devaluation combined with long-standing forestry practices to cut timber, send much of it to Japan, and lay off workers in U.S. mills.

During the postwar period, the federal government, which owns 191 million acres of timber in the United States, adopted policies to make cheap timber available to the logging and housing industry, providing jobs for the most job-intensive industry in America and inexpensive housing for would-be homeowners (see chapter 4).

The U.S. Forest Service, which oversees public forests, made cheap timber available to private industry in two ways. First, it sold timber for less than it cost the government to hire forest rangers and build access roads to timber stands. The Forest Service built and maintained 340,000 miles of heavy-duty roads, a network eight times longer than the interstate highway system, able to span the globe thirteen times. Instead of charging buyers for the full cost of its roads and other timber services, the Forest Service and taxpayers assumed much of the cost. For example, it amortized the cost of road building over many years, hundreds of years in some cases, so that buyers only had to cover artificially low annual costs. Between 1980 and 1991, the Forest Service lost $5.6 billion from below-cost timber sales.

Second, the Forest Service greatly increased the amount of public timber cut in the postwar period. It increased timber sales from 3.5 billion board feet (one board foot is twelve by twelve inches square by one inch thick) in 1950 to 8.3 billion board feet in 1960, then to 12 billion board feet in the late 1960s, a fourfold increase.[36] The infusion of large public timber supplies into the market kept prices low. Forest managers were encouraged to sell as much timber as possible by laws that based their operating budgets on the volume of timber sales from their districts. In many parts of the country, they did not practice sustained yield harvesting but cut trees faster than they grew back. Wilderness Society economist Jeffrey Olson estimated that, from 1980 to 1985, the Forest Service overcut Northwest woods by 61 percent, and private industry overcut their woods by 126 percent.[37] Over time, this practice led to declining timber supplies and rising prices. The timber sold by the Forest Service in the Pacific Northwest declined by 75 percent, from 8 billion board feet in 1986 to 2.5 billion board feet in 1992.[38] It was in this context that the 1985 dollar devaluation made its appearance in the Pacific Northwest.

The dollar devaluation made Northwest timber available to foreign buyers at bargain basement prices. For Japanese buyers, it represented a two-for-one sale. (The Japanese were the principal purchasers, though buyers in China, Taiwan, and South Korea also bought heavily.) As the dollar fell, Japanese purchases of Northwest timber increased from 3 billion board feet in 1986 to 4.2 billion board feet in 1988. By 1988, one of every four trees cut in the Northwest was shipped to Japan. In Washington State, 40 percent of the harvest was exported.

George Leonard, associate chief of the Forest Service, admitted that log exports affected the supply of timber in the Northwest. "But if we want to buy Sonys and Toyotas from Japan, we've got to sell them something they want," he said.[39]

Increased U.S. timber exports led to two problems: higher timber prices and fewer jobs. First, the sale of large quantities of timber to overseas buyers reduced domestic supplies and competition between domestic and foreign buyers, who could offer more. This competition led to higher timber prices in the United States. Domestic timber prices increased from about $250 per thousand board feet in the mid-1980s to $350 in 1992 ($474 in 1993), a 30 percent increase.[40] Because a 2,050-square-foot house uses 14,350 board feet of wood, a 30 percent increase in timber prices added $3,000 to the cost of the house. Higher costs made it more difficult for U.S. consumers to purchase a home (see chapter 4).

Second, foreign buyers insisted on buying and shipping whole, raw logs. Japanese buyers did not want U.S. lumber mills to cut the wood before shipping it overseas. Instead, they wanted to provide timber to the workers in Japanese mills, where they cut timber into the metric equivalent of two-by-fours. (U.S. mills do not use the metric system and do not cut timber to suit the Japanese construction industry.) Because the United States exported raw logs, not milled wood, employment in U.S. mills declined. Although estimates vary, between three and five jobs are lost for every million board feet of raw timber exported. Representative Peter DeFazio of Oregon calculated that the export of 4.3 billion board feet in 1988 resulted in the loss of between 13,800 and 23,000 jobs.[41] Between 1986 and 1991, 163 mills were closed in the Northwest.[42] "Decks at Japanese mills are piled high as Mount Fuji with logs from the Northwest, while mills here at home are scrapping for leftovers," said DeFazio. "We're facing the greatest timber supply crisis in our history while Japanese mills are running around the clock."[43]

In addition to export-related unemployment, lumberjacks and mill workers were laid off as the industry automated production, moved some mills to lower-wage countries such as Mexico, and ran out of wood to cut in this part of the country. The Forest Service estimated in 1990 that technological change alone would displace 13 percent of the workforce by the end of the century.[44] And Forest Service plans to set aside timber for the protection of spotted owls, a bird threatened by timber cutting in old-growth forests, and salmon, whose streams are threatened by soil erosion from heavily logged forests, will also reduce timber supplies and affect jobs. Although no one at the Plaza meeting considered or anticipated the impact of a dollar devaluation on U.S. natural resources, the one-two punch of Forest Service policy and dollar devaluation resulted in declining timber supplies, higher prices, and growing unemployment in the Pacific Northwest.

GLOBAL CONSEQUENCES OF DOLLAR
DEVALUATIONS, 1970–1990

Successive dollar devaluations did little to reduce U.S. trade deficits. They also had an adverse impact on mill workers and timber prices in the Pacific Northwest. Globally, devaluations had important consequences for oil-producing countries, contributing to inflation in the 1970s, falling oil prices in the 1980s, and war in the Persian Gulf during the 1980s and early 1990s.

OIL

Around the world, dollars are used to buy and sell oil, a legacy of the fact that the United States was the world's first big oil-producing country. Because the world oil trade was and still is conducted in dollars, dollar devaluations have played an important role in the contemporary history of oil, contributing to inflation in the 1970s and to war in the 1980s and 1990s.

The 1971 dollar devaluation lowered the revenues of oil-producing countries because the dollars they were paid with were worth less than before. Determined to regain lost revenues and to increase the price of oil in real terms, the members of OPEC responded in 1973 with an oil embargo during the Yom Kippur War between Egypt and Israel. This embargo, and a subsequent embargo during the Iranian revolution in 1979, increased oil prices to more than $35 a barrel. During the 1970s, then, the dollar devaluation helped trigger rising oil prices, which spurred inflation in the United States and around the world (see chapter 4).

Although the first dollar devaluation in 1971 contributed to oil price hikes and increased the power of OPEC, the 1985 devaluation had the opposite effect. The Plaza Accords led to falling oil prices, declining revenues for oil-producing countries, and the outbreak of war among its members.

Between 1980 and 1985, the price of oil declined slowly from $35 to just under $30 a barrel (still a high price compared to the 1970 price of $3 a barrel). Prices fell because countries discovered new oil in the North Sea or expanded production to take advantage of high prices. Increased supplies undermined the price of oil (see chapter 6). But oil prices did not fall below $30 because the Saudi Arabian government was determined to keep prices high for other OPEC countries. The Saudi Arabian government was willing, for a time, to curb its production so that an oil glut, and lower prices, did not materialize. But by 1985, increasing production by OPEC and non-OPEC countries exhausted the patience of the Saudi Arabians, who had seen their oil revenues decline from $119 billion in 1981 to only $26 billion in 1985.[45] In that year, to Saudi embarrassment, the United Kingdom produced more oil than Saudi Arabia. After a December 9, 1985, OPEC meeting, only two months after the Plaza meeting, the Saudi Arabians abandoned their low-production, price support policy and increased their production to recapture their market share. Within a few months, the price of oil had collapsed to $10.[46]

Although U.S. consumers welcomed lower oil prices, the domestic U.S. oil industry did not because it could not make money at $10 a barrel. Although the price that producers get for their oil is set at the world level, they each have different production costs. It costs very little to pump oil from shallow wells in Saudi Arabia, more to lift it from deeper wells in West Texas. At $10 a barrel, U.S. producers could not afford to pump oil from domestic wells. So U.S. firms quit drilling and pumping oil and laid off workers. The recession in the oil industry depressed the price of real estate in the Southwest, which contributed to the collapse of savings and loan organizations that had invested heavily in office buildings in the region (see chapter 4). "Moreover," explained Daniel Yergin, "if prices stayed down, U.S. oil demand would shoot up [as consumers drove more], domestic production would plummet, and imports would start flooding in again, as they had in the 1970s."[47]

To head this off, Vice President George Bush flew to the Middle East to persuade the Saudi Arabian government to *increase* oil prices. He later explained, "I think it is essential that we talk about stability and that we not just have a continued free fall [in prices] like a parachutist jumping out without a parachute. . . . I'm absolutely sure . . . that *low* prices would cripple the domestic American energy industries, with serious consequences for the nation [emphasis added]."[48]

To provide *higher* prices to U.S. and Saudi Arabian oil producers, the United States, Saudi Arabia, and some OPEC countries reached a consensus that oil prices should stabilize at $18, a considerable rise from $10. And their combined efforts eventually established new OPEC quotas, bringing OPEC and non-OPEC producers into line by 1987.

Of course, the decline in oil prices was accompanied in this same period by a devaluation of the dollar. In effect, the price of oil fell *twice*, first when rising oil supplies drove down prices, and second when devaluation forced down the *dollar* price of oil. In real terms, the price of oil had returned to about what it had been in 1973. As a result, the price of a gallon of gas, in inflation-adjusted 1993 dollars, was $1.12 in 1993 compared to $1.25 in 1973.[49]

But falling oil prices had different consequences for different countries. Oil *importing* did well, but the oil-*producing* countries fared badly.

Oil-Importing Countries

The United States saved money because the price of oil was cheaper. This helped reduce the U.S. trade deficit. U.S. consumers were pleased with lower gas prices at the pump. But while the United States saved money, the Japanese and Europeans saved money twice. They benefited from the falling *price* of oil and from the *devaluation* of the dollar, which further lowered its cost to them. So while the United States saw its bill for imported oil fall by about 30 percent, Japan saw its bill fall by 50 percent and West Germany by 57 percent in this period.[50] As James Sterngold noted, "The stronger yen also slashed Japan's import bills, since oil is paid for in dollars."[51] Because Japan worked hard to improve its energy efficiency and promote conservation during this period, while the United States did little, Japan actually reduced its dependence on foreign oil (see chapter 8 on global warming).

Japan and West Germany also captured other benefits. In the late 1980s, the U.S. government spent about $50 billion providing military and naval protection to Kuwait and Saudi Arabia, equal to about $100 per barrel of oil imported from the Persian Gulf. Energy economist Amory Lovins notes that "since Germany and Japan depend heavily on Persian Gulf oil (without incurring these tremendous annual military costs) America in effect subsidizes the economies of its two major trading competitors."[52]

Oil-Exporting Countries

For oil-exporting countries, the price decline and dollar devaluation drastically reduced revenues. Despite organizing collectively in OPEC and waging a two-decade campaign to increase oil prices and use the revenue to promote economic development, oil-producing countries in the late 1980s found themselves back where they started in 1973. As a result of falling prices and heavy spending, "The $121 billion in financial reserves amassed by Saudi Arabia [in the early 1980s] have almost vanished," the *New York Times* reported in 1993. "'The Saudis have been drawing down reserves for 10 years,' an American official said. 'They're a mere shadow of their former selves.'"[53]

War in the Persian Gulf

Although oil-producing countries with small populations (Saudi Arabia, Kuwait, Libya) were still relatively prosperous, the heavily populated oil-producing countries such as Nigeria, Iraq, and Iran saw their economic fortunes decline. Iraq, the second largest oil-producing country in OPEC, saw its oil revenues decline from $26 billion in 1980 to $12 billion in 1988, at a time when it was spending heavily to wage war with neighboring Iran. Iraqi dictator Saddam Hussein had earlier invaded Iran to capture its oil fields. If he had succeeded, he would have controlled enough of world oil production to demand higher prices in OPEC and recapture the revenues Iraq lost to price cuts and then dollar devaluation. But Hussein's decade-long campaign failed to defeat Iran's army and capture its oil. So having failed to captured Iran's oil, Hussein then invaded Kuwait to seize its oil fields in 1990. The United States and its allies then assembled a multinational army to drive Iraqi forces from Kuwait in 1991.

Although the 1985 dollar devaluation contributed to lower world oil prices, which benefited consumers in Western Europe, Japan, and the United States, it also contributed to war in the Middle East, leading to U.S. military intervention. In this context, the Plaza Accords had consequences and repercussions that policymakers did not intend, anticipate, or even imagine.

GLOBAL CONSEQUENCES, 1990–2000

The reverberations from dollar devaluations continued to be felt in the 1990s. They altered economic relations between the United States and Japan, contributed to global monetary instability and economic crises in countries around the world, and persuaded other countries to abandon their own currencies and adopt the U.S. dollar as their own, official domestic currency.

United States and Japan

Although the 1985 Plaza Accords considerably reduced the value of the dollar in relation to the yen (from Y250 = $1 to Y125 = $1), they did little to reduce the U.S. trade deficit and the job loss associated with it during the rest of the 1980s and beginning of the 1990s. But the value of the dollar fell again in the mid-1990s. It fell to Y105 = $1 in 1993 and then to Y80 = $1 in 1995, its lowest rate ever.

As the dollar devalued, the price of Japanese goods in U.S. markets rose sharply. Japanese manufacturers, particularly automakers, began losing ground to U.S. producers. Here's why: It cost Japanese automakers 1.43 million yen, on average, to build a car in Japan, plus $2,600 to ship and market the car in the United States. When the exchange rate was Y110 = $1, the cost to Japanese manufacturers, in dollars, was $13,000. But when the exchange rate fell to Y80 = $1, the cost to Japanese car makers rose to $17,875, a substantial price increase.[54] As the dollar fell in 1995, the *New York Times* reported that "Japanese corporate executives seem shellshocked by market trends over which they have no control."[55] Moreover, many small manufacturing firms in Japan began to go out of business or move abroad, where exchange rates and labor costs were more favorable.[56] Of course, this is what officials had hoped the 1985 Plaza Accords would accomplish. It just took a deeper devaluation and a longer time (ten years) than they had anticipated.

But just when exchange rates fell to the point where they *did* stem imports, reduce U.S. trade deficits, and redistribute manufacturing jobs, this time from Japan to the United States, policymakers in the United States and Japan reversed course. In mid-1995, monetary officials in the United States and Japan worked together to *increase* the value of the dollar, forcing it back up to

114Y = $1 in 1996. It then stayed at about this level for the rest of the 1990s and into 2001.

Of course, the *rising* dollar benefited Japanese, not U.S., manufacturers. One Japanese study found that for every dollar rise in the exchange rate, Japanese automakers reaped about $360 million in economic benefits.[57] By 1996, the *New York Times* reported that "Japanese manufacturers have [again] found themselves in the catbird seat with a choice of grabbing bigger profits, cutting prices to build market share, or both."[58]

Why on earth would U.S. and Japanese officials collaborate in 1995 to reverse the devaluation of the dollar, just when it had begun to alter the relation between U.S. and Japanese manufacturers? They did so for two reasons.

First, Clinton administration officials worried that a devalued dollar would hurt Japanese businesses, which were mired in a recession that had begun in 1990 (see chapter 2). If Japanese auto sales faltered in the United States, the recession in Japan might deepen. U.S. officials reasoned that this would slow the world economy and dim U.S. economic prospects. Because the U.S. economy was growing during this period, largely as a result of gains made from the reorganization of American business (see chapter 2), Clinton administration officials were in a generous mood. "I don't think there's any question about the health and competitiveness of [U.S.] industries compared with industries [in Japan and] all over the world," Treasury Secretary Robert Rubin argued.[59]

Second, U.S. officials did not want to antagonize the Japanese, who had made substantial purchases of U.S. government bonds during the decade since the 1985 Plaza Accords. Japanese negotiators warned that if U.S. officials did not help strengthen the dollar, Japanese investors might sell off U.S. bonds.[60] If Japanese investors sold U.S. bonds, the U.S. government would have to raise interest rates to attract new buyers. As we will see in chapter 4, higher interest rates can trigger a recession and force people out of work. This was something the Clinton administration was unwilling to do as the 1996 presidential campaign approached.[61]

Because the Japanese economy remained stuck in a recession, and because the U.S. government still needed foreign investors to purchase U.S. bonds, exchange rates remained at the 1996 level into 2001, and U.S. trade deficits grew to new heights. By 1998, the U.S. trade deficit rose to more than $350 billion, a staggering sum compared with the $2.3 billion deficit that triggered the first devaluation in 1971 and the $122 billion trade deficit that forced a second devaluation in 1985. Although they were first identified as a problem by Nixon in 1971, exchange rates remain an ongoing problem for the United States and its allies today.

Gender and Exchange Rates

Most imported products are manufactured goods (autos and oil) made by men in factories, not services performed by women in offices, hospitals, or restau-

rants. So changing exchange rates generally affect men in manufacturing industries more than they do women in service industries. This being the case, the
monetary policies adopted by government officials to alter exchange rates were
really about the redistribution of jobs held by *men* in Western Europe, the
United States, and Japan. Put simply: monetary policy is gendered; changing
exchange rates primarily affect men in manufacturing.

The loss of mill jobs in the Pacific Northwest provides a good example of this
because the workers hired to cut, transport, and mill timber are predominantly
male. Of course, the loss of male jobs also affected the women who lived with
men employed in these industries. When men lost manufacturing jobs during
the 1970s, 1980s, and 1990s, many women in working- and middle-class households looked for work in growing service industries. But in the Pacific Northwest, this proved difficult to do because few service industries were located in
mill and logging towns. Under these conditions, lost income from male employment was not easily replaced by female partners, living standards fell, divorce
rates climbed, and mill towns emptied as people searched elsewhere for jobs.

Monetary Instability and Economic Crises

When Nixon first devalued the dollar in 1971, he also destroyed the system of
fixed exchange rates established at Bretton Woods in 1944. After 1971, the values of currencies were not fixed in relation to each other but "floated" up and
down depending on the health of their respective economies. But they floated
up and down fairly slowly, largely because governments did much of the buying
and selling of currencies on global markets. But that began to change in the
1980s and 1990s, as investors began pouring money into currency markets and
trading currencies at an increasingly frenetic pace. They were able to invest
heavily in currency markets because many governments were forced to make
their currencies "convertible" as part of debt crisis management plans, and
because they agreed to open their economies to foreign investment and trade
(see chapters 5 and 11). By the 1990s, decisions by private investors (whether
to buy or sell a particular currency) could have a rapid and dramatic impact on
exchange rates, triggering a serious economic crisis. During the 1990s, when
currency traders sold off Mexican pesos, Thai baht, South Korean won, Indonesian rupees, and Russian rubles, they forced rapid and deep devaluations of
these currencies. Foreign investors who owned government bonds saw their
value decline and sold them off, leaving governments without the money they
needed. To persuade investors to buy bonds, government officials raised interest
rates to very high levels. But this sent their economies into deep recessions,
leading to widespread bankruptcy and job loss. "This is off the radar screens in
terms of severity," Allen Sinai, a global economist explained. "It is the single
most negative event since the Great Depression in the United States."[62]

Because the monetary instability associated with the floating system of exchange rates can cause serious economic problems, some effort has been made to develop a "new" Bretton Woods system of fixed rates. The Bretton Woods Commission, led by Paul Volcker, former chairman of the Federal Reserve (see chapter 4), argues that "there is good evidence that exchange rates fluctuate excessively" and do not accurately reflect a currency's underlying economic health.[63] The commission proposed reforms that would address some of the problems created by floating rates. But other economists opposed the project, arguing that "the world isn't capable of maintaining a true fixed exchange-rate system."[64] So far, efforts to reform global monetary relations have made little headway.

Countries Adopt the Dollar

In the absence of any global monetary reform, a growing number of countries have adopted the U.S. dollar as their own official currency in an effort to stabilize their exchange rates and curb inflation. In 2000, Ecuador abandoned the sucre and adopted the dollar as its official currency; El Salvador and Guatemala "dollarized" their economies in 2001.[65] In Argentina, Brazil, and Lithuania, governments have linked or "pegged" their currency to the dollar, keeping both their own currency and the dollar in circulation.[66] In other countries such as Russia, the dollar plays a strong, though unofficial role as a medium of exchange, largely because billions of U.S. dollars circulate in the economy.

Why have countries dollarized their economies? First, they have done so because they "have a tremendous need for a stable currency, and we [the United States] are providing them with a benefit they cannot get any other way," explained William Poole, an economist at Brown University.[67]

Second, they dollarize to curb inflation, which has reached astronomical rates in some countries. Because the supply of dollars is limited and foreign governments cannot print more dollars on their own, a switch to dollars makes it difficult to raise prices because people do not have enough dollars to pay higher prices. Third, countries adopt the dollar or link their currencies to it as a way to legalize the widespread use of dollars to conduct business or bank savings.

U.S. officials have welcomed the dollarization of foreign economies. In 2000, Treasury Secretary Lawrence Summers applauded El Salvador's decision to dollarize: "This step should help contribute to financial stability and economic growth in El Salvador and further its integration into the global economy."[68]

But several problems are associated with dollarization. First, when a country adopts the dollar as its own or links its own currency to the dollar, it surrenders its ability to make independent monetary policy and assigns this authority to another country: the United States. Moreover, when U.S. officials make decisions about monetary policy, they do so without consulting other countries or considering the impact of their decisions on other economies. In effect, governments that dollarize surrender monetary policy to the U.S. Federal Reserve

Board (see chapter 4).[69] "The Fed uses its control of interest rates to stimulate or cool the American economy, but does not directly consider the needs of other countries that use the dollar," observers have noted.[70] So officials in dollarized countries give up their ability to stimulate the economy, create jobs, reduce unemployment, or encourage investment or savings.

Second, when countries dollarize, they create discriminatory, two-tier economies. People with ready access to dollars obtain an important advantage over people without access to dollars. In many cases, access is closely related to occupation, gender, and geography. In Russia, for example, male taxicab drivers in big cities can obtain dollars from businessmen and tourists; female prostitutes in Moscow and other big cities do the same. "Those with access to hard currency or 'valyuta' flaunt that access in their choice of dress, shampoo or entertainment," one observer wrote, leading to what he called "dollar apartheid."[71]

People who have jobs or live in areas where dollars are hard to come by are disadvantaged, in part because people with dollars bid up the prices of local goods and services. These small-scale or selective inflations create hardships for people with few dollars. In Ecuador, for example, rural Indian populations protested violently against the dollarization in 2000 because they had little access to dollars and were preyed upon by currency traders and counterfeiters.[72] Many of them are illiterate, making it difficult for them to decipher U.S. coins, which do not use numbers to indicate their values ("quarter dollar," not 25 cents; "dime," not 10 cents).[73] As a result, dollarization tends to discriminate between groups based on gender, occupation, ethnicity, and geography.

Third, when countries dollarize, they tie their economic fortunes to U.S. exchange rates. So when rates change, as they did in 1971, 1985, and 1995 when the dollar was devalued, countries can experience serious problems. Panama provides a good example of this because it has long used the U.S. dollar as its official currency.

Panama

After 1985, Panamanians watched helplessly as the value of the dollar fell dramatically. This made it more difficult for them to import manufactured goods or oil from other countries. For rich people this meant that "they consumed more [domestic] rum and less [imported] whiskey. 'I used to eat caviar,' one wealthy Panamanian put it, 'Now I eat ham.'"[74] For the poor, it meant that the cost of tortillas and cooking fuels rose, and transportation costs also increased, resulting in a rapid decline in their standard of living.

The devaluation of the dollar came at a time of rising indebtedness and deteriorating relations between Panama and the United States. The U.S. government wanted to oust or arrest Panama's dictator, General Manuel Noriega, on drug trafficking charges, and the Bush administration applied economic sanctions on the country to force him to surrender power. The combination of intentional sanctions and unintentional devaluation crippled the economy, leading to a 17 percent decline in gross domestic product and 25 percent unemployment by 1989.[75] When Noriega refused to surrender power and his soldiers attacked U.S. military personnel, the United States invaded the country on December 20, 1989. Noriega was captured and deported for trial in Miami. Although civilian democrats assumed power after Noreiga was deposed, the economy remained in difficult circumstances as a result of debt, devaluation, embargo, and invasion.

The 1971 dollar devaluation marked the beginning of a twenty-five-year effort to improve U.S. competitiveness. But it also contributed to global monetary instability and led to serious problems for domestic workers in Northwest forests and Texas oil fields. It created problems for oil-producing countries and contributed to war in the Middle East. It also contributed to monetary crises in other countries around the world.

The year 1971 also marked the beginning of a long campaign against inflation. In some respects the fight against inflation was more successful than the fight against trade deficits and job loss in the United States. Efforts to curb inflation during the early 1980s successfully reduced inflation rates in the United States. But this was not without cost. The battle against inflation crippled the domestic savings and loan industry, which contributed to rising homelessness, and triggered a global debt crisis for countries around the world. The battle against inflation in the United States will be examined in chapter 4, and the far-reaching consequences of the debt crisis will be examined in chapters 5 and 11.

NOTES

1. Paul A. Volcker and Toyoo Gyohten, *Changing Fortunes: The World's Money and the Threat to American Leadership* (New York: Times Books, 1992).

2. "Transcript of President Nixon's Address on Moves to Deal with Economic Problems," *New York Times*, August 16, 1971.

3. Tsuru Shigeto, *The Mainsprings of Japanese Growth: A Turning Point* (Paris: Atlantic Institute for International Economics, 1989), 18.

4. Berch Berberoglu, *The Legacy of Empire: Economic Decline and Class Polarization in the US* (New York: Praeger, 1992), 56.

5. Volcker and Gyohten, *Changing Fortunes*, 38–39.

6. Volcker and Gyohten, *Changing Fortunes*, 79–80.

7. Volcker and Gyohten, *Changing Fortunes*, 81.

8. Volcker and Gyohten, *Changing Fortunes*, 346.

9. Berberoglu, *The Legacy of Empire*, 56.

10. Bill Orr, *The Global Economy in the 90s: A User's Guide* (New York: New York University Press, 1992), 261.

11. Matthew L. Wald, "After 20 Years, America's Foot Is Still on the Gas," *New York Times,* October 17, 1993.

12. Andre Pollack, "A Lower Gear for Japan's Auto Makers," *New York Times,* August 30, 1992.

13. Robert Gilpin, *The Political Economy of International Relations* (Princeton, N.J.: Princeton University Press, 1987), 331.

14. Volcker and Gyohten, *Changing Fortunes,* 229.

15. Berberoglu, *The Legacy of Empire,* 56; Gilpin, *The Political Economy of International Relations,* 157.

16. Gilpin, *The Political Economy of International Relations,* 194.

17. Gilpin, *The Political Economy of International Relations.*

18. Yoichi Funabashi, *Managing the Dollar: From the Plaza to the Louvre* (Washington, D.C.: Institute for International Economics, 1989), 263.

19. Funabashi, *Managing the Dollar,* 231.

20. Daniel Burstein, *Yen! Japan's New Financial Empire and Its Threat to America* (New York: Simon & Schuster, 1988), 142; Orr, *The Global Economy in the 90s,* 167.

21. Volcker and Gyohten, *Changing Fortunes,* 256.

22. Volcker and Gyohten, *Changing Fortunes,* 252.

23. Robert D. Putnam and Nicholas Bayne, *Hanging Together: The Seven-Power Summits* (Cambridge: Harvard University Press, 1984), 18; Volcker and Gyohten, *Changing Fortunes,* 329–30.

24. Putnam and Bayne, *Hanging Together,* 45–46, 48, 237; Peter I. Hajnal, *The Seven-Power Summit: Documents from the Summits of Industrialized Countries, 1975–1989* (Millwood, N.Y.: Kraus International, 1989), xxiii, xxiv.

25. Volcker and Gyohten, *Changing Fortunes,* 329–30.

26. Putnam and Bayne, *Hanging Together,* 17.

27. Peter T. Kilborn, "U.S. and 4 Allies Plan Move to Cut Value of Dollar," *New York Times,* September 23, 1985.

28. Orr, *The Global Economy in the 90s,* 91.

29. Volcker and Gyohten, *Changing Fortunes,* 294.

30. Burstein, *Yen!* 147.

31. Burstein, *Yen!* 148.

32. Volcker and Gyohten, *Changing Fortunes,* 270, Dilip K. Das, *The Yen Appreciation and the International Economy* (New York: New York University Press, 1993), 25–28.

33. Berberoglu, *The Legacy of Empire,* 42–43.

34. Das, *The Yen Appreciation,* 77.

35. James Sterngold, "Intractable Trade Issues with Japan," *New York Times,* December 4, 1991; James Sterngold, "Japan Shifting Investment Flow Back toward Home, *New York Times,* March 22, 1992.

36. "The Forest Service: Time for a Little Perestroika," *The Economist,* March 10, 1988.

37. Jeffrey T. Olson, *National Forests: Policies for the Future. Vol. 4. Pacific Northwest Lumber and Wood Products: An Industry in Transition* (Washington, D.C.: Wilderness Society, 1988), 10.

38. Jeff Pelline, "Timber Shortage Chops Industry," *San Francisco Chronicle,* July 13, 1992.

39. Timothy Egan, "With Fate of the Forests at Stake, Power Saws and Arguments Echo," *New York Times*, March 20, 1989.

40. Timothy Egan, "Export Boom Dividing Pacific Timber Country," *New York Times*, April 23, 1988.

41. Egan, "Export Boom."

42. Pelline, "Timber Shortage."

43. Egan, "Export Boom."

44. Ted Gup, "Owl vs. Man," *Time*, June 25, 1990.

45. Daniel Yergin, *The Prize: The Epic Quest for Oil, Money and Power* (New York: Simon & Schuster, 1991), 747.

46. Yergin, *The Prize*, 750.

47. Yergin, *The Prize*, 755.

48. Yergin, *The Prize*, 756–57.

49. Orr, *The Global Economy in the 90s*, 261; Wald, "After 20 Years."

50. Orr, *The Global Economy in the 90s*, 302–3; Das, *The Yen Appreciation*, 18.

51. James Sterngold, "Leaders Come and Go, but the Japanese Boom Seems to Last Forever," *New York Times*, October 6, 1991.

52. Amory B. Lovins and Joseph J. Romm, "Fueling a Competitive Economy," *Foreign Affairs* (Winter 1992–93): 49.

53. Stephen Engelberg, Jeff Gerth, and Tim Weiner, "Saudi Stability Hit by Heavy Spending over the Last Decade," *New York Times*, August 22, 1993.

54. Keith Bradsher, "Falling Yen Puts Car Makers in Japan in the Driver's Seat," *New York Times*, July 15, 1996.

55. Andrew Pollack, "Shellshocked by Yen, Companies in Japan Still Find Ways to Profit," *New York Times*, April 18, 1995.

56. Andrew Pollack, "Japan Inc.'s Dying Bit Players," *New York Times*, May 27, 1995.

57. Bradsher, "Falling Yen."

58. Bradsher, "Falling Yen."

59. Bradsher, "Falling Yen."

60. John Judis, "Dollar Foolish," *New Republic*, December 9, 1996, 23–24.

61. Judis, "Dollar Foolish."

62. David E. Sanger, "The World Looks at Bali and Sees Krakatoa," *New York Times*, January 18, 1998.

63. Peter Passell, "A Blast from the Exchange-Rate Past," *New York Times*, July 21, 1994.

64. Passell, "A Blast from the Exchange-Rate Past."

65. Larry Rohter, "Ecuador's Use of Dollars Brings Dollar's Problems," *New York Times*, February 5, 2001.

66. Thomas L. Friedman, "Never Mind Yen. Greenbacks Are the New Gold Standard," *New York Times*, July 3, 1994.

67. Friedman, "Never Mind Yen."

68. Joseph Kahn, "U.S. and I.M.F. Welcome Salvador's Adoption of Dollar," *New York Times*, November 25, 2000.

69. Rohter, "Ecuador's Use of Dollars," 70; Kahn, "U.S. and I.M.F. Welcome."

71. Steven Erlanger, "'Dollar Apartheid' Makes a Few Russians Rich but Resented," *New York Times*, August 23, 1992.

72. Rohter, "Ecuador's Use of Dollars."

73. Rohter, "Ecuador's Use of Dollars."

74. Steve C. Ropp, "Military Retrenchment and Decay in Panama," *Current History* (January 1990): 39.

75. Steve C. Ropp, "Panama: The United States Invasion and Its Aftermath," *Current History* (March 1991): 116.

4

Fighting Inflation

When President Nixon devalued the dollar to improve U.S. competitiveness, he also introduced wage and price controls to fight inflation. "The time has come for decisive action," he said in his August 15, 1971, speech, "action that will break the vicious circle of spiraling prices and costs."[1] His orders to "freeze . . . all prices and wages throughout the United States for a period of 90 days" opened the government's attack on inflation.

During the following decade, the government would wage two major campaigns to slow inflation. The first, in 1971, proved to be a failure. The second, which began in 1979, succeeded in curbing inflation. But the cost of victory was high. The policies used to fight inflation prompted a debt crisis in the Third World and contributed to the collapse of the savings and loan industry in the United States, and this led to rising homelessness in America.

In his speech, Nixon blamed inflation on the war in Vietnam. "One of the cruelest legacies of the artificial prosperity produced by the [Vietnam] war is inflation," he argued. "For example, in the four war years between 1965 and 1969, your wage increases were completely eaten up by price increases. Your paychecks were higher but you were not better off."[2]

Economists agree that government spending on the war in Vietnam contributed to rising inflation. But they argue that other factors also contributed to it. In the postwar period, most countries in Western Europe, North America, and Japan experienced modest inflation. This inflation was caused by government policies designed to keep unemployment low and to prevent the recurrence of prewar depression. During the 1930s, businesses had responded to recession by laying off workers to cut costs. But high levels of unemployment reduced the demand for goods. Without consumers to buy their goods, businesses could not increase production, rehire workers, and begin the steps to economic recovery.

After the war, governments in Western Europe, North America, and Japan developed programs designed to maintain demand and prevent widespread unemployment when normal business cycle recessions occurred. They did this by pumping money into the economy, through defense, social service, or public works programs. These policies, generally described as "Keynesian" after the British economist John Maynard Keynes who developed them, helped avert depression. But by pumping money into the economy, they also produced modest rates of inflation. When money was plentiful and demand high, businesses could raise prices. And because unemployment rates were low and labor was relatively scarce, workers could demand and get higher wages. These developments, and the fact that the United States was pumping dollars into Western Europe and Japan to promote economic recovery, (see chapter 2), produced modest rates of inflation in all three regions during the 1950s and 1960s.[3]

When the United States began waging the Vietnam War in earnest in 1965, U.S. military spending in the United States *and* overseas soared. But U.S. officials were unwilling to raise taxes to pay for the war. If they had, taxes would have taken away some of the money the government was putting into the hands of businesses and into the pockets of workers, which would have lowered *their* demand for goods. But because taxes stayed low, demand remained high. And when demand stayed high, businesses could raise prices and workers could ask for higher wages. As a result, inflation rose sharply.

If prices and wages rose in tandem, for everyone, inflation would not be regarded as a terrible social problem. But *inflation is a discriminatory economic process*, hurting some people more than others. Some businesses, for example, were better able to raise their prices than others, usually because what they produced was *more* of a necessity than other products. Oil, for example, was something that homeowners in wintry New England or drivers in suburban Los Angeles could not do without. It was more of a necessity than lawn chairs or vintage wine. By the same token, some workers were better able to demand and get higher wages, usually because they were organized in unions or performed services regarded as essential to others. So workers who belonged to the United Auto Workers union or worked for the local fire department or collected garbage were better able to bargain for pay raises than restaurant waiters or office workers who were not unionized or employed by the government.

Other groups were also disadvantaged by inflation. People living on fixed incomes or pensions—some twenty million Americans in 1971, according to Nixon—found it difficult to increase their incomes to keep pace with inflation. And people who derived their income from savings accounts and government bonds found that inflation eroded the value of their assets because the interest they received was fixed at fairly low levels (often below the rate of inflation). So, for example, if the rate of inflation was 6 percent annually, a savings account offering 4 percent was losing value, and a ten-year savings bond that provided a 6 percent return was not earning a dime.

Because inflation is discriminatory, affecting businesses, workers, pensioners, and investors in different ways, government officials regarded it as a social prob-

lem. Although people adversely affected by inflation despair of its consequences, *even* those who kept up with inflation complained about it. As
economist Anthony Compagna notes, "If someone's income increased by $1,000
(which he or she regards as due to merit, conveniently forgetting that inflation
boosts other people's income as well) and rising prices take away $500 of the
$1,000, the person is still better off but *feels cheated anyway* [because] $1,000
at the old prices would have meant a [more] significant increase in living standards."[4]

For these reasons, Nixon introduced wage and price controls to curb inflation,
then increasing at about 4 percent annually. When inflation rises 7 percent
annually, as it did during the rest of the decade, consumer prices and monthly
wages double in just ten years.[5] This is what occurred in the 1970s.

Nixon's wage and price controls, which remained in effect until April 1973,
briefly slowed but did not curb inflation.[6] As journalist William Greider
observed, "The inflation rate subsided for a time but still remained about 3 percent. By 1973, prices were escalating rapidly again and the consumer price index
rose by a new postwar record, 8.89 percent. The following year, 1974, OPEC
pushed up oil and the price level rose 12.2 percent."[7]

Several developments frustrated the Nixon administration's efforts to slow
inflation. Many economists believe that the wage and price control program was
not effectively managed, allowing exemptions to some businesses and workers
but not others. And when the controls ended, everyone scrambled to recover
lost gains.[8] Soviet crop failures in 1973 and 1974 increased the demand for grain
and sent food prices soaring (see chapter 7). At the same time, dramatically
increased oil prices followed successive oil crises—the first in 1974 following
the Yom Kippur War, and the second during the 1979 revolution that overthrew
the Shah of Iran and resulted in the capture of hostages at the U.S. embassy in
Tehran. The simultaneous rise of food and oil prices pushed inflation to record
heights. After each oil crisis, inflation in the United States hit double-digit figures, 12 percent in 1974, 13.3 percent in 1979, and 12.4 percent in 1980.[9] At
these rates, prices doubled every five or six years.

The burst of inflation at the end of the 1970s prompted government officials
to launch a second campaign against inflation. But instead of using wage and
price controls administered by the federal government, officials used high interest rates and the Federal Reserve, a semipublic agency, to curb inflation.

1979: THE SECOND BATTLE
AGAINST INFLATION

At the beginning of 1979, inflation was running at a rapid 11 percent annual
rate. "In a year's time, a dollar would buy only 89 cents' worth of goods. A $6,000
car would soon cost $660 more. And every wage earner would need a pay raise

of more than 10 percent simply to stay even," noted Greider.[10] By the summer of 1979, new OPEC price increases began to kick in, pushing the inflation rate to 14 percent. Rising inflation and lengthening lines at gas stations drove down President Jimmy Carter's popularity. By July, "barely a fourth of the voters approved of his performance as President."[11]

Faced with rising inflation and declining popularity, Carter took two steps. First, he made a stern speech criticizing American materialism:

> In a nation that was proud of hard work, strong families, close-knit communities and our faith in God, too many of us now tend to worship self-indulgence and consumption. Human identity is no longer defined by what one does, but by what one owns. But . . . owning things and consuming things does not satisfy our longing for meaning. We have learned that piling up material goods cannot fill the emptiness of our lives which have no confidence or purpose.[12]

Overnight, this speech boosted Carter's popularity by 10 percent, and "75 percent of voters agreed with the President's warning of spiritual crisis."[13] His increased popularity proved to be only temporary. After Iranian students seized hostages at the U.S. embassy in Tehran on November 4, 1979, his popularity again declined.

In addition to his speech, Carter took another step. On July 25, he appointed Paul Volcker, who had helped shape the Nixon administration's 1971 dollar devaluation and introduce wage and price controls (see chapter 3), to head the Federal Reserve System.[14] Volcker's subsequent decision to raise interest rates to curb inflation would have a long and lasting impact on U.S. economic fortunes. Although his high interest rate policies succeeded in bringing down inflation, they created other problems for the United States and other countries around the world. One important problem was an economic recession during an election year. This and the hostage crisis in Iran led to Carter's electoral defeat by Ronald Reagan one year later.

THE FEDERAL RESERVE SYSTEM
AND HIGH INTEREST RATES

The Federal Reserve System, established in 1913, acts as the central bank for the United States, controlling the supply of money and credit to private banks and financial institutions, supervising the industry, and managing the sale of U.S. bonds, which are used (along with taxes and fees) to raise money for the government so that it can pay its bills.[15] Its governors are appointed by the president, subject to Senate confirmation, to serve fourteen-year terms. As a result, the Federal Reserve System has considerable autonomy to shape economic policy.

In general, the "Fed" can use its control over money and credit to affect U.S. economic fortunes. If it increases the supply of government money and credit going to private banks, investors, and businesses, the "stimulated" economy usually grows. If the Fed decreases the money supply, making money and credit harder to get, then the "price" or interest rates that banks, investors, and businesses have to pay for money rises. The higher the price of money, and the higher the interest rate, the harder it is to borrow money, invest, or build new factories. As a result, the economy usually slows and unemployment increases.

After he was appointed to the Fed, Volcker adopted an anti-inflationary strategy. By tightening the supply of money and credit, he hoped to force up interest rates, slow economic growth, and curb inflation. Although he knew this would trigger an economic recession and increase unemployment, Volcker thought it necessary to act. "After years of inflation," he told an audience in the autumn of 1979, "the long run has caught up with us."[16]

So on October 6, 1979, Volcker announced that he would fight inflation by restricting the supply of money and credit and raising interest rates. "Appropriate restraint of the supply of money and credit is an essential part of any program to achieve the needed reduction in inflationary momentum and in inflationary expectations," he announced. "Such restraint . . . will help to restore a stable base for financial, foreign exchange and commodity prices."[17]

During the next six months, interest rates nearly doubled, rising from about 11 percent when Volcker became chairman to 20 percent in the summer of 1980.[18] But when the Fed eased off, inflation resumed, so Volcker pushed interest rates back up. And during the next two years, until the summer of 1982, interest rates rocketed up and down as the Fed used interest rates to wrestle with the tag team of inflation and recession.[19] In the end, the high interest rate policy pinned inflation, though recession remained standing. As Greider noted, "The Gross National Product contracted in real terms by more than $82 billion from its peak and, since 1979, the country had accumulated as much as $600 billion in lost economic output. The excess supply of goods, the declining incomes, the surplus labor—all had worked to force down wages and prices. Price inflation fell dramatically: from above 13 percent [in 1979] to less than 4 percent [in 1983]."[20]

Volcker's high interest rate policies, which triggered the deepest recession in the postwar period, had returned the U.S. economy to the kind of modest inflation that had first triggered Nixon's wage and price controls in 1971.[21] Recall that Nixon took action to curb inflation when it was running at about 4 percent. After 1982, inflation remained at this level, running about 4 percent during the 1980s and 1990s.[22]

In addition to a deep recession, the Fed's high interest rate policies also affected the fortunes of different social groups in the United States. Although everyone complained about its effect, inflation had been good for some groups— middle-income homeowners who had seen the value of their homes rise sharply—but bad for others. Wealthy investors, for instance, had seen the value of their assets, particularly bonds, decline sharply in the 1970s. As New York University economist Edward N. Wolf reported, "Inflation acted like a progressive tax, leading to greater equality in the distribution of wealth."[23]

But high interest rates and falling inflation changed that. High interest rates rewarded the wealthy, primarily because the top 10 percent of the population "owned 72 percent of corporate and federal bonds . . . plus 86 percent of state and local bonds."[24] As interest rates rose to record highs, and inflation fell to modest lows, their assets increased. "According to the U.S. Census, only families in the top 20 percent of the economic ladder enjoyed real increases in their after-tax household incomes from 1980 to 1983. The others, the bottom 80 percent, actually lost."[25]

Volcker anticipated this development. When farm representatives asked him to lower interest rates, Volcker responded, "Look, your constituents are unhappy, mine [banks and bond holders] aren't."[26]

Farmers were unhappy with high interest rates because many of them had borrowed heavily (at government request) during the 1970s to expand production and reap the high prices associated with repeated crop failures in the Soviet Union (see chapter 7). But during the early 1980s, Soviet harvests recovered and world grain prices fell, just when U.S. interest rates skyrocketed. The combination of falling prices and rising interest rates drove four hundred thousand farmers out of business during the early 1980s.

The ruin of small farmers across the Midwest had a huge impact on other small businesses and rural communities because farmers are really *big consumers*. The average farm family consumes more in a year than a steel worker household consumes in a lifetime. A farm household might borrow $100,000 each year to buy the fertilizer, seed, crop insurance, and equipment they need to plant and harvest their crops. A steel worker family might borrow this sum to buy a house only once every thirty years. So the bankruptcy of large numbers of small farmers had a devastating impact on other small businesses that provided goods and services to farmers. Moreover, the entry of men and women from struggling or bankrupt farms into local labor markets, as farmers sought "off-farm" income to keep their land, usually depressed wages for the jobs that remained. Small wonder, then, that farmers were angered by Volcker's high interest rate policies. Many felt betrayed because these policies were pursued by a Republican administration, which they had supported during the 1980 election (Midwest farm states traditionally vote Republican).

By squeezing the supply of money and credit and raising interest rates, the Federal Reserve triggered a deep recession and curbed inflation. But while high interest rates curbed inflation, they also contributed to an overseas debt crisis, rising U.S. budget deficits, and declining U.S. competitiveness.

DEBT, DEFICITS, AND DEVALUATION

When the Fed raised interest rates to record highs in the early 1980s, foreign and domestic investors rushed to buy U.S. bonds or "securities." They did so because they viewed them as "safe"—nothing is safer than U.S. government-backed securities—and profitable: a 15 to 20 percent annual return was higher than more risky investments in stock markets or real estate. High U.S. interest rates, which were substantially higher than what other governments offered in this period, acted like a magnet, attracting monies from around the world. The magnetism created by high U.S. interest rates had important consequences for different countries.

In Latin America, high U.S. interest rates resulted in increased debt and "capital flight." During the 1970s, businesses and governments borrowed money from the United States and from banks in Western Europe and spent it on economic development projects (see chapter 5). The interest rate they paid on borrowed money was tied to U.S. interest rates. So when the Fed pushed up U.S. interest rates, borrowers in Latin America saw their interest payments soar, which made it more difficult for them to repay their debts.

High U.S. interest rates also attracted Latin American investors, who spent their money on U.S. bonds rather than on development projects in their own countries. In 1978, before U.S. interest rates rose, Latin American investors sent about $7 billion overseas. But in 1980, Latin Americans invested nearly $25 billion overseas, most of it in the United States.[27] "Capital flight," as economists call it, was a problem for Latin American countries because it reduced domestic investment, which resulted in unemployment, and deprived governments of the currency they needed to run their countries and repay debts. In August 1982, the Mexican government ran out of money to manage its affairs or repay its $80 billion debt to foreign countries, and the Federal Reserve had to take emergency measures to prevent it from defaulting on its loans. If Mexico had declared bankruptcy, major U.S. banks would also have been forced into bankruptcy, and a global financial crisis would have ensued.[28] In subsequent years, the Fed and the U.S. government had to address a series of financial crises in Latin American countries, Eastern Europe, and Africa, known collectively as the debt crisis, which was partly a product of the Fed's high interest rate policies.

High U.S. interest rates also acted like a magnet for other first world investors, drawing huge sums of money from Western Europe and Japan. Although these countries did not have foreign debts, like Latin American countries, U.S. economists thought that the flight or migration of capital from Western Europe and Japan would deprive them of money to invest in public works or new factories in their countries, causing increased unemployment and reducing their ability to compete with the United States. But despite massive purchases of U.S. securities, these problems did not materialize in Western Europe and Japan because the U.S. government gave back to them through military spending what the Federal Reserve took away from them in capital flight.

When President Reagan took office, he promised to increase military spending and cut taxes. As foreign capital flooded into U.S. securities markets as a result of high U.S. interest rates, the administration found that it could deliver on both its promises. With high interest rates, the Reagan administration could sell bonds and raise the money it needed to increase military spending without raising the taxes to pay for it. By using the sale of U.S. bonds to borrow money from foreigners, the government increased military spending 50 percent, from $201 billion a year in 1980 to $311 billion in 1987.[29] Moreover, it could do this without raising taxes to pay for it. In fact, the Reagan administration cut taxes dramatically during much of this period.

Put another way, in 1985, the U.S. government spent about $79 billion more on defense than it had in 1980. And it received $71.4 billion from foreign investors. Thus the increases in military spending were almost entirely paid for by foreigners, which meant that the government did not have to use domestic taxes to raise this money.

This policy—increased military spending and lower taxes—had several important consequences in Western Europe, Japan, and the United States.

The Military Rebate

Western Europe and Japan have been U.S. military allies since World War II. To protect them from invasion by communist countries, the U.S. government had stationed troops and spent money on defense in these countries throughout the postwar period. Economists estimate that between 60 and 70 percent of *all* U.S. military spending was devoted to NATO, which defended Western Europe.[30] The United States spent a smaller though still large amount, defending U.S. allies in East Asia, Japan among them. As U.S. military spending increased under the Reagan administration, its spending in Western Europe and Japan also increased. By purchasing equipment and supplies from its allies, by paying the salaries of about 351,000 U.S. soldiers in Europe, and by providing military aid to its allies, the U.S. government injected huge sums of money into the economies of its allies.[31]

In 1985, for example, foreigners (mostly from Western Europe and Japan but also from Latin America) purchased $71.4 billion in U.S. securities.[32] That year, the United States spent $278.9 billion on the military.[33] If the United States spent 60 percent of its military budget for the defense of its First World allies (a low figure since some estimates of U.S. spending on NATO are higher and this figure does not include U.S. spending on Japan), then about $167.34 billion was spent on U.S. allies. This means that the United States "took in" less capital from its allies than it "gave back" in military spending. Total U.S. "giving" to U.S.

allies in that year amounted to $95.94 billion, a kind of massive military "rebate." So while the Federal Reserve's high interest rate policy pulled money out of European and Japanese economies, the Reagan administration's defense spending policies put much of it back. Moreover, the high U.S. interest rates, which U.S. economists expected to hurt other U.S. competitors, did not result in recession or high unemployment in either Europe or Japan.

High U.S. interest rates did not greatly reduce the availability of capital in Western Europe and Japan for another reason. Workers in these countries saved more of their money than Americans. They were more thrifty because high tariffs often made imported goods expensive, because their governments and banks did not make consumer credit as easily available as they did in the United States, and because they were more reluctant to go into debt than Americans. Because they put a higher percentage of their income in their savings accounts, their banks had more money available to invest. As a result, Japan substantially increased its domestic investments—building new roads and factories and creating more jobs—while *also* increasing its purchases of U.S. government securities in this period (see chapter 3).[34]

As a result of U.S. defense spending and their own thriftiness, Western Europe and Japan were able to benefit three times from high U.S. interest rates. First, they profited from interest rates that were higher than they could obtain at home. Second, they benefited from increased U.S. military spending in their countries. And third, the flood of foreign currency into the United States increased the value of the dollar, making it easier for them to sell their wares in the United States (see chapter 3). During the early 1980s, the stronger dollar made it more difficult for U.S. firms to sell their goods abroad, while making it easier for Western European and Japanese businesses to sell their products in the United States. Propped up by high U.S. interest rates, the stronger dollar undermined U.S. competitiveness and led, in 1985, to a second devaluation of the dollar through the Plaza Accords.

These developments were the product of two sets of policies. It was the combination of the Fed's *monetary* policy, which used high interest rates to fight inflation, and the Reagan administration's *fiscal* policy, which borrowed money from abroad to increase military spending while cutting taxes, that contributed to these different *global* developments: debt crisis in Latin America, Africa, and Eastern Europe (see chapter 5) and the redistribution of production from the United States to Western Europe and Japan (see chapter 2).

For the U.S. economy, the combination of the Fed's high interest rate policy and the Reagan administration's policy of increased military spending but lower taxes had important consequences. By increasing its spending and cutting taxes, the Reagan administration created large and growing budget deficits that contributed to a rapidly growing national debt. Because the government borrowed money to cover annual budget deficits at high rates of interest, interest payments grew, which also contributed to the size of total debt.

High interest rates also contributed to the collapse of the domestic savings and loan (S&L) industry. Widespread bankruptcies in this industry reduced investment in the housing industry. This outcome triggered a housing shortage and led to rising home prices and rents, which in turn led, by decade's end, to rising homelessness in America.

HOUSING AND HOMELESSNESS

During the thirty years before 1979, the housing industry built millions of inexpensive homes and apartments, making it possible for two-thirds of all Americans to purchase and own their homes. But in the ten years after 1979, the savings and loan organizations that provided money to the construction industry and to home buyers collapsed. Home building slowed, prices and rents rose, and homelessness increased. The Federal Reserve's 1979 decision to raise interest rates marked a turning point and played an important role in reversing the housing industry's fortunes.

High U.S. interest rates not only attracted money from Latin America and investors in Western Europe and Japan but also drew money out of domestic savings accounts. The flight of capital from the passbook savings accounts of domestic S&Ls created problems that led to the collapse of the industry, which had long been a mainstay of the housing industry. Although capital flight from the domestic S&L industry had been a minor problem since 1965, it became a major problem after 1979.

During the postwar period, S&Ls provided much of the money used by private construction companies and independent contractors to build homes and apartments. S&Ls differed from commercial banks in several important respects. Unlike commercial banks, they did not offer checking accounts or provide services to merchants or loans to businesses. Instead, they offered passbook savings accounts to local depositors and attracted customers by paying interest rates that were slightly higher than those offered by banks. (The federal government set these rates and made sure they were higher than those offered by commercial banks.) The S&Ls then took the money deposited in savings accounts and lent the money to contractors and home buyers at a slightly higher rate so they could build and buy homes and so S&Ls could profit from the loans. The income they received from construction loans and mortgage payments enabled the 5,500 S&Ls in the United States to pay their depositors interest on their savings account and make a small profit, which they used to pay salaries, rent, and dividends to shareholders.

Between 1950 and 1970, "31 million housing units were built, including 20 million single-family homes."[35] The large supply of inexpensive housing and the availability of cheap, low-interest, thirty-year home loans made it possible for most Americans to purchase homes. Although only 43.6 percent of Americans owned homes in 1940, 64.4 percent owned homes in 1980, a 50 percent increase.[36] By collecting the savings of small depositors and lending it out to builders and buyers, the S&Ls played an important role in postwar prosperity.

The industry's first real problems began in the mid-1960s. To fight the war in Vietnam, President Lyndon Johnson needed to increase military spending. But he was reluctant to increase taxes to pay for the war because he worried that tax increases would make the war more unpopular. To raise the money, Johnson persuaded the Fed to raise interest rates on government securities, much as Volcker did fifteen years later. Interest rose to a rate that was slightly higher than the rate S&Ls offered depositors on passbook savings accounts. In 1966, for example, the government's three-month Treasury bills (T-bills) paid 5.28 percent interest, while S&Ls provided only 4.75 percent interest on savings accounts (and commercial banks offered only 4 percent).[37]

As a result, some depositors began withdrawing their money from S&L savings accounts and investing it in government securities that offered a higher rate of return. When investors withdrew money from a financial institution, they reduced its assets and weakened its ability to make loans. The technical term for this process is *disintermediation*, but it might also be called a "slow run on the bank" or capital flight, which undermines the ability of financial institutions to operate as "intermediaries" between investors and borrowers.

Initially, investors drawn by higher U.S. interest rates withdrew only modest amounts of money from S&Ls, only $2.5 billion in 1966, a small sum compared to the more than $500 billion held by S&Ls. But disintermediation continued, growing to $4 billion in 1969. The federal government responded to this slow flight of capital by raising the interest rates S&Ls could offer on savings accounts to 5 percent in 1970 and 5.25 percent in 1973. They also made it more difficult to purchase T-bills by setting a $10,000 minimum on purchases, which was more than most small savers could afford.[38] But because the government's interest rates also increased, remaining one or two percentage points higher than S&L rates for much of the 1970s, the flow of money out of S&Ls continued at a moderate pace.

But in 1979, the Federal Reserve raised interest rates, and the return on three-month T-bills reached 12.07 percent in 1979, 15.66 percent in 1980, and 16.30 percent in 1981.[39] As a result, money flooded out of S&Ls offering depositors only one-half or one-third as much. In 1981, investors withdrew $21.5 billion from S&Ls, five times as much as they had in 1969. To stop this massive capital flight and to prevent the wholesale disintermediation of the S&L industry, government officials took two steps that would have fateful consequences.

As its first step, Congress in 1980 passed and President Carter signed the Depository Institutions Deregulation and Monetary Control Act. This bill allowed S&Ls to increase their interest rates on savings accounts (the federal government had previously limited interest rates) so they could win back runaway investors, and it increased the government's insurance on investors' deposits from $40,000 to $100,000.

Although higher interest rates prompted some investors to redeposit their money in S&L accounts, they created another problem. Recall that payments on home mortgages provided the income for S&Ls. If they took in money from borrowers at 8 percent and they paid depositors 5 percent on their savings accounts, the S&Ls earned 3 percent. But when they raised interest rates on savings accounts to, say, 10 percent, this increased their expenditures. But they could not easily raise their *income* from mortgage payments because they had made home loans at fixed rates for *long* periods of time. In the 1980s, S&Ls' income came from people who had borrowed money at 8 percent in the 1960s. Because they could not raise the mortgage payments of long-term borrowers to increase their income, the S&Ls began paying depositors (10 percent) more than they earned from borrowers (8 percent). As a result, they began to *lose* money, about $4.6 billion in 1981. And bankruptcies began to mount: 17 S&Ls failed in 1980, 65 in 1981, 201 in 1982. The assets of insolvent S&Ls grew from one-tenth of a billion dollars in 1980 to $49 billion in 1982, a 500 percent increase.[40]

Although disintermediation had been slowed, government policy had contributed to increasing bankruptcy. To address this problem, the Garn–St. Germain Depository Institutions Act was passed in 1982. This bill allowed S&Ls to offer checking accounts, issue credit cards, loan money to consumers for autos and personal purchases, make commercial loans to businesses, and invest in stocks and bonds. By allowing S&Ls to offer these services and become more like commercial banks, government officials expected S&Ls to increase their income. For example, the interest rates on credit cards or business or auto loans are much higher than interest rates on home loans. So if the S&Ls could make 15 percent from their credit card customers, government officials thought, they could pay depositors 10 percent and still make money. For a time it worked. S&Ls loaned money in new ways, at higher rates of interest, and paid depositors higher rates on their savings accounts. For a brief time they attracted investors and turned a profit. But two problems soon emerged.

First, increased commercial lending led to the widespread construction of office buildings, golf courses, and resort developments, particularly in the Southwest, where high oil prices in the early 1980s encouraged the expansion of the domestic oil industry and created a booming market for commercial real estate in cities like Dallas. But the massive construction of office towers and shopping malls created a glut of commercial properties, and the fall of oil prices after 1985 led to the collapse of the domestic oil industry, which crippled the real estate market (see chapter 3). The value of commercial real estate in the Southwest fell by nearly one-half between 1984 and 1989.[41] As the value of real estate fell, builders and developers found it difficult to repay their loans and many went bankrupt. When the S&Ls could not recover their loans from bankrupt borrowers, they, too, went bankrupt. As bankruptcy threatened, depositors began withdrawing their money, which led to renewed disintermediation. Profits plummeted, and the S&L industry began to collapse wholesale.

It did not help matters that the Reagan administration cut the budget for bank examiners during this period, which actually reduced the number of field agents and cut the number of federal examinations by 50 percent between 1980 and 1984.[42] Nor did it help that regulators ignored a 1983 government report warning that "the deregulation of the past few years . . . has substantially reduced the ability of regulatory agencies to constrain the risk-taking of insured institutions. . . . In light of the competitive pressures the industry will face in the next few years, this deregulation could result in substantial losses."[43]

When S&Ls went bankrupt, the Federal Reserve and U.S. government agencies seized control and paid off depositors, who were insured up to $100,000 (as a result of changes in the 1980 law). Investors who owned shares of bank stock were not covered by government insurance, and many lost their investments. The cost of repaying depositors in failed S&Ls, the government's bailout as it was called, was high. In 1990, Treasury Secretary Nicholas Brady testified to Congress that one thousand S&Ls, or 40 percent of the industry, would have to be seized and depositors repaid. He estimated that this would cost the government between $89 billion and $130 billion. Taxpayers will eventually cover this cost, amounting to $1,300 for each American household.[44] Other cost estimates are higher. Some economists calculated that the bailout cost taxpayers between $159 billion and $203 billion. If one included the interest payments on this debt, the cost climbed to between $325 billion and $500 billion, or about $5,000 for each American household.[45]

The government tried to recover some of these costs by selling off the assets of seized S&Ls. By 1992, it had sold off assets worth $144 billion. But the sale of 2,300 square miles of real estate, an area twice the size of Rhode Island, was difficult in a sluggish market.[46]

Second, the S&Ls' changed lending practices reduced the amount of money going to the housing industry. In the early 1970s, S&Ls loaned 60 percent of their assets to home builders and buyers. But as they shifted their emphasis to consumer and commercial loans, at higher rates of interest, they made only 40 percent of their money available to home buyers in 1984 and only 30 percent in 1988.[47] As money for the housing industry dried up, and the money that was available cost more (because of higher interest rates), fewer homes were built and fewer people could borrow money to purchase homes.

In 1972, the housing industry built 2.4 million new homes. But in 1984, when the population was larger and the demand for housing had grown, the industry built only 1.7 million homes.[48] During the 1990s, the industry built 1.1 million homes a year on average, only one-half as many as were built each year in the 1970s.[49] This was a *critical* development because the population was bigger and the housing supply smaller. This pushed up housing prices and rents across the country.

Inflation had pushed up the cost of housing during the 1970s. In the 1980s, inflation abated, but a shrinking supply of houses and a growing demand for houses continued to push prices up. As the price of housing and the cost of money to purchase a home rose in the early 1980s, fewer people could afford to buy a home, and the percentage of homeowners began to decline for the first time since 1940.

Many people who might have bought a home in previous decades kept on renting apartments. This development, and the decline in the construction of apartment units, increased the demand for rental units. The Joint Center for Housing Studies at Harvard University reported in 1989 that the number of poor renters had grown, but rental housing stock had declined, and this helped drive up rents. As a result, rents began to rise sharply after 1980, increasing from about $350 a month in the Northeast in 1980 to $420 a month in 1986, and from $380 a month in the West in 1980 to $480 by 1986.[50]

While rents rose, federal housing assistance to the poor declined. The Reagan administration cut housing assistance from $27 billion in 1980 to less than $8 billion in 1987, and the number of federally subsidized housing units declined from 200,000 to 15,000.[51]

As a result, the demand for rental housing outstripped the supply and rents rose. "In 1978 there were 370,000 more low-cost units (renting for $250 a month) than there were low-income renter households, but by 1985, there were 3.7 million fewer low-cost units than there were low-income renter households."[52] Government cuts in housing assistance and stagnant wages made it difficult for poor people to pay higher rents or compete for the available housing. In 1997, 5.4 million families paid more than one-half of their income for housing, a dangerously high level. "To make matters worse, the number of affordable housing units is shrinking just when it needs to expand," a federal government study warned.[53]

Poor people who could not afford rising rents were forced out of the housing market. Of course, before people hit the streets, they try to crowd into apartments with others or go to live with relatives if they can (this is a process familiar to college students, who cram into apartments or share houses to save on rent). But when these alternatives are exhausted, poor people, many of them working in minimum wage jobs, become homeless.

By 1990, there were between six hundred thousand and three million homeless people in the United States.[54] Of course, they were not all forced to wander the streets of American cities by high interest rates and the collapse of the S&L industry. A small homeless population had long existed in the United States, and its number increased as a result of personal choice or misfortune, economic recession, or government policies, such as the de-institutionalization of mentally disabled patients from state hospitals in the 1970s. But the growing percentage of homeless *families*, about 40 percent of the homeless population in 1993, indicated that economic developments during the 1980s played an important role in increased homelessness during the 1980s and 1990s.[55]

Gender and the Housing Crisis

High interest rates triggered the collapse of the S&L industry and crippled the residential construction industry, which had long relied on S&Ls to finance new construction. Construction is a very gendered industry. Of the 4.4 million workers employed in construction, the most labor-intensive industry in America, the overwhelming majority (more than 90 percent) are men.[56] Moreover, many of the workers in related industries—timber, furniture, landscape, hardware, plumbing, electrical, air conditioning, heating, painting, paving, flooring, and roofing—are also predominantly male. So the decline of the residential construction industry since 1971 has hammered occupations long identified with male workers. Although the S&L industry provided service jobs (tellers) for women, the number of women employed by S&Ls was small by comparison.

The rising price of homes and rents had rather different gender consequences. During the 1980s, the homeless population was predominantly male. This was due in part to the fact that the "old" homeless population, which consisted of derelict, alcoholic, and transient street people, was overwhelmingly male. During the 1980s, many of the "new" homeless were poor men who had lost their jobs in manufacturing and also construction industries. So in the 1980s, homelessness was closely associated with men. But this began to change in the 1990s, as the number of homeless women and children increased. By 2000, the number of women and children in the homeless population had grown considerably, to perhaps 40 percent of the total. In New York City, for example, of the 25,000 people who sought city-provided shelter each night in 2000, 18,000 of them were children and a parent, most of them women.[57] Of course, women and parents with children were more likely to seek, and obtain, shelter than single men. But the homeless population today is not identified only with men, as it once was, but with men, women, and children.

Although the Federal Reserve's high interest rate policy successfully curbed inflation, the victory was costly. The collapse of the S&L industry and the rise of homelessness have become major and continuing problems in the United States. While interest rates declined in the 1990s, it was difficult to revive the housing industry, increase the supply of homes and apartments, and decrease housing prices to levels where homelessness could be substantially reduced. Overseas, rising interest rates triggered a massive debt crisis, which is still a serious problem. It is to this development that we now turn.

NOTES

1. "Transcript of President's Address on Moves to Deal with Economic Problems," *New York Times*, August 16, 1971.

2. "Transcript of President's Address."

3. Michael R. Smith, *Power, Norms and Inflation: A Skeptical Treatment* (New York: Aldine de Gruyter, 1992).

4. Anthony S. Campagna, *The Economic Consequences of the Vietnam War* (New York: Praeger, 1991), 122.

5. Berch Bergeroglu, *The Legacy of Empire: Economic Decline and Class Polarization in the US* (New York: Praeger, 1992), 61.

6. Campagna, *The Economic Consequences*, 89.

7. William Greider, *Secrets of the Temple: How the Federal Reserve Runs the Country* (New York: Touchstone, 1987), 91.

8. Campagna, *The Economic Consequences*, 114.

9. Paul A. Volcker and Toyoo Gyohten, *Changing Fortunes: The World's Money and the Threat to American Leadership* (New York: Times, 1992), 115; Berberoglu, *The Legacy of Empire*, 61.

10. Greider, *Secrets of the Temple*, 14.

11. Greider, *Secrets of the Temple*.

12. Greider, *Secrets of the Temple*.

13. Greider, *Secrets of the Temple*, 15.

14. Greider, *Secrets of the Temple*, 46–47.

15. *The World Almanac and Book of Facts 1990* (New York: Pharos, 1990), 83; Greider, *Secrets of the Temple*, 32–33.

16. Greider, *Secrets of the Temple*, 104.

17. "Test of Fed's Announcement on Measures to Curb Inflation," *New York Times*, October 8, 1979; Steven Rattner, "Anti-Inflation Plan by Federal Reserve Increases Key Rate," *New York Times*, October 7, 1979.

18. Greider, *Secrets of the Temple*, 148–49.

19. Greider, *Secrets of the Temple*, 219.

20. Greider, *Secrets of the Temple*, 507.

21. Bill Orr, *The Global Economy in the 90s: A User's Guide* (New York: New York University Press, 1992), 257.

22. Orr, *The Global Economy in the 90s*, 258.

23. Greider, *Secrets of the Temple*, 44.

24. Greider, *Secrets of the Temple*, 372.

25. Greider, *Secrets of the Temple*, 577.

26. Greider, *Secrets of the Temple*, 676.

27. Manuel Pastor, Jr., *Capital Flight and the Latin American Debt Crisis* (Washington, D.C.: Economic Policy Institute, 1989), 9.

28. Greider, *Secrets of the Temple*, 517.

29. Orr, *The Global Economy in the 90s*, 287.

30. Ruth Sivard, *World Military and Social Expenditures, 1987–88* (Washington, D.C.: World Priorities, 1987), 37.

31. "U.S. Official Affirms a 40% cut in Troops Based in Europe by '96," *New York Times*, March 29, 1992.

32. Norman J. Glickman and Douglas P. Woodward, *The New Competitors: How Foreign Investors Are Changing the U.S. Economy* (New York: Basic Books, 1989), 116.

33. Orr, *The Global Economy in the 90s*, 287.

34. David E. Sanger, "Japan Keeps Up the Big Spending to Maintain Its Industrial Might," *New York Times*, April 11, 1990.

35. David Kotz, "S&L Hell: Loan Wolves Howl All the Way to the Bank," *In These Times*, August 8, 1989, 20.

36. Kotz, "S&L Hell."

37. Lawrence J. White, *The S&L Debacle: Public Policy Lessons for Bank and Thrift Regulation* (New York: Oxford University Press, 1991), 63.

38. White, *The S&L Debacle*, 62, 64.

39. White, *The S&L Debacle*, 68.

40. Kotz, "S&L Hell," 21.

41. White, *The S&L Debacle*, 111.

42. White, *The S&L Debacle*, 88–89.

43. White, *The S&L Debacle*, 92.

44. David E. Rosenbaum, "How Capital Ignored Alarms on Savings," *New York Times*, June 6, 1990.

45. Rosenbaum, "How Capital Ignored."

46. Leslie Wayne, "The Great American Land Sale," *New York Times*, November 30, 1992.

47. Kotz, "S&L Hell," 21.

48. Greider, *Secrets of the Temple*, 654.

49. Richard W. Stevenson, "Market Place. The Gospel According to Greenspan: Rising Home Prices," *New York Times*, November 3, 1999.

50. Ann Mariano, "Fewer Can Buy Homes, Study Finds: Poor Seen Trapped in Rent Cost Squeeze," *Washington Post*, June 24, 1989.

51. Kevin Phillips, *The Politics of Rich and Poor: Wealth and the American Electorate in the Reagan Aftermath* (New York: Random House, 1990), Appendix 1.1; Richard Sweeney, *Out of Place: Homelessness in America* (New York: HarperCollins, 1993), 89.

52. E. J. Dionne, Jr., "Poor Paying More for Their Shelter," *New York Times*, April 18, 1989.

53. Michael Janofsky, "Home Prices Are Out of Reach for Many," *New York Times*, June 12, 2000.

54. Michael Levitas, "Homelessness in America," *New York Times Magazine*, June 10, 1990.

55. William Clairborne, "Big Increase in Homeless Families," *San Francisco Chronicle*, December 22, 1993.

56. Lawrence Mishel and David M. Frankel, *The State of Working America, 1990–91* (Armonk, N.Y.: Sharpe, 1991), 104.

57. Nina Bernstein, "Shelter Population Reaches Highest Level Since 1980s," *New York Times*, February 8, 2001.

5

Debt Crisis and Globalization

On March 27, 1981, Polish government officials in London told representatives of five hundred Western banks that Poland could not repay the $27 billion it had borrowed from them. In July, the Romanian government followed suit, suspending payments on its more modest $7 billion debt to Western banks.[1] The financial problems created by these defaults were dwarfed a year later, in August 1982, when Mexico's finance secretary, Jesus Silva Herzog, announced that Mexico could no longer make payments on its $90 billion foreign debt. During the next year, more than forty other countries, most of them in Latin America, ran out of money and announced they could no longer repay the interest or principal on huge debts owed to private banks and government lending agencies in first world countries. Collectively, countries in Latin America, Africa, and Eastern Europe owed $810 billion in 1983, a twelvefold increase from the $64 billion they owed in 1970.[2] "Never in history have so many nations owed so much money with so little promise of repayment," *Time* magazine observed.[3]

The sudden inability of so many countries to repay their debts created a "debt crisis" that threatened first and third world countries alike. If countries like Poland, Mexico, and Brazil could not repay loans made by banks in Western Europe and North America, then major banks could fail, creating widespread bankruptcy, financial chaos, and possibly, global economic depression. Moreover, if borrowing countries in Latin America, Africa, and Eastern Europe defaulted on their loans and declared bankruptcy, they could no longer obtain the money they needed to pay for essential food and oil imports or develop the industry they needed to provide jobs for growing populations.

Although the debt crisis, which became acute in the early 1980s, threatened rich and poor countries alike, measures taken to address the crisis had different consequences for northern creditors and southern debtors. The threat of bankruptcy for lenders in the North has receded. In 1994, the *New York Times* even announced that the debt crisis was "officially" over. But while the crisis may have ended for lenders, it continues for debtors, who found themselves even deeper in debt in 2000, despite having made every effort to repay debts accumulated in the 1970s.

But how did a collective crisis produce such different outcomes? As we will see, debts in Latin America, Africa, and Eastern Europe increased rapidly during the 1970s, because rich countries wanted to lend and poorer countries wanted to borrow large sums of money. Although the transfer of money from northern lenders to southern borrowers proved beneficial to both in the 1970s, it proved troublesome in the early 1980s as a result of two developments. First, rising interest rates, which were designed to fight inflation in the United States, increased the amount that borrowers were expected to pay northern lenders. Second, falling commodity prices for the goods southern countries exported to the North decreased the incomes of countries in the South, making it more difficult for them to repay northern lenders. Increasing costs and falling incomes made it difficult for borrowers to repay their debts, and a debt crisis ensued. To solve this crisis, northern creditors, and the global monetary institutions that represented them (the IMF and World Bank), demanded that southern borrowers adopt strenuous economic measures to repay their debts. These global institutions took the opportunity presented by the debt crisis to remake the economies of debtor countries along neoliberal market lines. So the debt crisis indirectly became a force for globalization. Although the creditors were able to avert a financial crisis, the debt crisis caused enormous economic hardship for borrower countries and left them even deeper in debt. Since the onset of the crisis, debt doubled from $639 billion in 1980 to $1,341 billion in 1990.[4] In Latin America, the region with the largest share of debt, "total indebtedness . . . now equals about $1,000 for every man, woman and child" in the continent, this in a region where $1,000 is more than most families earn in a year.[5]

Although countries around the world experienced a debt crisis, Latin America will be the focus of the discussion here because the countries with the largest outstanding foreign debts (Mexico and Brazil with $90 billion each) are in Latin America and because the continent owes more than half of the total outstanding debt.[6] By contrast, for example, Eastern European countries collectively owed $92.8 billion in 1981, equal to Mexico's debt,[7] and African countries together owed $82 billion in 1985, less than either Mexico or Brazil.[8]

GETTING INTO DEBT

In the 1970s, the amount of money loaned to countries in Latin America, Africa, and Eastern Europe increased dramatically. Between 1970 and 1973, banks in Western Europe and the United States lent $23.4 billion to Latin America, more money than had been loaned in the previous thirty years.[9] During the next decade, Latin America multiplied its debts more than twelve times. Debt expanded rapidly in the 1970s because lenders had large supplies of money that they were eager to lend and because countries around the world had great demand for borrowed money. "Indebtedness is a two-sided relationship," New York investment banker Richard Weinert observed. "It depends not only on a willing borrower, but equally on a willing lender. Indebtedness results as much from the need of lenders to lend as from the need of borrowers to borrow."[10] But conditions that in the 1970s encouraged rich countries to lend, and poorer countries to borrow, changed dramatically in the 1980s.

The Lenders

After World War II, government agencies and institutions such as the IMF and the World Bank made the majority of the loans to poor countries. They did not lend large amounts (about $20 billion to Latin America between 1950 and 1970), they attached strict conditions to the loans, and they loaned money primarily to promote financial stability or to finance large-scale development projects like dams and ports. During the 1970s, private banks in Western Europe and North America began lending increasing amounts of money, increasing their share of total lending from about one-third to more than one-half of all loans by the end of the decade.[11] Private banks lent large sums of money to Latin American countries because they saw it as a way to invest profitably the growing pool of money available to them in "Eurodollar" or European currency markets.

During the 1970s, governments and private investors from around the world deposited U.S. dollars and other "hard currencies" they had earned in trade with the United States in Western European banks and in U.S. banks with subsidiaries in Europe. Some of the first dollar deposits were made by the Soviet Union. They were joined by investors in Latin America, Japan, and other countries around the world, who deposited dollars in these accounts because they regarded them as safe and because they were not subject to the same kind of government regulations that applied to currencies deposited in the accounts of domestic banks.[12]

The money available in this Eurodollar banking pool grew from about $10 billion in 1960 to $110 billion in 1970.[13] Then, in the 1970s, money from another source began to deepen and expand this monetary pool. After the 1973 OPEC oil embargo sent oil prices soaring, OPEC countries received huge amounts of dollars from industrialized countries in payment for their oil, as much as $100 billion a year. "Since $100 billion a year is hard to spend," one writer observed, "even on Cadillacs, private 747s, and sophisticated missiles," the OPEC countries deposited much of their money in Western European and U.S. banks, and this money found its way into the Eurodollar market.[14] OPEC countries did this because they wanted to earn interest on their newfound wealth and because they regarded Western European banks as safe havens for their money. With the influx of dollars from oil-producing countries, often called Petrodollars because they were dollars used to pay for OPEC oil, the pool of money in the Eurodollar market grew to $1,525 billion by the 1980s.[15] (Precise estimates vary enormously because government regulatory agencies have a difficult time monitoring or tracking this money. Still, the rate of increase during the 1970s is the same regardless of the figures used.)[16]

As the money available to Western banks grew, bank officials searched for profitable ways to invest or loan it. Large U.S. banks became particularly active in Latin America, where banks had numerous subsidiaries and a fairly long history of involvement in local economies. "The nine largest U.S. banks, whose total capital is $27 billion, have lent over $30 billion (or more than their net worth) to private and government borrowers in just three countries: Mexico, Brazil and Argentina," the *Wall Street Journal* wrote in 1984.[17] The banks loaned money from Eurodollar pools, from U.S. depositors in their branch banks, and from smaller banks that joined loan syndicates.

Public and private lenders in the North lent money to countries in the South for a variety of reasons. Banks made loans so that poor countries could purchase goods made in Western Europe and North America. In the 1970s, for example, "42 percent of [Britain's] construction equipment, 33 percent of new aircraft and 32 percent of British textile machinery went to third world markets. In the United States, by 1980, the third world market accounted for . . . 20 percent of U.S. industrial product and about one-quarter of gross farm income."[18]

The U.S. government's Export-Import Bank, for instance, loaned money to Latin American governments so they could purchase U.S. airplanes. As Boeing Aircraft President Malcolm Stamper explained, "the Ex-Im Bank . . . was created to help promote exports . . . to help foreign firms and their nations to buy big-ticket goods that would be of social and economic benefit. Airplanes certainly meet this description. . . . Airplane exports are also very good business for this country's own economy, by the way."[19]

Private lenders also discovered that they could make more money loaning money to foreign borrowers than to domestic borrowers. "While the ten largest U.S. banks had a phenomenal expansion of international earnings [from Latin American loans] in 1970 to 1976, profitability in the domestic market ran generally flat. By the mid-1970s, most of the large banks had 50 percent or more of their earnings from abroad. In the case of Citicorp . . . by 1970 over 80 percent of their earnings came from their international operations."[20]

U.S. bankers in the 1970s did not worry greatly about the risks associated with foreign loans for several reasons. First, most of their money was loaned to Latin American dictatorships, which maintained close and friendly ties to the United States and seemed unlikely to renege on their debts (see chapter 11).[21] Second, they observed that the prices of many southern commodities, particularly oil, were *rising* in the 1970s, which helped their economies grow. This suggested that, as their incomes grew, borrower countries would be able to repay old debts and shoulder new ones without difficulty. Third, because governments had the authority to raise money by taxing their citizens, they could still repay loans should economic problems develop. Explaining why his bank was bullish on foreign loans, Citicorp Chairman Walter Wriston told the *New York Times* in 1982, "A country does not go bankrupt."[22]

Not everyone was so optimistic. *Euromoney* observed in 1975 that "a purely technical analysis of the current financial position [of many borrowing countries] would suggest that defaults are inevitable; yet many experts feel this is not likely to happen [because] the World Bank, the IMF and the governments of major industrialized nations . . . would step in rather than watch any default seriously disrupt the entire Euromarket apparatus."[23]

Despite their enthusiasm for foreign loans, northern banks worried about the risks associated with mounting debt. So they hedged their bets, insisting in the late 1970s that borrowers agree to readjust interest rates on new *and* old loans every six months and bring interest rates into line with current market rates.[24] By 1983, nearly 70 percent of all loans in Latin America were subject to floating interest rates, which would rise or fall depending on the interest rates set in the United States.[25] Although interest rates were then stable, which meant that borrowers did not worry greatly about accepting this new condition, the bankers' insistence that floating interest rates be adopted by borrowers would have important consequence for both lenders and borrowers in the early 1980s.

The Borrowers

Not only were bankers willing to lend; governments and corporations in Latin America were eager to borrow money in the 1970s. Public and private borrowers had substantial and diverse needs for northern loans. Much of the money they borrowed was simply used to repay lenders. "Between 1976 and 1981," Sue Branford and Bernardo Kucinski wrote:

> Latin America borrowed an enormous $272.9 billion. But over 60 percent of this, $170.5 billion, was immediately paid back to the banks as debt repayments or interest. Another $22.9 billion remained with [northern] banks as reserves [against potential losses], which were a kind of additional guarantee for the debt itself. And an estimated $56.6 billion was quickly sent abroad as capital flight. Only $22.9 billion effectively entered the continent to be used (or not) in productive investment.[26]

Of the $88 billion Mexicans borrowed between 1977 and 1979, only $14.3 billion was actually available for use in the country.[27]

Although estimates of the amount of borrowed money actually available for use in any given country vary considerably, the money that remained was put to different uses by public and private borrowers.

In their effort to promote economic growth, governments borrowed money to pay for "essential" imported goods such as oil, food, and machinery. Rising oil prices in the 1970s forced countries without oil to pay more for imported oil. U.S. economist William Cline estimated that oil price increases cost southern countries an extra $260 billion in the years between 1974 and 1982, a figure comparable to the $299 billion acquired by these same countries during this period.[28]

Of course, some Latin American countries, such as Mexico, had large oil supplies of their own. But while Mexico did not pay more for imported oil, it borrowed heavily to develop its oil fields and become a major producer, expecting that increasing oil prices would enable it to pay off mounting debts. As we will see, this expectation did not materialize, and falling oil prices after 1980 helped trigger Mexico's debt crisis.[29]

The cost of imported food also rose in the 1970s. Rising oil prices increased the cost of growing food because farmers rely heavily on gasoline-powered tractors and petroleum-based fertilizers and pesticides. Moreover, poor harvests in the Soviet Union during the mid-1970s increased the demand and therefore the price of food on world markets (see chapter 7). "For low-income countries, the increased cost in these years . . . of food imports from [first world] countries far exceeded the increased cost of oil imports," argued Shahid Burki.[30]

As we have seen, with money provided by northern lenders, southern governments also purchased tractors and textile machines to expand commodity production in fields and factories and built roads, ports, and airports—and the aircraft to use them—to facilitate the transport of commodities, business managers, and bankers. Many of these activities provided jobs to northern manufacturers of imported goods and employment for domestic users of these products in the South. By building huge mining, hydroelectric, irrigation, and industrial projects, governments could put people to work and increase their income from project revenues and worker taxes.

In addition to paying for essential imports, governments used borrowed money to build up hard currency reserves and stabilize their currencies, to subsidize or lower the cost of fuel, food, and transportation so that domestic consumers would not be adversely affected by rising oil and food prices, and sometimes to balance their budgets.[31] As one Latin American finance minister recalled, "I remember how the bankers tried to corner me at conferences to offer me loans. If you are trying to balance your budget, it's terribly tempting to borrow money instead of raising taxes."[32]

Of course, not all the money was used for essential or legitimate government purposes. Some of it was used to increase military expenditures, wasted on boondoggle development projects, or siphoned off for personal gain. Military spending by Latin American countries doubled during the 1970s, despite the fact that they faced no external threats. Military spending in Africa increased by one-third.[33] Many development projects proved to be boondoggles. A huge development project providing electricity from the Inga dam on the Zaire River to a copper–cobalt mining complex in Shaba province cost nearly $1 billion, but when it was finished, the electricity it delivered was no longer needed at the mines.[34] Moreover, in some countries, government corruption was widespread. In Zaire, a country described by some writers as an "absolutist kleptocracy," President Mobutu Sese Seko stashed away about $5 billion in personal Swiss bank accounts, a sum equal to his country's total foreign debt.[35] In Brazil, President Fernando Callor de Mello was impeached for corruption in 1992.

Governments were not the only borrowers. Private borrowers acquired a substantial portion of Latin American debt. In Latin America, "private debt rose from $15 billion in 1972 to $58 billion in 1981," accounting for about 20 percent of the total ($272.9 billion in 1981).[36] During the 1970s, domestic owners of Latin American farms and factories, often "the principal national monopolistic groups of the country," borrowed heavily to finance the expansion of their businesses.[37] In Mexico these groups acquired one-quarter of the country's total debt.

Alongside private domestic borrowers, subsidiaries of businesses in Western Europe and North America also borrowed money, and when they did, they increased the debt of southern countries. So, for example, General Motors, Ford, Union Carbide, Pepsico, and Volkswagen were all important borrowers in Mexico, adding $750 million of debt to Mexico's total.[38]

Like northern lenders, southern borrowers were confident they could repay mounting debts. Inflation in northern countries meant that real interest rates were fairly low and stable in the 1970s, commodity prices for the raw materials and goods they produced were rising, and their economies were growing. But these favorable conditions, which encouraged both lenders and borrowers in the 1970s, did not last. When conditions changed—when interest rates rose and commodity prices fell—in the 1980s, they triggered a crisis that proved earlier assumptions wrong.

THE CRISIS: RISING INTEREST RATES, FALLING COMMODITY PRICES

When Paul Volcker, head of the Federal Reserve, raised U.S. interest rates in 1979 to fight inflation in the United States, he did not intend to create a global debt crisis. But rising U.S. interest rates, and the rising London Interbank Offered Rate (LIBOR), which set interest rates for Eurodollar lending, greatly increased the cost of southern loans, most of them now tied to floating rates set by the United States or LIBOR.[39]

Rising interest rates had two important consequences. First, they increased interest payments on accumulated debt. "Mexico's interest bill tripled from $2.3 billion in 1979 to $6.1 billion in 1982 . . . for the region as a whole, interest payments more than doubled, from $14.4 billion in 1979 to $36.1 billion in 1982."[40] High interest rates made it harder for borrowers to pay back their debts. U.S. economist William Cline estimated that high interest rates in the 1980s cost indebted countries $41 billion more than they would have paid had interest rates remained at the average level between 1961 and 1980.[41] Other economists have estimated that Latin American countries paid out more than $100 billion in "excessive" interest between 1976 and 1985.[42]

A second problem was that high U.S. interest rates acted like a magnet, attracting money from around the world. U.S. officials understood that capital flight from other countries would reduce investment abroad and undermine the competitiveness of other countries. As we have seen, it did not greatly weaken Western Europe and Japan because they had higher savings rates, which meant they had more capital available to them, and because the U.S. government returned some of this capital to them in the form of U.S. military spending. Unfortunately, countries in Latin America, Africa, and Eastern Europe did not have these advantages, because they had low savings rates and a huge demand for capital (which is why they had been borrowing money from abroad). And except for Panama, where the United States stationed a large military force, the United States returned little of the money it acquired from Latin American investors in the form of military spending. As Volcker observed, "In many [indebted countries], their excessive debt burdens can be traced in large part to a flight of capital by their own citizens discouraged from investing at home."[43] He might have added that U.S. policies, which were under *his* control, also encouraged them to invest their capital in the United States.

High interest rates attracted $150 billion in capital from Latin America between 1973 and 1987, the bulk of it after 1979, when as much as $25 billion annually "flew" to the United States to purchase Treasury bonds.[44] Massive capital flight created several problems for Latin American countries: it deprived them of money they might have used to invest in their own countries, pay for imports, or repay debt, and it eroded their country's tax base as investors withdrew taxable savings from Latin American banks and placed them in tax-free deposits in U.S. banks.[45] During the height of Mexico's debt crisis, "a Mexico City newspaper published the names of 537 Mexicans each with over a million dollars on deposit with foreign banks."[46] As a result, capital flight deprived indebted countries of money at a time when they needed it most.

Just as interest rates increased, commodity prices began to fall. During the 1970s, the price of commodities typically exported by third world countries— metals, raw materials, and foodstuffs—generally rose. They could then use the hard currencies they earned by selling these goods to northern countries to repay their loans, which had to be repaid in hard currencies. Lenders insisted on repayment in dollars or other hard currencies (deutsche marks, pounds, yen), not in pesos or astrals, because they worried that indebted governments would

simply print more money and use inflation to repay loans in worthless, depreci-
ated currency.

Generally speaking, the prices Latin American countries could get for their
commodities fell slowly between 1950 and the mid-1970s, when the OPEC
embargo and weather-related food shortages began to increase commodity
prices, particularly of oil and food. Commodities then began to fall dramatically
in the 1980s.[47] Between 1980 and 1982, world commodity prices fell by more
than one-third, "to their lowest level in 30 years, a disastrous development for
countries that expected commodity exports to pay their way," noted sociologist
John Walton.[48] "The beef that Argentina [exported] fell from $2.25 a kilogram
. . . in 1980 to $1.60 by the end of 1981. Sugar from Brazil and the Caribbean
fell from 79 cents a kilo to 27 cents by 1982. And copper, a big-ticket item for
the likes of Chile and Zaire, fell from $2.61 a kilo to $1.66," one writer
observed.[49]

Falling prices reduced the ability of borrower countries to repay debts, which
were being pushed up by higher interest rates. Prices continued to fall during
the rest of the 1980s. A World Bank index of raw material prices, which started
at 168.2 in 1980, fell to 100 by 1990, and 86.1 in 1992, the lowest prices in real
terms since 1948.[50]

The price of oil also fell, slowly after 1980 and then sharply after 1985. Mexico, which borrowed heavily to become a major oil producer because it believed
oil prices would continue to climb, found itself with mounting debt and declining revenues.[51] "Given the deterioration in the terms of trade, Latin Americans
sell more and get less," observed Mexico's finance minister, Jesus Silva Herzog.[52]

Why did commodity prices fall so dramatically in the 1980s, crippling the
ability of borrowers to repay their debts? They did so because high U.S. interest
rates triggered a global recession that reduced demand for their goods. They also
fell because northern countries had begun to develop new supplies or to substitute materials for southern commodities (we will examine these developments
in greater detail in the next chapter). In the case of oil, the discovery of new
oilfields in the North Sea increased the supply and helped lower global prices,
while energy conservation measures reduced demand. Commodity prices also
fell because southern countries collectively produced *more* of these goods in the
1980s. Remember that, in the 1970s, borrowers used northern money to expand
their production of oil (Mexico), coffee (Colombia), frozen orange juice (Brazil),
beef (Argentina), copper (Chile, Zaire), and tin (Bolivia). With money and hard
work, they succeeded in producing more of these goods. But as production
expanded, supplies increased and prices fell. The irony is that the harder they
worked and more they did what they set out to do, they earned less and fell
deeper into debt.

Mounting debt and a growing inability to repay loans threatened to bankrupt
the major U.S. and Western European banks. If that occurred, financial chaos
and a global economic crisis would have ensued. To avert such a catastrophe,

lenders acted quickly to manage the crisis. The IMF and the World Bank quickly took the lead, assuming responsibility for managing the debt crisis and ensuring that borrower countries repay all of their debts, both public and private. As Princeton economist Robert Gilpin observed, "Interest payments on the debt would not be decreased across the board nor world commodity prices received by debtors be increased. The burden of solving the problem would continue to rest squarely on the debtors."[53]

For much of the postwar period, the World Bank and IMF were fairly obscure institutions. The World Bank made modest loans to promote economic development in poor countries; the IMF helped manage the occasional crisis that emerged when poor countries ran out of the hard currencies they needed to purchase foreign goods. But the debt crisis thrust these Bretton Woods institutions into the forefront of efforts to manage the debt crisis. The IMF, in particular, was asked to assume a new, expanded, global role. Not only was it asked to manage crisis in dozens of countries simultaneously, it was also expected to reshape the government policies and economic structures of those countries. The IMF required governments to abandon decades-old development policies and adopt new, neoliberal market policies in their place. These new policies and practices contributed to the globalization of these economies.

If the IMF had not taken the lead, if individual banks had tried to collect debts or seize assets on their own, chaos would have ensued and debtors might have been able to play lenders against each other. Instead, by forming what Gilpin calls a "creditor's cartel," which was led by the IMF and World Bank, northern lenders could practice a "divide and conquer strategy" and "impose their will on the debtors."[54] They were able to do this because private lenders could speak with one voice, through the IMF, in negotiations with foreign borrowers. The lenders also possessed two important advantages: they alone could lend borrowers the money they needed to make ends meet and they alone possessed accurate information on the debts and economic conditions of borrowing countries (most debtor governments lacked key financial information on private debt in their own country).[55] The existence of powerful global institutions, unity of purpose, and control of economic data enabled the lenders to bargain with debtors from a position of strength.

While IMF officials managed the debt crisis in dozens of countries, private lenders moved to protect themselves from the consequences of the crisis by reducing credit and shifting the burden of financing new loans to public agencies and making taxpayers assume some losses.

During previous Latin American debt crises, lenders simply stopped lending to borrowers, sometimes for decades. During the 1980s, private banks greatly reduced their lending, though they did not cut off credit entirely. Capital flows to Latin America fell by one-third between 1980 and 1984 as private lenders began to cut and run.[56] The problem was that borrowers desperately needed new loans, at least in the short term, so they could get their finances in order and take steps that would eventually enable them to repay debts. Public lending agencies urged private bankers to continue lending money. U.S. treasury secretary James Baker, whose 1985 Baker Plan attempted to advance a comprehensive settlement of the debt crisis, argued that "increased lending by the private banks in support of comprehensive economic adjustment programs" was essential in order to make it possible for borrowers to repay their debts. As Baker told bankers, "I would like to see the banking community make a pledge to provide these amounts" ($20 billion over the next three years) on a "voluntary basis."[57]

Because private banks did not respond to Baker's invitation, the Baker Plan failed.[58] So the U.S. government and international lending agencies had to pick up the slack, which meant that taxpayers in Western Europe and the United States had to shoulder increasing responsibilities for debt crisis management.

Private lenders also protected themselves by declaring "losses" on foreign loans, which enabled them to reduce their taxes. But while they claimed losses, they could still demand full repayment from borrowers, so they could declare losses, receive tax breaks, *and* recover their original investment.[59] Although the tax laws that allow banks to take "provisions" or make "loan-loss reserves," as they are called, differ from country to country, the savings to banks can be substantial. One economist estimated that between 1987 and 1990, "over $20 billion of U.S. bank debt on the third world was charged off and provisioned under federal mandate. Since the corporate tax rate on U.S. banks is 34 percent, this sum would give rise to tax credits of at least $6.8 billion."[60] British banks received about $7 billion, German banks $10 billion, and French banks $10.9 billion as a result of similar laws.[61] Altogether, private banks probably received between $44 billion and $50.8 billion in tax credits in this period, all at taxpayer expense.[62]

Taxpayers not only assumed responsibility for revenues lost in this fashion but also had to foot the bill when their governments agreed to provide debt relief to some borrowers, as the U.S. government did when it discharged $7 billion of Egypt's debt for agreeing to participate as a U.S. ally in the 1990–1991 Persian Gulf war.[63]

Although the stockholders of some banks experienced losses when it became apparent that their banks had lent heavily to debtors and the value of their bank stocks declined, private banks emerged from a potentially devastating crisis relatively unscathed. No major Western bank failed as a result of the debt crisis. But while lenders averted serious problems, borrowers did not.

DEBTORS FALL APART

When borrowers in Latin America, Africa, and Eastern Europe ran out of money to repay their debts, they faced serious problems. Without foreign currency, they could not pay for imported fuel or food, and owners of domestic capital began to send it abroad. Without imported or domestic capital, agricultural and industrial businesses would grind to a halt and lay off workers, and the economy would collapse. To avert these economic disasters, borrower governments, under IMF direction, took steps to get the hard currency they needed to purchase imported goods and repay lenders.

As a condition for receiving a continued influx of money, borrower governments were asked to assume responsibility for repaying *private* debts that they did not themselves incur. In Venezuela and Argentina, nearly 60 percent of the total debt had been acquired by private businesses, domestic *and* foreign.[64] Although private borrowing in Latin America as a whole accounted for 20 percent of the outstanding debt, about $58 billion, governments and taxpayers were asked to repay this debt as if it were their own. According to Harvard economist Jeffrey Sachs, "In country after country, governments took over the private debt on favorable terms for the private sector firms, or subsidized the private debt service payments, in order to bail out the private firms. This 'socialization' of the private debt resulted in a significant increase in the *fiscal* burden of the nation's foreign debt."[65]

This situation was unfair because it imposed on the people of these countries debts not of their making. Not only did governments bail out private sector firms in their own country, many of them subsidiaries of northern corporations, but they effectively bailed out private northern banks because these banks would not otherwise have been able to recover private debts in foreign countries. Once they knew potential losses were averted and private debt responsibilities assumed by southern governments, private lenders agreed to continue making loans during the debt crisis, though, as we have seen, they reduced their share of new loans.

With the money they needed to avert the immediate crisis, southern governments were then forced to adopt painful economic policies, which the IMF insisted would allow them to repay debts in the long term. Although the specific IMF policies varied, most governments adopted similar structural adjustment programs (SAPs), or "austerity programs," as they were called, trying to create "trade surpluses" and government "budget surpluses" to raise the money they needed to repay their debts.

Indebted governments were first required to increase their trade surpluses. If they could export more goods than they imported, they could acquire a larger amount of hard currency, which they could then use to repay old debts and reduce their need to borrow money to pay for imported goods. To create trade surpluses, they tried simultaneously to increase exports and reduce imports. To increase exports, governments urged agricultural and industrial businesses to expand production and export more of their goods. They assisted this process by devaluing their currencies. When the United States devalued the dollar, government officials hoped that this would make U.S. exports cheaper abroad and make Japanese goods more expensive in America (see chapter 3). They expected the devaluation to increase U.S. exports and discourage U.S. consumers from buying imported Japanese goods, thereby reducing the U.S. trade deficit. Latin American governments hoped their own currency devaluations would have the same effect, helping them create a trade surplus that would provide them with much-needed currency.

Latin American countries did export more goods, though falling prices for those commodities, global recession, which reduced demand, and northern restrictions or tariffs on many southern goods meant they had a difficult time keeping exports at 1980 levels. From 1980 to 1985, Latin American countries increased the volume of goods they exported by 23 percent, but the value of these exports remained about the same.[66] Latin American countries exported between $90 billion and $100 billion worth of goods between 1980 and 1984. Exports then fell to about $78 billion from 1984 to 1986, mostly as a result of falling oil prices, before recovering to the $100 billion level by 1988.[67]

With exports holding steady (despite increased efforts), the only way Latin American governments managed to create trade surpluses in the 1980s was by cutting back on imported goods. Whereas Latin American countries imported between $90 billion and $100 billion worth of goods in 1980, they imported only $60 billion by 1982, staying at this level throughout much of the mid-1980s.[68] By slashing imports, they created a trade surplus that gave them between $30 billion and $40 billion, which they used to repay lenders. As Mexican finance minister Silva Herzog observed, "The much heralded improvement in Latin America's current accounts therefore is attributable mostly to import reduction, rather than to export increase."[69]

Because indebted governments were responsible for repaying public *and* private debts, they also had to find ways of raising money to repay lenders. The IMF instructed them to raise money by selling off state assets to foreign or domestic buyers and by creating budget surpluses.

During the 1960s and 1970s, many southern governments created state-run business to promote economic development. Governments could borrow money to derive revenue from their operations. These businesses—the government-owned phone, airline, bank, oil, or cement company, the state coffee board—often enjoyed monopoly status, either because they provided services that private businesses could not profitably provide or because monopoly eliminated "wasteful" domestic competition and allowed these firms to compete with large TNCs. In debt crisis negotiations, the IMF insisted that indebted governments sell off or "privatize" state-owned businesses, both to increase "competition" and to raise money to pay off debts. They also insisted that governments change their laws so that TNCs could purchase these assets when they were offered for sale. Many southern governments had long restricted foreign investment because they worried that key sectors of the economy would fall under the control of foreign owners.

At IMF insistence, Latin American governments began selling off state-owned businesses. By 1990, for example, the Mexican government sold off 875 of the 1,155 enterprises that it had owned all or part of in 1982.[70] This pattern was repeated around the continent, with governments selling off airlines, port facilities, phone companies, and chemical plants. Of course, currency devaluations played an important role in this process.

As in the United States, where the 1985 dollar devaluation made U.S. assets available for sale to Japanese investors at one-half their previous price, currency devaluations in Latin America enabled foreign investors to purchase important economic assets at bargain basement prices. Privatization and currency devaluations worked more to the advantage of foreign investors, though Latin American investors who had placed their money in the dollar accounts of Western banks during the great capital flights of the early 1980s could also acquire state assets at advantageous prices. So, for example, Mexico sold Teléfonos de México, the government's telephone company, for $1.76 billion to a French, American, and Mexican communications consortium.[71] Because the Mexican government had devalued the peso, foreign investors got a real bargain.

Although governments could raise money to repay debts by selling public assets, this was a one-time way to raise money. To raise the money they needed, governments had to create continuing budget surpluses. They did this by increasing taxes and cutting public spending. In general, the burden of tax increases and spending cuts typically fell on poor and middle-income taxpayers.

During the 1970s, many Third World governments used borrowed money to keep oil and food prices low so that transportation, cooking fuel (kerosene), and basic foodstuffs would remain affordable for poor and working people at a time when world oil and grain prices were climbing. But to create budget surpluses, they were forced in the 1970s to eliminate these "subsidies," which accounted for a considerable proportion of government spending, and to increase taxes. Generally speaking, taxes on corporations and the rich were reduced (as they were in the United States in this same period) while excise and sales taxes, which fell most heavily on the poor, and income taxes on middle-income groups increased. "A 1986 study of 94 [IMF]-supported adjustment programs implemented between 1980 and 1984 found [that] 63 percent . . . contained wage and salary restraints; 61 percent included transfer payment [for Social Security and unemployment programs] and subsidy [for food and fuel] restraints; . . . and 46 percent included personal income tax measures," writes economist Howard Lehman.[72]

The SAPs administered by the IMF provided important benefits for the North. First, they ensured that lenders would be repaid by southern borrowers, which averted a financial crisis in the North. Second, they increased the flow of goods from South to North. Because the increased supplies helped lower the price of these goods, producers and consumers in the North paid less, reaping a substantial benefit. Third, the sale of industries in the South, at cheap, devalued prices, meant that northern investors could snatch up some real bargains and increase their control of economies in the South. SAPs contributed to the alization of the South, a development that provided important benefits for the North.

THE CONSEQUENCES

The steps taken by lenders and borrowers had important economic, social, and political consequences for indebted countries. They undermined economic development, setting them back decades, accelerated environmental destruction, and adversely affected women and female children. The silver lining in this otherwise black cloud was that debt crisis also contributed to the fall of dictatorship and rise of democracy in many countries (a development we will examine in chapter 11). Let us review some of the important social consequences of the debt crisis.

Deeper in Debt

In economic terms, indebted countries managed to repay their debts but found themselves deeper in debt. Moreover, their strenuous efforts to repay debt exhausted their economies, prompting some economists to describe the 1980s as a "lost decade." As Volcker said, "Even a decade later, the wounds in Latin America itself have not fully healed. For some of those countries (and for those similarly affected in Africa), the 1980s was a lost decade in terms of growth and price stability."[73]

How could borrower countries "repay" their debts yet end up deeper in debt? Between 1982 and 1990, lenders sent $927 billion to southern borrowers. In the same period, borrowers repaid lenders $1,345 billion in principal and interest. As a result, indebted countries paid $418 billion more than they received. British economist Susan George argues that this sum is six times greater in real terms than the amount of money the United States transferred to postwar Europe through the Marshall Plan.[74] Yet despite these massive repayments, borrowers found themselves "61 percent more in debt than they were in 1982."[75]

Mexico, for example, paid lenders $100 billion in debt service between 1982 and 1988, $10 billion more than it owed when the crisis struck in 1982. But while it repaid vast sums to first world lenders, it owed even more: $112 billion in 1988. How could this happen? It is similar to what happens when people buy a house. Home buyers understand that if they borrow $100,000 at 10 percent interest for a thirty-year period, they will actually pay $300,000 in all, two-thirds of it as interest and one-third as the principal (the amount of the original loan). The bank, of course, insists that the borrower repay the interest first. After ten years, the borrower has repaid $100,000 but still owes $200,000, which is still larger than the original loan. In the same way, Mexico had made substantial payments but still had a lot left to repay.

Latin American debt has increased from about $280 billion in 1982 to $435 billion in 1993, and total Third World debt climbed from $639 billion in 1980 to $1,341 billion in 1990. Most borrowers will continue to repay debt into the foreseeable future.

In Argentina, debt grew from $40 billion in 1982, when the debt crisis began, to $132 billion in 2001. At IMF request, the government introduced repeated austerity programs. But its debts grew anyway, despite its two-decade effort to repay them. The most recent austerity program, announced in 2001, required the government to cut salaries and pensions for government workers. Teachers have not been paid for months, schools can no longer afford to boil water to make powdered milk for malnourished children, and public health officials no longer vaccinate dogs for rabies, leading to a widespread outbreak of the disease.[76] "Argentina is a country without credit," President Fernando de la Rua admitted.[77]

Although indebted governments successfully repaid lenders in the 1980s, they drained their economies. Instead of growing, most Latin American economies actually shrank by about 10 percent while their populations continued to grow.[78] In Mexico, the real incomes of average workers fell 40 percent between 1981 and 1988, while the incomes of government employees fell even more, nearly 50 percent.[79] In most Latin American countries, wages fell, while unemployment rose, prices and taxes increased, and hunger grew. In 1986, 20 million more people in Latin America were living below the poverty line than in 1981, 150 million people in all.[80] Not surprisingly, declining incomes and rising unemployment persuaded many Latin Americans to emigrate to the United States in search of jobs. According to Sachs, "As for the debtor countries, many have fallen into the deepest economic crisis in their histories. . . . Many countries' living standards have fallen to levels of the 1950s and 1960s. A decade of development has been wiped out throughout the debtor world."[81]

Gender and the Debt Crisis

The debt crisis adversely affected men and women across the South. But, for a variety of reasons, SAPs were particularly hard on women and female children.[82]

First, the IMF encouraged governments to expand the production of export crops so they could earn hard currency to repay debt. But the expansion of land devoted to export crops often reduced the amount of land devoted to subsistence agriculture and in-common uses: forests for firewood, land for gardens, water for domestic consumption (see chapter 7). Women in many countries grow food for their families, forage for firewood to cook their meals, and draw water to bathe their children and wash their clothes. The conversion of agricultural land and forests from subsistence production to export agriculture, and the use of water from rivers to grow water-intensive crops, has made it harder for women to provide these goods and resources for their families.[83] Women and female children have had to walk farther, forage longer, and pay more for resources they need. So SAPs have increased female work burdens substantially.

Second, governments eliminated subsidies for food, fuel, and transport, forcing people to pay more for these goods. Higher costs have meant that many families must do with less of each. But when families cut back, men cut back less and women more. Women cut back more because, in most patriarchal families, men command a greater proportion of household income and resources than women. Women typically work longer hours (twelve to fourteen hours a day compared to eight to twelve hours for men) and devote a greater share of their earnings to the household. Economists have found that women in Mexico contributed 100 percent of their earnings to the family budget, but men contributed only 75 percent of theirs. As the World Bank reported, "It is not uncommon for children's nutrition to deteriorate while wrist watches, radios and bicycles are acquired by the adult male household members."[84] Throughout the South, the adverse impact of rising prices, a product of SAPs, was disproportionately felt by women.

Third, governments cut back on public services, particularly education and health care. Again, these cuts adversely affected men, but hurt women more because in patriarchal households, families more often send male children to school or send males to seek medical treatment, neglecting the needs of women and girls. In hard times, women and girls do without. The result is that fewer girls attend school, and illiteracy among women has increased. As public health care services have declined, government-sponsored campaigns against AIDS or female genital mutilation (in Africa) have languished, and infant mortality rates, particularly for girls, have increased.[85] The IMF-directed decline of public services has been particularly detrimental for women and female children.

Environmental Destruction and Debt

Governments also increased the rate of deforestation so they could export hardwood timber or beef raised on cleared rain forests. Brazil and Mexico, the two largest debtors, are also major deforesters. Brazil is ranked number one and Mexico number six in the world. In Mexico, much of this deforestation has occurred in Chiapas, the southern state where Zapatista peasants revolted in 1994. Both have increased deforestation rates dramatically in the past two decades: Brazil up 245 percent, Mexico up 15 percent.[86]

Debt and Protest

These social and environmental problems frequently led to social conflict, what some scholars have called "IMF riots," when people protested government "structural adjustment" policies. University of California sociologist John Walton recorded fifty major "protest events" in thirteen countries between 1976 and 1986. He found that when governments cut subsidies for food and basic necessities, increased fares on public transportation, or eliminated government jobs, riots sometimes resulted. In September 1985, for example, "hundreds of Panamanian workers invaded their legislature chanting: 'I won't pay the debt! Let the ones who stole the money pay!'"[87]

Debt and Democracy

Although the debt crisis had disastrous economic and social consequences for indebted countries, it had some positive political consequences. The debt crisis and structural adjustment programs imposed by the IMF discredited the dictators who had borrowed and ruled most Latin American countries. When debt crises struck, civilian democrats demanded and received political power in return for their support for arduous debt crisis management programs. As we will see (chapter 11), debt crisis contributed to the democratization of much of Latin America in the 1980s. So while the debt crisis was an economic disaster, it was also a political opportunity.

Impact on the North

Although indebted countries experienced great difficulties as a result of the debt crisis, people in northern countries also experienced debt-related problems. As we have seen, Latin American borrowers increased trade surpluses, which provided them with much-needed cash, by reducing their imports. Because many of these imports were goods made or grown in northern countries, import reductions contributed to unemployment in Western Europe and the United States.

Between 1980 and 1986, U.S. exports to Latin America fell by $10 billion. One economist estimated that this resulted in the loss of 930,000 jobs in the United States.[88] U.S. Trade Representative William Brock calculated that 240,000 U.S. jobs were lost as a result of the Mexican debt crisis alone.[89] Senator Bill Bradley observed that Latin American debtors had made a "Herculean effort" to service their debts. But he noted, "The price the United States has paid for Latin America's ability to meet its new debt schedules has been the collapse of Latin American markets for U.S. products . . . and the loss of more than one million [U.S.] jobs."[90] So while private lenders managed to cover their assets, workers and taxpayers have had to foot some of the bill.

Debt Relief?

Although lenders averted a global economic crisis, borrowers continue to wrestle with the consequences of the debt crisis. From the lenders' perspective, borrowers still owe them a great deal. But from the borrowers' perspective, they have already repaid their debts. Some economists have suggested that remaining debts could be forgiven or reduced without great harm to lenders. They also note that continued indebtedness undermines the ability of indebted countries to purchase imports, which is essential for the health of economies in Western Europe and the United States. Former World Bank president Robert McNamara argued, "The evidence that growth and progress in the developing countries now has a measurable impact on the economy of the United States reflects the importance of the developing countries to the United States as export markets and as customers of U.S. commercial banks."[91]

The continued insistence on full repayment of debt, the objective of bankers, conflicts in the long run with the sale of northern goods in southern markets, which is the objective of farmers and manufacturers in the North. The problem in coming years will be how to resolve the conflicting objectives and needs of different groups, North and South.

One proposal, advanced by the IMF in the late 1990s, would be to provide debt relief to some of the poorest countries. The money would come in part from the sale of gold reserves held by the IMF.[92] For extremely poor countries such as Uganda, which "spends $3 per inhabitant on health annually, and about $17 a person on debt repayment," debt relief would be extremely welcome.[93] But German, Japanese, and other officials in the Group of Seven have objected to the plan, arguing that the IMF should not sell off even a small part of its $40 billion in gold.[94] Countries in Africa, the poorest of the debtor countries, would receive most of the relief outlined in recent IMF plans.[95] But they would receive only a partial reduction of their debt, and then only if their governments adopted new structural adjustment programs.

The debt crisis was not anticipated either by lenders in the North or by borrowers in the South. But when it occurred, institutions in the North seized the opportunity to reshape the South along neoliberal lines, a process that contributed to contemporary globalization.

If the prices that producers in the South received for the goods they made had *increased* during the 1980s and 1990s (as they did in the 1970s), it would have been much easier for indebted countries to repay their debts. But prices did not rise; they *fell* dramatically. So it became very difficult for them to repay debt or advance economically. In the next chapter, we will examine why commodity prices fell so sharply during the last twenty years, a development that has had extremely important consequences for people around the world.

NOTES

1. Iliana Zloch-Christy, *Debt Problems of Eastern Europe* (Cambridge: Cambridge University Press, 1987), 29, 34; Christopher A. Kojm, *The Problem of International Debt: The Reference Shelf*, vol. 56, no. 1 (New York: Wilson, 1984), 8.

2. John Walton, "Debt, Protest and the State in Latin America," in *Power and Popular Protest: Latin America Social Movements*, ed. Susan Eckstein (Berkeley: University of California Press, 1989), 301.

3. Robert Gilpin, *The Political Economy of International Relations* (Princeton, N.J.: Princeton University, 1987), 317.

4. Steven Greenhouse, "Third World Markets Gain Favor," *New York Times*, December 17, 1993.

5. Paul Kennedy, *Preparing for the 21st Century* (New York: Random House, 1987), 204.

6. Kojm, *The Problem of International Debt*, 10.

7. Zloch-Christy, *Debt Problems of Eastern Europe*, xiii.

8. Trevor W. Parfitt and Stephen Riley, *The African Debt Crisis* (London: Routledge, 1989), 16, 17.

9. Sue Branford and Bernardo Kucinski, *The Debt Squads: The US, the Banks and Latin America* (London: Zed, 1988), 47.

10. Michael Moffitt, *The World's Money: International Banking from Bretton Woods to the Brink of Insolvency* (New York: Simon & Schuster, 1983), 98.

11. Branford and Kucinski, *The Debt Squads*, 47; Jacobo Schatan, *World Debt: Who Is to Pay?* (London: Zed, 1987), 9.

12. Branford and Kucinski, *The Debt Squads*, 58.

13. Branford and Kucinski, *The Debt Squads*, 58. See also Stephany Griffith-Jones and Osvaldo Sunkel, *Debt and Development Crises in Latin America: The End of an Illusion* (Oxford: Clarendon, 1986), 72.

14. Kojm, *The Problem of International Debt*, 36.

15. Branford and Kucinski, *The Debt Squads*, 58.

16. Robert Cherry, *The Imperiled Economy. Book 1: Macroeconomics from a Left Perspective* (New York: Union for Radical Political Economics, 1987), 202; Gilpin, *The Political Economy of International Relations*, 315.

17. Kojm, *The Problem of International Debt*, 18.

18. Richard W. Lombardi, *Debt Trap: Rethinking the Logic of Development* (New York: Praeger, 1985), 91.

19. Lombardi, *Debt Trap*, 90.

20. Robert Devlin, *Debt and Crisis in Latin America: The Supply Side of the Story* (Princeton, N.J.: Princeton University Press, 1989), 36, 38.

21. Lombardi, *Debt Trap*, 76–77.

22. Lombardi, *Debt Trap*, 74.

23. Cherry, *The Imperiled Economy*, 201.

24. Branford and Kucinski, *The Debt Squads*, 59; Schatan, *World Debt*, 7.

25. Branford and Kucinski, *The Debt Squads*, 56.

26. Branford and Kucinski, *The Debt Squads*, xiv; Cherry, *The Imperiled Economy*, 200.

27. Branford and Kucinski, *The Debt Squads*, 78; Griffith-Jones and Sunkel, *Debt and Development Crises in Latin America*, 107.

28. Branford and Kucinski, *The Debt Squads*, 64; Vincent Ferraro, "Global Debt and Third World Development," in *World Security: Trends and Challenges at Century's End*, ed. Michael T. Klare and Daniel C. Thomas (New York: St. Martin's, 1991), 329.

29. Nora Lustig, *Mexico: The Remaking of an Economy* (Washington, D.C.: Brookings Institution, 1992), 20.

30. Shahid Javed Burki, "The Prospects for the Developing World: A Review of Recent Forecasts," *Finance and Development* 18, no. 1 (March 1981): 21.

31. Walton, "Debt, Protest and the State in Latin America," 305.

32. Walton, "Debt, Protest and the State in Latin America," 305.

33. Branford and Kucinski, *The Debt Squads*, 75.

34. Schatan, *World Debt*, 83.

35. Lombardi, *Debt Trap*, 86.

36. Parfitt and Riley, *The African Debt Crisis*, 79.

37. Arturo R. Guillen, "Crisis, the Burden of Foreign Debt and Structural Dependence," in *Latin American Perspectives*, Issue 60, no. 16, 1 (Winter 1989): 38.

38. Guillen, "Crisis, the Burden of Foreign Debt and Structural Dependence."

39. Guillen, "Crisis, the Burden of Foreign Debt and Structural Dependence," 40.

40. Jeffrey D. Sachs, *Developing Country Debt and the World Economy* (Chicago: University of Chicago Press, 1989), 302; Devlin, *Debt and Crisis in Latin America*, 50; Jackie Roddick, *Dance of the Millions: Latin America and the Debt Crisis* (London: Latin America Bureau, 1988), 35.

41. Branford and Kucinski, *The Debt Squads*, 95; Kojm, *The Problem of International Debt*, 15; Schatan, *World Debt*, 10.

42. Ferraro, "Global Debt and Third World Development," 329.

43. Schatan, *World Debt*, 110; Branford and Kucinski, *The Debt Squads*, 96.

44. Frank E. Morris, "Disinflation and the Third World Debt Crisis," in *World Debt Crisis*, ed. Michael Claudon (New York: Ballinger, 1986), 83.

45. Manuel Pastor, Jr., *Capital Flight and the Latin America Debt Crisis* (Washington, D.C.: Economic Policy Institute, 1989), 8–9.

46. Pastor, *Capital Flight*, 11–12.

47. Roddick, *Dance of the Millions*, 65.

48. Bill Orr, *The Global Economy in the 90s: A User's Guide* (New York: New York University Press, 1992), 262; Sachs, *Developing Country Debt*, 303, 309–10.

49. Walton, "Debt, Protest and the State in Latin America," 306; Griffith-Jones and Sunkel, *Debt and Development Crises in Latin America*, 13; Howard Lehman, *Indebted Development: Strategic Bargaining and Economic Adjustment in the Third World* (New York: St. Martin's, 1993), 15; Parfitt and Riley, *The African Debt Crisis*, 2–3.

50. Darrell Delamaide, *Debt Shock: The Full Story of the World Credit Crisis* (New York: Doubleday, 1984), 28; Schatan, *World Debt*, 41.

51. Lombardi, *Debt Trap*, 10; Filipe Ortiz de Zevallos, "Manana Has Arrived: Latin America Recovers from the Lost Decade," *The World Paper* (October 1993): 5.

52. Kojm, *The Problem of International Debt*, 16–17; Robert A. Pastor, *Latin America's Debt Crisis: Adjusting to the Past or Planning for the Future?* (Boulder, Colo.: Rienner, 1987), 13; Lustig, *Mexico*, 24–25, 39.

53. Pastor, *Latin America's Debt Crisis*, 35.

54. Gilpin, *The Political Economy of International Relations*, 326.

55. Gilpin, *The Political Economy of International Relations*, 319–20.

56. Roddick, *Dance of the Millions*, 10.

57. Branford and Kucinski, *The Debt Squads*, 8; Gilpin, *The Political Economy of International Relations*, 327.

58. Pastor, *Latin America's Debt Crisis*, 151–52.

59. Branford and Kucinski, *The Debt Squads*, 120–21.

60. Susan George, *The Debt Boomerang: How Third World Debt Harms Us All* (Boulder, Colo.: Westview, 1992), 65–66.

61. George, *The Debt Boomerang*, 74.

62. George, *The Debt Boomerang*, 79–81.

63. George, *The Debt Boomerang*, 82.

64. George, *The Debt Boomerang*, 156.

65. Roddick, *Dance of the Millions*, 71, 110–11.

66. Sachs, *Developing Country Debt*, 13.

67. Branford and Kucinski, *The Debt Squads*, 5.

68. Pastor, *Latin America's Debt Crisis*, 35–36; Clyde H. Farnsworth, "Latin America Records Some Economic Gains," *New York Times*, September 11, 1989.

69. Farnsworth, "Latin America Records Some Economic Gains."

70. Pastor, *Latin America's Debt Crisis*, 36.

71. Lustig, *Mexico*, 105.

72. Lustig, *Mexico*, 106.

73. Lehman, *Indebted Development*, 44–45.

74. Paul A. Volcker and Toyoo Gyohten, *Changing Fortunes: The World's Money and the Threat to American Leadership* (New York: Times, 1992), 187.

75. George, *The Debt Boomerang*, xv.

76. Clifford Krauss, "Argentina's Provinces Struggle to Stay Afloat," *New York Times*, November 18, 2001.

77. Clifford Krauss, "Argentine Leader Announces Debt Revision and Subsidies," *New York Times*, November 2, 2001.

78. Krauss, "Argentine Leader Announces Debt Revision and Subsidies."

79. Griffith-Jones and Sunkel, *Debt and Development Crises in Latin America*, 6.

80. Lustig, *Mexico*, 69.

81. Branford and Kucinski, *The Debt Squads*, 24.

82. Mariarosa Dalla Costa and Giovanna F. Dalla Costa, *Paying the Price: Women and the Politics of International Economic Strategy* (London: Zed, 1993).

83. C. George Caffentzis, "The Fundamental Implications of the Debt Crisis for Social Reproduction in Africa," in *Paying the Price*, 28.

84. Lester Brown, *State of the World 1993* (New York: Norton, 1993), 64.

85. Caffentzis, "The Fundamental Implications of the Debt Crisis for Social Reproduction in Africa," 34; Andre Michel, "African Women, Development and the North-South Relationship," in *Paying the Price*, 65–66.

86. Ferraro, "Global Debt and Third World Development," 333.

87. George, *The Debt Boomerang*, 10–11.

88. Walton, "Debt, Protest and the State in Latin America," 200, 316.

89. Ferraro, "Global Debt and Third World Development," 335.

90. Lombardi, *Debt Trap*, 91; Delamaide, *Debt Shock*, 12.

91. Pastor, *Latin America's Debt Crisis*, 70.

92. Paul Lewis, "Debt-Relief Cost for the Poorest Nations," *New York Times*, June 10, 1996.

93. Paul Lewis, "World Bank Moves to Cut Poorest Nations' Debts," *New York Times*, March 16, 1996.

94. Lewis, "Debt-Relief Cost for the Poorest Nations."

95. "Rich Nations Pledge to Double Countries Getting Debt Relief," *New York Times*, September 17, 2000.

6

Falling Commodity Prices

During the past twenty years, commodity prices have fallen dramatically. This has been an extremely difficult problem for people who grow sugar, mine copper, or pump oil in Africa, Asia, Latin America, and the Middle East. Falling prices have reduced incomes for the workers, businesses, and government that produce "commodities"—food and agricultural products, raw materials, and minerals—around the world. As we have seen, falling prices have made it difficult for people in the South to repay debt or develop economically (see chapter 5). Indeed, falling commodity prices have made poor people poorer, creating hardships for the hundreds of millions of people who labor in fields, forests, and mines across the globe.[1]

In the South, tens of millions more people work in factories and mills, producing manufactured and finished goods for domestic markets. But during the last twenty years, manufacturing industries in many countries have collapsed, and the jobs they provided have disappeared. The widespread destruction of these "old" industries has reduced incomes for urban workers, particularly males.

During this same period, there has been an expansion of some export manufacturing in "free trade" enclaves called *maquiladoras* (named after zones in Mexico) and the growth of service industries, particularly tourism. These "new" manufacturing and service industries have provided some jobs for women and girls. But the apparent gains made by women in these industries have not offset the massive job and income losses associated with falling commodity prices and the collapse of "old" manufacturing industries. Moreover, where tourism has been linked to the sex industry, it has not helped the women and girls it "employs."

Why did commodity prices fall in the South? Commodity prices fell because supplies from the South increased and because new technologies developed in the North reduced the demand for many raw materials. New technology, particularly electronic and computer technologies, is often heralded as the engine of "globalization." But computer technologies did *not* play a major role in these developments. Instead, more prosaic, nonelectronic technologies, and changed consumer behavior, contributed to falling prices.

Why did manufacturing industries collapse? Many of the industries that produced goods for domestic markets collapsed because the structural adjustment programs introduced by the IMF during the debt crisis exposed these industries, for the first time, to foreign competition with powerful transnational corporations from the North (see chapter 5). As domestic markets were opened to foreign trade, many manufacturers in the South proved unable to compete with TNCs based in the North. Their failure led to widespread deindustrialization in the South. To appreciate these developments, and their impact on women and men, let us first examine the fall in commodity prices.

COMMODITY PRICES, 1950–1979

During the 1950s and 1960s, commodity prices fell, but they did so slowly. They fell because producers in Africa, Asia, Latin America, and the Middle East planted more sugar, cotton, and coffee; mined more copper, tin, and gold; and pumped more oil.[2] Increased production swelled world supplies. Postwar economic recovery and growth in the United States, Western Europe, and Japan increased demand for these commodities, but it did not quite keep pace with growing supplies, so prices gradually fell. Early on, scholars and government officials in the South recognized that commodity prices would fall and worried that the incomes of countries that relied on commodity exports would deteriorate, worsening the terms of trade between North and South. In the 1950s, the prominent Latin American economist Raul Prebisch argued that a long-term decline in the terms of trade for commodity producers was "not casual or accidental, but deeply ingrained in the world trading system itself."[3]

Across the South, government officials, many of them employed either by capitalist or communist dictators, heeded the warnings of Prebisch and other "dependency theorists." So they took two steps to protect themselves from falling commodity prices, which threatened to undermine their economic growth and development. First, they built manufacturing industries that produced goods for domestic markets. They hoped that, by producing goods for domestic consumers, these industries could reduce the need to import expensive goods manufactured in North America and Western Europe, a process described by economists as "import substitution."[4] Domestic manufacturing industries helped dictatorships reduce their spending on imported goods, provide jobs for domestic male workers, and provide income and revenue for the state, which could be reinvested in the economy and used to provide jobs in the regime's bureaucracy and army. To protect newly established industries from competition with northern TNCs, regimes slapped high tariffs on imported goods and provided generous subsidies to private and state-owned firms to get them up and running. This strategy was widely adopted by capitalist dictatorships and communist regimes alike.

As a second step, officials tried to organize commodity cartels. They tried to persuade officials from countries that produced particular commodities to join organizations or cartels that could *limit* supplies and establish supply quotas among members. By agreeing to limit supplies, commodity producers hoped to strengthen their bargaining position with core buyers, which were dominated by large, postcolonial TNCs, and thereby stabilize or even increase the commodity prices they received. OPEC, which was founded in 1960, became the most famous of these commodity cartels. But it was not alone. Producers of coffee, sugar, tin, and tropical timber also organized cartels.[5] But cartels had little success during this period. OPEC, for example, was unable to stabilize oil prices, which fell from $5.38 a barrel in 1951 to only $2.09 in 1970. OPEC's first attempt to embargo oil during the 1967 Arab-Israeli war was a conspicuous failure. But OPEC fortunes, and those of commodity producers throughout the periphery, would improve dramatically in the 1970s.

In 1971, President Richard Nixon devalued the dollar (see chapter 3). This cut prices for oil producers because they were paid for their oil in dollars. To deal with falling prices, OPEC reorganized, enlisting the support of oil-producing countries such as Indonesia and Nigeria, which had ignored its call for an embargo in 1967. During the 1973–1974 Yom Kippur War, OPEC members agreed to cut their oil deliveries to the West, a move that drove prices up to $16.48, an eightfold increase.[6] Meanwhile, Soviet grain shortages reduced food supplies, which helped increase the price of agricultural and other commodities to levels not seen since World War II.[7]

Rising prices were generally good for commodity producers in the South, particularly for oil-producing states. But for poor countries without any oil of their own, skyrocketing oil prices were a great hardship. Still, while rising oil prices created an economic crisis for many poor countries, they also provided a solution to the problems they caused. Oil-producing countries deposited their flood of oil revenues in banks in Western Europe, creating a giant and growing pool of money in the "Eurodollar Market." The Eurodollar market grew from $110 billion in 1970 to $1.5 trillion by 1980.[8] To earn money and repay depositors, Western banks then loaned much of this money—$810 billion between 1970 and 1983—to borrowers in the South (see chapter 5). Regimes there used borrowed money to pay for higher-priced imported oil. They also used it to provide low-cost food and services to working people, which helped purchase some political support for dictatorship, increase military spending to contain any domestic opposition, and expand commodity production to take advantage of unusually high prices.[9]

Although workers in the North experienced the global inflation of the 1970s as a period of relative "scarcity," workers in the South experienced it as a time of relative "plenty."[10] In the South, economic growth accelerated, state revenues increased, and worker incomes grew in real terms, for the first time in a generation. Economists described these events as "miraculous," arguing that poor countries had finally found a path to real development.[11]

But the U.S. decision to raise interest rates in 1979 triggered an economic crisis of hurricane proportions in the South. This storm would sweep away all of the economic gains made in the 1970s and wreck the dictatorships that had used borrowed money to finance growth. The winds it generated created waves of change that continue to buffet the South.

Higher interest rates increased costs for peripheral borrowers, who had converted their fixed, low-interest loans to loans with floating rates in the late 1970s at the insistence of Western lenders. So when interest rates rose sharply in the early 1980s, interest payments increased fivefold, draining money out of borrower countries. Investors in the South also purchased high-interest U.S. securities. This flow of money out of the South, what was called "capital flight," reduced the hard-currency stocks that businesses and states needed to repay loans.

While higher interest rates drained money from the South, they also triggered a recession in the North. This reduced demand in the North for goods from the South and pushed down commodity prices. Because their (interest payment) costs increased at a time when their (commodity) income fell, regimes soon ran out of hard-currency reserves and faced bankruptcy, first in Poland and Bolivia (1981), then in Mexico (1982), and soon thereafter in countries throughout Africa, Eastern Europe, and Latin America. This acute economic crisis combined with various political crises to force dictators from power during the next decade. Regimes transferred power to civilian democrats, who were forced to adopt measures designed to repay debt (see chapter 11). Democratization (a political good) was joined with austerity or "structural adjustment programs" (an economic evil). Austerity programs then contributed to both the collapse of commodity prices and the deindustrialization of import-substitutionist manufacturing industries.

COLLAPSING COMMODITY PRICES, 1980–2000

After 1980, commodity prices fell heavily. They collapsed because commodity supplies from the South increased, while demand in the North weakened. Commodity supplies increased for a variety of reasons. During the 1970s, supplies increased because southern states used borrowed money to expand production so firms could take advantage of high prices. For example, world coffee production increased from 3.8 million tons in 1970 to 4.9 million tons in 1979, world cotton production grew from 11 to 14 million tons, and world sugar production increased from 585 to 754 million tons.[12] Then in the 1980s, as indebted countries searched desperately for ways of earning the hard currency they needed to repay debt, they redoubled their efforts. The austerity programs developed by the IMF and adopted by democratizing states played an important role in expanding commodity supplies because they required states to increase exports to earn the money they needed to pay their bills. Between 1980 and 1988, "the volume of primary products exported by developing countries rose by over 20 percent," the economist Alfred Maizels observed.[13] But growing supplies only glutted markets and produced no real gain for commodity producers.

Global monetary institutions and TNCs also played a role in expanding commodity supplies. They frequently financed the expansion of commodity production to diversify their sources of supply, secure long-term supply relations, and weaken the ability of producers in the South to organize commodity cartels. So, for instance, TNCs and core states financed projects to grow coffee in Vietnam, where it had not previously been cultivated. In 1990, Vietnam produced only one million bags of coffee. But by 2000, it produced thirteen million bags, making it the second largest coffee producer in the world, behind Brazil and ahead of Colombia.[14] The sixty coffee-growing countries around the world now produce 115 million bags annually, more than the 108 million bags consumed by coffee drinkers from Seattle to Karachi.[15] The oversupply is due primarily to the World Bank–sponsored expansion of coffee production in Vietnam. Because supply grew faster than demand by 2000, prices fell, from 95 cents a pound in 1999 to only 30 cents a pound in 2001, its lowest level in thirty years.[16]

But while IMF austerity programs and World Bank lending policies are partly responsible for impoverishing commodity-producing countries, they were not wholly to blame. Deflationary policies in the North, the introduction of new technologies, and changing consumer behavior in the North have also played critical roles. They helped reduce the demand for commodities just when supplies expanded.

In the early 1980s, the demand for commodities fell because deflationary policies (high interest rates) forced Western European and North American economies into a recession. This "slowed down substantially the growth of demand for all industrial inputs, including primary commodities."[17] But when economies in the North recovered, and began to grow again in the mid- to late 1980s, demand did not revive. It did not because the introduction of new technologies in the 1970s and 1980s enabled producers in the North to replace southern commodities with goods made in the North, a process of "substitution" or "dematerialization."[18] Dematerialization occurs when fewer raw materials are needed to produce the same quantity of goods, a kind of raw materials "conservation."[19] In 1984, for example, Japan "consumed only 60 percent of the raw materials required for the same volume of production in 1973."[20]

Product substitution and dematerialization were not entirely new developments. In the early twentieth century, coal tar distillates were used to create industrial dyes that replaced vegetable and mineral dyes; vegetable oils were used to make margarine that replaced butter; oil-based technologies were used to make synthetic rubber to replace natural rubber and synthetic fibers that replaced cotton, wool, jute, and sisal. But the invention and adoption of a new set of technologies in the 1970s and 1980s set the stage for the widespread replacement of southern commodities. New technologies in hand, producers in Japan, North America, and Western Europe did more with less.[21]

To illustrate this process and its impact on peripheral commodity producers and workers, let us briefly describe how new technologies affected the demand for a few important peripheral products: sugar, copper, oil, and gold.

Sugar

In the mid-1960s, scientists in Japan and the United States developed enzymes to produce fructose sugar from the starch in corn. The new high-fructose corn sweeteners (HFCS) replaced cane and beet sugars in many products. HFCS technology was taken off the laboratory shelf when world sugar prices quadrupled in the 1970s and producers in the North began using HFCS instead of cane and beet sugar. The decision by Coca-Cola and Pepsi in the early 1980s to use HFCS in their beverages was a turning point. In 1970s, U.S. per capita consumption of HFCS was only 0.7 pounds. But it grew to 29.8 pounds by 1983, and in 1985 reached 60 pounds, equaling the consumption of cane and beet sugar for the first time ever.[22]

The demand for cane and beet sugar was undermined not only by HFCS technology but also by new dietary sweetener technologies, particularly aspartame, which captured 13 percent of the U.S. sugar market by 1988. As U.S. producers switched from cane and beet sugars to HFCS and dietary sweeteners, U.S. imports of sugar grown in the South dropped, falling from 4.8 million metric tons in 1970–1991 to only 1.7 million metric tons in 1989–1990.[23]

Copper

In the mid-1960s, the electrical industry in the core began using aluminum to replace copper wire, and aluminum cables captured 2 percent of the market by 1974. But because aluminum is also a southern product, the use of aluminum to replace copper in some goods resulted in the substitution of one southern product for another. More important for copper producers has been the development of fiber optic cable, wireless communication, and recycling technologies in the North.

In 1970, Corning scientists began developing glass fiber that could transmit laser light efficiently enough to make "wave guides," fiber optic cables that could transmit phone calls and other electronic communications. Still, it would be twelve years before Corning would sell fiber optic cable in quantity, largely because the phone giant AT&T was not ready to junk its copper wire phone system and replace it with new fiber optic cable. But the 1982 breakup of AT&T's phone monopoly and the rising cost of copper, which had doubled in price during the inflationary 1970s, encouraged AT&T's new competitors to build new communications networks using fiber optic cable. Demand for the new cables has become so great since then that core producers have trouble keeping pace.[24] The subsequent adoption of wire*less* cellular phone and data networks has meant that businesses have eliminated the need for copper wire for many uses. In addition, producers in the North have developed new conservation and recycling technologies that enable them to *reuse* the copper they already possess, rather than purchase new copper from primary producers. By 1985, the United States obtained half of the copper it needed from recycled copper scrap. Although copper is still used, new technologies have replaced copper for many uses, and world demand has weakened dramatically.

Oil

Successive oil embargoes and skyrocketing oil prices stimulated the development and introduction of myriad new oil-replacing technologies. Government tax credits encouraged industries and consumers in the North to adopt new energy conservation technologies for transport, manufacturing, office buildings, and dwellings, improvements described by some as a *"nega*watt revolution."[25] Automakers, after much delay, improved gas mileage. Electric utilities found ways to meet new demand with existing energy systems and alternative power sources. Architects and builders redesigned offices and homes and developed new lighting and refrigeration systems that reduced office and residential energy consumption 16 percent between 1973 and 1985. Overall, U.S. demand for energy fell 20 percent in this period, and demand fell even more in Western Europe and Japan, where conservation policies were more aggressively promoted.

Gold

Even gold is not immune from technological innovation. For centuries gold was seen as a repository of value, the "ultimate form of payment."[26] But in recent years, other monetary instruments—U.S. securities, stocks, and corporate bonds, as well as more sophisticated and obscure ways to store value (money market funds, mutual funds, hedge funds, etc.)—have been developed. These new monetary *technologies* have persuaded many investors, even private banks and central government banks, to dispense with gold, which is mined primarily by men of color in the South. Central banks in Argentina, Belgium, the Czech Republic, England, and the Netherlands have sold some of their gold reserves in recent years. Even the IMF has announced plans to shed gold assets. One reason that the IMF has considered selling its gold and using the proceeds to assist the poorest, most desperate indebted countries (see chapter 5), is that the *value* of its gold is declining. IMF managers reason that it would be better to sell gold now, before prices fall further. The irony, of course, is that IMF policies contributed both to the demonetization of gold and to falling gold prices. As one money manager argued, gold "has essentially been de-monetized by the modern financial economy."[27] One economist has gone further. "Inexorably," Niall Ferguson has argued, "we are moving towards a demonetization of gold comparable with the demonetization of silver that began in the 1870s."[28]

The weakening demand for gold by central banks and other investors in the North has further eroded the price that producers, particularly in South Africa, could obtain for the not-so-precious metal. When the Bank of England sold 25 *tons* of gold from its vaults—the first lot of a planned sale of 415 tons—South African miners picketed the British embassy in Pretoria. They demonstrated because falling gold prices between 1997 and 1999 had cost 103,000 black male workers their jobs in South African gold mines. In London, gold dealers opposing the sale hung a banner that read: "Precious metal, Give Away Prices."[29]

Three important points can be made about substitutionist technologies. First, the introduction of new technologies was spurred by high commodity prices. This means that attempts by commodity producers to raise prices will likely contribute to the development and introduction of new technologies that help the North abandon these goods, thereby weakening demand and forcing down prices.

Second, while new technologies reduced the demand for primary goods, they did not wholly eliminate them. Synthetic rubber has not eliminated the need for natural rubber in large truck and airplane tires (the larger the tire, the more natural rubber it needs); synthetic fabrics have not eliminated the demand for cotton denims; HFCS has not replaced cane sugar in baked goods, confectionery, and candies (hard candies need real sugar to set properly); and new energy technologies have not yet eliminated the demand for oil, which continues to grow as the world car fleet expands. This means that producers and consumers in Japan, North America, and Western Europe still need *some* commodities from the South, but they do not need as much as they once did.

Third, because producers in the North have vast public universities and private research institutes at their disposal, they have the scientific and engineering means to invent and deploy new substitutionist technologies. The patent protection provided investors by government laws and new free trade agreements means that they can reap the benefits of new substitutionist technologies (see chapter 9). New technologies have also helped TNCs mine other advantages. HFCS technologies enabled U.S. firms to use corn grown in Iowa and Illinois as their raw material, which strengthened the demand for this important U.S. crop. So new technologies can assist commodity producers (farmers) in the North, while undermining farmers in the South.

The demand for southern commodities has been reshaped not only by new technologies but also by consumers in the North. In recent years, changed consumer preferences and diets have reduced the demand for many commodities. In recent years, U.S. consumers drank less coffee, and per capita consumption dropped one-third between 1975 and 1991.[30] Although they drank less coffee, they increasingly preferred "more subtle, higher quality arabica coffees" that are lower in caffeine than robusta.[31] This was generally good for producers of "fine" arabica coffees in Colombia but bad for robusta growers, particularly in Africa, where robusta is the principal coffee variety.[32]

Changed dietary preferences have also reduced the demand for southern commodities while increasing the demand for northern substitutes. Diet-conscious consumers in the North have increasingly shunned fat-heavy tropical oils and switched to low-cholesterol temperate oils grown in the North. They eat fewer candy bars with cocoa butter and palm oil (grown in the tropics) and more candy made from vegetable and cotton seed oils (grown in the Midwest). They have abandoned sugared gum for sugar*less* gums that use aspartame. In the United Kingdom, for example, sugarless gum's share of the market increased from only 6 percent in 1977 to 60 percent in 1993.[33] Health-conscious consumers have sound medical reasons for adopting diets that are lower in caffeine, sugar, and fat. But what is good for worker health in the North is bad for worker pocketbooks in the South, where workers had come to depend on the jobs provided by the export of tropical products.

The growing supply of commodities and the falling demand for those goods have combined to slash prices. Real commodity prices fell 50 percent between 1980 and 1992. They fell another 20 to 30 percent in the late 1990s.[34] Losses for commodity producers in this period were greater than they were during the Great Depression. In the 1930s, prices fell heavily for commodity producers, but they also fell for manufacturers in the North. By contrast, in the 1980s and 1990s, prices fell *only* for commodities, not for manufacturers from the North. So the current deflation is *selective*, affecting the South and not the North, and it is worse than any other downturn in this century.[35]

Plummeting commodity prices have had catastrophic consequences for workers and states in the South. Once you know that fifty million people work in the sugar industry and twenty million people grow coffee, the impact of new HFCS technology and changed consumer diets and preferences becomes evident.[36] Although social scientists marvel at the changes associated with new computer and electronic technologies, the global impact of these technologies is rather small compared to the changes associated with more prosaic HFCS technologies or consumer habits.

GENDER AND FALLING COMMODITY PRICES

Of course, the impact of falling commodity prices on women and men varies enormously, depending on how different commodity-producing industries organize work along gender lines. Falling prices have their biggest impact on labor-intensive industries like sugar, which requires up to six workers per ten hectares in cane fields, most of them male. In Brazil, the world's largest sugar producer, the number of people working in the industry fell by almost half, from 1.2 million to only 700,000, in the 1990s.[37] During the 1980s, 400,000 sugar workers lost their jobs in the Philippines. A 1985 Catholic Church study found that "an overwhelming majority of the displaced sugar plantation and mill workers . . . are suffering from severe malnutrition, starvation, disease, and lack of medical care, decent clothing and shelter."[38] In Trinidad and Tobago, two small islands where eight thousand sugar workers lost their jobs, the prime minister argued, "If current conditions are maintained, we shall be confronting a situation that could lead to the destruction of the sugar industry in most developing nations."[39]

Other labor-intensive commodities, such as rubber and vanilla, are also threatened by substitutionist technologies and falling prices. If *in vitro* production of natural rubber becomes a reality, as scientists expect, the jobs of twelve to sixteen million workers in East Asian rubber plantations will be put at risk.[40] In this industry, women make up a significant portion of the work force, though it remains predominantly male. The development, meanwhile, of artificial vanilla threatens the livelihood of the one hundred thousand natural vanilla farmers in Madagascar, where most of the world's supply is grown by women and men in independent farming households.[41]

Generally, where commodity production is organized on large-scale plantations, men make up most of the work force. Where production is organized by small-scale farmers, women play a much larger role. The way production is organized also varies by region, even for the same commodity. For instance, bananas grown in Central America are typically grown on large plantations by large TNCs (Dole) that employ mostly male workers. But bananas on Caribbean islands are typically grown by small farmers that rely on male and female household members. Coffee in Vietnam is grown on large-scale plantations that employ men; coffee in Colombia is grown by small farmers, both men and women. So falling prices have different gender consequences, depending on the way that producers organized production.

In commodity-producing industries such as copper, oil, and gold, the number of workers affected by falling prices is much smaller because they are much more capital intensive. Mining and mineral extraction industries typically employ *only* men. Women rarely work in mines or oilfields anywhere in the world. But the impact of falling prices on male workers in these industries has been devastating. In Chile, copper mines have been shut down, workers have lost jobs, and those who still work have seen wages fall. Mario Olivares earned $400 a month mining copper ore. But after he was laid off, he earned only a dollar a day as a street vendor.[42] In South Africa, the number of male gold miners fell by half—from 514,000 to 180,000—in the last decade, and widespread unemployment in mining districts has contributed to increased rates of violence against women, rape, and divorce.[43] Layoffs in the mining industries of Chile, Poland, Russia, South Africa, and Zambia have devastated the workers who had organized unions and demanded an end to authoritarian, apartheid, and communist regimes in those countries. Falling prices and economic change have crippled one of the main political constituencies for democratization (see chapter 11).

The impact of falling commodity prices is not restricted only to the South. Falling copper prices have also affected male miners and oil workers in the United States and Canada. Since 1980, the number of male workers in U.S. gas and oilfields fell by more than half, from 425,000 to less than 200,000.[44] Falling oil prices threw 25,000 wildcatters out of work in Wyoming and tens of thousands more in Texas, where they organized a "Starving Oil Workers March" on the state capitol in 1999.[45] Still, the number of workers affected by falling commodity prices in the North is relatively small compared to the South, where a large number of people labor in commodity-producing industries.

In the South, falling prices had different consequences for men and women workers. Where goods are produced on large scale plantations (sugar, rubber, soybeans) or in capital-intensive mines (copper, gold, oil), men make up most if not all the workforce. In these industries, men lost jobs and wages as prices fell. But where goods are produced primarily by independent small farmers, industries that rely much more heavily on female participation (sisal, jute, palm oil, vanilla), falling prices directly affect male *and* female workers. In Africa, women constitute 47 percent of the workforce in agriculture, 40 percent in South Asia and the Caribbean, and 18 percent in Latin America.[46]

The current trade dispute over bananas illustrates the complex character of change for men and women in different settings. In the late 1990s, the United States demanded that Western Europe reduce its tariffs on banana imports from Central America so that U.S. corporations with large plantations in the region could sell more bananas in Western Europe. The European Community refused to lower tariffs because they imported from independent small farmers in their former colonies in the Caribbean. In gender terms, the Europeans were asked to abandon the 145,000 men and women who grow bananas in the Caribbean and buy bananas instead from U.S. plantations in Central America, which employ mostly men.[47]

Falling prices have not only reduced worker incomes but also ruined businesses, particularly those with higher production costs. As prices fell, the first producers affected were ones that had poorer soils, deeper mines, poorer ore, thicker oil, and, therefore, higher costs. So falling prices gradually shifted the *location* of production, from high-cost copper producers such as Mexico and Peru to lower-cost producers in Indonesia and Papua New Guinea; from high-cost oil producers in Wyoming and Texas to lower-cost producers in Saudi Arabia and Nigeria.

Falling prices also reduced revenues for commodity-dependent countries. In

Arabia, the state's oil revenues fell 40 percent or $20 billion during the ⌐Js, and the government ran a $13 billion budget deficit in 1999.[48] "The boom days are over," Crown Prince Abdullah complained, "and they will not come back."[49] Chile was forced to cut $685 million from its budget in 1998 as copper prices and export earnings fell.[50] And in South Africa, economists estimated that the government lost $200 million in revenue for every $10 fall in the price for an ounce of gold.[51] As revenues fell, it became more difficult for governments to repay their foreign debts or provide services and benefits to domestic workers. World Bank economists concluded in 1998 that lower commodity prices "may produce an increase in the financial vulnerability of [commodity-dependent] countries."[52]

The expansion of agricultural commodity production has also contributed to hunger and migration. As southern farmers devoted more land to the production of export crops (cotton, bananas, sugar, coffee, fresh fruits and flowers), less land was available for the production of subsistence foods (wheat, corn, millet, rice, beans, potatoes), which local populations consumed as a central part of their diet (see chapter 7). As the supply of subsistence foods fell, prices rose, and people found it harder to purchase the food they needed. Malnutrition and hunger then became a persistent problem. Moreover, the use of Green Revolution agricultural technologies on these export crops typically increased productivity and consolidated land in the hands of large farmers who had access to the credit needed to purchase these inputs. The consolidation of land forced farm households to seek work as wage laborers on large-scale farms and plantations or migrate. Dispossessed workers either moved to urban areas, where their search for work depressed wages in local labor markets, or moved to marginal rural lands, where their attempts to wrest food from jungle forests and desert fringes wreaked environmental havoc.

STRUCTURAL ADJUSTMENT AND DEINDUSTRIALIZATION

In addition to falling commodity prices, workers in the South have also experienced widespread deindustrialization. The destruction of domestic manufacturing industries has resulted in massive job loss, particularly for urban males.

Before 1980, dictators in the South used foreign investment (much of it provided by TNCs to their subsidiaries) and loans (from Western banks and global monetary institutions) to build manufacturing industries that provided jobs and produced goods for *domestic* markets. Governments used high tariffs on manufactured goods imported from the North to protect domestic industries from foreign competition and force domestic consumers to purchase domestic goods. This set of policies and practices, which were supposed to reduce dependence on the North and promote indigenous economic development, was known as "import-substitutionist industrialization." Many of these domestic industries were owned and managed by the state, often by the military, which controlled most countries in Africa, Asia, Latin America, and Eastern Europe in this period. Government officials used this industrial sector to create jobs, generate income and revenue for the state, and, frequently, enrich corrupt elites. A few states in East Asia—South Korea, Taiwan, and Singapore—even managed to produce goods that could be *exported* to markets in Japan and the United States. But manufacturing industries in most southern countries produced goods that could *only* be sold to captive domestic consumers.

After 1980, the conditions that allowed domestic manufacturing industries to flourish in the South were fundamentally changed by debt crisis, deflation, and democratization. When dictators fell, the newly installed civilian governments adopted a common set of economic policies they believed would help them repay debt, solve their economic problems, and lay the ground for real development sometime in the future. The neoliberal globalization policies adopted by countries around the world had three important features. First, they opened economies to foreign investment and trade. Second, they sold public or state assets to foreign and domestic entrepreneurs, a process known as "privatization." And third, they cut military spending and demilitarized their economies.[53] Unfortunately, the neoliberal globalization policies they adopted as part of IMF austerity programs led to the widespread *de*industrialization of the domestic manufacturing sector, which had long provided jobs for urban males.

Opening Economies

Government officials opened their economies to foreign investment and trade by easing restrictions on private investment and capital flows, and slashing tariffs on *imported* manufactured goods. Officials hoped these measures would encourage foreign investment and force domestic firms to increase the quality of their goods, so they could survive in a more competitive environment. But foreign investment generally failed to materialize. Investors either continued to invest heavily in the North or invested *selectively* in just a few countries: East Germany, China, and, to a lesser extent, Brazil and Mexico. And as tariffs fell, domestic consumers rushed to buy "higher quality" imported goods. Across Latin America, where average tariffs fell from 39 to 15 percent between 1989 and 1992, the new policy "unleashed a consumer boom, as Latin Americans . . . flocked to snap up imported goods."[54]

In the South, consumers played an important role in recent economic developments, often to their own detriment. In Mexico, for instance, binge buying by consumers created a $23 billion trade deficit in 1994. The government then devalued the peso to increase the cost of imports and slow consumer purchases of foreign goods. But this made foreign investors lose confidence in the economy, and they withdrew their money. This further lowered the value of the peso and threatened the government with ruin. Financial crisis was averted when the U.S. government intervened with a $50 billion rescue plan. One element of this plan was that the Mexican government had to raise interest rates to restore foreign investor confidence. But higher interest rates caused a recession and increased debt payments for households that had borrowed money. The buying binges of Mexican consumers eventually led to recession, job loss, and a debt crisis for heavy-spending worker households. This would become a common pattern in the 1990s. Tariff reduction and binge buying frequently led to financial crises and, more important, deindustrialization.

When consumers *started* buying "high-quality" imports, they *stopped* purchasing domestic goods they regarded as inferior. Many domestic industries, when confronted with competition from goods from the core, unceremoniously collapsed. Particularly hard hit were the domestic steel and auto industries, which had long employed male workers.[55] In Yugoslavia, for instance, the state-owned auto company, Zastava, produced the cheap, boxy Yugo for many years. But when the economy was opened to foreign car imports, consumers abandoned Yugos and purchased Fiats instead. The market for Yugos collapsed and more than half of its male work force was laid off.[56]

In Latin America, the proportion of the work force employed by large manufacturing firms "fell from 44 percent to 32 percent between 1980 and 1990."[57] In Tanzania, domestic industrial production declined by as much as 80 percent in the wake of debt crisis and structural adjustment programs.[58]

Privatization

Government officials across the South sold public assets to private investors. They hoped to use the money they raised from the sale of government-owned firms to repay debts and balance budgets, and they believed that private management would improve efficiency and quality. Between 1989 and 1992, Brazil sold 92 firms and a port for $52 billion, while Argentina and Mexico together sold 173 companies for $32.5 billion.[59] National banks, airlines, telephone companies, shipping lines, trucking firms, steel mills, cement factories, and port facilities were commonly offered for sale.

But the widespread sale of public assets created a glut on global markets, and many went unsold. Of the 123 firms put on the market by the new democratic government in the Philippines, only 58 were sold, and they earned the government considerably less than their book value.[60]

In many countries, the sale of government-run businesses was accompanied by currency devaluations. Government officials commonly devalued their currencies, either to promote exports (so they could repay debts) or to slow binge buying by consumers. But currency devaluations made domestic goods cheaper for *foreigners*, not for *domestic* buyers. So when governments offered domestic firms for sale, devaluations cut their real price for foreigners, and they were snapped up by foreign investors. As the economist Andre Gunder Frank explained, "The real market value of [public] properties and goods is suffering a classical and severe deflation in terms of world currencies, [so that] property and land . . . can be and is bought by Westerners 'for a song.'"[61]

Across the South, foreign investors creamed off the best manufacturing industries, and dissolved the rest. In Argentina, for example, U.S. investors—Citicorp Equity—bought the government's Acros Zapla steel plant. In 1992, Citicorp began modernizing the plant, but also cut its work force, from 5,000 to only 709.[62] The same thing happened when the government's oil company was privatized. Between 1990 and 1996, 4,500 workers lost their jobs; only 500 remained.[63]

Demilitarization

Where civilian governments took power, they quite sensibly cut military spending. They did so to make it harder for the military to mount coups and intervene in political affairs and to reduce the heavy burden of military spending on weak economies. They recognized that military spending had contributed to heavy debt loads and had done little to promote economic growth. They agreed with the findings of scholars like A. F. Mullins, who concluded, "In general, those states that did best in GNP growth . . . paid less attention to military capability than others."[64]

Across the South, governments reduced the size of armed forces, cut military spending, and privatized firms controlled by the army.[65] Military spending in Latin America, for example, fell by one-quarter in the late 1980s. But while reductions in military spending were beneficial for democratic governments and ailing economies, they also resulted in job loss for the males who were conscripted or enlisted to serve in the armed forces. As a result, demilitarization also contributed to male job loss.

Neoliberal globalization policies led to widespread deindustrialization, particularly for manufacturing firms that had been owned by the state. Firms that were subsidiaries of businesses based in the North—and there were a large number of these in Latin America—fared better. They took advantage of their access to foreign capital to expand their operations, taking over the local markets of collapsing enterprises. But while they continued to provide jobs for male urban workers, most of the other economic benefits were captured by core firms.

The decline of many manufacturing industries in the South resulted in high levels of unemployment and falling wages for male workers employed in the firms that survived.[66] In Argentina and Brazil, *un*employment in manufacturing rose to nearly 20 percent by the late 1990s, a threefold increase.[67] "The recession is only going to get worse," explained Moises Selerges, Jr., a member of a manufacturing union in Brazil. "We're in the boat. Water's coming in, and we're sinking."[68]

ENCLAVE MANUFACTURING, TOURISM, AND THE TRAFFIC IN WOMEN

Falling commodity prices and the deindustrialization of domestic manufacturing resulted in massive job and income loss for workers, primarily men in rural and urban settings. These two events have been accompanied by a third development, which has frequently been seen as beneficial for workers and governments. The expansion of export manufacturing, in "free trade" enclaves or *maquiladoras*, and the growth of service industries, principally tourism, has provided some new jobs, primarily for women. But the gains made by women in export manufacturing and tourist enclaves have *not* offset the loss of jobs and income in the primary-commodity and domestic manufacturing industries. So while some "new" jobs were created, they did not replace the "old" jobs that were lost.

Maquilas

Export-manufacturing in free trade enclaves has been around for decades. Mexico was among the first country to introduce them. After the United States ended its Bracero Program (which recruited Mexican workers for U.S. agriculture), U.S. officials encouraged Mexico in 1965 to set up export-processing maquiladoras along its northern border to provide jobs for the two hundred thousand Mexican workers who had been expelled from jobs in U.S. agriculture.[69] Employment in *maquilas* grew from 3,087 in 1965 to 56,253 in 1975, and then to 500,000 in 1990.[70] At first, maquilas produced clothing, toys, luggage, and furniture, but they eventually produced electrical appliances, electronics, and auto parts in large quantity.[71] The U.S. and Mexican firms that operated maquilas mostly hired *women*, and they "constituted about 85 percent of the work force" in the first decade.[72] The percentage of women in maquilas has since declined, to 64 percent in 1988, but this is still a very high percentage compared to women's employment in other manufacturing industries in Mexico.[73]

Maquilas in Mexico employ about one-third of the total number of workers in maquila industries around the world.[74] Worldwide employment in export manufacturing zones grew from 866,000 in 1983 to 1.3 million in 1986.[75] They grew rapidly in this period because government officials wanted to expand the production of export goods so they could earn the hard currency they needed to repay their debts.[76] As in Mexico, the maquilas in most countries employ women to manufacture apparel and electronic goods, largely because they can be paid less than men.

Although employment for women has grown rapidly in the maquilas of Mexico and other countries, it has not compensated for the loss of male jobs in primary-commodity and domestic manufacturing industries.[77] Given the fact that export-manufacturing firms employ only 10 percent of all manufacturing jobs in Mexico and, on average, only 2 percent of manufacturing jobs in the 48 peripheral countries that have maquilas, it is easy to see why they cannot.[78] Moreover, because export-manufacturing firms are owned primarily by northern TNCs, manufacturing profits are captured by others. Maquilas do provide hard-currency earnings for indebted governments, but officials also agree to forgo considerable tax revenues—these zones are, by definition, duty-free—when they are established.

Of course, maquilas have provided jobs for women and income for households, income that is sorely needed, particularly where men have lost jobs and seen their incomes fall. But because maquilas pay low wages and provide employment for only short periods of time—usually for women workers between eighteen and twenty-five years of age—the income provided women workers is small and the relief it can provide households is usually temporary. In Indonesia, the sociologist Diane Wolf found that wages did not even cover the cost of subsistence for the young female workers employed in export factories. Parents actually had to *subsidize* their employment.[79] But they did so because employment provided *cash* wages, which they could not otherwise obtain in rural subsistence economies, cash they needed to pay taxes and purchase goods that they could not make themselves or obtain through barter.

Tourism

Faced with falling prices, widespread deindustrialization, and the limited gains provided by export manufacturing, it is not surprising that government officials in many countries have come to view tourism as a panacea. Many have spent heavily to promote this important service industry, which is now said to provide more jobs worldwide than any other industry.

Like export manufacturing, tourism takes place in enclaves, near sunny beaches and important historical-cultural sites. Like maquilas, tourism provides considerable employment for women.[80] Like export manufacturing, employment in the tourist industry has grown rapidly in recent years. But unlike maquilas, tourism has provided a much larger number of jobs. Worldwide, the number of people working in the tourist industry increased from 197 million in 1990 to 250 million in 1999.[81] In 1999, tourists spent $4.2 trillion, a level of spending that promised enormous benefits to the workers, businesses, and governments that could capture a slice of the trade. Unfortunately, try as they might, workers, businesses, and states have not captured many of the benefits that the industry provides. Why? There are several reasons.

Most of the world's tourists are workers from Japan, North America, and Western Europe. Although they spend a lot—U.S. tourists spent $52.6 billion on travel abroad in 1996—they spent most of it in other rich countries.[82] Countries in the North captured 65 percent of all international arrivals and 72 percent of all tourist receipts in 1989.[83] Because tourists from the North traveled primarily to other countries in the North—France, the United States, Spain, Italy, and United Kingdom were the top five destinations—they provided jobs and income for workers and businesses there. More tourists visited Disney's Epcot Center in Florida than all of Latin America and the Caribbean, excluding Mexico. Even if countries in the South spent heavily to develop their tourist industries, they would find it difficult to compete with high-tech, Euro-Disney destinations or the European "homelands" of white ethnic groups in the United States, who yearn to visit the lands of their immigrant forebears.

When tourists from the North *do* travel to southern destinations, *most* of the money they spend is captured by airlines, hotels, and cruise lines, which are generally owned by TNCs based in the North. For example, 97 percent of all tourists flying to the Bahamas "arrived on an American-owned airline," 90 percent of them stayed at hotels owned by TNCs, and most of the food and drink (steak and Scotch) they consumed was *imported* from the North.[84] Access to tourist destinations is largely controlled by travel agents and package tour companies in the North, so it is difficult and expensive for businesses in the South to market their destinations to northern tourists.[85] When they arrive in the South, tourists spend a relatively small percentage of their vacation dollars on goods or services provided by local workers, businesses, or states. This is particularly true when they travel on cruise ships or stay in all-inclusive resorts, which prevent dollars or deutsche marks from leaking out into local economies.

The expansion of tourist industries in the South has also created a glut of beach resorts and hotels. So the industry is subject to the same diminishing returns as other commodity-producing industries. Where supplies are high, prices tend to fall. Some countries can attract more tourists if they devalue their currencies. Tourists from the North look for bargains, traveling to countries where the local currency is weak, the hard currencies they earn go far, and they can live like kings. But while currency devaluations may sometimes increase travel to southern countries, they also reduce the value of the industry as a hard-currency earner. Tourists like cheap destinations. But they shun places where poverty is rampant, the infrastructure is decayed, and the threat of violence or crime is high—the condition of many poor countries today. The influx of hard currency into tourist enclaves is also a problem because it creates a two-tier economy. Workers employed in the tourist industry have access to dollars and francs. They typically use the hard currency they earn to bid up the price of domestic goods. This behavior creates miniature, selective inflations that hurt workers who do not have access to dollars and are paid only in local currencies. Nor does work in tourist industries replace the jobs lost in other industries. In the Caribbean, for example, more jobs were lost in the declining sugarcane industry than were created in the tourist industry.

THE SEX INDUSTRY AND
TRAFFICKING IN WOMEN

Prostitution has long existed in many countries.[86] But until recently it was relatively small scale, with local men purchasing the sexual services of women from domestic and rural settings. But two developments associated with contemporary globalization have contributed to the expansion of sex industries, which are designed to provide sexual services to domestic men *and* foreign male tourists, and which draw women and girls, from domestic *and* foreign countries, to work in the industry. The practice of enlisting women from distant countries, primarily by regional mafias, has contributed to a large-scale "trafficking in women."[87]

It is important to note that the term "trafficking in women" is contentious among feminists and other scholars who study the sex industry. For some, the term reflects the forced and coercive character of the industry and describes the cross-border transport of women to its centers.[88] For others it is a pejorative term, which fails to appreciate the fact that many women "voluntarily" participate in the industry and deprives women of the respect that they deserve as "sex workers."[89] This debate in part reflects the character of the sex industry in different settings around the world. In East Asia, the sex industry is fairly "coercive" and relies heavily on children. In the Caribbean, by contrast, participation in the industry is fairly voluntary, and the industry relies primarily on adults, not children.

In any event, between three and four million women and girls work in the sex industries of Thailand, South Korea, the Philippines, Taiwan, and Japan.[90] Many of these women work outside their country of origin. Many are held in debt bondage by employers, who often purchase young women or girls from poor households (one-third of these three to four million are children under age seventeen) and lure or force them into the sex industry, where they are held until they repay their debts or until they are too ill or aged to work in the industry.[91] In Thailand, a sex industry agent will advance a payment to the girl's parents, and the young women who enter this service are obligated to repay twice that amount.[92]

Why has the sex industry, not just in East Asia but in the Caribbean and Western Europe, expanded in recent decades? It has done so largely as a result of two kinds of globalization: (1) the spread of U.S. military bases overseas during the 1950s, 1960s, and 1970s and (2) the adoption of SAPs during the 1980s and 1990s.

The Military and the Sex Industry

After World War II, the U.S. government established 1,500 military bases outside the United States "to support 340,000 soldiers in Europe, 144,000 in the Pacific and Asia, and thousands more on land and sea in the Caribbean, the

Middle East, Africa, and Latin America."[93] Sex and entertainment industries often grew up alongside these bases, the most prominent or notorious among them were located next to naval ports in the Philippines and Marine bases in Okinawa, Japan.[94] In Olongapo City, next to the massive Subic Bay naval facility in the Philippines, twenty-five thousand women worked in the entertainment and sex industry in 1987, and five thousand more women joined the workforce when American aircraft carriers docked in port.[95] U.S. servicemen not only patronized the sex industry in large numbers but also fathered, and then left, children conceived with women prostitutes or romantic partners. In Okinawa, four thousand children of these liaisons were abandoned by U.S. servicemen.[96] This has been a problem because their mothers could not obtain financial support from departed fathers and because biracial children were shunned and tormented by Japanese children at school.[97] And when they grew up, many outcast, biracial youths joined the sex industry to survive.

During the late 1960s, the escalation of war in Vietnam, which increased the number of U.S. troops there to half a million, expanded the sex industry in Vietnam and contributed to its rise in other countries, particularly Thailand and Taiwan, where soldiers were sent for rest and recreation.[98] The sex industry in Thailand became perhaps the biggest in the world. After the war in Vietnam ended in 1975, Thailand became the principal global destination for sex tourists, mostly businessmen from East Asia, but also from Western Europe and North America. The number of sex trade establishments in Bangkok grew from 977 in 1980 to 5,754 in 1994, and the number of women working in the industry grew from 400,000 to perhaps 1.5 million, producing about $5 billion in annual revenue.[99] Many Thai women also traveled to work in the sex industries of other countries, where they were regarded as "exotic" by men who preferred foreign women. As one analyst observed, "One thing that stands out but stands unexplained [in the literature] is that a large percentage of sex customers seek sex workers whose racial, national or class identities are different from their own. . . . sex industries today depend on the erotization of the ethnic and cultural 'Other.'"[100] During the 1980s, for example, "There was a switch from white Dutch women to Asian, African, and Latin American women in the red-light districts [in Amsterdam]."[101]

Although the U.S. military withdrew from Vietnam and closed some overseas bases—Subic Bay was closed in 1992—U.S. servicemen overseas continued to patronize and promote sex industries in countries around the world. Then during the 1980s and 1990s, the sex industry in many countries expanded as a result of developments associated with debt crisis and structural adjustment programs.

Structural Adjustment and the Sex Industry

In many countries, the sex industry emerged in the wake of debt crisis, SAPs, and falling commodity prices. In Jamaica, for example, debt, austerity programs, and falling prices ruined the bauxite and sugar industries during the 1980s.[102] To compensate, the government aggressively promoted the tourist industry, which by 1990 employed one of every four workers in the country.[103] A large, diverse sex industry grew up alongside the tourist industry, though Jamaican *men*, not just women, participated in the trade as "Beach Boys" for female tourists and gay male tourists.[104] In Jamaica, many male and female sex workers enter the industry "voluntarily," without the kind of coercive debt contracts common in East Asia, and children do not comprise a large percentage of the workforce, as they do in East Asia.[105]

The sex industry in the Dominican Republic also expanded at about the same time as it did in Jamaica, and for the same reasons. The number of women in the sex industry doubled from twenty-five thousand in 1986 to fifty thousand in 1996, and another fifty thousand worked in sex industries overseas.[106] Women in this latter group often *do* work under more coercive conditions than domestic sex workers. Foreign agents advertise regular jobs in other countries, pay the cost of travel to foreign destinations, seize women's passports on arrival, and then demand women repay their "debt" by working in the sex industry. This practice—the trafficking in women—is common in East Asia and in Western Europe. Women from poor, indebted countries in the Philippines and Indonesia are drawn to metropolitan centers of the sex industry in Japan and Taiwan; women from Eastern Europe and the former Soviet Union are drawn into the sex industry in Western Europe and Israel. By promising high wages to women in poor countries—most of them recently hit by debt-crisis, austerity programs, deindustrialization, and falling commodity prices—sex industry agents have been able to meet the growing demand for workers in the global sex industry.[107]

Left unexplained in the literature is this: why has the demand by men for sex industry workers in Japan, North America, and Western Europe expanded in recent years? No doubt the decriminalization of prostitution has played some role. And some anecdotal evidence suggests that where women have made substantial economic, legal, and political gains and have become more "independent" as a result, men have increasingly patronized sex industry workers, seeking women who are less independent and more "compliant." Little is known about this because most scholars examine the female "supply" side of the sex industry, not the male "demand" side.

In any event, the sex industry has been "globalized" in recent years as a result of several developments. The problem for women is that many work under coercive and degrading conditions, and they risk violence and disease, particularly AIDS. Women in the industry (and women generally) have great difficulty protecting themselves from AIDS by insisting on condom use. A UN report on AIDS in 2001 concluded that "the gender dynamics of the epidemic are far reaching due to women's weaker ability to negotiate safe sex."[108] The fact that spending on disease prevention and public health has declined in the wake of debt crisis and SAPs in many countries has made matters worse.

CONSEQUENCES: GROWING POVERTY

Falling commodity prices and widespread deindustrialization have resulted in huge job and income losses, which have not been made good by increased employment in the export-manufacturing and tourist industries. Although women with jobs in maquilas and tourism have increased their contribution to household incomes, they have not been able to prevent household incomes from falling significantly. Millions of households have been swept into poverty and debt.

As income from commodity production and wages fell—for example, by 40 percent in Mexico and 65 percent in Tanzania during the 1980s—poverty increased.[109] Half of Peru's twenty-four million people live in poverty, and the number of poor workers in Latin America increased by sixty million between 1980 and 1993, "leaving 46 percent of the population, nearly 200 million people, living in poverty."[110] There are more poor people living in India—312 million in 1994—than in all of Latin America and Africa combined.[111] Where malnutrition is rampant, infectious diseases have made a comeback: cholera in Latin America; plague in India.

Like households in the United States, which borrowed heavily to maintain standards of living, many middle-income households in the South borrowed money to purchase homes, buy consumer goods, or start businesses. But when interest rates rose (they rose in the early 1980s when the United States lifted interest rates, and they rose in the 1990s when currency crises forced governments to raise domestic interest rates to attract foreign investors and prevent capital flight), households that had borrowed money were ruined. In a sense, the debt crisis of peripheral states became also a debt crisis for individual households. Teresa and Guillermo Lasso, a middle-income couple, owned a beauty parlor and veterinary practice in Mexico. They borrowed $79,000 to build a house. But as the economy worsened, "people were just letting their [pet] dogs and cats die," Dr. Lasso explained. His practice collapsed, and the interest payments on their mortgage increased from $660 a month to $2,125, considerably more than their $1,250 monthly income. Because Mexican banks can charge interest on outstanding interest, they now owe the bank $113,000. They stand on the verge of bankruptcy and risk losing everything.[112]

Workers who borrowed money to purchase less expensive consumer goods—cars, motor bikes, televisions—have also been affected by domestic interest rate hikes. As a result, most households have cut back. "Everybody is working the maximum to spend the minimum," explained Luiz Henrique Afonso, a government worker in Brazil. "I don't know anybody whose budget isn't being pinched or who isn't cutting back in some way or another," he said in the wake of currency crisis, interest rate hikes.[113] For some this meant cutting back on consumer purchases or food. Ricarda Martinez de Suarez and her husband, who survive on a pension in Mexico, stopped buying chicken heads and feet from the market and started raising chickens to provide meat.[114] For others, it meant cutting back not only on consumer goods but also on the number of children they bear.

Declining Fertility Rates

In many countries, fertility rates have fallen dramatically in recent years. Women have decided to have fewer children in Muslim countries such as Bangladesh, Egypt, and Indonesia and in Catholic countries such as Colombia and Mexico.[115] Demographers attribute the change to a combination of events: economic crisis, television, and contraceptives. In Mexico, declining fertility rates were closely associated with economic crisis, falling from 6.5 births per women just before the onset of the debt crisis in 1980 to 3 births per woman in 1995.[116] "Small families live better," Gloria Munoz Castro said, explaining her decision to stop reproducing after having two children. "We didn't want to spend all our money just to feed and clothe children." Her sister-in-law concurred, saying she would not have any children because "food is expensive, the oil is running out, water is scarce. The future's just too bleak."[117]

The general decline in fertility rates reflects this economic assessment. In one survey, nearly one-half of all Mexican households decided "to stop or postpone having children" between 1982 and 1988.[118] Demographers studying the rapid decline of fertility rates in Brazil, which "has experienced the largest self-induced drop in human history," have argued that women reduced family size because their incomes declined (largely as a result of the debt crisis) at a time when their economic expectations rose (largely as a result of watching TV).[119] They were able to have fewer children because they began using contraceptives or had themselves sterilized. To get more with less, women have, in effect, downsized their immediate families by having fewer children, this despite opposition from the Catholic Church and the absence of any family planning programs sponsored by the government.[120]

Debt Bondage

For the very poorest workers, debt may not only mean cutting back on consumption or family size, it may also mean entering into debt bondage or slavery. When extremely poor households in Bolivia, Brazil, India, or Thailand lose a crop or a job and face ruin and starvation, they can sometimes borrow money to stave off extinction. But because they have no assets or credit, they can only borrow under extremely disadvantageous and onerous conditions. Lenders typically require children, adults, or entire families to work in charcoal furnaces, brick foundries, carpet factories, or brothels until their debts are repaid.[121] Social scientist Kevin Bales estimated that twenty-seven million people worldwide are "enslaved," most of them by debt.[122] In India, for example, between three hundred thousand and one million children, who work twelve to sixteen hours a day, are held captive in carpet factories to repay household debts.[123] Because lender-owners keep the accounts and refuse to let illiterate workers or borrowers review them, they can keep the children in thrall until they are no longer useful. Unlike slavery in the colonial era, workers today are not enslaved for life but are instead discarded when their productivity declines.[124] This practice is particularly evident in industries where children and young girls are held in debt bondage, in carpet factories and sex industry brothels.

Migration

Across the South, tens of millions of workers are persuaded by falling commodity prices, deindustrialization, and the expansion of enclave manufacturing and tourism to migrate in search of work. The overwhelming majority of migrants moved from rural to urban settings *within* the same country. There are seventy to one hundred million workers who annually migrate within China.[125] A small number moved in the opposite direction, from fertile agricultural areas to remote marginal lands: the Amazon in Brazil; the mountain jungles in Peru and Central America; desert fringe areas in the Sahel; interior jungles in Central Africa; remote islands in the Indonesian archipelago.[126] There they practice swidden agriculture and subsistence farming, mining, or forestry. Of those who moved from rural to urban areas, a small percentage migrated across international borders, seeking work in the North. If they evaded capture and deportation and found work, they typically sent money to family members back home.

Contrary to popular belief, immigration has provided important economic benefits to countries in the North. A 1997 National Academy of Science study found that immigration added "perhaps $10 billion a year to the U.S. economy."[127] But perhaps more significantly, migrant worker remittances provided a vital source of income for households and governments, which benefited from hard-currency inflows. Indeed, migrant worker remittances may have been one of the very few ways that have actually promoted real development. In some countries—the Philippines, Cuba, Vietnam—migrant workers provided *more* money for investment than TNCs, Western banks, and the World Bank *combined*.[128] Unlike the investments and loans made by Western businesses and banks, the money sent by workers goes directly to households, who use the money carefully. A good example is provided by migrants from Chinantlan, Mexico.

In 1945, two brothers from Chinantlan hitchhiked to New York City, where they found jobs mopping floors.[129] Pedro and Fermin Simion established a base there for other relatives, who traveled singly or in groups to join them in New York over the next fifty years. There they helped each other find work, shared apartments, pooled income, and, importantly, sent money home. They tithed a portion of their earnings and formed a committee to raise money for specific development projects in Chinantlan. They bought bricks for the town square and spent $100,000 for a new potable water system. "Our priority is to give this little town its most basic needs," explained Abel Alonso, the New York committee's president. By the late 1990s, the New York–based migrant community sent Chinantlan $2 million each year, and its leaders functioned like a government-in-exile. "We have no other source of income besides New York," Chinantlan's mayor Dr. Francisco R. Calixto explained.

The migrants returned regularly to the town for vacations and holiday celebrations, and many built homes and retired there. Their Social Security checks and pensions provided an ongoing source of hard currency for the local economy and helped create jobs in local small businesses. Could the World Bank, U.S. corporations, or the indebted Mexican state have done as much for the development of this small town? They could have, but they did not ever try.

SELECTIVE GLOBALIZATION

People in the South adopted different strategies they hoped would promote economic development and close the yawning gap between rich and poor countries. But they have repeatedly failed, and the distance between countries in the South and North has widened. Some government officials and scholars have hoped that "globalization," the neoliberal policies adopted by most governments in the 1980s and 1990s would promote development. But it is unlikely to do so because economic growth requires, at a minimum, substantial private or public investment. For most poor countries, this investment will not be forthcoming.

During the 1950s and 1960s, the South received some private investment and public aid from the North. In 1960, about 32 percent of all foreign investment flowed into southern economies.[130] But notice that the bulk of global invest ment—68 percent—was invested in the North. Of the money invested in the South, much of it was concentrated in only a few states. The $18.6 billion invested by the United States in South Korea and Taiwan between 1962 and 1978 was *greater* than U.S. investment and aid to *all* of Africa ($6.89 billion) and India ($9.6 billion) or to *all* of Latin America ($14.8 billion).[131] Still, with relatively few external resources, many poor countries managed to construct domestic manufacturing industries that provided jobs for urban male workers and produced goods for domestic markets.

Then in the 1970s, poor countries received a boost from two sources. First, they receive a massive influx of money in the form of loans. Second, commodity prices rose, raising their incomes substantially. The money from loans and the income from high commodity prices provided jobs, increased wages, and provided substantial benefits to workers and governments for the first time in the postwar period. But it did not last. Deflationary policies in the North increased the cost of borrowed money. And the expansion of commodity production by countries in the South, often at the behest of the IMF and World Bank, created gluts, which forced down prices. The crisis that ensued has not yet been ameliorated. The debts owed by governments in the South continue to mount—debt doubled from $639 billion in 1980 to $1,341 billion in 1990—while their income from commodities continued to fall.

During the 1980s and 1990s, governments across the globe opened their economies, sold public assets, and cut military spending. These neoliberal "globalization" policies were supposed to stimulate investment and promote growth. But they could work only if investment was made. It seemed a promising strategy because there was a lot of money available in Eurodollar markets, corporate accounts, development agencies, and government aid programs. Open-door policies in the South made it easier for these institutions to invest in or assist poor countries. The trouble for the South was that global investors have been extremely selective. They have been selective in three ways.

First, the bulk of global investment finances economic development in the North. And the percentage is increasing. The North received 67.3 percent of direct investment available worldwide in 1960, but it received 75.5 percent in 1983 and 83.1 percent in 1989.[132] Whereas Western Europe and Japan were the chief beneficiaries of investment and aid in the 1950s and 1960s, the United States is now the major beneficiary of global investment flows, which is one important reason why it has improved its competitiveness and grown in recent years.[133] Although most of this money comes from Western Europe and Japan, a substantial amount comes from the South in the form of capital flight. Domestic investors in Latin America, for example, have invested more than $300 billion in the core, most of it in the United States.[134] In many cases, the measures designed to facilitate the *import* of capital into southern countries has actually made it easier for capital to *exit*. In this way, the undeveloped South contributes to the improvement of the already-developed North.

Second, while some investment has been made in the South, the percentage is diminishing. This investment, too, has been selective. Most of it has gone to China. In 1996, China received $42 billion in foreign investment.[135] While that was a huge sum, keep in mind that this would not pay the cost of installing a telephone in every house in China. But this sum dwarfs investment elsewhere in the South. In the same year, Mexico received $6 billion worth of investment, and India, with nearly one billion people, received only $3 billion.[136]

Third, when money from global financial pools trickles into peripheral economies, it is concentrated in enclaves, in the export manufacturing and tourist industries. Although this investment creates some jobs for women, it creates more jobs and larger revenues for the TNCs that organize and monopolize manufacturing and tourism in the South. Workers and states in the South have vast needs. But they should not expect that their economic development will be assisted by global investors, whose selective patterns of investment deny them what they require. When they "globalized" their economies, they expected some economic reward. But economic rewards have not been forthcoming.

The investment that has been available globally has not been distributed widely. It has instead been distributed selectively. As such, it is more appropriate to describe contemporary change as a process of "selective globalization," which contributes to *diverging* economic circumstances, *not* converging economic fortunes, as many theorists of contemporary "globalization" suggest.[137]

Of course, development in the capitalist world economy has always been "selective," contributing to the diverging fortunes of North and South. Colonialism was the primary form of globalization for several centuries. After World War II, the cold war and *neo*colonialism defined the shape of globalization. Since the onset of the debt crisis and the end of the cold war, globalization has taken a new form, which can be described as "selective globalization."

Contemporary global change has *not* united the world economically. It has integrated Japan, North America, and Western Europe and linked them with some manufacturing and commodity-producing enclaves in the South. But it has also *detached* the North from much of the South. For centuries, Western states conquered, colonized, and compelled slaves, servants, and workers in the South to furnish them with raw material, agricultural products, and industrial goods they desired. Until recently, the West needed to exercise its political and military authority—what was called "imperialism"—to compel workers and, after decolonization, compel governments to furnish the goods that they required. But this relationship has fundamentally changed.

The introduction of new technologies means that the North no longer needs many products from the South. In fact, the North requires fewer and fewer goods from the South. Economically, this means that the North has little incentive to invest in the South, except where essential goods are still produced, manufactured, or procured or where profitable markets for northern goods still exist. These markets are hard to find because consumers in the periphery are generally poor. TNCs would much rather invest in the expansion of markets in the North, where they can access consumers with credit cards, than consumers in the South, where their meager earnings are held in depreciating currencies. TNCs would rather sell expensive running shoes to the twenty million U.S. schoolchildren with allowance money in their pockets than furnish inexpensive shoes to every person living in Africa.

Politically, this means that government officials in the North can view economic and political events in the postcolonial South with increasing detachment and relative indifference. Except under exceptional circumstances, Western governments are no longer willing to invest or intervene in the South to secure their geopolitical interests. The North's declining economic and political interest in the South has resulted in what may be called "indifferent imperialism."[138] Governments in the North are still sometimes willing to exercise their political and military power where their vital interests are threatened, as they did in Iraq in 1990–1991 or in Afghanistan in 2001, but most of the South hardly matters at all.

This point has important implications for theories of "development." I agree with Peter Drucker, who has argued, "For if primary products are becoming of marginal importance to the economies of the developed world, traditional development theories and policies are losing their foundations."[139] From this perspective, globalization is not simply the latest model of development for the world at large. It is the *end* of development, in the traditional sense, for much of the world.

NOTES

1. John T. Passe-Smith, "The Persistence of the Gap between Rich and Poor Countries: Taking Stock of World Economic Growth, 1960–1993," in *Development and Underdevelopment: The Political Economy of Global Inequality*, ed. Mitchell A. Seligson and John T. Passe-Smith (Boulder, Colo.: Rienner, 1998), 33. This area has been called the "Third World" but also the "developing" world and, more recently, the "emerging" world. But whatever it is called, "The great majority of developing countries depend for their welfare and livelihood on the production and export of primary commodities." Alfred Maizels, *Commodities in Crisis: The Commodity Crisis of the 1980s and the Political Economy of International Commodity Prices* (Oxford: Clarendon, 1993), 1.

2. Deniz Kandiyoti, *Women in Rural Production Systems: Problems and Policies* (Paris: United Nations Education, Scientific and Cultural Organization, 1985), 62.

3. Maizels, *Commodities in Crisis*, 105–6.

4. Duncan Green, *Silent Revolution: The Rise of Market Economies in Latin America* (London: Cassell, 1995), 16–17.

5. Barbar Dinham and Colin Hines, *Agribusiness in Africa* (London: Earth Resources Research, 1983), 56, 72.

6. Lester Brown, *State of the World, 1984* (New York: Norton, 1984), 43–44.

7. Kenneth L. Peoples, David Freshwater, Gregory D. Hanson, Paul T. Prentice, and Eric P. Thor, *Anatomy of an American Agricultural Credit Crisis: Farm Debt in the 1980s* (Washington, D.C.: Farm Credit Assistance Board, 1992), 23.

8. Barbar Stallings, *Banker to the World: U.S. Portfolio Investment in Latin America, 1900–1986* (Berkeley: University of California Press, 1987), 298; Sue Brandford and Benardo Kucinski, *The Debt Squads: The U.S., the Banks and Latin America* (London: Zed Books, 1988), 58.

9. Robert Schaeffer, *Power to the People: Democratization around the World* (Boulder, Colo.: Westview, 1997), 88.

10. Robert K. Schaeffer, "Success and Impasse: The Environmental Movement in the United States and Around the World," in *Ecology and the World-System*, eds. Walter L. Goldfrank, David Goodman, and Andrew Szasz (Westport, Conn.: Greenwood, 1999), 201.

11. William C. Smith, *Authoritarianism and the Crisis of the Argentine Political Economy* (Stanford, Calif.: Stanford University Press, 1989), 259; Ewrnst J. Olivari, *Latin American Debt and the Politics of International Finance* (Westport, Conn.: Praeger, 1989), 8–9.

12. Robert K. Schaeffer, "Technology and Work in the Third World," in *Research in the Sociology of Work. Volume 6: The Globalization of Work,* ed. Randy Hodson (Greenwich, Conn.: JAI, 1997), 76.

13. Maizels, *Commodities in Crisis,* 17.

14. Juan Forero, "The Caprice of Coffee: World Glut Takes Toll on Latin American Economy," *New York Times,* November 8, 2001.

15. Michael Wines and Sabrina Tavernise, "Russian Oil Production Soars, for Better and Worse," *New York Times,* November 21, 2001.

16. David Gonzalez, "A Coffee Crisis' Devastating Domino Effect in Nicaragua," *New York Times,* August 29, 2001.

17. Maizels, *Commodities in Crisis,*15.

18. David Goodman, Bernardo Sorj, and John Wilkinson, *From Farming to Biotechnology: A Theory of Argo-Industrial Development* (London: Blackwell, 1987), 2–4, 580.

19. H. Guyford Stever and Janet H. Muroyama, "Overview," in *Globalization of Technology,* eds. Janet H. Muroyama and H. Guyford Stever (Washington, D.C.: National Academy Press, 1988), 5.

20. Umberto Colombo, "The Technology Revolution and the Global Economy," in *Globalization of Technology,* 26.

21. Niels Thygesen, Yutaka Kosai, and Robert Z. Lawrence, *Globalization and Trilateral Labor Markets: Evidence and Implications* (New York: Trilateral Commission, 1996), 85.

22. Schaeffer, "Technology and Work in the Third World," 78–79.

23. Schaeffer, "Technology and Work in the Third World," 79.

24. Seth Shiesel, "Fiber Optic Cable Demand Outstrips Supply," *New York Times,* November 4, 1996.

25. Schaeffer, "Technology and Work in the Third World," 80–81.

26. Jonathan Fuerbringer, "An Icon's Fading Glory," *New York Times,* June 15, 1999.

27. Fuerbringer, "An Icon's Fading Glory."

28. Niall Ferguson, *The Cash Nexus: Money and Power in the Modern World, 1700–2000* (New York: Basic Books, 2001), 326.

29. Donald G. McNeil, Jr., "As Britain Sells Some Gold, South Africa Howls," *New York Times,* July 7, 1999.

30. Robert J. Samuelson, "The Trouble with Steak," *Newsweek,* April 7, 1997.

31. See Michael Barratt Brown and Pauline Tiffen, *Short Changed: Africa and World Trade* (London: Pluto, 1992), 32.

32. Brown and Tiffen, *Short Changed.*

33. A. Pitotrowski, "Sugar-Free Gum: A Success Story," in *Sugarless—Towards the Year 2000,* ed. Andrew J. Rugg-Gunn (Cambridge: Royal Society of Chemistry, 1994), 184–91.

34. Jonathan Fuerbringer, "Swamped by Asia's Wake," *New York Times,* July 11, 1998; Alfred Maizels, Robert Bacon, and George Mavrotas, *Commodity Supply Management by Producing Countries: A Case-Study of the Tropical Beverage Crops* (Oxford: Clarendon, 1997), 8; Fuerbringer, "An Icon's Fading Glory"; Jonathan Fuerbringer, "Commodities' Price Slide Victimizes Economies of Several Nations," *New York Times,* December 11, 1998; Jonathan Feurbringer, "No Refuge in Plunging Commodity Prices," *New York Times,* August 28, 1998.

35. Maizels, *Commodities in Crisis*, 27–29.

36. Calestous Juma, *The Gene Hunters: Biotechnology and the Scramble for Seeds* (Princeton, N.J.: Princeton University Press, 1989), 143.

37. James G. Brown, *The International Sugar Industry: Developments and Prospects*, World Bank Staff Commodity Working Paper 48 (Washington, D.C.: World Bank, 1987), 2; Simon Romero, "Spoonfuls of Hope, Tons of Pain," *New York Times*, May 21, 2000.

38. G. Hawes, *The Philippine State and the Marcos Regime: The Politics of Export* (Ithaca, N.Y.: Cornell University Press, 1987), 85; Michael Redclift and David Goodman, "The Machinery of Hunger: The Crisis of Latin American Food Systems," in *Environment and Development in Latin America: The Politics of Sustainability*, eds. David Goodman and Michael Redclift (Manchester: Manchester University Press, 1991), 66; Maizels, *Commodities in Crisis*, 38.

39. Henk Hobbelink, *Biotechnology and the Future of World Agriculture: The Fourth Resource* (London: Zed, 1991), 74; Frederick Claimonte and John Cavanagh, *Merchants of Drink* (Penang, Malaysia: Third World Network, 1988), 167.

40. Food and Agricultural Organization, *Agricultural Raw Materials: Competition with Synthetic Substitutes*, FAO Economic and Social Development Paper 48 (Rome: Author, 1984), 7.

41. Juma, *The Gene Hunters*; Suzanne Daley, "Vanilla Farming? Not as Bland as You Might Think," *New York Times*, January 19, 1998.

42. Clifford Krauss, "Pinching Pennies in a Land of Copper," *New York Times*, December 21, 1998.

43. Donald G. McNeil, Jr., "Gold Breaks Its Promise to Miners of Lesotho," *New York Times*, June 16, 1998; Rachel L. Swarns, "A Bleak Hour for South Africa Miners," *New York Times*, October 10, 1999.

44. Agis Salpukas, "Roughnecks of Distinction," *New York Times*, July 8, 1998.

45. Allen R. Meyerson, "Soft Oil Prices Take Their Toll on Wildcatters," *New York Times*, January 2, 1999; Agis Salpukas, "Refining Entrepreneurship," *New York Times*, June 9, 1998.

46. Lynne Brydon and Sylvia Chant,*Women in the Third World: Gender Issues in Rural and Urban Areas* (New Brunswick, N.J.: Rutgers University Press, 1989), 69.

47. Larry Rohter, "Where Banana Is King: A Land Revolt," *New York Times*, July 22, 1996; Larry Rohter, "Trade Storm Imperils Caribbean Banana Crops," *New York Times*, May 9, 1997.

48. Douglas Jehl, "For Ordinary Saudis, Days of Oil and Roses Are Over," *New York Times*, March 20, 1999.

49. Douglas Jehl, "Where Oil Is Plentiful but Cash Is Short," *New York Times*, January 16, 1999.

50. Jonathan Fuerbringer, "Swamped by Asia's Wake," *New York Times*, July 11, 1998; Sam Dillon, "Loss of 3,000 Mexican Steel Jobs Has an Asian Connection," *New York Times*, July 28, 1998.

51. Schaeffer, "Technology and Work in the Third World," 205.

52. Fuerbringer, "Swamped by Asia's Wake."

53. Schaeffer, "Technology and Work in the Third World," 218–45.

54. Green, *Silent Revolution*, 138–39.

55. Dillon, "Loss of 3,000 Mexican Steel Jobs"; Bill Orr, *The Global Economy in the 90s: A User's Guide* (New York: New York University Press, 1992), 83.

56. Charlotta Gall, "Free Market's Assembly Line Carries Hard Choices," *New York Times*, October 8, 2001.

57. Green, *Silent Revolution*, 95; Philip McMichael, *Development and Social Change: A Global Perspective* (Thousand Oaks, Calif.: Pine Forge, 1996), 130; Robert Cohen, "Argentina Sees Other Face of Globalization," *New York Times*, February 6, 1998.

58. Reana Jhabvala, "Self-Employed Women's Association: Organising Women by Struggle and Development," in *Dignity and Daily Bread: New Forms of Economic Organizing among Poor Women in the Third World and the First*, ed. Sheila Rowbotham and Swasti Mitter (London: Routledge, 1994), 142.

59. Green, *Silent Revolution*, 72.

60. Andre Gunder Frank, "Soviet and Eastern European 'Socialism': What Went Wrong?" in *Regimes in Crisis: The Post-Soviet Era and the Implications for Development*, eds. Barry Gills and Shahid Qadir (London: Zed, 1995), 105.

61. Frank, "Soviet and Eastern European 'Socialism,'" 105.

62. Cohen, "Argentina Sees Other Face of Globalization."

63. Cohen, "Argentina Sees Other Face of Globalization."

64. A. F. Mullins, Jr., *Born Arming: Development and Military Power in New States* (Stanford, Calif.: Stanford University Press, 1987), 103.

65. Jenne Vickers, *Women and the World Economic Crisis* (London: Zed, 1991), passim.

66. Faruk Tabak, "The World Labour Force," in *The Age of Transition: Trajectory of the World-System, 1945–2025*, eds. Terence K. Hopkins and Immanuel Wallerstein (London: Zed, 1996), 111.

67. Calvin Sims, "A Saint Besieged: Heavan Knows, Many Need Help," *New York Times*, August 8, 1997; Diana Jean Schemo, "Economic Detour in Brazil," *New York Times*, September 26, 1998.

68. Sims, "A Saint Besieged"; Schemo, "Economic Detour in Brazil."

69. Susan Tiano, *Patriarchy on the Line: Labor, Gender, and Ideology in the Mexican Maquila Industry* (Philadelphia: Temple University Press, 1994), 19; Ira C. Magaziner and Mark Patinkin, *The Silent War: Inside the Global Business Battles Shaping America's Future* (New York: Vintage, 1990), 319–20.

70. Jorge A. Bustamente, "Maquiladoras: A New Face of International Capitalism on Mexico's Northern Frontier," in *Women, Men, and the International Division of Labor*, ed. June Nash and Maria Patricia Fernandez-Kelly (Albany: State University of New York Press, 1983), 241; Enrique Martin Del Campo, "The Case of the American Hemisphere," in *Globalization of Technology*, 95; Patricia A. Wilson, *Exports and Local Development: Mexico's New Maquiladoras* (Austin: University of Texas Press, 1992), 43; Maria Patricia Fernandez-Kelly, "Broadening the Scope: Gender and the Study of International Development," in *Comparative National Development: Society and Economy in the New Global Order*, eds. A. Douglas Kincaid and Alejandro Portes (Chapel Hill: University of North Carolina Press, 1994), 157.

71. Magaziner and Patinkin, *The Silent War*, 322.

72. Tiano, *Patriarchy on the Line*, 24.

73. Tiano, *Patriarchy on the Line*.

74. Wilson, *Exports and Local Development*, 10; Linda Y. C. Lim, "Women's Work in Export Factories: The Politics of a Cause," in *Persistent Inequalities: Women and World Development*, ed. Irene Tinker (Oxford: Oxford University Press, 1990), 101.

75. Wilson, *Exports and Local Development*, 10; Lim, "Women's Work in Export Factories," 101.

76. Helen I. Safa and Peggy Antrobus, "Women and the Economic Crisis in the Caribbean," in *Unequal Burden: Economic Crises, Persistent Poverty, and Women's Work*, ed. Lourdes Beneria and Shelley Feldman (Boulder, Colo.: Westview, 1992), 63.

77. Emilio Carillo Gamboa, "Globalization of Industry through Production Sharing," in *Globalization of Technology*, 97.

78. Kamudhini Rosa, "The Conditions and Organisational Activities of Women in Free Trade Zones: Malaysia, Philippines and Sri Lanka, 1970–1990," in *Dignity and Daily Bread*, 80.

79. Diane L. Wolf, *Factory Daughters: Gender, Households Dynamics, and Rural Industrialization in Java* (Berkeley: University of California Press, 1992), 180.

80. David Harrison, "Tourism, Capitalism and Development in Less Developed Countries," in *Capitalism and Development*, ed. Leslie Sklair (London: Routledge, 1994), 238; Diane E. Levy and Patricia B. Lerch, "Tourism as a Factor in Development: Implications for Gender and Work in Barbados," *Gender and Society* 5, no. 1 (March 1991): 69.

81. Barbara Crossette, "Surprises in the Global Tourism Boom," *New York Times* April 12, 1998.

82. Crossette, "Surprises in the Global Tourism Boom."

83. Harrison, "Tourism, Capitalism and Development," 233.

84. Harrison, "Tourism, Capitalism and Development," 241.

85. Harrison, "Tourism, Capitalism and Development," 242.

86. Sipiporn Skrobanek, Nataya Boonpakdee, and Chutima Jantateero, *The Traffic in Women: Human Realities of the International Sex Trade* (London: Zed, 1997).

87. Emek M. Ucarer, "Trafficking in Women: Alternate Migration or Modern Slave Trade?" in. *Gender Politics in Global Governance*, eds. Mary K. Meyer and Elisabeth Prugl (Lanham, Md.: Rowman & Littlefield, 1999), 230–31; Philip Shenon, "Feminist Coalition Protests U.S. Stance on Sex Trafficking Treaty," *New York Times*, January 13, 2000.

88. Skrobanek et al., *The Traffic in Women*.

89. Alison Murray, "Debt-Bondage and Trafficking: Don't Believe the Hype," in *Global Sex Workers: Rights, Resistance, and Redefinition*, eds. Kamala Kempadoo and Jo Doezema (New York: Routledge, 1998), 52–56.

90. Marina Budhos, "Putting the Heat on Sex Tourism," *Ms. Magazine*, March 1997, 10; Andrew Sherry, "For Lust or Money," *Far Eastern Economic Review*, December 14, 1995, 23.

91. Sherry, "For Lust or Money," 12; Elizabeth Olson, "U.N. Urges Fiscal Accounting Include Sex Trade," *New York Times*, August 20, 1998.

92. Skrobanek et al., *The Traffic in Women*, 66.

93. Cynthia Enloe, *Bananas, Beaches and Bases: Making Feminist Sense of International Politics* (Berkeley: University of California, 1989), 66.

94. Edward A. Gargan, "Traffic in Children is Brisk (Legacy of the Navy?)" *New York Times*, December 11, 1997.

95. Enloe, *Bananas, Beaches and Bases*, 86–87.

96. Calvin Sims, "A Hard Life for Amerasian Children," *New York Times*, July 23, 2000.

97. Sims, "A Hard Life for Amerasian Children."

98. Skrobanek et al., *The Traffic in Women*, 8.

99. Skrobanek et al., *The Traffic in Women*, 57; Enloe, *Bananas, Beaches and Bases*, 35–36; Kamala Kempadoo, "Introduction: Globalizing Sex Worker's Rights," in *Global Sex Workers*, 6.

100. Julia O'Connell Davidson and Jacqueline Sanchez Taylor, "Fantasy Islands: Exploring the Demand for Sex Tourism," in *Global Sex Workers*, 37.

101. Skrobanek et al., *The Traffic in Women*, 14; Kempadoo, "Introduction: Globalizing Sex Worker's Rights," 4.

102. Beverly Mullings, "Globalization, Tourism, and the International Sex Trade," in *Global Sex Workers*, 60.

103. Mullings, "Globalization, Tourism, and the International Sex Trade," 62.

104. Mullings, "Globalization, Tourism, and the International Sex Trade," 66.

105. Mullings, "Globalization, Tourism, and the International Sex Trade," 66–67.

106. Kamala Kempadoo, "Continuities and Change: Five Centuries of Prostitution in the Caribbean," in *Global Sex Workers*, 15.

107. Carlotta Gall, "Macedonia Village Is Center of Europe Web in Sex Trade," *New York Times*, July 28, 2001.

108. Barbara Crossette, "In India and Africa, Women's Low Status Worsens Their Risk of AIDS," *New York Times*, February 26, 2001.

109. Aili Mari Tripp, "The Impact of Crisis and Economic Reform on Women in Urban Tanzania," in *Unequal Burden*, 164.

110. Green, *Silent Revolution*, 91; Hazel J. Johnson, *Dispelling the Myth of Globalization: The Case for Regionalization* (New York: Praeger, 1991), 2; Of course, rates of poverty vary considerably, from 22 percent in Costa Rica to 77.5 percent in Guatemala. Patricia Baeza, "Introduction," in *The Power to Change: Women in the Third World Redefine their Environment*, ed. Women's Feature Service (London: Zed, 1992), 2.

111. John F. Burns, "India's Five Decades of Progress and Pain," *New York Times*, August 14, 1997.

112. Sam Dillon, "Peso Crisis Bites Into Mexico's Long-Ruling Party," *New York Times*, July 4, 1997.

113. Larry Rohter, "Once More, Barzilians Tighten Belts for a Rough Ride," *New York Times*, February 14, 1999.

114. Anthony De Palma, "In Mexico, Hunger and Woe in Crisis," *New York Times*, January 15, 1995; William K. Stevens, "3d-World Gains in Birth Control: Development Isn't Only Answer," *New York Times*, January 2, 1994.

115. De Palma, "In Mexico, Hunger and Woe in Crisis"; Stevens, "3d-World Gains in Birth Control."

116. Sam Dillon, "Smaller Families to Bring Big Change in Mexico," *New York Times*, June 8, 1999.

117. Dillon, "Smaller Families."

118. Lourdes Beneria, "The Mexican Debt Crisis: Restructuring the Economy and the Household," in *Unequal Burden*, 94.

119. "Latin America's Birth Surprise," *New York Times*, June 13, 1999.

120. James Brooke, "Births in Brazil Are on Decline, Easing Worries," *New York Times*, August 8, 1989; Amartya Sen, "Populations: Delusion and Reality," *New York Review of Books*, September 22, 1994, 70.

121. Clifford Krauss, "When Even an Economic Miracle Isn't Enough," *New York Times*, July 12, 1998.

122. Kevin Bales, *Disposable People: New Slavery in the Global Economy* (Berkeley: University of California, 1999), 23.

123. Bales, *Disposable People*, 23.

124. Bales, *Disposable People*, 15.

125. Ann Tyson and James Tyson, "China's Human Avalanche," *Current History*, September 1996, 277.

126. Seth Mydans, "Indonesia Resettles People to Relieve Crowding on Java," *New York Times*, August 25, 1996.

127. Robert Pear, "Academy's Report Says Immigration Benefits the United States," *New York Times*, May 18, 1997.

128. Safa and Antrobus, "Women and the Economic Crisis in the Caribbean," 72.

129. Deborah Sontag, "A Mexican Town That Transcends All Borders," *New York Times*, July 21, 1998.

130. Arthur S. Alderson, "Globalization and Deindustrialization: Direct Investment and the Decline of Manufacturing Employment in 17 OECD Nations," *Journal of World-Systems Research* 3, no. 1 (1997): 5.

131. Bruce Cumings, "The Northeast Asian Political Economy," in *The Political Economy of the New Asian Industrialism*, ed. Frederic C. Deyo (Ithaca, N.Y.: Cornell University Press, 1987), 67.

132. Torry D. Dickinson, "Selective Globalization: The Relocation of Industrial Production and the Shaping of Women's Work," in *Research in the Sociology of Work, Volume 6: The Globalization of Work*, ed. Randy Hodson (Greenwich, Conn.: JAI, 1997), 118; Alderson, "Globalization and Deindustrialization," 5; Priyatosh Maitra, *The Globalization of Capitalism in Third World Countries* (Westport, Conn.: Praeger, 1996), 93.

133. Satoshi Ikeda, "World Production," in *The Age of Transition*, 46.

134. Chander Kant, *Foreign Direct Investment and Capital Flight*, Princeton Studies in International Finance, No. 80 (Princeton, N.J.: Princeton University Press, April 1996), 1; Christel Lane, *Industry and Society in Europe: Stability and Change in Britain, Germany, and France* (Aldershot, U.K.: Elgar, 1995), 85.

135. David E. Sanger, "Study Shows Jump in Investing in China and Revival in Mexico," *New York Times*, March 24, 1997.

136. Sanger, "Study Shows Jump"; Burns, "India's Five Decades of Progress and Pain."

137. Dickinson, "Selective Globalization," 124. See William Greider, *One World, Ready or Not: The Manic Logic of Global Capitalism* (New York: Simon & Schuster, 1997), passim. Brazil in 1999 received foreign investments worth about $26 billion. Simon Romero, "Carrying the Flag for Free Trade," *New York Times*, December 2, 1999.

138. Robert K. Schaeffer, "Free Trade Agreements: Their Impact on Agriculture and the Environment," in *Food and Agrarian Orders in the World-Economy*, ed. Philip McMichael (Westport, Conn.: Praeger, 1995), 267.

139. Peter F. Drucker, "The Changed World Economy," *Foreign Affairs* (Spring 1986): 774–75; N. Peritore, "Biotechnology: Political Economy and Environmental Impacts," in *Biotechnology in Latin America: Politics, Impacts, and Risks*, ed. N.Peritore and A. K. Golve-Peritore (Wilmington, Del.: SR Books, 1995), 20–21.

7

Technology, Food, and Hunger

During the past century, successive technological revolutions have increased food supplies in the United States and around the world. But while agricultural technologies have increased world food production, which has grown even faster than world population, they have also displaced U.S. farmers and contributed to hunger around the world.

Agricultural revolutions in the United States raised farm costs and lowered the prices farmers earned for their crops. These developments forced millions of farmers off the land, with important consequences for rural communities, urban consumers, and the environment. In the South, the introduction of agricultural technologies greatly increased the volume of food produced. But because technology was typically used to grow crops for export and for animal feed, it displaced staple crops and small farmers, contributing to widespread hunger. The irony is that growing food supplies and gnawing hunger go hand in hand in the modern world. In this chapter, we will examine the social and environmental problems associated with technological change in agricultural settings, first in the United States, and then around the world.

TECHNOLOGICAL REVOLUTIONS

Three technological revolutions in agriculture have occurred during the past century, and we are on the verge of a fourth. The first began in the 1920s, with the introduction of tractors and soybeans. The second got under way in the 1940s, with the introduction of chemical fertilizers and pesticides, hybrid seeds, animal antibiotics, and government-supplied power and water, all elements of what came to be known as the "Green Revolution." The introduction of Green Revolution technologies began in the United States. The introduction and adoption of these technologies by farmers around the world resulted in a third agricultural revolution during the 1960s and 1970s. A fourth revolution, which is associated with the introduction of new biological and genetic technologies, is just now getting under way.

Each of these technological revolutions transformed agriculture and increased food production. The first revolution began in the 1920s, at a time when seven million family farmers worked the land, using horses for traction. The typical 150-acre farm planted 50 acres of corn or wheat, grew another 50 acres of oats to feed the horses, and kept 50 acres in pasture to rest the land, though farmers grazed their beef or dairy cattle on this fallow pasture.[1] The arrival in the United States of immigrants from Europe, Latin America, and Asia swelled the population and kept the demand for farm products strong and prices high. Indeed, the prices farmers received were as high as at any time during this century. Because their expenses for land, horses, and housing were low and stable, and prices were high—wheat sold for $100 a ton and corn for $76 a ton—farmers could support their families and foster vibrant rural communities nearby.[2]

Although farm supplies fluctuated annually, depending on the weather, the relation between supply and demand remained fairly close or balanced from the farmers' perspective. Moreover, the existence of millions of small farms supported local banks, small businesses, and neighborly towns across the country. But during the 1920s, the introduction of cheap tractors made by the emerging auto industry transformed U.S. agriculture, leading in the 1930s to glut and crisis.

In 1910, only 1,000 farmers used tractors. But by 1920, with earnings from high wartime food prices, farmers had purchased 250,000 tractors from Henry Ford and John Deere, and by 1930, 900,000 farmers owned the new, hardworking machines.[3] The introduction of tractors on the farm was important because it eliminated the need for horses and for the oats they consumed. Farmers could stop growing oats for horses and, instead, plant corn or soybeans. "As powered machinery replaced the horse, more land became available for cash crops," noted Peter Phillips, an agricultural economist.[4] In the 1920s and 1930s, many farmers began planting soybeans. Because this legume fixes nitrogen, it can be used in rotation with corn to replenish corn-depleted soil. And because its oils can be used in industry (for paints and varnishes), in food processing (for cooking oil and margarine), and in animal feed (its protein-rich residue can be fed to cows), soybeans often took over former oat fields.

These developments enabled farmers to increase the volume of food supplies enormously. In a sense, the widespread adoption of tractors and soybeans "was equivalent to the discovery and development of a new continent, of a new North America, in the 20th century," argues Jean-Pierre Berlan, an agricultural economist.[5]

The problem was that the new tractor-based agriculture produced huge supplies of food, leading to gluts and lower *prices*. Meanwhile, the cost of buying and maintaining the new machinery significantly increased *expenses* for farmers.

When industry in the United States and around the world laid off millions of workers during the Great Depression that followed the 1929 stock market crash, the demand for food weakened and agricultural prices fell. Wheat prices fell 20 percent, to $79 a ton, in the 1930s.[6] Under these conditions—mounting food supplies and falling demand, at a time when the cost of growing food was rising—many farmers could not earn enough money to survive. As they lost their ability to lease land or repay loans, they were forced to abandon their farms in droves. Perhaps 1.5 million farmers were driven out of farming as a result of the Depression, a process depicted in John Steinbeck's *The Grapes of Wrath*.[7]

Things for farmers might have been even worse if the drought of 1934–1936 had not also reduced supplies: "The calamitous years, which wiped out almost half the corn crop and a large segment of the wheat crop were, in their own peculiar way, an economic blessing since they restored the balance of supply and demand, a prerequisite for economic recovery. No government agricultural policy would have dared to do what the weather did."[8] The problems associated with this farm crisis were solved, temporarily, by the outbreak of World War II. Because the worldwide war disrupted or destroyed agricultural production in many countries, global food supplies fell. And because war-related industries hired millions of workers and the military drafted millions more into service, the demand for food greatly increased. As a result, prices rose to their highest level in the twentieth century. With wheat prices soaring to $122 a ton and corn to $94 a ton, "net farm income quadrupled, rising from $4.5 billion to $12.3 billion between 1940 and 1945."[9] U.S. farmers prospered.

After the war, U.S. agriculture was transformed by a second technological revolution. Whereas the introduction of the tractor spurred a substantial increase in food production in the 1920s and 1930s, new biological and chemical technologies greatly increased food supplies in the postwar period. The new hybrid seeds, chemical fertilizers, pesticides, and antibiotics, which were developed by government-sponsored research scientists and then produced and marketed by the emerging seed and agricultural chemical industries, dramatically improved crop yields and increased food supplies.[10] Together with the tractors and farm machinery developed during the earlier period, and the extension of government irrigation projects in the arid West and the provision of electrical power to rural communities, these technological innovations transformed agriculture, resulting in a series of changes known collectively as the "Green Revolution."

The Green Revolution enabled farmers to increase yields 2 percent per acre annually since 1948. They increased corn yields from 38.2 bushels an acre in 1930 to 118 bushels in 1985, soybeans from 21.7 to 34.1 bushels, and wheat from 16.5 to 37.5 bushels in the same period. Milk production per cow increased from 5,314 pounds in 1950 to 13,786 pounds in 1987.[11] The new technologies created food supplies equal to that produced by *another* North American continent.

The extension of U.S. Green Revolution technologies around the world created a *third* agricultural revolution. Farmers in Europe began adopting the new agrochemical technologies in the 1950s and 1960s. They were assisted in this effort by the European Community's Common Agricultural Program (CAP)—a government subsidy program designed to increase food supplies, promote free trade among member countries, and equalize food prices throughout Western Europe. By 1972, European farmers, assisted by new technologies and government subsidies, produced enough food to feed Europe without importing U.S. food, and were on the verge of creating regular surpluses. By 1985, they would export one-third of the food they grew.[12]

The diffusion of Green Revolution technologies in the South took hold more slowly. But by the 1980s, the new technologies began having an impact on food supplies. Aided by Green Revolution technologies, populous poor countries such as India, Pakistan, Indonesia, and China posted major increases in food supplies. India increased grain production by nearly 20 percent, from 131.15 million metric tons (mmt) in 1980 to 190.23 mmt in 1989.[13] China increased its grain harvest from 240 mmt in 1970 to 320 mmt in 1980, then to 407 mmt in 1984[14]; Indonesia from 33.65 mmt in 1980 to 49.11 mmt in 1989; Pakistan from 16.86 to 21.07 mmt in the same period.[15]

The advent of new genetic and electronic agricultural technologies in the 1980s and 1990s is resulting in a fourth revolution. Scientists using genetic engineering are splicing genes from one plant to another, creating "transgenic" products that can increase yields. Computerized mapping of soils and the use of satellites to position farm machinery allow farmers to work the land with greater precision.[16] Some scientists are also trying to use genetic material from wild and previously neglected local crop varieties to make popular varieties hardier and more productive.[17] Donald Plucknett, a science adviser to the Consultative Group on International Agricultural Research, conducted a 1993 study that found annual yields of grain rising sharply in the late twentieth century. "We all know that there is a biological limit to yield out there somewhere," said Plucknett. "But what surprised me in doing this research is that some of the highest-yielding countries don't seem to be close to it."[18]

Other scientists are dubious about these claims. Elaine Ingham, a plant pathologist at the University of Oregon, responded to the study by saying, "We can keep dumping fertilizer and chemicals on farmland but at what cost to the rest of the ecosystem? Long before we hit the maximum on crop productivity, we are going to have problems with clean water."[19]

As part of a fourth revolution, they may be a resurgence of food production in Russia in coming years. At the beginning of the twentieth century, Russia exported large quantities of grain. Under communism, food production faltered and the Soviet Union began importing food, particularly during the 1970s. But grain production has recently recovered. The privatization of land and new investment in agriculture may eventually increase production in the former Soviet Union. If it does, world food supplies could receive an important boost.[20]

FALLING PRICES, RISING COSTS, FAILING FARMERS

Successive agricultural revolutions greatly increased food supplies. New technologies enabled U.S. farmers to grow three times as much corn in 1985 as they had in the 1950s, probably five times as much as they could in 1920.[21] And because technology enabled farmers to convert land they had once rested in fallow or used to grow feed for horses, they could devote more of their land to corn (the largest crop in the United States) or wheat. In 1989, for example, U.S. farmers produced so much food (278.98 million tons of grain) that they could feed more than half of it to cows, export nearly one-third of it to other countries, and still have enough left over to produce cereal, toast, pasta, and corn chips for U.S. consumers at the lowest prices in the world.[22]

But while new technologies increased food supplies, they created a series of problems for farmers: falling prices, rising costs, and farm failures.

First, rising food supplies resulted in lower prices. In 1920, farmers earned $103 a ton for their wheat.[23] Rising supplies created by tractors and soybeans and falling demand during the Great Depression drove wheat prices down to $79 a ton. High demand during World War II boosted prices up to $122 a ton for wheat and $94 a ton for corn. But after the war, as Green Revolution technologies were introduced, prices fell slowly: to $95 a ton for wheat and $80 a ton for corn in 1954; to $65 a ton for wheat and $53 for corn in 1960; to $62 for wheat and $57 for corn in 1965; and to $54 for wheat and $46 for corn in 1972.

During the 1970s, prices rose again as a result of poor harvests and grain shortages in the Soviet Union, to $110 for wheat and $79 for corn in 1974.[24] But when Soviet agriculture recovered somewhat in the late 1970s, and farmers in the European Community and the South used Green Revolution technologies to expand their production, prices fell again, to $66 for wheat and $50 for corn in 1980, then to $50 for wheat and $46 for corn in 1984.[25] Expressed in a different way, real prices for wheat, coarse grains, and soybeans declined by one-half between 1945 and 1985.[26]

Falling prices were compounded by a second problem. The new technologies generally raised the *cost* of growing food. In 1940, it cost farmers about $20 billion to grow their crops. Their costs doubled during the next thirty years, to $40 billion in 1970. Then, during the 1970s, costs rose rapidly, reaching $60 billion in 1980, a 50 percent increase in just ten years.[27] Today it costs farmers three times as much to grow their crops as it did in 1940.

Farm costs doubled between 1940 and 1970 because farmers purchased new machinery and agrochemical technologies to increase production on their farms. Then, in the 1970s, they borrowed substantial sums of money to purchase land or buy new machinery and agrochemical technologies so they could grow and sell more food while prices were high. This sharply increased their costs again.

Whereas farmers, on average, drove thirty-five-horsepower tractors in 1963, they drove sixty-horsepower tractors in 1983.[28] Of course, more powerful tractors are more expensive to buy and maintain. The cost of machinery alone increased 40 percent between 1950 and 1980.[29] Farmers also greatly increased their use of agrochemical technologies, particularly chemical fertilizers and pesticides. Farmers used about two million tons of nitrogen fertilizer in 1950, but nearly twelve million tons in 1980, a sixfold increase, and their use of pesticides tripled between 1965 and 1985.[30] Because the cost of oil quadrupled between 1973 and 1980, the cost of operating tractors and applying oil-based fertilizers and pesticides increased sharply during the 1970s. And because farmers used about 50 percent more fertilizer to grow food and paid more for the fertilizer they used, their fertilizer costs rose from $1.6 billion in 1970 to $8.6 billion in 1981.[31]

Of course, technology was not wholly responsible for increasing the cost of growing food in this period. Farmers also borrowed money, not only to buy technology but to purchase land, especially after 1970. Rising debt sharply increased farmers' costs in the 1970s.

Between 1950 and 1970, farm debt—half of it borrowed to purchase technology and half of it to buy land—grew from $12 billion to $53 billion, a fourfold increase.[32] Then during the next twelve years, it quadrupled again, to $216 billion, a sum equal to the debt incurred by *all* of Latin America in this period.[33] And because the Federal Reserve raised interest rates to curb inflation in 1979, the cost of repaying debt increased sharply, raising the cost of producing food (see chapter 4).[34] Whereas farmers collectively devoted only 4 percent of their income to pay the interest on their debts in 1950, and 23 percent in 1970, they spent 75 percent of their income on interest payments in 1980 and 98.9 percent in 1982.[35]

Of course, some farmers borrowed more heavily than others. Generally speaking, young farmers, particularly in the midwestern corn and soy belt states, went heavily into debt.[36] Encouraged by high prices during the Soviet grain shortages of the mid-1970s, many farmers borrowed heavily to purchase land so they could expand production. They were encouraged to do so by bankers, who offered this same advice to both U.S. farmers and governments in the South. "The [Farmers Home Administration] almost hauled you in and stuffed money down your shirt," observed Michigan farmer Morie Kranz.[37]

Bankers were eager to lend money both because commodity prices were high and because the value of farm land was increasing. On average, the value of agricultural property escalated from $216 billion in 1970 to $754 billion in 1980, and an acre of farmland rose from $600 to nearly $1,200 during the decade.[38] Bankers felt confident lending money so long as the value of farmland—the collateral for their loans—was rising. But when farm prices began to fall, many farmers could not afford to meet rising interest payments and began to go bankrupt. To recoup their loans, bankers foreclosed and sold off farms. Because farmland was sold in large quantities, the price of land began to fall. As farmland prices fell, bankers became less willing to extend loans, and many farmers found it difficult to borrow the money they needed to survive.[39] Like the savings and loans during the same period (see chapter 4), many agricultural banks also failed: 79 in 1984, 120 in 1985, and 138 in 1986.[40] But a wholesale collapse of the farm credit industry did not occur because government agencies that also loaned money to farmers did not go bankrupt—though they did need a financial bailout to cover their losses during this period—so lending to farmers continued.[41]

Still, "one-fourth of all farm loans—$33.7 billion—from the Farmers Home Administration, federal land banks, production credit associations, commercial banks and life insurance companies were non-performing or delinquent in 1984 and 1985. The farm credit system lost $4.6 billion in 1985 and 1986."[42] As Kenneth Peoples, president of the Farm Credit Assistance Board, noted, "By the mid-1980s, there were from 200,000 to 300,000 farmers [one of every five commercial farms] who had exhausted their options to adjust to adversity and who failed financially. This is perhaps the outstanding statistic of the farm credit crisis."[43]

The falling prices and rising costs associated with the introduction of new technologies created a third problem for farmers: falling farm incomes. Between 1950 and 1990, farm incomes declined by half. Measured in constant 1990 dollars, net farm income declined from $80 billion in 1950 to $60 billion in 1970. Then it rose to $100 billion in 1974, before falling to $35 billion in 1980 and $20 billion in 1982. It then rose to $30 billion in 1985 and $40 billion in 1990, about one-half its 1950 level.[44]

As farm income declined, farmers were forced into bankruptcy and driven off the land. During the past sixty years, declining incomes drove the great majority of U.S. farmers out of business: "From a peak of 7 million farms in 1930, the number of farms declined to 6 million in 1945 and then to 5.6 million in 1950."[45] In 1970, only 2.9 million farms remained. By 1980, there were 2.2 million and by 1994, there were just 1.9 million, the lowest number since 1850.[46] All told, two-thirds of all U.S. farms have disappeared in the past sixty years. By 2000, there were only about 1.5 million farms left.[47]

The elimination of four or five million farms actually understates the case because the bulk of food produced in the United States is now grown by only 125,000 farmers, only a fraction (6 percent) of the "surviving" farmers.

Although the rate at which farms disappeared would slow over time—220,000 farms disappeared in 1951, 138,000 in 1961, and only 33,000 in

1983—farms in the 1980s were much bigger (about four hundred acres on average) than farms were in the 1950s (about two hundred acres on average).[48]

As farmers were driven off the land, surviving farmers purchased their land and expanded. Average farm size grew from two hundred acres in 1940 to nearly five hundred acres in 1990.[49] Large farmers increased their share of goods grown in the United States. As anthropologist Laura DeLind noted, "[In 1992], a mere 6 percent of all farms (less than 170,000 farms) account for 60 percent of the nation's commodity production and receive 84 percent of the net farm income."[50] A 1991 U.S. Department of Agriculture (USDA) study found that 124,000 farmers owned 47 percent of all U.S. farmland.[51]

The displacement of most U.S. farms and the concentration of farming in the hands of a small group of surviving farms had important consequences for agricultural communities that depended on farming as an industry and a way of life. As the Office of Technology Assessment reported in 1991, "The shrinking number of farms and landowners will contribute further to the decline of rural communities and may affect markets for commodities and factors of production."[52]

Rural communities will be adversely affected because when farms disappear, so, too, do the businesses in agricultural towns. "On average, every time seven farms go under, one business serving a rural community folds," reports Dan Levitas of Rural America.[53] As Iowa farms disappeared in the 1980s, "Farm implement sales in Iowa dropped 42 percent . . . [and between 1980 and 1986] the state lost more than a third of its farm implement dealers."[54]

The decline of farm-related businesses led to declining employment in rural areas, which led to falling incomes for many farm families that had long relied on off-farm income to keep their farms. As David Goodman and Michael Redclift note:

> Rural communities in agriculturally dependent regions have been severely affected by the farm financial situation. . . . Further declines in rural wage rates and increases in unemployment could serve to harm rural places and to reduce the viability of multiple job holding among farm households, which has over the past two decades come to constitute the backbone of farm members in America.[55]

Although many people moved off the farm and into cities, many remained in agricultural areas, where they lived in poverty. "Of the 54 million people living in rural America [in 1990], over 9 million exist below the poverty line, a level of poverty that is nearly as high as in the nation's blighted inner-city neighborhoods," observed Osha Davidson.[56] And of the country's 150 worst "'Hungry Counties,' 97 percent are in rural areas."[57]

In some regions, whole communities are drying up and blowing away. "The Great Plains is creating a new era of ghost towns," says one scholar.[58] And some counties have fewer residents today than they did in 1890. Declining rural populations—the population decreased in 77 percent of Nebraska's towns between 1980 and 1992—made it hard for those who remain.

The plight of Morland, Kansas, illustrates these developments. As wheat farms and cattle ranchers went out of business, the population of Morland fell by half between the 1970s and 1990.[59] As people left, housing prices fell. "How can you sell houses to people who aren't there?" Fred Pruitt, a local real estate agent asked.[60] Falling home prices lowered the assessed property values in the county, reducing tax revenues for the government and the schools. In 2000, the high school, home of the Morland Tigers, was forced to close, and its nineteen students were sent to a school in a neighboring town. "We kept waiting for people to walk in the door [and register for school]," principal Shelly Swayne said, "But they never came."[61] The lone elementary school closed in 2001, and the state abolished the school district.[62] Of course, when the schools closed, teachers lost their jobs, further weakening the local economy. "I think the loss of the high school is the beginning of the end for this community," teacher Becky Ellis observed.[63]

Gender and the Farm Crisis

As prices fall and costs increase, farmers and ranchers lose money. But before they sell out or declare bankruptcy, many try to hold on to their land as best they can. One common strategy is for women in farming households to seek off-farm jobs that can generate income that can be used to keep the farm afloat. In recent years, many women found jobs as teachers, in city or county government offices, or in local service jobs: cashiers, waitresses, and sales clerks. But women seeking jobs in rural economies faced a number of problems. Their entry into private sector service jobs created a labor surplus, lowering wages to the minimum and making it hard for them to generate enough money to keep the family farm solvent. The loss of schools has closed off teaching opportunities for women. And as rural populations declined, local and county governments have tried to merge or consolidate their services, reducing employment for women in government.[64] Women must then travel long distances to find work in larger towns, but job opportunities there are declining, just as they are in smaller towns, and for the same reasons. As a result, it has become harder and harder for women to find jobs that can help families keep their farms.

For men, the prospect of securing off-farm income is equally dismal. Moreover, as people leave rural areas, the number of women in rural communities has declined. One reporter noted that "as women become scarce in rural America . . . the men left behind on farms are facing a difficult time finding marriage partners. This epidemic of bachelorhood has led some towns, like Herman, Minnesota, to advertise their surplus of marriageable men in hope of attracting female suitors."[65] Evidently, conditions today are not unlike a century ago, when frontier farmers advertised for mail-order brides.

Government officials have not been indifferent to these developments. Beginning in the 1930s, government officials took steps to address the problems associated with rising supplies, falling prices, and the displacement of U.S. farmers. But while the policies developed to deal with these problems were expensive and complex, they did little, in the end, to solve them.

GOVERNMENT FARM POLICIES

Between 1950 and the 1970s, government officials tried to deal with the problems associated with growing food supplies by introducing two kinds of policies. First, they developed programs designed to increase the demand for U.S. food around the world. Second, they developed programs to curb U.S. food supplies. By increasing demand and reducing supplies, they hoped to keep farm prices from falling too rapidly and avert a rapid displacement of farmers.

In the 1950s, government officials developed two strategies to increase demand for U.S. food around the world: (1) they helped other countries purchase U.S. food at bargain prices or gave it to them free of charge, and (2) they developed new markets for U.S. food.

"Food aid" was the first and most important way that government officials increased the demand for U.S. food in the post–World War II period. In 1954, Congress passed Public Law 480, or the Agricultural Trade Development and Assistance Act. The act was designed to "develop and expand markets for U.S. agricultural commodities, to use the abundant agricultural productivity of the United States to combat hunger . . . and to encourage economic development in the developing countries."[66]

The new law gave government officials two ways to increase the demand for U.S. food in foreign countries. Under Title I of the act, the U.S. government could sell food to foreign governments on favorable or "concessional" terms, meaning that the U.S. government could sell them food at bargain prices or loan them money at low interest rates to purchase food. The foreign governments would then sell U.S. food in their country and pay for the food (or repay the loan) in their own currency. The U.S. government would then spend the money it earned in the foreign country, using it to build "dams or roads, to buy supplies for [U.S.] military bases or any other projects that involved locally produced goods and services. It had a multiplier effect on American foreign aid appropriated by Congress and it could be directed to projects independent of Congressional approval."[67]

U.S. officials also provided U.S. food free of charge to select countries under Title II of the act. Since 1955, the government has *given* away about 30 percent of the food exported under the act and *sold* 70 percent on "concessional" terms.[68] But agricultural economist Robert Wood argued that despite giving food away or selling it at low prices, "this program probably cost the U.S. nothing at all because the cost of price support and storage in the absence of the food aid program would have amounted to about as much as 'giving' it away."[69]

U.S. food aid helped increase foreign demand for U.S. food. As Watkins notes:

> PL 480 paved the way for U.S. world market domination and established an outlet for the farm sector's problematic surplus productive capacity. Between 1954 and 1960, the U.S. share of international grain trade rose from 26 percent to 41 percent, with concessional sales accounting for almost a third of the total. These subsidized exports became a critical source of income support for the U.S. farm sector, which relied increasingly on foreign demand.[70]

By providing cheap or free food to other countries, the U.S. government helped cultivate a taste for First World foods such as wheat, which were not previously a staple part of the diet of many people around the world. Massive food aid to Taiwan during the 1950s and 1960s created "such a taste for wheat" that "U.S. commercial food exports to Taiwan increased by 531 percent between 1967 and 1974," when U.S. food aid was phased out.[71]

Besides feeding people with cheap surplus food, the U.S. food aid program was also used to promote other economic and political objectives. In her study of seventy-nine countries that received food aid between 1950 and 1990, geographer Janet Kodras found that

> the relative abundance of food resources . . . and the flexibility of food aid as a foreign policy vehicle [made] PL 480 . . . an important mechanism in the pursuit of American global objectives. U.S. food aid has been used in war (the Vietnam conflict) and as a bargaining chip in peace negotiations (the Middle East Accords) . . . as long-term support for an ally (Israel throughout the post-war era) and as an immediate *quid pro quo* for favors gained (establishing military bases in Iceland during the 1950s and Somalia during the 1980s). U.S. food aid has been sent to recalcitrant socialist states (Yugoslavia and Poland in the 1950s) and to staunchly capitalist regimes (El Salvador, Costa Rica and Honduras during the 1980s). It has been used to build commercial markets for U.S. agriculture (wheat in Taiwan) and to protect U.S. manufacturing concerns (copper in Chile). In these and many other cases . . . food aid was distributed to pivotal states in the dynamic foreign agenda of the U.S. government.[72]

A second way to increase demand was to find new markets for U.S. food in countries where people were able to pay for food. During and after World War II, U.S. farmers found ready markets for their food in Western Europe and Japan. But the recovery of farmers there and the adoption of food self-sufficiency policies, which sometimes excluded U.S. agricultural imports, slowed demand for U.S. food in Western Europe and Japan.

In the 1950s and 1960s, government officials provided credits and loans to countries that did not need direct or indirect food aid so they could more easily purchase U.S. food.[73] During the 1960s, they sought to stimulate demand in poor countries, and by 1971, countries in Latin America, Asia, and Africa (excluding Argentina and Japan) "accounted for almost half of world imports, on the eve of the first large Soviet purchases."[74] But government officials were reluctant to sell food to communist countries, even though their demand for U.S. food was strong.

As a result of Cold War policies, U.S. government officials did not actively seek new markets in communist countries until the 1970s. But then they did with new enthusiasm. During the 1970s, they also increased sales to East Asian countries such as South Korea and Taiwan, where rapid economic growth increased the demand for food.[75]

While government officials tried to increase the demand for U.S. food, they also tried to curb U.S. food supplies by paying farmers to take land out of production, imposing tariffs on some imported foods to keep domestic supplies low (and prices high), and using subsidy and loan programs to displace farmers slowly.

Government officials tried to reduce food supplies by encouraging or requiring farmers to take land out of production, particularly land that was vulnerable to soil erosion, or by helping farmers store surplus grain in silos. In bad years, when harvests were poor, or in good years, when demand was strong, these two methods of reducing supply were little used. Acreage restrictions were typically lifted in bad years so farmers could produce more to make up possible shortfalls. They were abandoned in very good years to meet new demand. During the 1960s, between ten and twenty million acres were idled under various government programs to reduce supplies, but this land was brought back into production when Soviet grain shortages dramatically increased the demand for U.S. grain in the mid-1970s.[76]

The trouble with acreage reduction programs was that farmers often took some of their land out of production and then used more fertilizer on the land that remained, thereby actually increasing the volume of food they produced. As Peoples explained:

> Envision the paradox of a mid-1950s farmer receiving a $1,000 subsidy from the U.S. government for setting aside 50 acres of corn ground to reduce the grain surplus, and then using the subsidy check as a down payment on a $5,000 tractor to make . . . the farm more efficient and productive. In effect, the government provided the down payment and then the banker provided the remainder of the financing that enabled the farmer to invest in new machinery to produce higher grain yields on the remaining planted acres.[77]

When too much grain was produced, and falling prices threatened, the government helped farmers store their surplus in the farmer's own silos by offering nonrecourse loans. The government provided low-interest loans so farmers could survive until they sold their grains at a later date for a higher price.[78] "The nonrecourse feature meant that a farmer who obtained the loan had a choice of two alternatives: to deliver the farm product (the security for the loan) in lieu of payment or to pay off the loan in cash with accumulated interest and storage costs, if any."[79] Although this program reduced supplies by helping farmers store their surpluses, it was limited by the amount of storage space available to farmers, and this space was insufficient to store supplies that accumulated in the United States during the postwar period.

In a variation on the theme of storing surplus food, the government also bought some commodities like dairy products and either stored them or gave them away through food stamp and school lunch programs in order to reduce the volume of milk and cheese available on the market.[80]

In a second set of farm programs, government officials curbed domestic U.S. supplies by using tariffs (taxes on imported goods) or quotas (limiting the volume of imported produce) to restrict food imports. Restricting foreign imports would cause domestic supplies to be smaller, and prices higher, than they would have been otherwise. Under Section 22 of the Agriculture Adjustment Act of 1951, Congress allowed government officials to impose tariffs or quotas on any farm commodity whose supply the government was trying to manage, and a 1955 amendment allowed officials to place restrictions on any imported foods that interfered with U.S. subsidy programs.[81]

In practice, the government placed stiff tariffs and quotas on dairy products and tobacco during this period, while putting low tariffs on grain. Tariffs on tobacco were very high—50.5 percent in 1988—"reflecting and enhancing the success of the tobacco lobby in acquiring strong support in Congress," while imported dairy products had tariff rates of 12.3 percent and grains of only 2.3 percent.[82]

Although many farmers would have liked the government to reduce the supplies of other food in this way, the government has been unwilling to use tariffs to limit supplies because officials believed that the use of tariffs by other countries would limit overall demand. And the government tried throughout the postwar period to increase overseas demand for burgeoning U.S. food supplies. So it used tariffs to reduce the supply of only a few, politically important crops. Because tobacco and dairy farmers were concentrated in just a few states, they had more political clout than farmers scattered across many different states.

The third important way that government programs limited food supplies was by reducing the number of farms through subsidy and loan programs. These programs were designed to weed out "inefficient" farmers and take their land out of production, thereby reducing food supplies.

During the postwar period, falling farm prices and rising costs would have rapidly ruined many farmers, creating a 1930s-style crisis in the 1950s and 1960s. To avoid this, government officials used subsidy and loan programs, developed in the Agricultural Act of 1947, to raise the price that farmers received through "deficiency payments."[83] Each year, USDA officials calculated what it would cost the "majority" of farmers (not all farmers) to produce their crop.[84] The government then agreed to pay farmers the difference between the low market price and the higher "target price," a price that was supposed to cover their costs and provide them with enough income to live. But many farmers, a "minority," had higher costs. Perhaps they were more deeply in debt, or their land was more difficult to farm, or they had higher living expenses (medical bills, college tuition for their children). In these cases, government "deficiency payments" did not cover their costs. So every year, a minority of "inefficient" farmers were forced out of farming. Because government officials typically set target prices *below* what many families needed to earn to survive—government officials usually set prices about one-third less than farmers received during the "golden years" of farm prices (1910–1914, 1940–1952)—about 150,000 farmers were driven into bankruptcy and forced off the land every year between 1950 and 1970.

The eviction of millions of farmers occurred *despite* large government payments, or subsidies, to farmers. "The annual budget of farm programs had risen from an average of $2 billion in the 1950s to over $5 billion by the mid-1960s," writes James Wessel.[85] So despite large subsidies, or rather because of the way government subsidy programs were designed, one-half of all U.S. farmers were forced out of farming between 1950 and 1970, the number of farms falling from six million to three million in just twenty years.[86] While the government spent billions of dollars on subsidy programs—$6.2 billion in 1968—the program kept half of the farmers in business but helped drive the other half out of business.[87]

Many government officials and industry leaders argued that "inefficient" farmers *should* go out of business. They reasoned that the land of bankrupt farmers would be taken out of production, food supplies reduced, and the farmers who survived would eventually be able to earn money without the need for government subsidy. The Committee for Economic Development, a corporate think tank, recommended in 1962 that "excess resources (primarily people) . . . move rapidly out of agriculture" and urged the government to adopt a program that "would involve moving off the farm about two million of the present farm labor force, plus a number equal to a large part of the new entrants who would otherwise join the farm labor force in the next five years."[88]

During the next ten years, nearly two million farmers left farming as a result of falling prices, rising costs, and government subsidy programs designed to smooth and facilitate this process. As agricultural economist Jane Adams has written, government policies "adopted in 1954 allowed commodity prices to decline, with a concomitant sharp drop in farm income."[89] Total farm income fell by half, from $70 billion in 1950 to $35 billion in 1970 (in 1982 dollars).[90] But because the total farm income was divided among a smaller number of farms (three million fewer farms), the income of the remaining farmers increased slightly, from about $10 billion to $12 billion in the same period.[91] As

Adams noted, "Only the larger, technologically advanced farmers with large volume and increasing production could survive as farm prices fell."[92]

But while government subsidy programs both displaced "inefficient" farmers and conserved "efficient" ones, the removal of three million farmers did not greatly reduce foods supplies because the "efficient" farmers frequently purchased the land of their bankrupt neighbors and expanded their own operations, producing the same or even greater volume of food on bigger farms.

Government farm policy changed dramatically in the 1970s. Because poor Soviet harvests greatly increased the demand for food, government officials no longer viewed food surplus as the central problem for U.S. agriculture. Instead they thought the primary problem in subsequent decades would be one of shortage. As a result, they radically changed their approach to agriculture. Rather than trying to reduce U.S. food supplies, they encouraged farmers to expand production. And rather than stimulate demand through food aid programs, they cut back dramatically on the provision of cheap or free food to others and demanded instead that countries now pay for higher priced U.S. food, a development that forced many poor countries to borrow heavily to pay for food imports.

To expand U.S. food supplies, government officials curtailed soil conservation and land set-aside programs and encouraged farmers to plant the 23.8 million acres of farmland idled in 1972.[93] They offered easy credit and low-interest loans to farmers so they could purchase land, expand production, purchase new machinery and agrochemical inputs, and increase yields.

During this period, there was little need for deficiency payments and nonrecourse loans because, for most crops, the market price regularly exceeded both the government's target price and the cost of producing food for the vast majority of U.S. farmers. The government did not scrap these programs, but they fell into disuse. "With high market prices, loan rates and target prices became irrelevant."[94]

To take advantage of sharply rising world demand, the U.S. government also abandoned its hostility to selling food to communist countries and aggressively pursued new markets in communist countries and rapidly developing countries like South Korea and Taiwan. U.S. agricultural sales were greatly assisted by Nixon's 1971 dollar devaluation, which enabled U.S. grain exporters to undercut other important first world grain producers like Australia, Argentina, and the European Community, and increase the U.S. share of world grain markets. As a result, "exports of agricultural commodities exploded during the 1970s," increasing sixfold, from about $7.3 billion in 1970 to $43.3 billion in 1981.[95] The share of world wheat exports increased from 36 percent in 1970 to 51 percent in 1980, and its share of coarse grain exports rose from 40 percent to 72 percent in the same period.[96]

During the 1970s, the U.S. government virtually abandoned its food aid program, forcing poor countries to purchase food at rising world prices, food that had previously been sold or given to them on concessional terms.

In 1965, the U.S. government had delivered eighteen million tons of food to poor countries through the PL 480 program. U.S. officials reduced this to about ten million tons in the 1970s.[97] But when surging demand pushed up food prices in 1972, the government cut way back so that this food could enter commercial markets. By 1974, the United States provided only three million tons of food through this program, and two-thirds of this went to only two countries: South Vietnam and Cambodia.[98]

As U.S. food aid disappeared, poor countries that had come to rely on first world imports were forced to buy food on global markets at world prices. To do this, many of them borrowed money from the World Bank and commercial banks in first world countries to pay for increasingly costly food imports. Poland, Argentina, Mexico, and Brazil made major grain purchases during this period, using money borrowed from multilateral and commercial banks to finance grain imports.[99] As we have seen, this contributed to rising indebtedness in the 1970s (see chapter 5).

But the high prices of the 1970s did not last, and food prices fell again at the end of the decade, leading to what the USDA called "the worse economic crisis [for agriculture] since the Great Depression."[100] As a result, the U.S. government reintroduced policies it had abandoned in the 1970s and introduced some new ones.

To reduce supplies, government officials renewed land set-aside measures in 1977 and took further steps in 1983 through the Payment in Kind (PIK) program.[101] "Taking land out of production, reducing supplies and thereby boosting prices are old methods of farm income support," Joseph Belden notes. "The PIK program renewed this approach by offering farmers not cash, but government-owned surplus grain, in exchange for taking acreage out of production. Farmers could then the sell the grain or hold it in hopes that prices would rise."[102] In 1983, for example, farmers took 82 million acres out of production, 36 percent of the total, and enrolled in the PIK program.[103]

As prices fell, the government's deficiency program kicked back into gear. But because the government wanted to drive "excess" farmers off the land as a way of reducing food supplies, it set very low target prices that did not cover the costs of many farmers, and it made farm credit difficult to obtain and placed onerous conditions on outstanding debts. U.S. farm debt quadrupled, from $52.8 billion in 1970 to $206.5 billion in 1983.[104] Higher interest rates in the 1980s forced heavily indebted farmers into bankruptcy.

But while U.S. officials renewed or modified long-standing programs to reduce supplies, they also spent considerable effort and money to reduce the supplies of *other* farmers in the European Community.

Like the United States, the European Community (EC) had used technological innovation and government subsidies to increase supplies produced by European farmers. By the early 1980s, they were exporting grain in large quantities and competing directly with U.S. farmers for markets in the South.

Although U.S. farmers could produce food more cheaply, on average, than EC farmers, the EC could deliver food for the same price because it provided more generous subsidies to EC farmers. So the EC could sell at low, world market prices and still provide a livable income for a majority of EC farmers.[105] In 1980, for example, the EC spent about 83 percent more on its farm program than did the U.S. government.[106] This enabled EC farmers to compete for Soviet grain sales, and by 1984, EC and U.S. farmers were "each selling 6.1 mmt of wheat to the USSR."[107]

Although subsidies put EC and U.S. farmers on equal footing, the rise in the value of the U.S. dollar after 1980, a strengthening due primarily to high U.S. interest rates, made it more difficult for U.S. farmers to compete in export markets. So to deal with these problems, U.S. officials took two steps in 1985.

First, they adopted the Export Enhancement Program (EEP) in May 1985, subsequently modified by the Food Security Act and Food Security Adjustments Act of 1986. Under the EEP, officials made government-owned food stock available to exporters at no cost so they could more easily compete with the EC. As Katie Snoden, an economist at the Rocky Mountain Institute, explained,

> If Brazil wants to buy 300,000 bushels of wheat . . . but will do so only if it is allowed to pay, say two-thirds of the U.S. market price for it, [U.S.] exporters can petition the [USDA to give them] 100,000 bushels of free wheat. This allows the exporters to buy [other] American commodities at the higher U.S. market rate, and sell them abroad at the lower world price and still make a profit.[108]

Of course, the use of new export subsidies to sell U.S. grain was matched by the European Community, resulting in a subsidy war between the two major first world food suppliers. U.S. officials believed they could use export subsidies to force up EC subsidies to a point where they would become onerous to European taxpayers. U.S. agriculture secretary John Block described this strategy as "squeezing the CAP until the pips squeak."[109]

The EEP did raise the cost of farm subsidies to the EC. "In 1986, for example, the EC subsidy for wheat exports was $82.68 per metric ton, while the U.S. subsidy was only $26.56; in January 1987, it rose to $120.25 while the American subsidy rose to $42.89."[110]

The effect of this farm subsidy war, and the rising cost of both deficiency payments (a result of rapidly falling prices) and the PIK program (the result of providing commodities to farmers who had removed huge amounts of land from production), was to raise the cost of U.S. agricultural subsidies to $30 billion in 1986, ten times the 1980 level.[111] The cost of EC subsidies, meanwhile, rose to about $40 billion.[112] Although subsidies hurt the European Community, they probably hurt the United States more because the United States was experiencing massive budget deficits and growing debt in this period while EC countries had much lower deficits.

As a second step, the Reagan administration initiated a second devaluation of the dollar in 1985 through the Plaza Accords. U.S. officials hoped that this would improve farmers' ability to sell food on foreign markets. By waging a subsidy war with the EC and devaluing the U.S. dollar, the Reagan administration hoped to reduce the supplies of other European farmers.

During the mid-1980s, government officials tried to reduce the supplies of U.S. farmers through subsidy and acreage restriction programs and to limit the supplies of EC farmers. But U.S. supplies mounted, and EC farmers continued to produce vast quantities of food. In 1991, for example, the EC had stockpiled 23.5 mmt of grain and 290,000 tons of butter, while the U.S. government in 1985 had stockpiled 500 million bushels of wheat and 1.3 million tons of dairy products at a cost of $400 million.[113] The cost of food subsidy programs rose, contributing to large budget deficits in the United States. The U.S. share of world food markets did not greatly improve despite subsidy programs and a massive dollar devaluation. The USDA reported, "Due to a combination of a weaker dollar and export subsidies, agricultural exports turned up again in quantity in 1987 and made further gains during 1988 in both quantity and value. But rising imports have kept the agricultural balance of trade lower than in the early 1980s."[114]

Between 1980 and 1987, the U.S. share of world agricultural exports had declined from 18 percent to 12 percent, while the EC's share grew from 35 percent to 39 percent. And in the important wheat market, the U.S. share fell from 44.7 percent in 1981 to only 28.6 percent in 1986.[115]

Because these remedies proved ineffective, U.S. officials developed a new approach to the problem of excess supply and insufficient demand. In the late 1980s and early 1990s, they began negotiating free trade agreements (FTAs) that would reduce supply and increase demand simultaneously (see chapter 9).

In negotiations to revise multilateral trade agreements with more than one hundred countries through the GATT and to create new bilateral trade agreements first with Canada (the U.S.–Canada Free Trade Agreement) and then with Canada and Mexico (the North American Free Trade Agreement, or NAFTA), U.S. officials argued that agricultural subsidies would be abolished or greatly reduced and that tariff barriers on food and other commodities would be eliminated.

U.S. officials reasoned that if farm subsidies were eliminated in both Europe and the United States, U.S. farmers and grain producers in Canada, Australia, and Argentina would regain their "natural" competitive advantages over EC farmers, who were more heavily subsidized. If subsidies were eliminated, many small farmers in Europe would be forced out of business. Whereas U.S. officials had long tried to displace "inefficient" farmers in Iowa and Kansas, in the late 1980s they sought to eliminate "inefficient" farmers in France and Japan.

Long negotiations, which began in 1987, were concluded in 1993 with the adoption of NAFTA and the signing of a revised GATT in 1994. Although measures that would reduce agricultural subsidies and eliminate tariff barriers were bitterly contested by EC negotiators and EC farmers, which delayed negotiations for several years, the agreement reached substantially reduced subsidies (see chapter 9).

The Freedom to Farm Act

After reducing farm subsidies in trade negotiations, the U.S. government then took steps to eliminate subsidies in the United States. In 1996, a Republican Congress passed, and a Democratic president signed, the Freedom to Farm bill. This measure promised to phase out all government subsidies to farmers, which had amounted to $7.3 billion in 1995, and leave the remaining farmers to prosper or fail on their own.[116] Government officials hoped this measure would strengthen the U.S. bargaining position in trade negotiations with the Europeans, and many believed that the farmers who had survived the decades-long winnowing process were hardy enough to prosper without government largess

But the Freedom to Farm bill was a disaster. After the bill was adopted, falling prices and shrinking markets threatened U.S. farmers, and they demanded new relief. Although the number of farmers is small (1.5 million), compared, for example, with the 12.5 million poor people on welfare in 1996, they are powerful politically because they are scattered across a large number of states, each with two senators determined to protect their interests. (By contrast, poor women and their children on welfare are concentrated in large cities in a few large states, and their political representatives attend to other constituencies.) Farmers lobbied successfully for new "emergency" relief programs that provided direct payments to farmers. Government farm subsidies grew from $7.3 billion in 1995 to $23 billion in 1999, and then jumped to $32.2 billion in 2000.[117] This is "far more than the federal government spent on elementary and secondary school education, school lunches, and Head Start combined," one writer observed.[118] Indeed, it is a sum larger than all the aid (welfare, food stamps, housing allowances) given to poor people in America.

There are several problems with new farm subsidies. First, they made liars or fools out of the political representatives who promised to end subsidies in 1996. Second, new U.S. subsidies have antagonized the EC, which has argued that U.S. subsidies violate the intent and purpose of new trade laws, which were supposed to curb agricultural subsidies. So large U.S. subsidies threatened to ignite a new, expensive farm subsidy war between the United States and the European Community.[119] Third, the new subsidies were distributed unfairly, with large farmers grabbing a disproportionate share. "The data shows that government subsidies are tilting the playing field in favor of the largest firms," said Clark Williams-Derry, an analyst at the Environmental Working Groups, which studies subsidies.[120] Only 10 percent of U.S. farmers, the largest farmers, received 61 percent of all subsidies.[121] "Congress talks about saving the family farm, but it pours the money disproportionately to larger farms," observed John A. Schnittker, an agricultural economist. "As you subsidize these large farms, they can pay more in buying land, and they can pay more in renting land. And so the system we have now really concentrates farming among the large operators."[122]

FARMERS AND CONSUMERS

The problem with government policies since World War II is that food supplies grew and prices fell despite their efforts to increase demand and curb supplies. One U.S. official described the failure of government efforts to deal with mounting food supplies in the 1950s: "We sold what we could for cash. What we couldn't sell for cash we would for credit. What we couldn't sell for dollars we sold for foreign currency. What we couldn't get money for we bartered. What we couldn't get anything for we gave away—what we couldn't export by any means we stored. And still the stocks increased."[123] In the end, government policies did not help demand keep pace with rising supplies, did not prevent prices from falling, did nothing to reduce farm costs, and did not prevent farmers from being displaced.

Throughout this period, government officials assumed that the displacement of millions of inefficient farmers would take land out of production, reduce the total amount of food grown, and shrink the supply of food. But the ruin of millions of farmers did little to reduce growing food supplies in the United States and around the world. Indeed, the postwar period is quite remarkable in that millions of farmers were eliminated, agricultural communities were undermined, and the environment was compromised *without* substantially reducing food supplies or raising prices.

The displacement of millions of farmers was an inefficient way to deal with rising food supplies because it did little to slow the introduction of new agricultural technologies, which were primarily responsible for increasing food supplies and lowering prices. It was also unfair because it eliminated small farmers and helped concentrate food production in the hands of very large farmers—not because they were "better" farmers but simply because they were "bigger." As a 1980 USDA study pointed out, "Growth you now see in farm size has little to do with efficiency. Above about $40,000 to $50,000 in gross sales . . . there are no greater efficiencies of scale. Medium-sized farms are as efficient as the large farms."[124]

While the falling prices associated with successive technological revolutions were bad for a majority of U.S. farmers, they did benefit urban consumers, though not as much as one might expect. Although the prices farmers received fell by more than one-half between 1950 and 1990, the real prices consumers paid at the grocery store did not fall nearly as far.

U.S. consumers spent 20 percent of this disposable income on food in the 1950s and only 14 percent in the mid-1980s.[125] But if the price they paid for food had declined by one-half, as it did for farmers in this period, consumers would have spent only 10 percent of their income on food. So while consumers generally benefited from falling farm prices, they did not benefit as much as they might. They did not because the food-processing industry has not lowered its prices as rapidly as farmers have lowered theirs, and the gap between the price of food at the farm gate and the grocery shelf has grown. In 1950, farmers received about 50 cents on every dollar paid by consumers at the checkout counter.[126] But by 1987, they earned only 25 cents on every dollar spent on food by consumers.[127]

The grain trade and food-processing industry has been able to increase the gap between farm prices and sticker prices because it is fairly concentrated, which means that it can bargain down farmers while maintaining consumer demand for its products. Because businesses that purchase and produce food are relatively few in number, while farmers are quite numerous, they are able to drive a hard bargain with farmers and keep prices low. They are in much the same position with food retailers—grocery stores—and consumers. The concentration of industry and the use of massive advertising to maintain consumer demand mean businesses are able to keep sticker prices higher than they would if the food-processing industry were less concentrated and more competitive. Between 1950 and 1978, the fifty largest food-processing firms increased their control of industry assets from 36 percent to 64 percent. And grocery chains of more than one hundred stores increased their share of all supermarket sales from 27 percent to 41 percent.[128]

As a result of growing concentration in the industry, food processors were able to increase the gap between farm prices and supermarket prices, despite an overall reduction in the amount that urban consumers paid for food. "Between 1980 and 1987, when farmers' earnings on the wheat in a box of cereal fell by 33 percent, the consumer price of cereal rose 84 percent."[129] As DeLind noted, "In 1990 alone, grain prices declined an average of 11 percent, but commercial cereal prices increased by 6 percent. . . . Stated in a somewhat different manner, a farmer must produce and sell 104 pounds of corn to buy a 25 oz. package of frosted flakes."[130] Put another way, the price that consumers pay for cereal has increased from $2.40 per pound in 1988 to $3.07 per pound in 1992, this at a time of *falling* grain prices.[131]

In contrast to farmers, who have seen their costs rise and their prices fall, which has led to declining farm incomes, "the 50 food processing firms listed in a *Forbes* magazine industry survey had an average return on equity of 15.1 percent from 1981 to 1986."[132]

Falling farm prices have been good for the grain-trade and food-processing industry, and beneficial to consumers, though less so, and to the industries that employ consumers as workers. Other industries benefit from lower farm and food prices either because it lowers the cost of their raw materials (cornstarch is used as glue in the packaging industry) or because it helps keep wages low. But falling farm prices, coupled with rising costs, have not been good for the majority of U.S. farmers.

HUNGER IN POOR COUNTRIES

Technological revolutions have increased world food supplies and allowed farmers in the South to make real gains. World food supplies have increased from 631 million tons in 1950 to 1,650 million tons in 1984, a 260 percent increase.[133] As a result, there is more food available *despite* rapid population growth. The amount of grain available per person has increased from 251 kilograms in 1950 to 380 kilograms in 1985.[134] "History records no increase in food production that was remotely comparable in scale, speed, spread or duration," British economist Michael Lipton has written.[135] Nonetheless, hunger is also widespread. In 1988, the World Bank calculated that one billion people were hungry and malnourished, four times as many people as live in the United States, one of every five people living on the planet.[136]

The number of hungry people is the subject of considerable debate, with estimates of world hunger ranging from 550 million to 1.3 billion. But whatever the exact figure, people in Africa, Asia, Latin America, and the Middle East are hungry *not* because population growth has outstripped the available food supply. The problem for people in the South has been that their effective demand for food has not kept pace with rising supplies, despite rapid population growth. As T. Kelley White, a USDA official, put it in 1989, "Food crises [in poor countries] will likely continue to be . . . the consequences of . . . lack of effective demand, rather than a failure of supply."[137]

"On a global basis, it has become an indisputable fact of our times that hunger can no longer be blamed on a shortage of food," writes Joseph Collins, codirector of the Institute for Food and Development Policy. "The telling fact is that in the early 1980s, the number of hungry people was accelerating precisely at a time when global food stocks were building up to record levels."[138] And he notes that it would not take a large amount of food, "only 15 to 20 million tons . . . of the 1,660 million tons [produced in 1987] . . . to raise the diets of . . . the world's undernourished to adequate levels."[139]

According to Collins, "a mere 5.6 percent of the country's food supply, if eaten by the hungry, would make an active life possible for everyone. For Indonesia . . . only 2 percent of the country's food supply would make the difference. . . . A redistribution of only 1.6 percent of . . . Brazil's [supply] would meet all the needs of the 86 million Brazilians estimated in 1984 to be undernourished."[140] But if world food supplies have increased even faster than the world's population, and if the world's hungry could be fed with a fraction of total supplies, why are so many people hungry?

There are several reasons. First, while new agricultural technologies increased food supplies, their introduction displaced many small farmers. Second, new technologies were typically used to expand the production of export crops and animal feed. This increased the total volume of food but also reduced the domestic supply of staple foods, which poor people eat to survive. Finally, the debt crisis reduced incomes and raised prices for poor people, making it more difficult for them to purchase the food that was being produced in ever-greater volume. These developments undermined the poor's "entitlement" to food, which reduced effective demand.

The concept of declining "entitlements" to food was introduced by the economist Amartya Sen in his 1981 book, *Poverty and Famines*. In it he argued that postwar famines were not usually the result of food "shortages" or the product of inadequate food "distribution." He notes that many devastating famines occurred despite the fact that harvests were good and food was widely distributed and readily available. Indeed, some of the worst famines have taken place with no significant decline in food availability per head. To say that starvation depends "not merely" on food supply but also on its "distribution" would be correct enough, though not remarkably helpful. The important question then would be: what determines distribution of food between different sections of the community?[141] According to Sen, people starved because their "entitlement" to land to grow food or income to buy food changed as a result of *economic* developments. He argues that "the entitlement approach views famines as economic disasters, not just as food crises."[142]

THE ECONOMICS OF FAMINE

During the Great Bengal Famine of 1943, when 1.5 million people died, Sen found that people starved not because harvests were poor—"the [food] supply for 1943 was only about 5 percent lower than the average of the preceding five years"—but because inflation induced by massive government spending on the British war effort in India raised rice prices dramatically, while the wages of agricultural workers who did not own land to produce food and of fishermen and rural craft workers did not rise to keep pace with increasing food costs.[143] The price of rice, using 1939–1940 as an index of 100, increased from 109 in 1941 to 385 in 1942, while the wages of rural agricultural and craft workers rose only from 110 to 125 in the same years. This meant that their ability to purchase enough rice to survive fell precipitously.[144] Poor sharecroppers did not suffer, even though they may have been equally "poor" (in terms of annual income), because their "income" was paid in rice, so its rising price did not affect them.[145] When famine became widespread among rural wage laborers, farmers and merchants also began hoarding rice, further increasing its price. High prices encouraged farmers to grow more rice in 1943 and 1944. The irony of this was that "while the famine killed millions . . . Bengal was producing the largest rice crop in history in 1943."[146] The problem for rural workers was that "institutional arrangements, including wage systems, were slow to adjust to the new reality [of higher prices]."[147] In this case, inflation, not food shortage, led to famine for many.

Thirty years later, in 1974, Bengal, now Bangladesh, was again struck by famine. Although the famine followed a large-scale flood, the harvest was good and food was widely available. The problem this time was that agricultural workers could not work during the summer flood, at the time of their highest annual earnings, and their incomes fell. Farmers and merchants, meanwhile, began hoarding food because they *thought* that the harvest would be poor and that prices would rise. As a result, prices rose at a time when the incomes of many workers had fallen. The fact that farmers had increasingly paid their workers in cash, rather than in kind (in food), made matters worse. As Sen notes, cash wages were "more modern" but they made wage-dependent workers "more vulnerable."[148]

The situation in the 1972–1974 Ethiopian famine was the result of somewhat different circumstances.[149] Although a drought reduced food supplies somewhat in one part of the country—the Wollo region—there was plenty of food in the country as a whole, and food prices did *not* rise. The problem was not that food prices rose but that poor people's entitlement to income to buy food or to land to grow food was reduced.[150] Many tenant farmers were evicted, household servants fired, and cow herders prevented from grazing their cows on land recently brought under cultivation for commercial export crops. "About 50,000 hectares of good land in the Awash Valley were 'developed' in 1970–71 for growing . . . cotton and sugar by a few big companies—mostly foreign owned," Sen records.[151] As a result, these groups lost the means to purchase or grow food. Cattle herders who had been deprived of access to traditional grazing land tried to sell their cows before they died from the drought. But this glutted the market and caused beef prices to fall, which meant that their ability to purchase grain declined substantially. "The pastoralist, hit by the drought, was decimated by the market mechanism," says Sen.[152] "A remarkable feature of the Wollo famine is that food prices in general rose very little, and people were dying of starvation even when food was selling at prices not very different from pre-drought levels."[153]

Although famines of the kind that Sen describes still occur with alarming frequency around the world—most recently in Somalia—*hunger* is the more common problem for poor people in the South. Hunger has increased because, borrowing from Sen, the poor's entitlement to food has been eroded by technological developments that displaced farmers and reduced the production of staple foods, as well as by developments that reduced the income of poor people in different settings.

REDUCING ENTITLEMENTS
TO LAND AND FOOD

The introduction of Green Revolution technologies in the South helped some farmers to produce more food, earn more money, and expand their landholdings. But the introduction of new mechanical and agrochemical technologies benefited some farmers more than others. Because Green Revolution technologies were designed to increase the production of some First World crops—wheat, corn, and soybeans—farmers who grew these crops realized substantial gains, while farmers growing "traditional" staple foods—beans, cassava, millet—found that the new technologies did not greatly assist them. As Keith Griffin noted:

> Far too much attention has been devoted to the effects of the "Green Revolution" in increasing output of one or two commodities and not enough attention has been given to the performance of the agricultural sector as a whole. For example, in India between 1964 and 1969, wheat production increased 90 percent, but rice production increased by only 4 percent, i.e., less than the population.[154]

Typically, "the development of high-yielding varieties of millet and sorghum has lagged far behind, even though these traditional food crops are considerably more drought-resistant and nutritionally balanced than maize."[155]

Large farmers growing new technology-friendly crops also benefited from better access to government credit and training programs, while their ability to produce on a large scale gave them greater market access and higher prices.[156] Agricultural economist Andrew Pearse has called these collective benefits

> the talents-effect after the well-known Biblical parable in which it is recounted that one servant receives ten talents [a form of money] from his master and is able to invest and prosper, while the insecurity of his humbler fellow restrains him from utilizing the single talent entrusted to him, which is wrathfully reappropriated by the master and given to the successful investor: "For unto everyone that hath shall be given, and he shall have abundance; but for him that hath not shall be taken away even that which he hath." (Matthew 25, 29)[157]

As a result, "the new technology has hastened the process of [class] differentiation [and] served to consolidate the rich peasantry as a powerful and dominant class" in many third world countries.[158] The expansion of technology-assisted farmers has concentrated land into fewer hands and displaced millions of farmers from the land. In northwestern Mexico, for instance, "the birthplace of Green Revolution technologies, the average farm size over 20 years jumped from

200 to 2,000 acres, with over three-quarters of those working in agriculture deprived of owning, or even renting, any land at all," notes Collins.[159] "The highly skewed landownership patterns now found in countries like Brazil, where 2 percent of the farmers own 57 percent of the arable land and more than half of all agricultural families own none, are but the most obvious legacies of such shifts," writes Lester Brown, head of the Worldwatch Institute.[160]

Because small, wealthy elites and prosperous, technology-assisted farmers have increased their ownership of and control over land in the postwar period, millions of farmers have been displaced from the land. "A 1975 . . . UN survey of 83 Third World countries found that typically only 3 percent of all landowners control a staggering 79 percent of all farmland, depriving most rural families of owning any land at all," says Collins.[161]

What happens to small farmers displaced by the concentration of landownership? Many of them remain in agricultural areas as landless workers, seeking employment on large farms and estates. In India, for example, the number of rural *households* (on average six people per household) who neither own nor lease land nearly doubled between 1961 and 1981, rising from fifteen million to twenty-six million, meaning that an additional sixty-six million people had become landless in that period.[162] Of course, as Sen has noted, it is this group of people who are particularly vulnerable to famine when employment declines or food prices rise sharply.

Because farmers using new machinery and agrochemical technologies typically need less labor and fewer workers than farms using traditional methods, there is not enough work in agricultural areas to support displaced farmers. "In the very areas of northwest Mexico where agricultural production boomed, the average number of days of employment for a farm worker shrank from 190 to 100" between 1973 and 1983 as a result of the introduction of tractors.[163]

When there is little work in agricultural areas, many displaced or landless farmers move in other directions, either to marginal land or to cities. Many displaced farmers move to more marginal forest, desert, or mountainous lands, where they try to grow subsistence crops. In Brazil, for example, farmers displaced from the fertile São Francisco valley migrate to the Amazon; in Central America they move out of the valleys and up into the hills and mountains; in Sahelian Africa they move into arid grasslands; and in Indonesia they move from the heavily populated island of Java to one of the country's many distant and less populated islands. In some countries, like Brazil and Indonesia, the governments actively encourage "transmigration" programs, providing migrating households with minimal supplies, transportation, and the promise of free land on distant "homesteads."[164] They do this in part because many farmers displaced from agricultural settings would otherwise crowd into the cities, swelling already large urban populations.

Of course, farming on marginal land can have serious environmental consequences. The burning of rain forest and the raising of cattle contribute to global climate change (see chapter 8). In addition, farming on marginal land often depletes and erodes the soil, reducing the ability of farmers to grow food. Eventually farmers have to move to new land and start again, usually with the same results.

Across the South, the influx of people displaced from agricultural regions has increased the size of cities. In Africa, for instance, Cairo was the only city with more than one million inhabitants in 1950. But by 1980, there were nineteen cities with one million people; by 2000, there were more than sixty such cities.[165]

The problem is that few countries have been able to provide employment for displaced agricultural workers in urban areas. This group, like landless agricultural workers, can be adversely affected by economic developments that reduce employment opportunities (such as recession), or raise food prices (inflation), or increase the cost of imported food (currency devaluations). Displaced poor become vulnerable to hunger and famine.

A second problem is that the new agricultural technologies have primarily been used to expand the production of export crops and animal feed, an expansion that has reduced the availability of "staple" foods or "subsistence" crops.

Most small farmers grow "staple" crops, foods that comprise the heart of their daily diet. The foods that people eat on a daily basis vary around the world, depending on climate and custom. People in Latin America depend on maize (corn) and beans; in sub-Saharan Africa, on sorghum, millet, and maize; in northern Africa, on wheat; and in India, on rice in wet regions and sorghum and millet in dry parts of the country.[166]

Prior to World War II, when many countries were ruled as colonies by European states, farmers were encouraged or forced to grow crops that could be exported to foreign markets: bananas from Central America, cotton from Egypt and Sudan, sugar from the Caribbean, and rubber from Southeast Asia. Generally, the amount of land given to the production of these export crops remained relatively small as a proportion of the total. But as government officials in newly independent countries tried to develop their economies after World War II, they expanded the production of export crops so they could obtain the hard currencies they needed to purchase machinery and import other capital and consumer goods.

By 1975, countries such as Costa Rica, Panama, Ghana, and Uganda devoted more land to the production of export crops like coffee, bananas, cocoa and cotton than to staple cereals that people in those countries typically consume. In extreme cases, such as the island country of Mauritius, 90 percent of all arable land was given over to the production of just one crop: sugar.[167] Countries such as Brazil, Colombia, Egypt, and Indonesia devote one-third or more of their land to export crops.[168]

In the postwar period, many countries began producing "new" export crops, such as soybeans. Brazil, which grew only 61,000 tons of soybeans in 1950, increased its production to more than fifteen million tons by 1980 on its way to becoming one of the world's largest producers.[169] Brazil's soybean crop is either exported or used to feed cows, which are then exported (see chapter 8).

In Brazil and across the South, farmers are increasingly growing crops that feed cows, not people. In a study of twenty-four countries in 1990, economist David Barkin found that "at least 5 percent of the total land cultivated in grain showed a shift from human cereal production to commercial grain production for other uses in the past 25 years."[170] He discovered that the "most accelerated rates of conversion from food to feed [were] occurring in Mexico and Central America, upper South America, eastern and southeastern Asia, northern Africa and western Asia."[171]

Large farmers in poor countries grow animal feed rather than food crops because the local demand for food crops is weak, and because cows turn plentiful feed into a higher-value food: beef, which can be sold to consumers in the North or eaten by domestic elites.

The production of feed rather than food crops has increased dramatically in the past twenty years. In 1970, only 11 percent of the food produced by poor countries was used to feed cows. But by 1990, more than 18 percent was grown for animal feed.[172]

Of course, as farmers grew more feed crops, less of the land was available to produce staple grains. As farmers grew more feed between 1961 and 1986, Barkin found that the production of staple cereals fell: 5 percent in Brazil, 26 percent in Colombia, 40 percent in Venezuela, 10 percent in South Africa, 16 percent in Tanzania, 10 percent in Thailand, and 11 percent in the Philippines.[173]

As feed supplies increased and subsistence supplies declined, the price of staple foods *rose*.[174] Barkin says of these developments in Colombia, "retail prices for all food grains rose dramatically during the [inflationary 1970s], but prices of [the staple] maize rose faster than did those of rice and wheat."[175]

The increased production of feed crops during the past twenty years or, in the 1980s, of fresh fruits and vegetables that are shipped from southern countries during their summer season to northern consumers during their winter, or of crops to produce ethanol for car fuel, makes staple food less available and more expensive to the poor.[176] As a result of these developments, the poor's entitlement to subsistence food supplies is slowly diminished. "The middle classes and wealthy eat an increasingly rich diet," Barkin concludes, "while undernutrition and malnutrition are common in poor farming communities and urban slums throughout the third world."[177]

The irony is that while Green Revolution technologies increase the volume of world food supplies, they have displaced small farmers and reduced the production of staple foods, on which poor people depend. Both developments contribute to hunger.

A third problem is that the income of poor people has generally declined in recent years, making it difficult for them to purchase food that is available.

As we have seen, U.S. officials tried to increase the demand for first world foods after World War II by making large quantities of food available to poor countries, either by giving it away or by selling it cheaply. Although this made cheap food available for many poor people, much of the benefits associated with food aid programs were obtained by a relatively small group of countries. During the 1950s and 1960s, cheap food and food aid programs *probably increased* the poor's ability to demand or obtain food, and this helped reduce hunger among the world's poor.

But two developments—the Soviet grain shortages in the 1970s and the debt crisis in the 1980s—weakened the poor's ability to obtain food through the market.

In the early 1970s, government officials reduced the amount of food being provided through U.S. food aid programs and tried to persuade recipients to purchase U.S. food instead. The Soviet grain shortages accelerated this process because large Soviet demand led to the sale of U.S. food at high prices, leaving little food left over to be given away through food aid programs.

To obtain the food they had previously received at little or no cost, many southern governments borrowed money from northern lenders—government agencies and commercial banks—to purchase food grown in the North. They wanted to continue buying food from the North because wealthy and middle-class consumers in their countries had come to prefer grains like wheat over traditional domestic varieties. They then used borrowed money to purchase food imports and to subsidize domestic food prices. Many governments provided food subsidies so that urban workers would not demand higher pay, thereby keeping the cost of industrial goods and exports competitive.[178] By borrowing money, governments in the South could maintain the demand for food even though food provided by U.S. aid programs had disappeared.

But the policy of purchasing food by borrowing money ran into difficulty when U.S. officials raised interest rates and commodity prices began to fall in the early 1980s, events that triggered a debt crisis for many indebted countries.

In the 1980s, the World Bank asked borrowers to take steps to repay their enormous debts to lenders. As part of "structural adjustment" programs designed to assist repayment, officials reduced or eliminated government subsidies for food and fuel, and cut the wages of government employees so they could raise more money to repay debt.

These policies helped governments repay their debts, but they reduced effective demand and undermined the poor's ability to obtain food. As government food subsidies declined, the cost of food rose, while falling wages meant that the poor found it more difficult to purchase food. These developments eroded the poor's entitlement to food by weakening their ability to demand the food that was available.

At the same time, many governments were also forced to devalue their currencies (see chapters 3 and 6).[179] This was done to make their exports cheaper, allowing them to sell more of their goods abroad so they could earn foreign currencies that could be used to repay debt, and to make imports more expensive, which would reduce domestic demand for imported goods. This would create trade surpluses that could be used by governments to repay their debts.

But domestic currency devaluations increased the price of imported food, grains that people had made part of the daily diet. They also lowered the price that farmers who grew export crops could obtain for food or feed stuffs. Because farmers had greatly increased the supply of export crops during the 1970s, prices had already begun to fall in the early 1980s.[180]

For farmers growing export crops, prices fell twice, first as a result of growing food surpluses and then as a result of domestic currency devaluations. To maintain their income as prices fell, many farmers tried to increase their production of export crops. But this only increased supplies and forced prices downward again. Together these developments reduced the ability of the rural poor, urban workers, and even export farmers to demand food through global and domestic markets.

As a result of these developments, many people go hungry and some starve. Chronic hunger hits children hardest. "Undernutrition affects nearly 40 percent of all children in developing nations and contributes directly to an estimated 60 percent of all childhood deaths," writes Katrina Galway, a U.S. AID official.[181] Typically, children and adults suffering from malnutrition get sick from other diseases.[182] Jeremy Rifkin notes that "chronically malnourished children generally develop smaller body frames and often smaller brains than normal children. If the malnutrition occurs within the first years of their lives, the physical and mental retardation becomes irreversible."[183] The poor survival rates for hungry children is the main reason that the average life expectancy in sub-Saharan Africa is only forty-seven years.[184]

Gender and Hunger

"Gender inequality," Amartya Sen has written, "has many distinct and dissimilar faces."[185] By this he meant that women are disadvantaged by different kinds of inequality—for example, the preference in many cultures for male babies and the practice of aborting girl fetuses during pregnancy, the inclination to send boys to school but not girls—*and* that the particular kind of disadvantages that girls and women face vary widely from one setting to another.[186] Gender inequalities, in Sen's view, are the product of diverse patriarchies around the world. Gender inequality is also expressed through the distribution of food in poor households, a patriarchal distribution that commonly results in malnutrition and hunger for girls and women. In South Asia, for example, Sen found that girls were "being underfed as compared with boys," resulting in lower weight and poorer health.[187] Girls also received less medical treatment than boys.[188]

The unequal, gender-based distribution of food in poor households affected not only girls but also women, particularly pregnant women. The "high incidence of maternal malnourishment in South Asia," Sen argued, has several important consequences for women. Underfed mothers risk anemia, and they often bear underweight children. "In terms of weight for age, around 40 to 60 percent of the children in South Asia are undernourished . . . [so] the children start deprived and stay deprived," Sen observed.[189] But maternal malnourishment also has adverse consequences for men. The irony is that *maternal* undernourishment leads eventually to a high incidence of cardiovascular illness among their *male* children. "In sum: what begins as a neglect of the interests of women ends up causing adversities in the health and survival of all, even at an advanced age," Sen writes. "Gender inequality can hurt the interests of men [in the form of cardiovascular disease] as well as women."[190]

SUMMARY

During the postwar period, food supplies have grown even faster than the population. But growing food supplies have displaced millions of farmers and have contributed, along with economic developments that undermine the poor's entitlement to food that is relatively cheap and widely available, to hunger and sometimes famine. In the view of agronomist Dale Johnson, these problems are the result of the fact that "a significant fraction of world farm output is being produced in the wrong place," in the North, not in the South where a majority of the world's poor and hungry reside.[191]

"In 1980," one scholar noted, "Third World nations had 75 percent of the world's people, but only 50 percent of the cereal production, 35 percent of the arable land, 35 percent of the meat and eggs, 22 percent of the milk and 15 percent of the tractors."[192] Global climate change may exacerbate this (see chapter 8). In 1994, scientists in the United States and United Kingdom concluded that global warming, if it occurs, would actually help *increase* food production in temperate northern countries (where food surpluses have been a persistent problem) but *decrease* food production in tropical southern countries (where the availability of subsistence foods has declined). They estimated that "because of global warming, an additional 60 to 350 million people, most of them in the developing world, could face critical food shortages by the year 2060."[193]

The irony is that global warming is caused primarily by countries in the North. In the United States, for example, the per capita production of carbon emissions (five tons annually) is ten times that of China (half a ton) and one hundred seventy times greater than Zaire.[194]

If global warming followed this pattern, it would simultaneously exacerbate the problem of food surpluses in the North and of persistent hunger in the South, problems that have persisted and grown sharper during the second half of the twentieth century.

NOTES

1. Nick Butler, *The International Grain Trade* (New York: St. Martin's, 1986), 12; William H. Friedland, Lawrence Busch, Frederick H. Buttel, and Alan P. Rudy, *Towards a New Political Economy of Agriculture* (Boulder, Colo.: Westview, 1991), 122.

2. Malcolm H. Forbes and Louis J. Merrill, *Global Hunger: A Look at the Problem and Potential Solutions* (Evansville, Ill.: University of Evansville Press, 1986), 117.

3. Friedland et al., *Towards a New Political Economy of Agriculture*, 122–23.

4. Peter W. B. Phillips, *Wheat, Europe and the GATT: A Political Economy Analysis* (New York: St. Martin's, 1991), 20.

5. Forbes and Merrill, *Global Hunger*, 117.

6. Forbes and Merrill, *Global Hunger*.

7. Butler, *The International Grain Trade*, 12.

8. Friedland et al., *Towards a New Political Economy of Agriculture*, 117.

9. David Goodman and Michael Redclift, *Refashioning Nature: Food, Ecology and Culture* (London: Routledge, 1991), 123.

10. Andrew Pearse, *Seeds of Plenty, Seeds of Want: Social and Economic Implications of the Green Revolution* (Oxford: Clarendon, 1980), 8.

11. Committee on the Role of Alternative Farming Methods in Modern Production Agriculture, *Alternative Agriculture* (Washington, D.C.: National Academy Press, 1989), 34.

12. Butler, *The International Grain Trade*, 32.

13. Bill Orr, *The Global Economy in the 90s: A User's Guide* (New York: New York University Press, 1992), 65, 66.

14. Butler, *The International Grain Trade*, 133.

15. Orr, *The Global Economy in the 90s*, 65.

16. Barnaby J. Feder, "Out of the Lab, a Revolution on the Farm," *New York Times*, March 3, 1996.

17. David l. Wheeler, "The Search for More-Productive Rice," *Chronicle of Higher Education*, December 1, 1995, A12.

18. David L. Wheeler, "Expansion of Agricultural Research Said to Have Fueled Dramatic Increases in Yields of Corn, Rice and Wheat," *Chronicle of Higher Education*, September 22, 1993, 10.

19. Wheeler, "Expansion of Agricultural Research."

20. Sabrina Tavernise, "Farms as Business in Russia," *New York Times*, November 6, 2001.

21. Mary Summers and Edward Tufte, "The Crisis of American Agriculture: Minding the Public's Business," unpublished paper, January 10, 1988, 16; Committee, *Alternative Agriculture*, 32.

22. Sicco Mansholt, "The GATT Agricultural Negotiations: A Time to Ponder the Consequences," unpublished paper, no date, see table.

23. Forbes and Merrill, *Global Hunger*, 117.

24. Forbes and Merrill, *Global Hunger*; Robert E. Long, *The Farm Crisis: The Reference Shelf*, vol. 59, no. 6 (New York: Winston, 1987), 14; Raymond F. Hopkins and Donald J. Puchala, "The Global Political Economy of Food," *International Organization* 32, no. 3 (Summer 1978): 584; Summers and Tufte, "The Crisis of American Agriculture," 7.

25. Forbes and Merrill, *Global Hunger*, 117.

26. Forbes and Merrill, *Global Hunger*, 117; Jeremy Rifkin, *Beyond Beef: The Rise and Fall of the Cattle Culture* (New York: Dutton, 1992), 160–61; William J. Hudson, "Population, Food and the Economy of Nations," in *Food and Natural Resources*, eds. David Pimentel and Carl W. Hall (San Diego: Academic Press, 1989), 284.

27. Summers and Tufte, "The Crisis of American Agriculture," 15; Committee, *Alternative Agriculture*, 32.

28. Committee, *Alternative Agriculture*, 37.

29. Kenneth L. Peoples, David Freshwater, Gregory D. Hanson, Paul T. Prentice, and Eric P. Thor, *Anatomy of an American Agricultural Credit Crisis: Farm Debt in the 1980s* (Washington, D.C.: Farm Credit Assistance Board, 1992), 23.

30. Peoples et al., *Anatomy of an American Agricultural Credit Crisis*; Osha Grey Davidson, *Broken Heartland: The Rise of America's Rural Ghetto* (New York: Free Press, 1990), 42; Diane Flaherty, "The Farm Crisis," in *The Imperiled Economy. Book II: Through the Safety Net*, ed. Robert Cherry et al. (New York: Union for Radical Political Economics, 1988), 41.

31. Flaherty, "The Farm Crisis," 40–41; James Wessel, *Trading the Future: Farm Exports and the Concentration of Economic Power in Our Food Economy* (San Francisco: Institute for Food and Development Policy, 1983), 84.

32. Joseph N. Belden, *Dirt Rich, Dirt Poor: America's Food and Farm Crisis* (New York: Routledge & Kegan Paul, 1986), 32.

33. Belden, *Dirt Rich, Dirt Poor*; Friedland et al., *Towards a New Political Economy of Agriculture*, 115.

34. Peoples et al., *Anatomy of an American Agricultural Credit Crisis*, 14.

35. Belden, *Dirt Rich, Dirt Poor*, 34.

36. Peoples et al., *Anatomy of an American Agricultural Credit Crisis*, 49–58.

37. Wessel, *Trading the Future*, 41–42.

38. Long, *The Farm Crisis*, 19; Peoples et al., *Anatomy of an American Agricultural Credit Crisis*, 25.

39. Peoples et al., *Anatomy of an American Agricultural Credit Crisis*, 40.

40. Davidson, *Broken Heartland*, 56.

41. Peoples et al., *Anatomy of an American Agricultural Credit Crisis*, 43.

42. Committee, *Alternative Agriculture*, 92.

43. Peoples et al., *Anatomy of an American Agricultural Credit Crisis*, 92.

44. Peoples et al., *Anatomy of an American Agricultural Credit Crisis*, 18.

45. Peoples et al., *Anatomy of an American Agricultural Credit Crisis*, 4, 12; Steve H. Murdock and F. Larry Leistritz, *The Farm Financial Crisis: Socioeconomic Dimensions and Implications for Producers and Rural Areas* (Boulder, Colo.: Westview, 1988), 30–31; Ingolf Vogeler, *The Myth of the Family Farm: Agribusiness Dominance of U.S. Agriculture* (Boulder, Colo.: Westview, 1981), 4.

46. Steven A. Holmes, "Farm Count at Lowest Point Since 1850: Just 1.9 Million," *New York Times*, November 10, 1994; Vogeler, *The Myth of the Family Farm*, 4.

47. Long, *The Farm Crisis*, 78.

48. Long, *The Farm Crisis*, 10; Committee, *Alternative Agriculture*, 54.

49. Peoples et al., *Anatomy of an American Agricultural Credit Crisis*, 12.

50. Laura DeLind, "Cheap Food: A Case of Mind Over Matter," paper prepared for

conference on "Diversity in Food, Agriculture, Nutrition and Environment," organized jointly by the Agriculture, Food and Human Values Society and the Association for the Study of Food and Society, June 4–7, 1992, East Lansing, Michigan, 8; Nora L. Brooks, Thoams A. Stucker, and Jennifer A. Bailey, "Income and Well-Being of Farmers and the Farm Financial Crisis," *Rural Sociology* 51, no. 4 (1986): 396; Murdock and Leistritz, *The Farm Financial Crisis*, 33.

51. "U.S. Says Number of Farm Owners Is at Lowest Level in the Century," *New York Times*, December 29, 1991.

52. "U.S. Says Number of Farm Owners."

53. Wessel, *Trading the Future*, 71.

54. Davidson, *Broken Heartland*, 55.

55. Philip Raikes, *Modernizing Hunger: Famine, Food Surplus and Farm Policy in the EEC and Africa* (Portsmouth, N.H.: Heinemann, 1988), 80.

56. Davidson, *Broken Heartland*, 73–74.

57. Davidson, *Broken Heartland*, 77.

58. Thomas Heath, "Once-Thriving Small Towns on Plains Face Extinction," *San Francisco Chronicle*, November 11, 1995, A9; John Margolis, "The Reopening of the Frontier," *New York Times Magazine*, October 15, 1995, 52.

59. Peter T. Kilborn, "Bit by Bit, Tiny Morland, Kan., Fades Away," *New York Times*, May 10, 2001.

60. Kilborn, "Bit by Bit."

61. Kilborn, "Bit by Bit."

62. Associated Press, "State Board Approves Dissolving School District," *Manhattan Mercury*, December 13, 2001.

63. Kilborn, "Bit by Bit."

64. Leonard Bloomquist, personal interview, December 11, 2001.

65. Dirk Johnson, "Home on the Range (and Lonely, Too)," *New York Times*, December 12, 1995.

66. Butler, *The International Grain Trade*, 26.

67. Henry Bernstein, Ben Crow, Maureen Mackintosh, and Charlotte Martin, *The Food Question: Profits versus People* (New York: Monthly Review Press, 1990), 18; Rachel Garst and Tom Barry, *Feeding the Crisis: U.S. Food Aid and Farm Policy in Central America* (Lincoln: University of Nebraska Press, 1987), 21; Mitchell Wallerstein, *Food for War—Food for Peace: United States Food Aid in a Global Context* (Cambridge, Mass.: MIT Press, 1980), 36.

68. Peter J. Taylor, "The Globalization of Agriculture," *Political Geography* 12, no. 3 (May 1993): 254–55.

69. Robert E. Wood, *From Marshall Plan to Debt Crisis: Foreign Aid and Development Choices in the World Economy* (Berkeley: University of California Press, 1986), 36.

70. Kevin Watkins, "Agriculture and Farm Trade in the GATT," *CAP Briefing*, 20 (London: Catholic Institute for International Relations, March 1989), 3.

71. Taylor, "The Globalization of Agriculture," 239.

72. Taylor, "The Globalization of Agriculture," 243–44; Robert L. Paarlberg, *Food Trade and Foreign Policy: India, the Soviet Union and the United States* (Ithaca: Cornell University Press, 1985), 116.

73. Katie Soden, *U.S. Farm Subsidies* (Snowmass, Colo.: Rocky Mountain Institute's Agricultural Program, 1988), 16.

74. Goodman and Redclift, *Refashioning Nature*, 154.

75. Friedland et al., *Towards a New Political Economy of Agriculture*, 84–85; Paarlberg, *Food Trade and Foreign Policy*, 131. Butler, *The International Grain Trade*, 55.

76. Lester Brown, *State of the World 1989* (New York: Norton, 1989), 57; Wallerstein, *Food for War—Food for Peace*, table 1.1; Goodman and Redclift, *Refashioning Nature*, 124.

77. Peoples et al., *Anatomy of an American Agricultural Credit Crisis*, 2.

78. Soden, *U.S. Farm Subsidies*, 10.

79. Gale D. Johnson, *World Agriculture in Disarray* (London: Macmillan, 1973), 35.

80. Soden, *U.S. Farm Subsidies*, 7.

81. Watkins, "Agriculture and Farm Trade in the GATT," 2.

82. Peter J. Taylor, "The Globalization of Agriculture," *Political Geography* 12, no. 3 (May 1993): 254–55.

83. Johnson, *World Agriculture*, 36.

84. Committee, *Alternative Agriculture*, 74.

85. Wessel, *Trading the Future*, 29.

86. Vogeler, *The Myth of the Family Farm*, 4.

87. Johnson, *World Agriculture*, 50.

88. *An Adoptive Program for Agriculture* (New York: Committee for Economic Development, 1962), 25, 59.

89. Jane H. Adams, "The Decoupling of Farm and Household: Differential Consequences of Capitalist Development on Southern Illinois and Third World Family Farms," *Comparative Studies in Society and History* 30, no. 3 (July 1988): 465.

90. "Good Times Are Back on the Farm, for a Bit," *The Economist*, March 10, 1990, 25; Belden, *Dirt Rich, Dirt Poor*, 42.

91. "Good Times Are Back on the Farm, for a Bit," 25.

92. Adams, "The Decoupling of Farm and Household," 465.

93. Brown, *State of the World 1989*, 57.

94. Peoples et al., *Anatomy of an American Agricultural Credit Crisis*, 31.

95. Ronald T. Libby, *Protecting Markets: U.S. Policy and the World Grain Trade* (Ithaca, N.Y.: Cornell University Press, 1992), 50.

96. Butler, *The International Grain Trade*, 16.

97. Wallerstein, *Food for War—Food for Peace*, 54.

98. Wallerstein, *Food for War—Food for Peace*; Taylor, "The Globalization of Agriculture," 241; Hopkins and Puchala, "The Global Political Economy of Food," 633; Wallerstein, *Food for War—Food for Peace*, 15.

99. Long, *The Farm Crisis*, 68; Wood, *From Marshall Plan to Debt Crisis*, 21.

100. Kevin Danaher, "U.S. Food Power in the 1990s," *Race and Class* 30, no. 3 (1989): 31.

101. Wallerstein, *Food for War—Food for Peace*, 17.

102. Belden, *Dirt Rich, Dirt Poor*, 44.

103. Belden, *Dirt Rich, Dirt Poor*, 44.

104. Committee, *Alternative Agriculture*, 91.

105. Libby, *Protecting Markets*, 37.

106. Libby, *Protecting Markets*, 83.

107. Libby, *Protecting Markets*, 62.

108. Soden, *U.S. Farm Subsidies*, 15.

109. Kevin Watkins, "Changing the Rules: The GATT Farm Trade Reform and World Food Security," *GATT Briefing* 4 (London: European Network on Agriculture and Development, 1990), 2.

110. Libby, *Protecting Markets*, 73.

111. Watkins, *RAPE*, 40.

112. Secondo Tarditi, Kenneth J. Thomson, Pierpalo Pierani, and Elisabetta Croci-Angelini, *Agricultural Trade Liberalization and the European Community* (Oxford: Clarendon, 1989), 2.

113. Roger Cohen, "Life Can Be Sweet on Europe's Subsidized Farms," *New York Times*, April 12, 1992.

114. Jane M. Porter and Douglas E. Bowers, *A Short History of U.S. Agricultural Trade Negotiations* (Washington, D.C.: U.S. Department of Agriculture, 1989), 19.

115. Libby, *Protecting Markets*, 13.

116. John W. Fountain, "Rising Fuel Costs Join Growing List of Troubles for Struggling Farmers," *New York Times*, May 19, 2001.

117. Elizabeth Becker, "Treaties May Curb Farmers' Subsidies," *New York Times*, August 31, 2001.

118. Nicholas D. Kristof, "As Farm Life Worsens, the Toughest Wither," *New York Times*, April 2, 2000.

119. Becker, "Treaties May Curb Farmers' Subsidies"; Elizabeth Becker, "88 Billion Farm Bill Wins Approval of Senate Panel," *New York Times*, November 16, 2001.

120. Elizabeth Becker, "Far from Dead, Subsidies Fuel Big Farms," *New York Times*, May 14, 2001.

121. Becker, "Treaties May Curb Farmers' Subsidies."

122. Kristof, "As Farm Life Worsens."

123. Paarlberg, *Food Trade and Foreign Policy*, 108.

124. Adams, "The Decoupling of Farm and Household," 465.

125. Lester Brown, ed., *State of the World 1992* (New York: Norton, 1992), 68; Friedland et al., *Towards a New Political Economy of Agriculture*, 126–27.

126. Friedland et al., *Towards a New Political Economy of Agriculture*, 126. See Butler, *The International Grain Trade*, 18.

127. Rifkin, *Beyond Beef*, 163.

128. Belden, *Dirt Rich, Dirt Poor*, 5.

129. Friedland et al., *Towards a New Political Economy of Agriculture*, 128.

130. Wessel, *Trading the Future*, 158.

131. "Does Cereal Cost Too Much?" *Weekly Reader* 77, no. 2 (September 15, 1995): 1–2.

132. Brown, *State of the World 1992*, 77.

133. Lester Brown, "Natural Limits," *New York Times*, July 24, 1993; Lester Brown, ed., *State of the World 1987* (New York: Norton, 1987), 59; Amartya Sen, *Poverty and Famines: An Essay on Entitlement and Deprivation* (Oxford: Clarendon, 1981), 158; William K. Stevens, "Feeding a Booming Population without Destroying the Planet," *New York Times*, April 5, 1994.

134. Marcia Pimentel, "Food as a Resource," in *Food and Natural Resources*, 426.

135. Paul Lewis, "Food Production and the Birth Rate in a New Race," *New York Times*, May 10, 1992.

136. Joseph Collins, "World Hunger: A Scarcity of Food or a Scarcity of Democracy," in *World Security: Trends and Challenges at Century's End,* ed. Michael T. Klare and Daniel C. Thomas (New York: St. Martin's, 1991), 345; Hopkins and Puchala, "The Global Political Economy of Food," 812; Keith Griffin, *World Hunger and the World Economy: And Other Essays in Development Economics* (London: Macmillan, 1987), 4; David Grigg, *The World Food Problem 1950–1980* (London: Blackwell, 1985).

137. Bruce Stokes, "Crowds, Food and Gloom," *National Journal,* September 16, 1989, 2263.

138. Collins, "World Hunger," 346.

139. Collins, "World Hunger," 346.

140. Collins, "World Hunger," 346–47.

141. Sen, *Poverty and Famines,* 7.

142. Sen, *Poverty and Famines,* 162.

143. Sen, *Poverty and Famines,* 52, 75.

144. Sen, *Poverty and Famines,* 54, 63, 54, 66.

145. Sen, *Poverty and Famines,* 69–70.

146. Sen, *Poverty and Famines,* 77–78.

147. Sen, *Poverty and Famines,* 78.

148. Sen, *Poverty and Famines,* 50.

149. Sen, *Poverty and Famines,* 86.

150. Sen, *Poverty and Famines,* 96.

151. Sen, *Poverty und Famines,* 104.

152. Sen, *Poverty and Famines,* 105, 107.

153. Sen, *Poverty and Famines,* 112.

154. Keith Griffin, *The Political Economy of Agrarian Change: An Essay on the Green Revolution* (London: Macmillan, 1974), 62–63.

155. Brown, "Natural Limits," 72.

156. Danaher, "U.S. Food Power in the 1990s," 39.

157. Pearse, *Seeds of Plenty, Seeds of Want,* 5.

158. Friedland et al., *Towards a New Political Economy of Agriculture,* 194. Pearse, *Seeds of Plenty, Seeds of Want,* 165.

159. Collins, "World Hunger," 350.

160. Brown, "Natural Limits," 71.

161. Collins, "World Hunger," 350.

162. Brown, *State of the World 1987,* 29–30.

163. Collins, "World Hunger," 350, 360.

164. Philip Shenon, "Rearranging the Population: Indonesia Weighs the Pluses and Minuses," *New York Times,* October 8, 1992.

165. Timberlake, 1985, 42.

166. David Barkin, Rosemary L. Batt, and Billie R. DeWalt, *Food Crops vs. Feed Crops: Global Substitution of Grains in Production* (Boulder, Colo.: Rienner, 1990), 17.

167. Dinham and Hines, 1983, 187.

168. Hopkins and Puchala, "The Global Political Economy of Food," 260.

169. F. LaMond Tullis and W. Ladd Hollist, *Food, the State and International Political Economy: Dilemmas of Developing Countries* (Lincoln: University of Nebraska Press, 1986), 133; David Goodman and Michael Redclift, *The International Farm Crisis* (New York: St. Martin's, 1989), 277, 275.

170. Barkin et al., *Food Crops vs. Feed Crops*, 18; Brown, *State of the World 1992*, 76.

171. Barkin et al., *Food Crops vs. Feed Crops*, 20.

172. Hopkins and Puchala, "The Global Political Economy of Food," 599.

173. Barkin et al., *Food Crops vs. Feed Crops*, 120.

174. Barkin et al., *Food Crops vs. Feed Crops*, 27.

175. Barkin et al., *Food Crops vs. Feed Crops*, 34.

176. Tullis and Hollist, *Food, the State and International Political Economy*, 147. Forbes and Merrill, *Global Hunger*, 154; Pan A. Yotopoulous, "Middle-Income Classes and Food Crises: The 'New' Food-Feed Competition," *Economic Development and Cultural Change* 33, no. 3 (April 1985): 480.

177. Barkin et al., *Food Crops vs. Feed Crops*, 1.

178. Goodman and Redclift, *The International Farm Crisis*, 209.

179. Goodman and Redclift, *The International Farm Crisis*, 52.

180. Dinham and Hines, 1983, 189, 193.

181. Rifkin, *Beyond Beef*, 177; Barry, 1987, 17.

182. Timberlake, 1985, 48.

183. Rifkin, *Beyond Beef*, 178.

184. Timberlake, 1985, 48.

185. Amartya Sen, "The Many Faces of Gender Inequality," *New Republic*, September 17, 2001, 40.

186. Sylvia Nasar, "Indian Wins Nobel Award in Economics," *New York Times*, October 15, 1998.

187. Sen, "The Many Faces of Gender Inequality," 38.

188. Sen, "The Many Faces of Gender Inequality."

189. Sen, "The Many Faces of Gender Inequality."

190. Sen, "The Many Faces of Gender Inequality."

191. Johnson, 1973, 23.

192. Richard W. Franke, "The Effects of Colonialism and Neocolonialism on the Gastronomic Patterns of the Third World," in *Food and Evolution*, ed. Marvin Harris and Eric B. Ross (Philadelphia: Temple University Press, 1987), 463.

193. David E. Pitt, "Computer Vision of Global Warming: Hardest on the Have Nots," *New York Times*, January 18, 1994.

194. Robert M. Jackson, *Global Issues 94–95* (Guilford, Conn.: Dushkin, 1994), 81.

8

Global Climate Change

On June 23, 1988, NASA scientist James Hansen told Congress he was "99 percent certain" that global warming had begun. "It is time to stop waffling so much and say that the evidence is pretty strong that the greenhouse effect is here," he argued.[1]

Scientists first warned of global warming a century ago. Nobel laureate scientist Svante Arrhenius argued in 1896 that increasing levels of carbon dioxide in the atmosphere would raise its temperature.[2] Since then, the amount of carbon dioxide in the atmosphere has increased about 27 percent, from 280 parts per million to 356 parts per million, as have other important heat-trapping gases such as methane, chlorofluorocarbons (CFCs), and nitrous oxide.[3] Hansen and others have argued that these gases, which were largely a by-product of human activity, retained heat from the sun, creating a "greenhouse effect" that has warmed the planet. The Earth's temperature is about one degree Fahrenheit hotter today than it was a century ago.[4] And the UN's Intergovernmental Panel on Climate Change (IPCC), a scientific task force first assembled in 1988 to assess the problem, predicts that global temperatures will increase between 1.4 and 6.3 degrees during the next century unless drastic steps are taken to curb greenhouse gas emissions.[5] If this occurs, the IPCC reported, "the rate of change is likely to be greater than that which has occurred on Earth any time since the end of the last ice age."[6]

Rapidly rising temperatures could create serious problems for people in different settings, scientists argue. Rising temperatures could melt polar ice and raise sea levels, inundating islands and low-lying coastal plains where millions live. A one-meter rise would flood deltas on the Nile, Po, Ganges, Mekong, and Mississippi Rivers, displacing millions of people and swamping the croplands now used to feed them.[7] Higher sea levels could drown coral reefs, destroying the fish and ruining the livelihood of people who depend on reefs in the Caribbean and the Pacific.[8] Warmer water could also increase the strength of hurricanes and typhoons, causing greater damage for people living along their path in the western Atlantic and western Pacific.[9] The insurance industry is particularly concerned about this prospect because windstorms caused $46 billion in losses between 1987 and 1993.[10]

Higher temperatures could also disrupt agriculture. While farmers in northern latitudes—North America and northern Europe and Asia—could benefit from higher temperatures, longer growing seasons, and higher levels of carbon dioxide (which plants use to grow), even modest increases could devastate farmers in tropical zones in Asia, Africa, and Latin America. Rice yields decline significantly if daytime temperatures exceed ninety-five degrees, and in many Asian countries, temperatures are already near this limit.[11] One group of scientists predicted that cereal prices could increase between 25 and 150 percent by the year 2060, a development that would cause hunger and starvation for between 60 million and 350 million poor people, most of them in the tropics.[12]

The prospect that global warming could have its most serious impact on people in relatively poor and populous tropic countries is ironic given the fact that most of the gases believed to contribute to global warming are generated by small populations in relatively rich northern countries, particularly the United States. In 1960, the United States produced one-third of all global carbon dioxide emissions and about 20 percent in 1987; its per capita annual production of 5.03 tons was nearly five times the world per capita average of 1.08 tons, but 13 times that of Brazil and 167 times that of Zaire.[13] This irony is not lost on poor countries, which are now being asked to reduce or defer fossil fuel consumption as a way to mitigate the effects of global warming. Brazil, for example, has rejected calls to reduce burning of tropical woods in the Amazon basin. President José Sarney argued that the industrial nations were conducting "an insidious, cruel and untruthful campaign" against Brazil to distract attention from their own large-scale pollution, acid rain, and "fantastic nuclear arsenal" that threaten life.[14] Chinese officials maintain that they need to consume vast quantities of coal to provide electricity for China's growing economy. At present, "the average Chinese consumes less than 650 kilowatt hours [annually], barely enough to burn a 75-watt bulb year round . . . and 120 million rural Chinese . . . live without electricity in their homes or villages."[15] But if it does expand coal-fired electricity production to light villages, run refrigerators, and power industry, as the government plans, China would overtake the United States as the world's largest producer of carbon dioxide sometime during this century.[16]

Because the environmental and social consequences of rising temperatures are not uniform, but unevenly distributed, it might be best to describe these developments as products of "global climate change" rather than "global warming," which suggests that temperature change will be experienced by people in much the same way everywhere.[17] Moreover, it might be better to use the phrase "global climate change," given the scientific uncertainties about the process and the debate surrounding claims that the world is warming significantly and that human activity is largely to blame.

Although Senator Al Gore, later vice president, asserted that "there is no longer any significant disagreement in the scientific community that the greenhouse effect is real and already occurring," global climate change remains the subject of scientific debate. While a majority of scientists share Gore's view that the greenhouse effect is demonstrable, a minority disagree, making two kinds of objections to the conclusions reached by the IPCC.[18]

First, some scientists argue that the Earth may not be warming much, if at all. S. Fred Singer, former director of the U.S. weather satellite program, notes that satellite data collected between 1979 and 1994 showed "no appreciable recent warming."[19] Other scientists agree that modest warming, about one degree, has occurred in the past one hundred years, but argue that this is well within the range of natural temperature change. They note that global temperatures in the 1980s, when some of the hottest years of the past century were recorded, were slightly lower than those recorded during the Middle Ages, some five hundred years ago, "when Scandinavians grew grain near the Arctic Circle," and more than two degrees cooler than global temperatures six thousand years ago.[20]

Second, some scientists argue that there is little proof that higher temperatures are the product of human activity and increased atmospheric concentrations of greenhouse gases. They note that global temperatures actually *declined* between 1940 and 1970, data that greenhouse proponents do not dispute, at a time when industry expanded and world carbon dioxide emissions tripled.[21] If human activity and atmospheric concentrations of carbon dioxide and other waste gases were closely related to temperature change, then global temperatures should have increased during this period, they maintain. The fact that they did not suggests that temperature change may be a result of "natural fluctuation" rather than a product of human activity.[22]

Because some scientists believe that the relation between human activity and temperature change is weak, they express little confidence in the computer models that use rising carbon dioxide levels to predict higher temperatures in the next century.[23] "I do not accept the model results [used by the IPCC and others] as evidence," Richard Lindzen of MIT says. Trusting them, he says, "is like trusting a ouija board."[24] Lindzen and others argue that computer models of climate change do not adequately account for natural variation or environmental processes—increased cloud cover, water vapor—that may mitigate warming tendencies. "I don't think we've made the case yet" that serious climate change is now occurring, he argues.[25]

This kind of skepticism finds some support in the IPCC report, which conceded in 1992 that "it is not possible at this time to attribute all, or even a large part, of the observed global-mean warming to the enhanced greenhouse effect [the extra warming attributable to human-produced gases] on the basis of the observable data currently available."[26] More recently, in 1995, the IPCC expressed greater confidence in the relation, writing that the warming of the past century "is unlikely to be entirely due to natural causes and that a pattern of climatic response to human activity is identifiable in the climatological record."[27] But criticism still persists. Lindzen argues that because computer models do not estimate natural variability accurately, there is "no basis yet for saying that a human influence on the climate has been detected."[28]

At issue, of course, is whether drastic steps should be taken to reduce the emission of greenhouse gases. If human activity does in fact contribute to global warming, as a *majority* of scientists believe, then their call for a 50 to 60 percent cut in greenhouse gas emissions, effectively returning emissions to 1950 levels, should be heeded. But if climate change is not a product of human activity, then efforts to reduce greenhouse emissions would be both ineffective and socially disruptive, particularly for poor countries that are trying to use carbon sources to promote economic growth. "Poverty is already a worse killer than any foresee-able environmental distress [associated with global warming]," Lawrence Summers, former chief economist of the World Bank, has argued. "Nobody should kid themselves that they are doing Bangladesh a favor when they worry about global warming."[29]

Although scientific uncertainty makes global climate change a difficult issue, it is nonetheless possible to develop a constructive approach. If steps were taken to solve environmental problems that are serious in their own right, problems that may also contribute to global climate change, then people could address real as well as potential problems, a strategy that would minimize both social and environmental risks. There are, for example, sound environmental and social reasons to reduce energy consumption and car use and slow deforestation. Because these activities also release vast quantities of carbon dioxide, efforts to curb the consumption of fossil fuels and wood might also reduce global warming. (The carbon dioxide released by these activities accounts for about half of all greenhouse gases.) The same is true for other activities that produce other greenhouse gases. A reduction of world cow herds would reduce hunger and deforestation, and also curb emissions of methane, which makes up about 18 percent of all greenhouse gases.[30] The ban on CFCs, which was scheduled to take effect in 2000, will slow destruction of the ozone layer, about which there is no serious scientific dispute, and reduce its contribution (about 14 percent) to global climate change. If nitrogen fertilizer use were curbed, the problems associated with groundwater pollution could be addressed and nitrous oxide levels in the atmosphere (about 6 percent of the total) could be reduced. However, in the case of nitrous oxide, fertilizer reductions could adversely affect global food supplies and contribute to hunger, which suggests that efforts to curb fertilizer use should be approached with great caution.

In this context, it is important not just to curb human activities that adversely affect the environment and may contribute to global climate change, but to do so in ways that are equitable and sensible. Any effort to address environmental problems should take into account the social impact of proposed solutions. With these issues in mind, let us look at pressing environmental problems that might be addressed, both because they contribute to known environmental and social problems and because they may contribute to global warming. We will look first at human activities that produce carbon dioxide, the main greenhouse gas, and then at activities that produce methane, CFCs, and nitrous oxide.

POWER, FORESTS, AND
CARS (CARBON DIOXIDE)

In the early 1970s, long before global warming became a concern, environmentalists urged energy conservation. They argued that the profligate use of coal and oil to generate electricity for home and industry contributed to serious environmental and economic problems.[31] (Coal and oil are used to generate more than one-half of the electricity around the world.) Because coal often contains sulfur, combustion in power plants contributes acid rain, which ruins forests near and far.[32] Although oil burns cleaner than coal, the production of oil creates toxic waste that is hard to discard safely, and the transport of oil across oceans frequently results in spills that harm marine life.

The use of oil to produce electricity or to fuel cars also contributes to serious economic problems, environmentalists argue. Countries that import oil spend vast sums to purchase it, contributing to trade deficits and sometimes debt. For the United States, "oil imports alone have accounted for three-fourths of [its] trade deficit since 1970," and the United States has paid $1 trillion between 1970 and 1990 for imported oil.[33] For countries without substantial domestic supplies, the economic costs can be higher. During the 1970s, many Latin American countries borrowed heavily and fell deeply into debt to pay for oil imports. Moreover, competition for control of oil supplies has recently led to two wars in the Persian Gulf—the 1980–1990 Iraq–Iran War and the 1990–1991 Gulf War—which forced consumer countries to increase defense spending and intervene militarily to protect supplies in the region. "Even before Iraq invaded Kuwait, U.S. forces earmarked for gulf deployment were costing taxpayers around $50 billion a year—yearly $100 a barrel for oil imported from the Persian Gulf."[34] The war to dislodge Iraqi troops cost tens of billions more.

Energy conservation can solve many of these environmental and economic problems. During the 1970s, when oil prices rose, it became cost-effective to curb energy use by persuading consumers to conserve and by introducing new technologies to produce and use electricity and fossil fuels more efficiently. Between 1973 and 1986, these steps—lowering thermostats, insulating homes, driving less, and improving gas mileage in cars—enabled the U.S. economy to grow without expanding energy use, a development that helped the environment and resulted in $150 billion in annual energy savings.[35] But as oil prices fell in the mid-1980s, many conservation measures were abandoned and technological improvements were deferred, resulting in growing levels of energy consumption. Energy consumption could again be curbed through consumer conservation programs and the introduction of new technologies—fuel cells, photovoltaic cells, computerized electricity distribution systems, gas turbine engines, and solar-hydro-geothermal technologies—to create what engineers call a "nega-watt revolution": producing more energy with less.[36] Some economists have urged U.S. officials to pursue energy-efficient policies in part because they would make U.S. industry more competitive with businesses in Europe and Japan, where ongoing conservation practices have lowered the real cost of energy for domestic industry.[37] If the rich countries developed and introduced energy-saving technologies, their cost would decline and they would become more affordable for poor countries. And because the power sector accounts for one-third of global carbon dioxide emissions, energy conservation would also help avert potential warming.

DEFORESTATION

During the early 1980s, environmentalists recognized that tropical deforestation had become a problem. Attention was first drawn to Brazil, where 33 percent of the world's tropical forests are located (58 percent are in Latin America, 23 percent in Southeast Asia and the Pacific, and 19 percent in Africa), and where deforestation was rapidly accelerating.[38]

In 1981, the United Nations estimated that 7.3 million hectares of tropical forest were burned or cut every year, and some environmental groups argued that as much as 11.3 million hectares were lost annually.[39] These figures were revised downward in the early 1990s, to about 1.5 million hectares.[40] But more recent studies indicate that deforestation has accelerated again, particularly in the Amazon.[41] But whatever the precise rate, deforestation remains a serious and growing problems, especially if the vast temperate Siberian forest (the size of the continental United States) is opened to intensive cutting, which experts expect to occur as a result of the breakup of the Soviet Union and the entry of foreign companies into the Russian economy (see chapter 11).[42]

Environmentalists have identified four problems with tropical deforestation. First, deforestation in the tropics, where rainfall is heavy—a one-hour downpour in Ghana can dump more rain than showers in London can deliver in a month—leads to rapid runoff, triggering floods and eroding soils.[43] Runaway forest soils fill streams with sediments, kill fish, and clog reservoirs behind dams, shortening their life span and reducing their ability to irrigate fields and generate electricity.[44]

Second, tropical woods do not easily recover from deforestation. Some scientists estimate that it takes tropical forests between 150 and 1,000 years to recover fully from a clear-cut, in contrast to temperate woods, which can be cut more often on a sustainable basis.[45] Because tropical forests do not easily recover, deforestation is typically associated with the loss of plant and animal species. Again, scientists debate the rate of extinction or argue that tropical rain forests are not the only or most important reservoirs of plant and animal species (one scientist argues that savannas may be more important for *mammal* species), but the fact is not disputed that deforestation leads to extinction in species-rich, tropical forest environments.[46] If Latin American forests are reduced to 50 percent of their original size, scientists estimate that 15 percent of forest plant species and 12 percent of bird species would be lost.[47] The problem with species loss is that it undermines the genetic base for cultivated plants and domestic species that are used by people throughout the world and for pharmacology, which relies on biological resources for human drugs.[48] For example, scientists recently discovered a primitive corn species in a tiny corner of a Mexican rain forest that was threatened with destruction. Because the surviving corn is a perennial, resistant to a variety of plant viruses, and hardy in cold and elevated climates, the plant holds great promise for plant geneticists who hope to infuse modern corn with some of the rain forest corn's genetic properties.[49] The irony is that species loss is reducing genetic resources just when genetic engineering technologies are being deployed to make effective use of them.[50]

Third, deforestation adversely affects indigenous Indian populations, particularly in Latin American and Pacific island forests. The destruction of rain forests and exposure to outside populations have reduced their number. In 1994, one entire village of Jaguapure Indians threatened to commit suicide unless seized lands were returned, and suicide rates among remnant tribes is high.[51] The opening of forests and the introduction of long-isolated cultures have resulted in the import and export of disease. River blindness and malaria have been taken into the forests, while scientists think that dengue fever, the Ebola virus, and perhaps AIDS have been brought out of disrupted rain forest environments.[52]

Deforestation also adversely affects other populations. In India and Africa, where there are few residual forest tribes, deforestation has increased fuel wood costs and forced poor people to forage further and longer for fuel to cook meals.[53]

Fourth, deforestation accelerates carbon dioxide emissions. Although undisturbed tropical forests emit carbon dioxide on balance, forest clearing and burning have greatly increased net carbon dioxide emissions, adding "perhaps 1 to 2.6 billion tons of carbon dioxide to the atmosphere annually, or between 20 and 50 percent as much as the burning of fossil fuels."[54] It matters, of course, how forests are cut. Selective cutting for valuable hardwoods produces less destruction and fewer emissions than conversion to tropical plantations. And these uses do less to destroy forest cover or release carbon dioxide than clear-cutting or burning, as occurred on a grand scale in 1976, when Volkswagen set twenty-five thousand hectares of Amazonian forest afire to clear land for a cattle ranch.[55]

Although there are good reasons to curb deforestation in the tropics and to prevent deforestation in temperate Siberian woods, different social solutions are needed because the economic causes of deforestation vary regionally.

In Latin America, the primary cause of deforestation is cattle ranching, from which beef is exported to the fast-food hamburger industry in the United States.[56] Central American ranchers, for example, export 85 to 95 percent of their beef to the United States.[57] The migration of poor farmers into the forests, where they engage in subsistence agriculture, also contributes to deforestation in Latin America. Governments in the region typically provide subsidies to cattle ranchers and assist the settlement of migrant farmers. They do so to promote beef exports that can be used to repay debt—deforestation accelerated after the onset of the debt crisis—and to provide land for small farmers displaced by the introduction of large-scale Green Revolution agriculture in the fertile valleys.[58]

In this context, deforestation might be slowed if the United States curbed consumption or imports of Latin American beef and if governments in the region introduced land reform to provide land to poor farmers and ease pressure on marginal agricultural environments. They might also encourage "sustainable" forestry—rubber tapping, nut harvesting—for indigenous and some settler groups already living in the woods. Of course, northern countries would probably have to extend substantial debt relief and economic aid to persuade governments in the region to conserve forests rather than use them as a source of export earnings or a way to absorb displaced rural populations.

The causes of deforestation in Southeast Asia are rather different. In Thailand, Malaysia, Indonesia, Papua New Guinea, and the Philippines, most tropical hardwoods are cut and exported to Japan, which imports 53 percent of the world's tropical hardwoods for use in construction and paper manufacture.[59] Taiwan and South Korea are also big tropical timber importers. Although timber exports are the main cause of deforestation in this region, conversion to tropical plantations—rubber, palm, and coffee—and the migration of subsistence farmers into the woods, which in Indonesia is directed by a government "transmigration" program designed to reduce population density on Java, also contribute to deforestation.[60]

In this context, deforestation might be slowed if Japan and the other tropical timber importers curbed hardwood consumption—much of the imported plywood is used once for concrete-building forms and then simply discarded—and if the Indonesian government emphasized birth control policies rather than "transmigration" programs. Thailand has banned the export of tropical timber, and other countries have banned the export of raw logs, in an effort to protect and manage their forests more effectively, though new free trade agreements may undermine their ability to use export controls to protect their resources (see chapter 9). And while conversion of forests to plantations contributes to species loss, it is less damaging than conversion to pasture or agriculture, and may represent a kind of compromise for countries needing export earnings.

In India and tropical Africa, the use of forests for fuel wood and subsistence agriculture is the main cause of deforestation, though countries in West Africa export some timber to European consumers.[61] The destruction of forests for fuel woods is particularly acute where population densities are high. In this context, birth control programs to reduce population density, the introduction of agroforestry programs—where villages are given resources to plant fast-growing trees for fuel—the provision of more efficient stoves to use fuel more effectively and, in some cases, the provision of cheap fuel alternatives, like kerosene, can help reduce pressure on the forests. These steps can improve conditions for poor women, who may spend hours searching for fuel woods or may switch to faster cooking but less nutritious foods where fuel is scarce or too expensive.[62] While these programs have proven effective, they are also costly for governments with few resources, which means that rich countries would have to provide economic aid if they were to be adopted widely.

Gender and Forests

In the South, deforestation generally hurts women because they are responsible in most poor, rural households for gathering firewood to cook food and warm family dwellings. Reforestation projects would mean that fuel supplies would be more plentiful and easier to obtain, which would same women considerable time, energy, and expense. In the North, as we have seen, deforestation generally hurts men because the logging, transport, milling, and pulping industries employ men, not women. Reforestation would provide employment for men, not women, though the growing reliance on technology and machinery in these industries means that reforestation could occur without significantly increasing job opportunities for men.

Automobiles

At the first Earth Day rallies in 1970, students sometimes bashed or buried cars, which they saw as symbols of environmental pollution and waste. Although smog and oil spills were then recognized as problems associated with cars, the explosive growth of the world car fleet and the widespread use of automobiles have since brought a host of other car-related environmental and social problems into sharp relief.

In 1950, there were fifty million cars worldwide, 75 percent of them in the United States. This number doubled by 1960, doubled again by 1970, and doubled again by 1990, an eightfold increase to more than four hundred million cars.[63] And experts predicted that the world car fleet would reach 530 million by 2000, with much of the growth occurring in the former communist countries.[64]

Of course, the exploding car population intensifies and widens the impact of cars on the environment. But perhaps more important is the extensive *use* of cars. By 1990, U.S. owners drove their cars two trillion miles every year, the equivalent of a round trip from Earth to Pluto every day of the year.[65]

The practice of driving interplanetary distances results in the consumption of vast quantities of oil, about six billion barrels a year. As has already been noted, the production, transportation, and use of oil are associated with a whole set of environmental, economic, and political problems. When burned to power a car, the oil is converted into a complex set of waste gases, carbon dioxide among them.[66] The average car produces its weight in carbon dioxide every year; the world car fleet generates about 14 percent of all carbon dioxide emissions.[67] But carbon dioxide emissions were long neglected because it is not a *toxic* gas, like most of the other one thousand assorted pollutants created by internal combustion engines.[68] Early efforts to reduce auto pollution focused on lead in gasoline, benzene, carbon monoxide, nitrogen oxides, unburned hydrocarbons, aldehydes, particulates, and trace metals because they contributed to smog and were known to have adverse effects on human health. More recent efforts have identified the release of CFCs from auto air conditioners (the number one source of CFC emissions in the United States) and carbon dioxide as problematic, even though they are not toxic to humans. Recently, more attention has been given to tiny particles of black carbon soot, which may be responsible for fifty thousand to sixty thousand deaths annually in the United States, affecting primarily young children with respiratory problems.[69] Carbon soot is also thought to make an important contribution to global warming, though the scientific evaluation of soot has only recently begun.

While cars release toxic pollutants, nontoxic gases, and particulates that adversely affect human health or the environment, they are also responsible for considerable death and injury. Worldwide, 265,000 are killed every year in auto accidents, and ten million more are injured.[70] Death rates are highest in poor countries, where cars share roads with pedestrians, bikes, and animals, and lower in rich countries where governments spend heavily to segregate traffic, police roads, improve auto safety and increasingly, prosecute drunk drivers.[71] But even in the rich countries, cars are prodigious killers. In the United States, cars kill about fifty thousand annually and have killed three million during the century since the car was invented. Nearly twice as many Americans have died on the highway than on the battlefield in all of this country's wars since 1776.[72]

In social and economic terms, the growth of car fleets has persuaded governments to build highways and transform cities to accommodate them, developments that have contributed to the deterioration of urban neighborhoods and downtown businesses, fueled urban sprawl, and consumed rural farms near cities. Because mass transit systems become more expensive and less efficient as cities sprawl—mass transit carries only as many people in the United States today as it did in 1900—people rely more heavily on the automobile for transport, at considerable personal expense.[73] A study by the Hertz Corporation reported that Americans devote 15 percent of their income on automobile transportation, and the average male spends 1,600 hours a year in his car.[74] The government too spends vast sums supporting private transportation, particularly on road construction, maintenance, and police services. The California Department of Transportation reported that the state spent $2,500 more for each vehicle on the road than it received from car owners in taxes and fees.[75] The cost to taxpayers of government automobile subsidies is now only becoming apparent, largely because the interstate highways and bridges (which were built in the 1950s) are now due for repair, at staggering cost.

During the 1970s, some of the problems associated with car use were addressed by government policy and market forces. Clean air legislation required cars to get better mileage and emit fewer pollutants. The elimination of lead from gasoline was particularly important, though U.S. manufacturers began exporting tetraethyl lead to other countries after the U.S. ban took effect. The introduction of safety belts, crash standards, and speed limits reduced fatalities 6 percent, even though the car population grew 50 percent.[76] At the same time, rapidly rising oil prices spurred technological innovation, resulting in smaller, more fuel-efficient cars, many of them from Japan, and reduced consumer use.

But many of the gains made during the 1970s eroded during the 1980s. The growing car population undermined technological improvements. "All of the progress we are making through technology is being eaten up by growth," one official of the California Air Resources Board reported.[77] The Reagan, Bush, and Clinton administrations cut mass transit systems, reduced fuel efficiency standards, and increased speed limits. These relaxed government policies undercut previous environmental and safety gains. After 1985, falling oil prices encouraged consumers to increase car use. In the past fifteen years, consumers have purchased trucks, jeeps, and minivans in increasing numbers, which is a problem because these vehicles get poor gas mileage, lowering the average fuel efficiency of the U.S. fleet. According to the Environmental Protection Agency, some forty million Americans live in cities that do not meet federal clean air standards, despite two decades of pollution reduction efforts.[78]

Many environmentalists and government officials have proposed higher taxes, tickets, and tolls as a way to curb auto use in the United States. They note that a 50-cent-a-gallon increase in the gas tax would produce $55 billion in annual revenue and discourage car use.[79] Although the Clinton administration raised the gas tax by only 4 cents, state officials around the country have increased registration fees, tickets, and tolls to raise money for strapped state budgets. In California, state officials raised registration fees and slapped a 40 percent penalty on drivers who paid one day late, while cities hiked parking tickets and tolls to finance budgets and reduce congestion. San Francisco, for example, increased its parking ticket revenues from $5.5 million in 1990 to $42 million in 1993, a sevenfold increase.[80]

The problem with this approach is that it is an inefficient and unfair way to reduce car use. The rising cost of fuel, fees, taxes, and tolls is felt first by low-income drivers, discouraging them from hitting the road. But this is not an efficient way to curb use because poor people own few cars and drive them sparingly. Families with annual incomes over $35,000 own three times as many cars, drive them three times as often and three times as far as families earning under $10,000.[81] The increasing popularity of gas-guzzling cars, vans, and trucks among well-to-do drivers means they consume more than three times as much gas. Higher costs are *inefficient* because they do little to curb use by people who have the greatest impact. They are also *unfair* because, in a country where mass transit systems are inadequate, poor people need cars to get to work just as much as wealthy families do. There are also regional inequalities. In Wyoming, the average commuter pays $243 a year in gas taxes, the average New Yorker only $91.[82] An across-the-board tax increase would have a greater impact on drivers in western states, where commutes are long, than on drivers in the East.

Gender and Automobiles

The rising cost of car ownership in the United States is socially unfair not only because it disadvantages poor people but also because it adversely affects poor women and single mothers. As a result of welfare reform in 1996, poor women who received government benefits were assigned jobs while looking for permanent employment. But the rising cost of car ownership made it difficult for poor women to own cars, making it hard for them to find or keep jobs that were far from home or could not easily be reached by public transit. It was even harder for women trying to get to work *and* child care providers. This problem has been exacerbated by the suburbanization of towns and industries, which has located jobs in places that require workers to own cars. So poor women and single mothers without cars have found it extremely difficult to keep assigned jobs or find permanent employment.

There is of course a way to curb car use that is efficient and equitable: gas rationing. But it is such an anathema to consumers and politicians—this despite demonstrable success during World War II—that it does not yet figure in any political discussion of car use.

Increasing car ownership and use in the United States and around the world is the source of serious environmental and social problems, global climate change among them. There are good reasons to reduce car use. But the automobile is so deeply embedded in the economic, social, and psychological life of the wealthy countries, particularly the United States, that it will be difficult to curb car ownership or use.

SWAMPS, RICE, AND COWS (METHANE)

After carbon dioxide, methane is the most important greenhouse gas, representing about 18 percent of all the gases with climate-changing potential.[83] Most of the methane in the atmosphere, about 65 percent, is emitted from "natural" processes, from anaerobic fermentation in wetlands, peat bogs, and swamps.[84] Human activity is responsible for about 35 percent of all methane emissions. Rice cultivation accounts for about 20 percent of this, and animal husbandry contributes about 15 percent.[85]

Although the use of synthetic fertilizer could lower methane emissions from rice cultivation, it would be difficult to reduce methane from this source without jeopardizing rice production, which feeds so much of the world.[86] But while it would be difficult to reduce rice production, there are sound human and environmental reasons to reduce animal herds, particularly of cows. Cows release about eighty million metric tons of methane into the atmosphere, considerably more than other domestic animals: ten times more than sheep, fifty times more than pigs.[87] Moreover, the expansion of the world cow herd, which increased from 500 million to 1.2 billion between 1950 and 1990, has contributed to two important human and environmental problems.[88]

First, cows consume vast quantities of grain that might otherwise feed a hungry and growing world population. Cows consume about one-third of the world's grain, nearly 70 percent of the grain grown in the United States.[89] In recent years, feed grain for cows has increasingly replaced grain grown for human consumption in poor countries, which has reduced the supply and increased the price of staple foods for hungry people.[90] Many countries, particularly in Latin America, have increased cattle production to supply beef for the U.S. market and earn money that can be used to repay debt. But the expansion of cattle ranching, with its resulting "protein flight," has reduced the amount of land devoted to agriculture and has led to rural job loss because ranching employs very few workers (one worker for every 47.6 hectares, compared with one worker for every 2.9 hectares in agriculture).[91] Cattle ranching has thereby contributed to rising prices and falling incomes for rural families in many countries, one reason why "one-third of rural families [in Mexico] never eat meat or eggs and 59 percent never drink milk."[92]

While the expansion of the world cattle herd contributes to hunger in poor countries, it also contributes to obesity and disease in wealthy countries where consumers eat vast quantities of beef.

Between 1945 and 1976, per capita beef consumption in the United States grew from 71 pounds to 129 pounds annually.[93] Nearly 40 percent of this was consumed as hamburgers, a postwar phenomenon associated first with the spread of backyard barbecue grills (unlike pork, which was preferred by Americans before the war) and later with the spread of fast-food hamburger franchises.[94]

The growing consumption of beef protein created a diet heavy in fat: 37 percent of calories in U.S. diets comes from fat.[95] As a result, obesity has become a serious problem. More than thirty-four million Americans are overweight, according to the Centers for Disease Control, and the number of women considered obese rose from 13.3 percent to 17.7 percent between 1960 and 1980.[96] More important, fat-heavy diets and obesity contribute to disease and death. The U.S. Surgeon General estimated that 1.5 million deaths in 1987 were related to dietary factors and said that diets high in saturated fat and cholesterol contributed to the high incidence of heart attack, colon and breast cancer, and stroke in America.[97]

Second, the world's cow herd contributes to a series of environmental problems. The expansion of cattle herds in tropical regions has led to extensive deforestation, particularly in Latin America, and increased carbon dioxide emissions. Outside rain forest settings, cattle grazing on desert fringe areas or on marginal lands can lead to desertification, as it has in the Sahel of Africa, or to the degradation of grasslands.[98] Cows also consume large quantities of water, far more than other domesticated animals, which can drain water resources in arid regions.[99] On pasture land, cattle waste can foul streams—"an ungrazed part of a stream in Montana produced 268 more trout than did a grazed part of the same stream"—while waste from feed lots can contaminate groundwater supplies—"the organic waste generated by a 10,000-head feed lot is equivalent to the human waste generated in a city of 110,000 people."[100]

But after increasing for many years, beef consumption in the wealthy countries fell in the past twenty-five years. From a high of 129 pounds per capita in 1976, U.S. beef consumption fell to 78.2 pounds by 1983, back to World War II levels.[101] This rapid decline was a product of two developments: rising grain prices during the 1970s and changing diets.[102] As Americans became more concerned about diet and health in the 1970s and 1980s, consumers reduced their purchase of beef, which was growing more expensive because feed prices had soared, and increasingly turned to chicken, fish, and pasta. As a result of falling consumer demand, the growth of the world cow herd slowed and then stabilized at about 1.25 billion head by 1990.[103]

While this was a welcome development in human and environmental terms, further cattle herd reductions would be possible and beneficial. A reduction in dietary fat in the United States, say, from 37 to 30 percent, a level most dietary scientists believe is necessary, would reduce beef consumption by another 20 percent.[104] And if fat made up only 14 percent of American diets, a level that some scientists believe is optimal because it would greatly reduce health risks, beef consumption would fall and the world cow herd could shrink dramatically, releasing large amounts of grain for human consumption. "If the 130 million metric tons of grain that are fed yearly to U.S. livestock were consumed directly as human food, about 400 million people—1.7 times larger than the U.S. population—could be sustained for one year," Cornell scientist David Pimentel estimated.[105] Of course, even scientists who argue that "we are basically a vegetarian species and should be eating a wide variety of plant food and minimizing our intake of animal food" do not argue for a completely vegetarian diet or an agriculture without animal husbandry.[106] Rather, they argue that consumption of animal protein should be reduced in wealthy countries, that consumers should rely on other animals that produce protein more efficiently (chickens and pigs), and that cow herds should be reduced but not eliminated so they can continue to provide milk, cheese, traction, and manure in many agricultural systems.

COOLANTS AND SPRAY CANS (CFCs)

In 1985, British scientists discovered that a set of gases called chlorofluorocarbons (CFCs) were responsible for depleting ozone in the atmosphere.[107] CFCs were first invented by DuPont scientist Thomas Midgley in 1930.[108] Because CFCs were nontoxic, nonflammable, noncorrosive, and inert, they soon found widespread application as coolants in refrigerators and air conditioners, propellants in spray cans, and blowing agents in plastic and Styrofoam. Later, related gases called halons found use in fire extinguishers: "Used in Army tanks, in which engine and munition fires can spread like lightning, [automatic] halon fire extinguishers . . . can snuff out a raging gasoline fire in thousandths of a second."[109]

In 1974, scientists warned that while CFCs were beneficial in many respects, when they were released into the atmosphere, sunlight would detach chlorine from the rest of the molecule, and chlorine would then attack and deplete ozone.[110] If this occurred, researchers warned, CFCs could weaken the ozone layer, the planet's protection against harmful ultraviolet radiation from the sun. They predicted that higher radiation levels would increase the incidence of skin cancer, particularly among Caucasians, make cataracts more common, and suppress the human immune system, which fights off viruses, tumors, and other infectious diseases.[111] Increased radiation would also harm plants, particularly crops like soybeans, and affect marine organisms in waters up to one hundred feet deep.[112] Scientists noted, however, that the effects would be hard to predict because radiation levels around the globe would increase unevenly, and because places with heavy cloud cover would block much of the radiation, whereas areas with direct sunlight would receive heavier doses.[113]

Scientists found evidence in 1985 that CFC levels and ozone depletion were closely related and discovered serious ozone depletion over Antarctica. This discovery of an "ozone hole . . . larger than the United States and taller than Mount Everest" spurred efforts to reduce and eventually ban CFCs and other ozone-depleting gases, halons, and later methyl bromide.[114]

In 1987, twenty-four countries adopted the Montreal Protocol on Substances That Deplete the Ozone Layer, agreeing to freeze CFC production at 1986 levels, followed by a 20 percent reduction by 1993 and another 30 percent reduction in 1998.[115] During the next few years, as evidence mounted that ozone depletion was accelerating and becoming more serious, signatories to the Montreal Protocol took additional steps. In 1989, they agreed to eliminate all CFC production by the end of the century and in 1992 moved the deadline up to 1996.[116] The rich countries also agreed to provide $500 million to poor countries to help them reduce their reliance on CFCs.[117] The Bush administration used provisions of the Clean Air Act to ban some substances not covered by the Montreal Protocol.[118] And in 1995, one hundred governments agreed to phase out methyl bromide, a powerful ozone-depleting pesticide used in agriculture.[119]

Governments acted with rare unanimity and considerable speed because the scientific evidence was not disputed (as it has been with global warming), because CFC contributed to ozone depletion but also to global warming (accounting for about 14 percent of greenhouse gases), because ozone depletion was accelerating rapidly—ozone was being depleted twice as fast in 1992 as it had been in 1985—and because the particular properties of CFCs made delay damaging. CFC have long atmospheric life spans: CFC 11 lasts 76 years in the upper atmosphere, CFC 12 for 139 years.[120] And because they are now stored in foams, refrigerators, and spray cans, they will be slowly released as these containers erode, pumping ozone-depleting gases into the atmosphere even after their manufacture has stopped. As a consequence, a CFC ban in 2000 would only reduce CFCs to current levels in 2073. By moving up the deadline to 1996, governments thought CFC levels would fall back to current levels much sooner, by 2053. These realities made for rare agreement. As U.S. delegate Richard Benedick explained, "We're seeing something completely unprecedented in the history of diplomacy. Politicians from every block and region of the world are setting aside politics to reach agreement on protecting the global environment."[121]

These developments produced real and immediate benefits and created fewer economic problems that many first expected. Scientists found that production and use of CFCs slowed even before the Montreal Protocol took effect and, as a result, that ozone depletion slowed dramatically. "Here is a beautiful case study of science and public policy working well," said NASA scientist James Elkins.[122] Moreover, the cost to industry and consumers of replacing CFCs with other technologies proved less expensive than industry officials first predicted. The switch to other technologies even resulted in energy-saving designs, which could result in savings of up to $100 billion during the next eighty-five years.[123] While efforts to reduce CFCs have been successful, it is important to note that they occurred not so much because they contributed to global warming but because they contributed to *other* serious social and environmental problems.

SYNTHETIC FERTILIZER (NITROUS OXIDE)

Synthetic nitrogen fertilizers emit nitrous oxide, a gas associated with global climate change. Natural sources of nitrous oxide emissions are also present in oceans and soils, but as with methane emissions, little can be done about them. About one-third of all nitrous oxide emissions are associated with human activity. Of these, synthetic fertilizer use is the most important source, though nitrous oxide is also produced during the manufacture of nylon.[124] The increasing use of nitrogen fertilizers—global fertilizer use grew from 14 million tons in 1950 to 121 million tons in 1984—contributes not only to global warming (about 6 percent of the total) but also to groundwater pollution and algae blooms, which deprive rivers, estuaries, and oceans of oxygen, killing fish, and other marine life.[125]

But while problems are associated with nitrogen fertilizers, global climate change among them, the use of fertilizer greatly increases world food production, which is essential for a growing population. As the World Watch Institute estimated, "Eliminating [synthetic fertilizer] use today would probably cut world food production by at least a third," an extremely serious problem for the "billion and a half people now fed with the additional food produced with chemical fertilizer."[126]

Under these circumstances, it is difficult to imagine or suggest that synthetic fertilizer use should be dramatically reduced or eliminated as part of an effort to reduce global warming. There are, however, some steps that could be taken to reduce fertilizer use and nitrous oxide emissions on the margins.

Because natural gas is used to produce synthetic fertilizers such as anhydrous ammonia, fertilizer prices rise and fall with energy prices. When energy prices rose in the 1970s, fertilizer use slowed somewhat, curbing pollution and nitrous oxide emissions.[127] Most agronomists also think that changed farm practices could reduce some fertilizer-related problems. They argue that farmers could apply fertilizers more carefully, an important consideration because their effectiveness is relatively ephemeral.[128] They urge farmers to use more natural manures for fertilizer, much of it now wasted in cattle, pig, and chicken feed lot systems, which do not apply waste to farmlands, because natural manures release less nitrous oxide and require less energy (and carbon dioxide emissions) to produce.[129] They also urge farmers to plant nitrogen-fixing crops like alfalfa along with nitrogen-depleting crops like corn to reduce synthetic fertilizer inputs and also reduce farmer costs, an important consideration if small-scale farmers are to survive.[130]

Because these practices would likely produce only modest reductions in synthetic fertilizer use, people concerned about global climate change will probably have to devote their attention to curbing *other* greenhouse gases, which in any event play a more significant overall role.

POLITICAL AND ECONOMIC SOLUTIONS

The scientific case for global warming persuaded government officials around the world to take steps to reduce greenhouse gas emissions. In 1992, government representatives meeting in Rio de Janeiro agreed that the industrialized countries would try to reduce greenhouse gas emissions to 1990 levels by 2000. President George H. Bush signed the agreement, which provided that measures taken to reduce greenhouse gases were voluntary, not mandatory.[131] Bush supported the agreement because he recognized that the United States, with only 5 percent of the world's population, was responsible for 25 percent of all greenhouse emissions.

In 1997, officials for 170 countries met in Kyoto, Japan, to hammer out a formal treaty that would set more ambitious goals and require signatory governments to take mandatory steps to reduce greenhouse emissions. At this meeting, representatives agreed to reduce emissions to 5 percent *below* 1990 levels by 2012, an approach endorsed by the Clinton administration.[132] The Kyoto Protocols, as the treaty was called, would take effect only after fifty-five countries, including countries responsible for 55 percent of all 1990 emissions, had signed the accord.

During the next four years, officials haggled over the details so that governments could sign the protocols and bring them into effect. But as negotiations neared their conclusion in 2001, President George W. Bush announced that the United States had reversed its position and would not endorse the treaty.[133] He argued that if the United States took steps required in the treaty, it would "have a negative economic impact, with layoffs of workers and price increases for consumers."[134] He also complained that the agreement was unfair because it required major reductions by the United States but none by poor, developing countries such as China and India.[135]

Negotiators had agreed to exempt India and China because their per capita production of greenhouse gases was only a fraction of that in the United States, Western Europe, and Japan. In 1998, per capita carbon dioxide emissions in the United States (20.1 tons) were ten times bigger than per capita emissions in China (2.3 tons).[136] If India and China were required to reduce emissions, they might be unable to provide even minimal supplies of electricity or fuel for transportation and heating. Moreover, while China was not obligated by Kyoto to reduce its greenhouse emissions, it did so anyway, reducing emissions by 17 percent between 1995 and 2001, even while its economy grew 36 percent.[137] "Even without undertaking binding commitments under an international agreement, China has nevertheless contributed substantially to reducing growth in greenhouse emissions," scientists at the Lawrence Berkeley National Laboratory reported.[138]

China was able to reduce emissions voluntarily because it ended government subsidies for fuel, which increased energy prices and reduced consumption, and because it promoted energy conservation, particularly in big cities where air pollution is a serious problem.[139] "We've done what we can to reduce emissions," Gao Feng, a Chinese official explained. "But it's not fair to ask the developing countries to take the lead."[140]

After the Bush administration pulled out of negotiations in the summer of

2001, adoption of the treaty was put in serious jeopardy. But negotiations continued in Marrakesh, Morocco, during the fall.[141] Finally, in November 2001, representatives of 164 countries announced that they had reached an agreement that would meet the approval of fifty-five countries, including countries responsible for 55 percent of global emissions.[142] With the United States on the sidelines, this meant crafting language that persuaded the EC, Japan, and Russia to sign on.

Although U.S. officials refused to participate, the treaty may still help reduce U.S. emissions even without government permission. That is because private businesses in the United States may voluntarily take steps that government officials are unwilling to take. Private corporations are moving on their own to reduce energy consumption and greenhouse emissions for a variety of reasons. First, many businesses and public utilities are converting from energy sources that are high in carbon (coal) to energy supplies that are lower in carbon (oil and natural gas).[143] When burned, natural gas produces only one-third as much carbon dioxide as coal, two-thirds that of oil.[144] Corporations practice this kind of "substitutionism" (see chapter 6) to take advantage of new technologies and reduce costs. The "decarbonization" of the energy system in the United States is being driven largely by market considerations, not government policy.

Second, many transnational corporations based in the United States do business in Western Europe, Japan, and in other countries that *are* signing onto the Kyoto Protocols. As a result, "many multinational companies plan to continue reducing emissions because they fact strong pressure to do so in Europe and Japan, fear rising energy costs, or want to promote their products as being friendly to the environment."[145]

TNCs recognize that if they do not take steps, their ability to compete with corporations in Western Europe and Japan may erode. This is particularly clear to U.S. automakers, who recognize that they must develop new, more energy-efficient, higher-mileage automobile designs if they are going to compete with automakers in Western Europe and Japan.[146] In the same spirit, DuPont and Alcoa have announced plans to reduce substantially their greenhouse gas emissions. DuPont said it would cut emissions to 65 percent *below* 1990 levels by the year 2010; Alcoa to 25 percent *below* 1990 levels by 2010.[147] These cutbacks would be more dramatic and more rapid than reductions called for in the Kyoto Protocols. It may be that U.S. businesses are willing to do what government officials cannot contemplate. In this case, the globalization of business may have positive environmental and social benefits. This is not always the case, as we will see in the next chapter when we examine the globalization of trade. But insofar as TNCs are taking steps to reduce greenhouse emissions, for whatever reasons, globalization in this context contributes to positive change.

NOTES

1. Philip Shabecoff, "Global Warming Has Begun, Expert Tells Senate," *New York Times*, June 24, 1988.

2. Jacqueline Vaughn Switzer, *Environmental Politics: Domestic and Global Dimensions* (New York: St. Martin's Press, 1994), 269.

3. Boyce Rensberger, "As Earth Summit Nears, Consensus Still Lacking on Global Warming's Cause," *Washington Post*, May 31, 1992.

4. William K. Stevens, "Experts Confirm Human Role in Global Warming," *New York Times*, September 10, 1995.

5. Christopher Flavin, "Slowing Global Warming," in *State of the World 1990*, ed. Lester Brown (New York: Norton, 1990), 17.

6. Paul Kennedy, *Preparing for the 21st Century* (New York: Random House, 1993), 108; William K. Stevens, "Earlier Global Warming Harm Seen," *New York Times*, October 17, 1990; Jeremy Leggett, "The Nature of the Greenhouse Threat," in *Global Warming: The Greenpeace Report*, ed. Jeremy Leggett (Oxford: Oxford University Press, 1990), 2.

7. Kennedy, *Preparing for the 21st Century*, 110.

8. William K. Stevens, "Violent World of Corals Is Facing New Dangers," *New York Times*, February 16, 1993.

9. Bill McKibben, *The End of Nature* (New York: Random House, 1989), 95–96.

10. Jeremy Leggett, "Gone with the Winds," *World Paper* (April 1993): 13.

11. Kennedy, *Preparing for the 21st Century*, 111–12.

12. David E. Pitt, "Computer Vision of Global Warming: Hardest on Have-Nots," *New York Times*, January 18, 1994; Claire Pedrick, "A Moveable Feast: Climate, Bread and Butter," *World Paper* (April 1993): 11.

13. Flavin, "Slowing Global Warming," 19; Kennedy, *Preparing for the 21st Century*, 117.

14. Marlise Simons, "Brazil, Smarting from the Outcry over the Amazon, Charges Foreign Plot," *New York Times*, March 23, 1989.

15. Patrick E. Tyler, "China's Power Needs Exceed Investor Tolerance," *New York Times*, November 7, 1994.

16. Patrick E. Tyler, "China's Inevitable Dilemma: Coal Equals Growth," *New York Times*, September 29, 1995.

17. William K. Stevens, "In a Warming World, Who Comes Out Ahead?" *New York Times*, February 5, 1991.

18. Patrick J. Michaels, *Sound and Fury: The Science and Politics of Global Warming* (Washington, D.C.: Cato Institute, 1992), 3; William K. Stevens, "Global Warming: The Contrarian View," *New York Times*, February 29, 2000; Andrew C. Revkin, "Debate Rises over a Quick(er) Climate Fix," *New York Times*, October 3, 2000.

19. S. Fred Singer, "Global Climate Change: Fact and Fiction," in *Environment 93/94*, ed. John L. Allen (Guilford, Conn.: Dushkin, 1993), 186; Richard A. Kerr, "Is the World Warming or Not?" *Science* 267 (February 3, 1995): 612; Michaels, *Sound and Fury*, 53.

20. Rensberger, "As Earth Summit Nears"; William K. Stevens, "In New Data on Climate Changes, Decades, Not Centuries Count," *New York Times*, December 7, 1993; William K. Stevens, "Climate Roller Coaster in Swedish Tree Rings," *New York Times*, August 7, 1990.

21. Williams K. Stevens, "With Climate Treaty Signed, All Say They'll Do Even More," *New York Times*, June 13, 1992; Singer, "Global Climate Change," 17; Lester

Brown, "A False Sense of Security," in Lester Brown, *State of the World 1985* (New York: Norton, 1985), 15.

22. Singer, "Global Climate Change," 186.

23. Flavin, "Slowing Global Warming," 17.

24. William K. Stevens, "A Skeptic Asks, Is It Getting Hotter, or Is It Just the Computer Model?" *New York Times*, June 18, 1996.

25. Stevens, "A Skeptic Asks."

26. Rensberger, "As Earth Summit Nears."

27. Williams K. Stevens, "Experts Confirm Human Role in Global Warming," *New York Times*, September 10, 1995.

28. Stevens, "Experts Confirm Human Role."

29. Sylvia Nasar, "Cooling the Globe Would Be Nice, but Saving Lives Now May Cost Less," *New York Times*, May 31, 1992.

30. Mick Kelly, "Halting Global Warming," in *Global Warming: The Greenpeace Report*, 86; Leggett, "The Nature of the Greenhouse Threat," 17.

31. Michael Renner, "Reinventing Transportation," in *State of the World 1994*, ed. Lester Brown (New York: Norton, 1994), 64.

32. Sandra Postel, "Protecting Forests," in *State of the World 1984*, ed. Lester Brown (New York: Norton, 1984), 82.

33. Joseph J. Romm and Amory B. Lovins, "Fueling a Competitive Economy," *Foreign Affairs* (Winter 1992–93): 47.

34. Romm and Lovins, "Fueling a Competitive Economy," 49.

35. Romm and Lovins, "Fueling a Competitive Economy," 48.

36. Renner, "Reinventing Transportation," 69.

37. Romm and Lovins, "Fueling a Competitive Economy," 50.

38. Catherine Caufield, *Tropical Moist Forests* (London: Earthscan, 1982), 7; Norman Meyers, "Tropical Forests," in *Global Warming: The Greenpeace Report*, 377.

39. Caufield, *Tropical Moist Forests*, 1; Sandra Postel and Lori Heise, "Reforesting the Earth," in *State of the World 1988*, ed. Lester Brown (New York: Norton, 1988), 85.

40. Stephen Budiansky, "The Doomsday Myths," in *Environment 95/96*, ed. John L. Allen (Guilford, Conn.: Dushkin, 1995), 35; "Instant Trees," *The Economist*, April 28, 1990, 93.

41. Diane Jean Schemo, "Burning of Amazon Picks Up Pace, with Vast Areas Lost," *New York Times*, September 12, 1996.

42. William K. Stevens, "Experts Say Logging of Vast Siberian Forest Could Foster Warming," *New York Times*, January 28, 1992.

43. Caufield, *Tropical Moist Forests*, 10.

44. Frec Pearce, "Hit and Run in Sarawak," *New Scientist*, May 12, 1990, 47; A. Kent MacDougall, "Worldwide Costs Mount as Trees Fall," *Los Angeles Times*, June 14, 1987; Postel, "Protecting Forests," 84.

45. Edward C. Wolf, "Avoiding a Mass Extinction of Species," in *State of the World 1988*, 110; Patrick Anderson, "The Myth of Sustainable Logging: The Case for a Ban on Tropical Timber Imports," *The Ecologist* 19 (September–October 1989): 166. Studies have shown that even temperate woods do not recover as easily or as fast as foresters have long assumed. Catherine Dold, "Study Casts Doubt on Belief in Self-Revival of Cleared Forests," *New York Times*, September 1, 1992.

46. Caufield, *Tropical Moist Forests*, 10; Budiansky, "The Doomsday Myths," 34; Charles Petit, "Scientist Argues against Focus on Rain Forests," *San Francisco Chronicle*, February 21, 1992.

47. Wolf, "Avoiding a Mass Extinction of Species," 103.

48. David Pimentel, Laura E. Armstrong, Christine A. Flass, Frederic W. Hopf, Ronald B. Landy, and Marcia H. Pimentel, "Interdependence of Food and Natural Resources," in *Food and Natural Resources*, eds. David Pimentel and Carl W. Hall (San Diego: Academic Press, 1989), 42.

49. Norman Meyers, "Loss of Biological Diversity and Its Potential Impact on Agriculture and Food Productivity," in *Food and Natural Resources*, 52–53.

50. Meyers, "Loss of Biological Diversity," 53.

51. Caufield, *Tropical Moist Forests*, 19; *San Francisco Chronicle*, March 11, 1996.

52. Caufield, *Tropical Moist Forests*, 33; Richard Preston, "Crisis in the Hot Zone," *The New Yorker*, October 26, 1992, 62.

53. Postel, "Protecting Forests," 83; MacDougall, "Worldwide Costs Mount as Trees Fall."

54. Postel and Heise, "Reforesting the Earth," 94.

55. Caufield, *Tropical Moist Forests*, 37.

56. Postel, "Protecting Forests," 77; Singer, "Global Climate Change," 86; Paul Harrison, *The Third Revolution: Population, Environment and a Sustainable World* (London: Penguin, 1993), 95–96.

57. Caufield, *Tropical Moist Forests*, 34.

58. "How Brazil Subsidizes the Destruction of the Amazon," *The Economist*, March 18, 1989, 69; Harrison, *The Third Revolution*, 96; Caufield, *Tropical Moist Forests*, 24–25.

59. Adam Schwarz, "Timer Troubles," *Far Eastern Economic Review*, April 6, 1989, 86; Caufield, *Tropical Moist Forests*, 29.

60. Caufield, *Tropical Moist Forests*, 28; Postel, "Protecting Forests," 77.

61. Postel and Heise, "Reforesting the Earth," 88–89.

62. Postel and Heise, "Reforesting the Earth," 88.

63. Motor Vehicle Manufacturers Association, *World Motor Vehicle Data, 1988 Edition* (Detroit: Author, 1988); Alan Attshuler, *The Future of the Automobile: The Report of MIT's International Automobile Program* (Cambridge: MIT Press, 1984), 2–3, 13; Lester Brown, Christopher Flavin, and Colin Norman, *Running on Empty: The Future of the Automobile in an Oil Short World* (New York: Norton, 1979), 86.

64. Attshuler, *The Future of the Automobile*, 113.

65. Alexandra Allen, "The Auto's Assault on the Atmosphere," *Multinational Monitor* (January–February 1990): 23.

66. Attshuler, *The Future of the Automobile*, 4.

67. Christopher Flavin, "Slowing Global Warming," in *State of the World 1990*, ed. Lester Brown (New York: Norton, 1990), 23; Attshuler, *The Future of the Automobile*, 58; Greenpeace, *The Environmental Impact of the Car: A Greenpeace Report* (Seattle: Author, 1992), 15.

68. Greenpeace, *The Environmental Impact of the Car*, 19.

69. Philip J. Hilts "Studies Say Soot Kills Up to 60,000 in U.S. Each Year," *New York Times*, July 19, 1993; Revkin, "Debate Rises over a Quick(er) Climate Fix."

70. Greenpeace, *The Environmental Impact of the Car*, 48; Attshuler, *The Future of the Automobile*, 5.

71. Wolfgang Zuckerman, *End of the Road: From World Car Crisis to Sustainable Transportation* (Post Mills, Vt.: Chelsea Green, 1993), 134.

72. Robert Schaeffer, "Car Sick: Autos Ad Nauseum," *Greenpeace Magazine* (May–June 1990): 15.

73. Schaeffer, "Car Sick."

74. Brown, Flavin, and Norman, *Running on Empty*, 17; Zuckerman, *End of the Road*, 85–86; Romm and Lovins, "Fueling a Competitive Economy," 86.

75. Zuckerman, *End of the Road*, 215.

76. Attshuler, *The Future of the Automobile*, 66–67, 70.

77. Ronal Brownstein, "Testing the Limits," *National Journal*, July 29, 1989, 1918.

78. Robert Reinhold, "Hard Times Dilute Enthusiasm for Clean Air Laws," *New York Times*, November 25, 1993; James Sterngold, "A Back-and-Forth Smog War," *New York Times*, September 12, 1996.

79. Matthew L. Wald, "50-Cents-a-Gallon Tax Could Buy a Whole Lot," *New York Times*, October 18, 1992.

80. Phillip Matier and Andrew Ross, "State Drives Up Car Costs," *San Francisco Chronicle*, June 21, 1993.

81. Motor Vehicles Manufacturer Association, *World Motor Vehicle Data, 1988 Edition*.

82. Wald, "50-Cents-a-Gallon Tax."

83. Anne Ehrlich, "Agricultural Contributions to Global Warming," in *Global Warming: The Greenpeace Report*, 401.

84. Ehrlich, "Agricultural Contributions to Global Warming," 402–3.

85. Ehrlich, "Agricultural Contributions to Global Warming," 403.

86. Ehrlich, "Agricultural Contributions to Global Warming," 407.

87. Ehrlich, "Agricultural Contributions to Global Warming," 404; McKibben, *The End of Nature*, 15; Alan Thein Durning and Holly B. Brough, "Reforming the Livestock Economy," in *State of the World 1992*, ed. Lester Brown (New York: Norton, 1992), 74.

88. Durning and Brough, "Reforming the Livestock Economy," 68.

89. Durning and Brough, "Reforming the Livestock Economy," 69–70.

90. Durning and Brough, "Reforming the Livestock Economy," 76; Steven E. Sanderson, "The Emergence of the 'World Steer': International and Foreign Domination in Latin American Cattle Production," in *Food, the State and International Political Economy: Dilemmas of Developing Countries*, eds. F. LaMond Tullis and W. Ladd Hollist (Lincoln: University of Nebraska Press, 1986), 133–34, 139–40.

91. Mark Edelman, "From Costa Rican Pasture to North American Hamburger," in *Food and Evolution*, eds. Marvin Harris and Eric B. Ross (Philadelphia: Temple University Press, 1987), 553, 554–55; Sanderson, "The Emergence of the 'World Steer,'" 146.

92. Sanderson, "The Emergence of the 'World Steer,'" 129.

93. Jimmy M. Skaggs, *Prime Cut: Livestock Raising and Meatpacking in the United States, 1607–1983* (College Station: Texas A&M University Press, 1986), 166.

94. Jeremy Rifkin, *Beyond Beef: The Rise and Fall of the Cattle Culture* (New York: Dutton, 1992), 260, 264.

95. Durning and Brough, "Reforming the Livestock Economy," 74.

96. Rifkin, *Beyond Beef*, 166.

97. Rifkin, *Beyond Beef*, 171.

98. Durning and Brough, "Reforming the Livestock Economy," 72–73; Kennedy, *Preparing for the 21st Century*, 98–99.

99. Vashek Cervinka, "Water Use in Agriculture," in *Food, the State and International Political Economy*, 148–49: Durning and Brough, "Reforming the Livestock Economy," 70–71.

100. Rifkin, *Beyond Beef*, 206, 221.

101. Rifkin, *Beyond Beef*, 206, 221.

102. Skaggs, *Prime Cut*, 181–82.

103. Ehrlich, "Agricultural Contributions to Global Warming," 405.

104. Durning and Brough, "Reforming the Livestock Economy," 81–82.

105. Pimental et al., "Interdependence of Food and Natural Resources," 36; Rifkin, *Beyond Beef*, 161.

106. Rifkin, *Beyond Beef*, 73–74.

107. Cynthia Shea, "Protecting the Ozone Layer," in *State of the World 1989*, ed. Lester Brown (New York: Norton, 1989), 77–78.

108. Shea, "Protecting the Ozone Layer," 85.

109. Malcome W. Browne, "As Halon Ban Nears, Researchers Seek a New Miracle Firefighter," *New York Times*, December 15, 1992.

110. Shea, "Protecting the Ozone Layer," 78–79.

111. Shea, "Protecting the Ozone Layer," 82–83; Tom Wicker, "Bad News from Above," *New York Times*, April 10, 1991.

112. Shea, "Protecting the Ozone Layer," 83; Malcome W. Browne, "Broad Effort Underway to Track Ozone Hole's Effects," *New York Times*, January 6, 1992.

113. William K. Stevens, "Clouds May Retard Ozone Depletion," *New York Times*, November 21, 1995.

114. Shea, "Protecting the Ozone Layer," 78.

115. Shea, "Protecting the Ozone Layer," 93.

116. Craig R. Whitney, "Banning Chemicals That May Harm Ozone," *New York Times*, March 3, 1989; David Perlman, "Scientists Discover Huge Increase in Threat to Ozone," *San Francisco Chronicle*, February 4, 1992; Craig R. Whitney, "80 Nations Favor Ban to Help Ozone," *New York Times*, May 3, 1989; William K. Stevens, "Threat to Ozone Hastens the Ban on Some Chemicals," *New York Times*, November 26, 1992.

117. Stevens, "Threat to Ozone"; Craig R. Whitney, "Industrial Countries to Aid Poorer Nations on Ozone," *New York Times*, May 6, 1989.

118. Keith Schneider, "Bush Orders End to Making of Ozone-Depleting Agents," *New York Times*, February 13, 1992.

119. William K. Stevens, "100 Nations Move to Save Ozone Shield," *New York Times*, December 10, 1995.

120. Shea, "Protecting the Ozone Layer," 88.

121. Malcome W. Browne, "Ozone Fading Fast, Thatcher Tells Experts," *New York Times*, June 28, 1990.

122. William K. Stevens, "Scientists Report an Easing in Ozone-Killing Chemicals," *New York Times*, August 26, 1993.

123. David Doniger and Alan Miller, "Fighting Global Warming Is Good for Business," Center for Global Change, College Park, University of Maryland, circa 1990.

124. Ehrlich, "Agricultural Contributions to Global Warming," 410–13; Keith Bradsher and Andrew C. Revkin, "A Pre-emptive Strike on Global Warming," *New York Times*, May 15, 2001.

125. William J. Hudson, "Population, Food and the Economy of Nations," in *Food and Natural Resources*, 201–3; Hilary F. French, "Clearing the Air," in *State of the World 1990*, ed. Lester Brown (New York: Norton, 1990), 106; Lester Brown, "Reducing Hunger," in *State of the World 1994*, 29.

126. "Reducing Hunger," 29; Ehrlich, "Agricultural Contributions to Global Warming," 419.

127. Brown, "Reducing Hunger," 31.

128. David A. Andow and David P. Davis, "Agricultural Chemicals: Food and Environment," in *Food and Natural Resources*, 195.

129. Andow and Davis, "Agricultural Chemicals," 195; Ehrlich, "Agricultural Contributions to Global Warming," 414, 416.

130. Norman Meyers, "Loss of Biological Diversity and Its Potential Impact on Agriculture and Food Productivity," in *Food and Natural Resources*, 59; Ehrlich, "Agricultural Contributions to Global Warming," 416.

131. William K. Stevens, "Greenhouse Gas Issue: Haggling Over Fairness," *New York Times*, November 30, 1997.

132. Andrew C. Revkin, "U.S. Move Improves Chance for Global Warming Treaty," *New York Times*, November 20, 2000.

133. David E. Sanger, "Bush Will Continue to Oppose Kyoto Pact on Global Warming," *New York Times*, June 12, 2001.

134. Sanger, "Bush Will Continue."

135. Sanger, "Bush Will Continue."

136. Erik Eckholm, "China Said to Sharply Reduce Emissions of Carbon Dioxide," *New York Times*, July 15, 2001.

137. Eckholm, "China Said to Sharply Reduce."

138. Eckholm, "China Said to Sharply Reduce."

139. Eckholm, "China Said to Sharply Reduce."

140. Eckholm, "China Said to Sharply Reduce."

141. Andrew C. Revkin, "Climate Talks Come Down to Haggling over Details," *New York Times*, November 9, 2001; Andrew C. Revkin, "Delegates Work Late on a Treaty to Battle Global Warming," *New York Times*, November 10, 2001.

142. Andrew C. Revkin, "Deals Break Impasse on Global Warming Treaty," *New York Times*, November 11, 2001.

143. William K. Stevens, "Moving Slowly toward Energy Free of Carbon," *New York Times*, October 31, 1999.

144. Stevens, "Moving Slowly."

145. Bradsher and Revkin, "A Pre-emptive Strike on Global Warming."

146. Bradsher and Revkin, "A Pre-emptive Strike on Global Warming."

147. Bradsher and Revkin, "A Pre-emptive Strike on Global Warming."

9

Free Trade Agreements

In 1986, U.S. officials asked other countries to negotiate new trade agreements that would open doors to U.S. goods around the world. U.S. officials were determined to conclude new agreements with their trading partners to solve a series of economic problems.

U.S. officials wanted to reduce the massive U.S. trade deficit, which had grown from $25.3 billion in 1980 to $122 billion in 1985. The 1985 dollar devaluation was designed to make U.S. goods cheaper to foreign buyers. If foreign consumers purchased more U.S. goods, the trade deficit would shrink. But in the year after the Plaza Accords, the U.S. trade deficit continued to rise, increasing from $122 billion to $155 billion. This development convinced U.S. officials that a currency devaluation would not alone increase the sale of U.S. goods abroad. They believed that restrictive trade policies and government practices in other countries made it difficult to sell even inexpensive U.S. goods in foreign markets. So U.S. officials asked governments around the world to adopt new trade rules that would open their doors to U.S. goods. As Carla Hills, the chief U.S. negotiator in trade talks from 1986 to 1992, put it, "I would like you to think of me as the U.S. Trade Representative with a crowbar, where we are prying open [the doors to foreign] markets, keeping them open so that our private sector can take advantage of them."[1]

U.S. officials were particularly keen on opening up markets for U.S. agricultural goods. They regarded this as a problem for two reasons. First, U.S. farmers were losing sales to European competitors—the U.S. share of the world wheat market declined from 55 percent in 1980 to 31.5 percent in 1986—which resulted in falling farm prices and declining incomes. Second, U.S. government spending on agricultural subsidies, which were used to help farmers compete with European farmers, had increased to $30 billion in 1986, a tenfold increase from 1980. Large agricultural subsidies contributed to large and growing government budget deficits. To increase agricultural sales, which would simultaneously reduce the U.S. *trade* deficit and the U.S. *budget* deficit, government officials proposed for the first time to open global agricultural markets.

In addition to agricultural trade, U.S. officials were determined to conclude trade agreements that would end foreign restrictions on food and raw material exports, eliminate their "tariffs" or taxes on U.S. goods that they imported, reduce regulations and restrictions that made it difficult to sell U.S. goods in foreign markets, make uniform government regulations that were necessary for the safe conduct of trade around the world, and prevent U.S. technology from being copied and used by competitors. "There is no question about it," Carla Hills said of far-ranging U.S. trade proposals. "This round of [trade] talks is a bold and ambitious undertaking."[2]

To reach agreement on trade issues with other countries, U.S. officials pursued negotiations in three settings. First, they initiated a new round of talks through the General Agreement on Tariffs and Trade (GATT), a set of global trade rules adopted in 1947. Members of GATT met periodically to revise the rules of the agreement in negotiations called "rounds." Until 1986, negotiations in most of GATT's successive rounds were concerned with the gradual reduction of tariffs or taxes on imported goods. In 1947, for example, governments around the world collected tariffs amounting to about 40 percent of the price of imported goods. By 1986, after seven rounds of negotiation, members had agreed to reduce tariffs to about 5 percent on average.[3] Because GATT sets trade rules for most, though not all countries (most communist countries did not participate in GATT during this period), U.S. leaders used GATT negotiations as a way to open doors for U.S. goods around the world. Called the "Uruguay Round," because the first meeting was held at a seaside resort in Uruguay, the global trade negotiations that began in 1986 would continue for seven years, ending in December 1993. The U.S. Congress would approve them one year later, on December 1, 1994. One year later, GATT was renamed the World Trade Organization (WTO).

Second, while a new GATT agreement was being negotiated by more than one hundred countries, U.S. officials also opened and concluded regional trade agreements with neighboring countries. The U.S.–Canada Free Trade Agreement, which was signed in 1988, and the North American Free Trade Agreement (NAFTA), which was ratified by the United States, Canada, and Mexico in 1993, were both designed to accomplish similar trade goals. U.S. officials used regional free trade agreements (FTAs) both as a model for GATT negotiations—they contained many provisions that U.S. officials wanted GATT members to adopt—and as a fall-back position should GATT members fail to adopt U.S. proposals. Because GATT negotiations deadlocked on several occasions, largely as a result of disputes over U.S. agricultural proposals, U.S. officials worried that the Uruguay Round might not revise trade rules sufficiently. So they decided to rewrite trade rules outside of GATT, beginning first with their closest neighbors and largest trading partners: Canada and then Mexico. (The United States conducts more trade with Canada than it does with Japan.)[4]

Third, U.S. officials used Section 301 of the Trade Acts of 1984 and 1988 to conduct one-on-one trade negotiations with other countries. If U.S. trade officials found that other countries denied U.S. corporations "reasonable" access to domestic markets, dumped their goods in the United States at below-market prices, or failed to protect the patents and copyrights of U.S. firms, Section 301 allowed them to impose retaliatory sanctions and tariffs on goods from these countries. The threat of "Super 301" sanctions frequently forced countries— most of them Third World countries—to begin bilateral negotiations with the United States to settle trade disputes. As one observer noted, "By 1990, more than half of the 32 cases under Section 301 investigation involved developing countries."[5] In these negotiations, U.S. trade officials asked that trade policies be revised to open doors to U.S. goods. In effect, Super 301 law was used to persuade other countries to comply with U.S. trade demands then being made in regional and global trade negotiations.[6]

By negotiating new trade relations through GATT and regional free trade agreements like NAFTA and applying U.S. trade laws, U.S. officials hoped to open doors to U.S. goods in foreign markets, expand trading opportunities, and solve a variety of economic problems for government and business. But while U.S. negotiators achieved many of their goals in the free trade agreements signed during the mid-1990s, they created a series of problems that triggered massive public protests against the WTO and FTAs by the end of the decade.

U.S. PROPOSALS TO SOLVE PROBLEMS

Generally speaking, U.S. officials used negotiations on global, regional, and bilateral free trade agreements to solve four problems related to agriculture, exports, taxes and regulation, and technology. Let us first examine agricultural issues.

Agricultural Subsidies

U.S. officials wanted to open doors to U.S. agricultural produce in foreign markets by eliminating subsidies for farmers in the United States and around the world. They wanted to eliminate agricultural subsidies because the large and growing cost of subsidies ($30 billion in 1986) contributed to massive U.S. budget deficits. Of course, a reduction of government subsidies would force many U.S. farmers out of business. But government officials had long viewed this as a good thing because they thought the elimination of "inefficient" farmers would reduce supplies and increase prices for farmers who remained in business. The problem was that officials thought it would be difficult and unwise to reduce

U.S. subsidies unilaterally because heavily subsidized European farmers would then undersell nonsubsidized U.S. farmers. As President Reagan argued, "No nation can unilaterally abandon current [subsidy] policies without being devastated by the policies of other countries. The only hope is for a major international agreement that commits everyone to the same actions and timetable."[7]

So U.S. officials proposed eliminating agricultural subsidies everywhere because they believed that U.S. farmers, and grain producers in Canada, Australia, and Argentina, could then undersell heavily subsidized European farmers. Without subsidies, many European farmers would go out of business. Because "the 12 countries of the European Community [have] more than 10 million farmers, compared with only two million in the United States," a smaller European farm population would reduce burgeoning food supplies, which would lead to higher prices for farmers who remained in business.[8]

Export Restrictions and Import Quotas

U.S. officials wanted to open foreign markets where governments restricted the sale or export of food, raw materials, and energy supplies. During the 1970s and 1980s, many poor countries began restricting the sale or export of their commodities, either to raise prices for their goods or to protect domestic industries. For example, oil-producing countries that joined OPEC used the organization to restrict the supply of oil and drive up its price. Coffee-producing countries used the 1958 International Coffee Agreement to establish export quotas for coffee-growing countries, restrict supplies and keep prices high. Although OPEC was better able to raise prices than the coffee cartel, the ability of countries to restrict exports by collaborating with other countries led to higher prices and sometimes to inflation in the rich countries that imported these goods. Poor countries also restricted the export of some raw materials to protect domestic industry. Indonesia and countries throughout Southeast Asia restricted the export of tropical timber because they wanted to build up their domestic plywood industries—Indonesia became the world's largest plywood maker—rather than export raw timber to plywood manufacturers in Japan.

U.S. officials wanted to reduce the ability of commodity cartels to limit supplies, which raised prices and contributed to inflation, so they proposed that export restrictions be prohibited in new trade agreements. Although this proved difficult to do with respect to OPEC in GATT negotiations, U.S. officials persuaded Canada and Mexico not to restrict the sale of food, energy, or raw materials to the United States. In NAFTA, for example, Canada agreed to provide natural gas and Mexico agreed to furnish oil to the United States at current levels, even if they faced energy shortages in their own countries.

Taxes and Regulations

U.S. officials also wanted to eliminate taxes and regulations that made U.S. goods more expensive or difficult to sell in foreign markets.

When GATT was founded in 1947, its members were determined to reduce "tariffs" or taxes on imported goods, and its name—General Agreement on *Tariffs* and Trade—reflected this goal. U.S. officials believed that tariffs were bad because they made U.S. goods more expensive and therefore harder to sell in foreign markets. But despite this ideology, countries around the world, the United States among them, imposed tariffs on imported goods both to raise money for the government (tariffs were the chief source of revenue for the U.S. government in the nineteenth century) and to protect domestic industry. If tariffs on imported goods made them cost more than products made by domestic industry, consumers would purchase domestic goods, even though foreign goods were more cheaply made. But high tariffs in the postwar period made it difficult for countries like the United States to export goods. This hurt employment in export-oriented industries and made consumers pay higher prices for the goods they purchased. So the United States and other GATT members agreed to reduce their tariffs on many, though not all, imported goods. Seven rounds of GATT negotiations reduced average tariffs from about 40 percent in 1947 to about 5 percent in 1985.[9] But many countries retained high tariffs on some imported goods such as textiles and agricultural produce to protect their textile industries and domestic farmers. In the case of agriculture, they were able to do so because the United States insisted in the 1950s that agricultural tariffs be *excluded* from tariff reduction negotiations in GATT.

In negotiations over new global and regional free trade agreements, U.S. officials sought to lower tariffs on manufactured goods, which were already pretty low, and reduce them on goods that were not previously covered, like agricultural produce. U.S. officials were particularly keen on reducing tariffs that made it difficult to sell U.S. beef and food to Japan.

U.S. officials also wanted to do more than reduce tariffs. They wanted to eliminate government *regulations* that made it difficult to sell U.S. goods in foreign markets even though they were not explicitly tariffs. Although GATT had slowly reduced tariffs, many countries used government regulations or "nontariff trade barriers" to restrict imports. "As tariff barriers within the GATT have fallen, nontariff barriers in most countries have risen," one trade economist explained.[10]

U.S. officials wanted to reduce nontariff trade barriers because they *acted like tariffs* even though they were not taxes. As United Technologies executive Harry Gray argued, "Such barriers as quotas, package and labeling requirements, local content laws, inspections procedures and discriminatory government procurement policies all inhibit world trade. We need conditions that are conducive to expanded trade. This means a world-wide business environment that's unfettered by government interference."[11]

To a large extent, U.S. proposals to reduce government regulations in other countries mirrored the Reagan administration's efforts to reduce costly and burdensome government regulations in the United States. But they represented a significant departure from GATT because GATT members had restricted previous negotiations to *tariff* reductions. Historically, GATT members paid little attention to nontariff barriers because they were harder to measure and because many countries argued that they did not have the same detrimental impact on economic activity that tariffs did. For example, governments in Japan and Germany restricted business hours, preventing shopkeepers from opening their doors after hours. This regulation was designed to protect family-run retail stores from big chain stores, who would keep their doors open longer and later to drive family firms out of business. In the United States, 7-Eleven was able to drive many mom and pop grocery stores out of business because it could keep longer hours than tired families could keep. U.S. negotiators wanted to end business hour regulations so that large U.S. chain stores like Wal-Mart could penetrate foreign retail markets and ruin small retailers, just as they had done in the United States.[12]

Of course, some government regulations are designed to ensure the safety and integrity of trade. Governments did not want to import contaminated foods or dangerous products that put consumers as risk, so they adopted health and safety restrictions that applied to imported goods. U.S. officials objected to some of these regulations, arguing, for example, that European restrictions on U.S. beef raised with hormones were unfair. "More and more governments are looking for and finding alleged problems about [food] composition or how it was grown," Hills argued in 1990. "As quotas and tariffs on farm products are reduced or eliminated as a result of the Uruguay Round, politicians will look for other ways to curb imports. If new and unjustified health and safety food standards are adopted, the U.S. will retaliate."[13]

While U.S. officials objected to some health and safety regulations, they recognized that others were necessary for trade. But the problem with *necessary* regulations was that *different* regulations applied to the same goods in different jurisdictions. Producers of everything from tomatoes to cars to aircraft found it costly and burdensome to comply with regulations that varied from one country to the next or, in the United States, from one state to another. To deal with problems caused by different kinds of regulation, U.S. officials argued that necessary regulations should be made uniform or "harmonized," as they put it, around the world. They then argued that international scientific organizations should be given authority to determine what regulations should be uniformly applied by all. As Carla Hills argued, "We want to abolish the right of nations to impose health and safety standards more stringent than a minimal uniform world standard."[14]

In the case of agriculture, U.S. officials proposed that responsibility for setting food safety standards be assigned to Codex Alimentarius, a scientific U.N. agency based in Rome. Codex sets regulatory standards for food, but compliance with its regulations was voluntary. U.S. officials proposed that countries around the world adopt Codex standards as their own and make these standards mandatory.[15]

Reagan administration officials also wanted to make government regulations more easily understood, more "transparent" to outsiders. Many countries established Byzantine regulations that only domestic firms could master, or they relied on "informal" or "arbitrary" rules and regulations that put importers at a disadvantage. U.S. officials argued that these rules should be codified and clarified so that importers could compete on a level economic playing field.

Patents and Piracy

The fourth problem that U.S. officials wanted to address in new free trade agreements was the unauthorized use of U.S. inventions by overseas competitors.

Although U.S. industries have higher labor costs than many foreign industries, they also possess more advanced and sophisticated technologies, which allow them to produce goods more cheaply than low-wage competitors. But during the 1970s and 1980s, U.S. firms found that benefits of advanced technology could be captured by others. They found that while a new technology—such as a new pharmaceutical drug, hybrid seed, computer chip, or Hollywood movie—was extremely costly to invent, test, and manufacture, it could be cheaply copied by others. Many countries did not recognize U.S. patent, copyright, and trademark laws, which assigned a monopoly to the inventor of a new technology for seventeen years and allowed them to sue others if they "infringed" on the patent by using their invention without permission or payment. Businesses in other countries frequently copied and used technologies invented elsewhere. So, for example, manufacturers in Southeast Asia made imitation Levi's jeans, reproduced copies of *Star Wars*, or manufactured generic drugs based on formulas patented elsewhere, thereby profiting from the sale of goods invented elsewhere.

U.S. officials were determined to safeguard the technological superiority of U.S. firms and prevent unauthorized use, or "piracy" as it was called, by foreign competitors. Gerald Mossinghoff, president of the Pharmaceutical Manufacturers Association, said that "patent piracy in just four countries—Argentina, Brazil, India and Turkey—cost U.S. research-based pharmaceutical firms almost $1 billion annually."[16] Altogether, U.S. companies would receive $61 billion a year if piracy of U.S. technological inventions or "intellectual property rights" as they are called were ended, according to the U.S. International Trade Commission.[17]

To protect inventions originating in the United States and other technologically advanced countries, U.S. officials argued that the protection given to inventors by U.S. patents, copyrights, and trademarks should be recognized by countries and their duration extended from seventeen to twenty years. In NAFTA negotiations, U.S. officials went further, proposing that copyrights, which protect songs like Madonna's "Material Girl" and movies like Disney's *Aladdin*, be extended to fifty years.

THE NEGOTIATIONS

Although U.S. officials made these ambitious and complicated proposals to solve U.S. economic problems, both foreign *and* domestic, they received crucial political support from other countries. A number of food-exporting countries outside Europe, which became known as the "Cairns Group" (Australia, Canada, New Zealand, Fiji, Brazil, Uruguay, Argentina, Malaysia, Indonesia, the Philippines, Thailand, Colombia, and Chile), supported U.S. agricultural proposals in heated disputes with members of the European Community. Although EC members opposed U.S. proposals on agricultural matters, they welcomed U.S. initiatives to end export restrictions, reduce tariff and nontariff barriers, and protect technological inventions from unauthorized use. EC members also wanted to reduce the economic power of commodity cartels, open doors to their goods in foreign markets, and protect their own technological advantages. Many governments around the world believed that they too would benefit from open doors and expanded trade. The civilian democrats that came to power in southern Europe, Latin America, East Asia, and Eastern Europe during the 1970s and 1980s agreed with U.S. officials that these proposals would expand trade and increase their own economic opportunities (see chapter 11). Then in the early 1990s, many former communist countries, which had previously not participated in GATT, became members, frequently supporting proposals initiated by the United States.

Of course, some countries objected to some or all of these proposals. But they were generally too small or isolated to have much impact on negotiations. "The big markets dictate the trading rules," one senior U.S. negotiator said. "The U.S. can't do it independently, and the EC can't do it independently, but when the two lock arms, they can determine the fate of the round."[18]

While GATT negotiations continued, the United States concluded free trade agreements with Canada in 1988 and then with Canada and Mexico in 1993. The first was relatively uncontroversial. But the second, NAFTA, was the subject of a brief, intense debate in Congress before it was ratified. Debate was brief in part because Congress allowed U.S. trade officials to negotiate regional and global free trade agreements under special "fast-track" authority. This meant that the president could conduct negotiations and then submit the finished agreement to Congress for approval within sixty days. Because they were "agreements," not "treaties," they needed approval by simple majorities in both houses, with the important stipulation that they could *not* be amended. Congressional representatives agreed to vote for or against the entire set of complex trade rules contained in the agreement. Presidents Reagan, Bush, and Clinton asked for, and Congress granted, special fast-track authority because they did not want individual representatives to complicate negotiations or obstruct the agreements reached.

The Uruguay Round negotiations were nearly completed in 1990, but they reached an impasse when U.S. and EC officials could not reach an agreement on reducing agricultural subsidies. After fits and starts, talks resumed and negotiations were eventually completed on December 14, 1993. The final document, which was 22,000 pages long and weighed 385 pounds, was signed by 109 countries on April 15, 1994.[19] "This [is] the single largest trade agreement ever," said President Clinton in April 1994. "It writes new rules of the road for world trade well into the next century."[20] The U.S. Congress approved GATT on December 1, 1994, and the WTO was established as its successor on January 1, 1995.

When GATT/WTO members signed the new agreement, they adopted many but not all of the proposals made earlier by U.S. officials. Export restrictions were banned, tariffs and quotas reduced, nontariff trade barriers restricted, some regulatory standards were made uniform, and patent protection was extended. But some important U.S. proposals were not adopted in full measure.

In agriculture, U.S. officials had proposed eliminating subsidies completely. But EC governments opposed this, largely because farmers in France mounted large and vehement protests against U.S. proposals. The dispute over agricultural subsidies very nearly led to the collapse of Uruguay Round negotiations. The EC agreed to reduce its sales of subsidized grain by 21 percent, far lower than the 100 percent reduction favored by the United States. "In the end, none of [the U.S.] negotiating objectives was achieved," said a disappointed Heinz Hutter, chief executive of Cargill, one of the world's largest grain-trading firms. "But it was unrealistic to think so much could be done so quickly against entrenched [European] interests."[21]

U.S. officials had greater success in negotiations with Canada and Mexico. Generally speaking, regional free trade agreements incorporated more of the U.S. proposals, and used stronger language and stricter provisions, than those reached in GATT.

Still, the free trade agreements adopted in 1993–1994 were generally a "success" for U.S. policymakers because they opened doors to U.S. goods in foreign markets, lowered prices and access to raw materials, and protected the technological advantages of businesses in the North.

PROBLEMS ASSOCIATED WITH FTAs

The new free trade agreements created a series of problems for people in different settings. After reviewing some of the problems related to specific provisions in the new agreements, we will discuss some of the general problems associated with them. Although FTAs have now been in effect for a number of years, it is difficult to assess their long-term impact. The main reason is that trade disputes among WTO members are addressed on a case-by-case basis, and each case typically takes several years to resolve while governments argue, contest, arbitrate, and appeal their case. So while FTAs set the rules, it takes some years before these rulings accumulate and their consequences become apparent. It was not until the WTO's 2001 meeting in Seattle that the consequences of rules made in the early 1990s became apparent to a wider public.

Reducing Subsidies

The first problem was related to the reduction of agricultural subsidies in GATT and the reduction of industrial subsidies in regional free trade agreements (the U.S.–Canada FTA and NAFTA). Although the EC agreed only to a partial reduction of its agricultural subsidies, the 21 percent reduction it conceded in GATT negotiations began to drive some of the EC's ten million farmers out of business. To some extent, European farmers began to experience a winnowing process like that experienced by U.S. farmers since World War II. The farmers most affected by reduced subsidies were farmers who received large subsidies, many of them in the United Kingdom, Portugal, Spain, Greece, Ireland, and Germany. Less affected were the more efficient Dutch and politically active French farmers. France is the largest agricultural producer in the EC, and its farmers are better organized and more efficient than most. They organized massive protests on a national scale and persuaded the government to hang tough in negotiations with the United States.

Provisions in regional FTAs did not eliminate agricultural subsidies, but they contained language that allowed member countries to sue one another if they thought that agricultural or industrial subsidies gave producers an unfair advantage or "distorted trade." Under the U.S.–Canada FTA, for example, U.S. timber producers complained that Canadian timber manufacturers received an unfair, trade-distorting subsidy because the government of British Columbia paid the cost of replanting trees cut down by Canadian firms in the province's forests. (U.S. timber companies must themselves pay the cost of replanting clear-cut forest on privately owned land in the United States.) This tree-replanting "subsidy" enabled Canadian firms to export and sell lumber in the United States at prices lower than U.S. firms.

Under regional FTAs and the WTO, firms cannot themselves sue other countries to force them to comply with provisions in the agreement. Only governments can. So U.S. timber producers asked U.S. trade officials to review their case and sue the Canadian government on their behalf. After "finding" that U.S. firms were "injured" by Canadian "subsidies," U.S. trade officials sued the Canadian government, asking it to remove the subsidies through the arbitration process established by the FTA. Arbitration panels, with trade experts nominated by both parties to a dispute, then meet in secret to determine whether a provision of the agreements has been violated.[22] They then issue a ruling if they believe it has. In this case, they ruled that the tree-replanting program was a subsidy that violated the agreement. Critics have argued that these secret arbitration panels are not open to public scrutiny or intervention by public groups that have a material interest in the outcome. In this case, environmental groups were excluded from the proceedings, though they would have been allowed to submit *amicus* briefs if the case were heard in U.S. or Canadian courts. "What we're talking about here is a secret government," Joan Claybrook, president of Public Citizen, has said of the arbitration panels established by FTAs.[23]

Once an arbitration panel has ruled on a dispute, different things can happen. In the timber dispute, the Canadian government could comply with the ruling and ask provincial authorities to stop funding the tree-replanting program. (Its ability to insist may depend on the constitutional relation between federal and provincial government in Canada. In the United States, the Constitution assigns considerable authority to the federal government, but also reserves important rights for state and local government.) But the Canadian government could also refuse to comply with the arbitration panel ruling. Because arbitration panels have no power to enforce their rulings, and because most FTAs do not have any organizational authority for insisting that governments change their trade policies, enforcement of arbitration panel rulings is usually left up to the "injured" party.

Free trade agreements allow governments injured by countries that violate the agreements to "retaliate" against the violator by imposing punitive taxes on goods imported from that country. (It is illegal to impose retaliatory tariffs without a favorable ruling.) So, in this case, the U.S. government could levy heavy tariffs on Canadian timber products, making it difficult for them to compete in U.S. markets. If the United States did so, the Canadian government could still refuse to comply. But high retaliatory tariffs would no doubt harm some Canadian manufacturers, who would then ask their own government to comply with the ruling so they could get on with business as usual. The arbitration and dispute resolution mechanism is designed to put economic pressure on governments to comply with trade agreements by enlisting both foreign governments and domestic manufacturers in the process. In this particular case, mounting economic pressure on the provincial government forced it to change its forest policy and end tree-replanting subsidies. Private companies in British Columbia must now bear this cost themselves.[24]

Environmentalists in Canada and the United States criticized the application of the free trade agreement in this case because it undermined what they regarded as a sensible way to ensure that clear-cut forests were replanted and the woods used on a more sustainable basis, something that might not occur if private firms have to pay for this themselves. Environmentalists and other consumer and labor groups also worried that this kind of ruling would set a precedent for attacks on other "subsidies" that they regarded as useful or necessary, and they warned that it could undermine the authority of state and local governments. They noted, for instance, that U.S. businesses have argued that Canadian health care, unemployment programs, and even the postal service violate free trade agreements. Because Canadian employers do not have to pay for health care benefits, as many do in the United States, U.S. businesses have argued that national health care in Canada unfairly aids Canadian firms and have asked the U.S. government to use the dispute resolution mechanism in NAFTA to challenge it. Because self-employed lobster fishermen in Canada can receive unemployment benefits in the off-season, while their U.S. counterparts cannot (self-employed workers cannot collect unemployment benefits in the United States), U.S. lobster men have argued that unemployment benefits underwrite Canadian lobster exports. And United Parcel Service (UPS), the private, U.S. delivery giant, has "filed a complaint contending that the very existence of the publically financed Canadian postal system represents unfair competition that conflicts with Canada's obligations under NAFTA," the *New York Times* has written. "Critics worry that if the tribunal upholds the U.P.S. claim, government participation in *any* service that competes with the private sector will be threatened [emphasis added]."[25] The rules attacking subsidies in FTAs have been used to wage a broad assault on government services, which many people regard as essential.

These disputes have not yet been resolved, but critics argue that language in free trade agreements permits a broad assault on important environmental and social programs. If, for example, U.S. proposals to eliminate agricultural subsidies completely had been adopted, programs that promote soil and water conservation, education and scientific research, farm credit and loans, and food aid to foreign countries could have been contested as unfair subsidies to trade.

Critics of new free trade agreements have also argued that rulings like that in the Canadian tree-replanting case and language in the new WTO could substantially undermine the authority of state and local governments. New WTO language, for example, requires contracting parties to "take such reasonable measures as may be available to it to ensure observance of the provisions of this agreement by regional and local governments and authorities within its territory."[26] And NAFTA requires members to "take all necessary steps, where changes to domestic laws will be required to implement their provisions . . . to ensure conformity of their law with these agreements."[27]

Former California governor Edmund G. Brown, Jr., has been one critic opposed to the preemption of state government by free trade agreements. "Our constitutional system rests on democratic accountability with significant legal and regulatory differences recognized among states and localities," he argued. "NAFTA . . . in the name of taking down trade barriers would curtail local preferences and thereby undermine the ability of diverse communities to control their own destiny."[28] The threat to public services and the authority of elected governments persuaded many groups in the United States, Canada, and Western Europe to mount or join protests against the WTO in the early twenty-first century.

Ending Export Restrictions and Import Quotas

A second set of problems was related to provisions in free trade agreements that reduced export restrictions on food, energy supplies, and natural resources and restricted import quotas on different commodities.

Many countries have limited the export of oil or coffee to reduce global supplies and thereby raise prices for the goods they sold. Although consumers around the world welcomed lower-priced gas and coffee, lower prices made it much more difficult for exporting countries to buy things from abroad, repay debts, invest their earnings in domestic development projects, raise standards of living, or close the growing economic gap between rich and poor countries. As we have seen, prices for oil, food, and natural resources fell dramatically during the 1980s (see chapter 6). Free trade agreements that prevent countries from reducing or managing the supply of these goods contributed to the downward pressure on prices. NAFTA, for example, prohibited Mexico and Canada from reducing their energy exports to the United States to a level below the average of the previous three years. This provision was designed to guarantee delivery of Mexican oil and Canadian natural gas and electricity to the United States.[29] By agreeing to maintain energy exports, Mexican and Canadian officials found it difficult to increase prices.

In the case of food, a prohibition of export restrictions could be particularly devastating. If a poor country experienced a bad harvest, and its government could not prevent other countries from buying and exporting its food, domestic food supplies could fall and prices rise. If food prices rise without a commensurate rise in income, many poor people might starve.

Without export restrictions, government officials in many countries had a harder time managing their natural resources. Pacific Rim countries belonging to the International Tropical Timber Organization banned the export of raw logs to Japan and restricted timber exports. They did so either to promote domestic industry, as Indonesia did to build up its plywood industry, or to manage its forest resources, as Thailand did to reduce the soil erosion and flooding associated with rapid deforestation.

The WTO ban on export restrictions affected not only poor countries; it also affected people and the environment in the North.

Japanese officials claimed that U.S. government restrictions on raw log exports from *federal* forests, which were designed to protect jobs at U.S. mills, and new federal restrictions on logging in old-growth forests, which were designed to protect endangered spotted owls, violated the WTO ban on export restrictions. Some U.S. forest industries supported the Japanese position. They urged an end to federal export restrictions and regulations because they wanted to get high prices from Japanese buyers as a result of dollar devaluations, which made it more profitable to cut and ship raw logs than to mill the wood first, and because they wanted greater access to public forest supplies (see chapter 3).[30] Membership in the WTO meant that it was very hard for U.S. officials to defend Forest Service restrictions and regulations that help manage public forests.

Just as free trade agreements attempted to reduce export restrictions, they also sought to eliminate import quotas, which restricted supplies and forced up prices. But this has had serious consequences for some businesses.

In Japan, for example, the end of restrictions on rice imports helped consumers, who previously paid more for staple foods than consumers in most of the world. But it has devastated the farm population and contributed to the migration of young people from rural areas to the cities. As journalist Roger Cohen observed:

> In opening its market to imported rice for the first time, Japan was taking more than a small trade step. Rice cultivation is central to Japan's religion, culture and folklore and the bar on imports symbolized its sacredness. Each spring, the Emperor plants the first seedling on the grounds of the Imperial Palace. But in the end, the Japanese government decided that access to markets outweighed these considerations.[31]

Despite large and determined protests by farmers, Japanese officials agreed to end the ban for a variety of reasons. Rice shortages had pushed up prices, which led consumers to support an end to the ban. Whereas only 41 percent of Japanese consumers supported an end to the ban in 1988, 62 percent did so in 1993.[32] They also responded to lobbying by Japanese industry. According to Andrew Pollack, "The big push [for an end to the ban] has come from Japan's powerful export-oriented industries," who argued that lower prices would benefit consumers and suppress worker demands for higher wages.[33]

But while they managed to reduce or eliminate restrictions on food, raw materials, textiles, and even cars in new free trade agreements, U.S. officials were unable to persuade other countries to lift import restrictions on Hollywood films and TV programs. "I am disturbed by the refusal of the EC to negotiate seriously," said Jack Valenti, president of the Motion Picture Association of America, the main lobbying group for the Hollywood-based entertainment industry. "I feel . . . disappointment that we were unable to reach a fair conclusion."[34]

European officials disagreed with this assessment. Jack Lang, France's minister of culture, said the decision *not* to eliminate restrictions on U.S. film, TV, and music imports was "a victory for art and artists over the commercialization of culture."[35]

Import restrictions on cultural goods were extremely contentious issues because Hollywood, the center of the U.S. communications industry, had captured global markets with film, TV, and music products. In France, for example, 60 percent of the films shown in theaters and 50 percent of the programs aired on French TV in 1990 were made in Hollywood.[36] Hollywood's cultural supremacy was even more pronounced in other countries around the world. In Brazil, eight of the ten top-grossing films in 1990 were made in Hollywood; in Hungary, Hollywood films captured nine of the top ten spots.[37] Hollywood earned more than $8 billion a year for its film and video exports, and growing income from foreign sales added jobs in Hollywood, where the film and TV industry employed 414,700 workers. Hollywood was able to capture foreign markets because it developed advanced technology and the means to raise and risk $50 million on the average film. Technology and capital enable it to attract skilled directors and actors from around the world (Louis Malle and Peter Weir, Arnold Schwarzenegger and Mel Gibson) and produce technologically sophisticated movies such as *Jurassic Park*, *Toy Story*, and *The Matrix*. Hollywood also bought or controlled distribution networks and theater outlets in other countries. In Indonesia, for example, the company that monopolized film distribution pushes Hollywood films. "As a result," writes journalist Philip Shenon, "the Indonesian film industry is dying, with fewer than 30 films expected to be produced [in 1992], half of [1991's] output."[38] Since World War II, the industry has been able to expand Hollywood's dominance at the expense of foreign film industries. Valenti once boasted, "The motion picture industry is the only U.S. enterprise that negotiates on its own with foreign governments."[39]

In Europe and elsewhere, government officials established import quotas on Hollywood products to protect domestic industries, preserve indigenous cultures, and restrict violence on television.[40] In recent years, France and Spain restricted the amount of time that could be devoted to Hollywood films and TV and radio programming in media outlets. They also levied taxes on film tickets to raise money to support their domestic film industries. Hollywood director Steven Spielberg criticized these moves, saying that "filmmakers can find no comfort when their film is barred or restricted or otherwise frustrated when they try to take out work to the global public."[41]

But a group of European directors led by Wim Wenders and Benardo Bertolucci responded by arguing:

> We are only desperately defending the tiny margin of freedom left us. We are trying to protect European cinema against its complete annihilation by Hollywood films like Spielberg's *Jurassic Park*, which swallowed up a huge share of European ticket sales in 1993. The dinosaurs of 1993, that's us. We are facing extinction and we are merely fighting for our survival. Do you seriously think that our European films are really so bad that they deserve to reach 1 percent of American audiences, while American films fill more than 80 percent of European screens?[42]

Reducing Tariffs

The reduction of taxes and regulations on imported goods, and the creation of uniform laws that are necessary to protect the health and integrity of trade, were a centerpiece of negotiations over new free trade agreements. Although the reduction and elimination of taxes and regulations that hinder trade were designed to benefit consumers, they contributed to three kinds of problems.

First, the reduction of tariffs on imported goods reduced government revenues. By reducing tariffs to zero, NAFTA cut U.S. revenues by about $4 billion a year and about $3 billion in tax revenues for Canada and for Mexico. The elimination of income from this source came at a time when each country faced large budget deficits and when they had to *increase* government spending to implement the agreement. Commerce Secretary Ron Brown estimated that the U.S. government would spend $2 billion a year for ten years to build roads, bridges, and sewers along the U.S.–Mexico border.

As it turned out, tariff reduction also provided tax relief for U.S. corporations. U.S. firms control about 40 percent of the Mexican and 40 percent of the Canadian export economy.[43] As economist Sidney Weintraub noted, "An important feature of the U.S.–Mexico industrial relationship is that more than one-half of their trade in manufactured goods takes place between affiliated companies. This is also true of U.S.–Canada industrial trade."[44]

Because U.S. corporations operating in Mexico and Canada export much of the goods they produce to the United States, or import goods from the United States to sell in Mexico and Canada, tariff reduction amounted to a large tax cut for U.S. firms operating in foreign countries. This tax relief was *not* available to U.S. firms that operated only in the United States.

Although U.S. firms operating in Canada and Mexico received substantial tax cuts, they did not necessarily pass along their savings to consumers in the form of lower prices. As Rene Osario, a Hewlett-Packard representative, said, "Tariff reduction will free investment for *other* things.[45]

The WTO does not entirely eliminate tariffs, allowing governments to retain some tariffs, though at lower levels. One issue that the new tariff reduction agreements did not address was the differential tariffs used by rich countries to discriminate against poor countries. Rich countries typically placed low tariffs on raw materials imported from poor countries, but very high tariffs on their manufactured goods. So, for example, rich countries placed a tiny 0.1 percent tariff on raw rubber imports, but levied a 16.5 percent tariff on manufactured rubber footwear.[46] Differential tariffs discouraged poor countries from making goods that could compete with producers in the North. Across-the-board tariff reduction benefited consumers, but it left discriminatory tariff structures in place, structures that often disadvantaged poor countries.

Tariff reductions can also result in huge jobs losses in poor countries. In India, the elimination in 2002 of tariffs on chicken imports will likely devastate the country's 100,000 chicken farmers and the 1.5 million people working in the chicken industry, and flood the country with chicken imported by U.S. firms such as Perdue and Tyson.[47] "Without the tariff, we [will be] in big soup," said

Anuradha Desai, chairwoman of the National Egg Coordination Committee in India.[48]

Second, the elimination of nontariff trade barriers or government regulations that act *like* tariffs because they make it more difficult to sell goods in foreign markets, has adversely affected consumers and the environment.

In 1992, for example, the Canadian government passed new regulations designed to protect the health of imported puppies. They did so because U.S. breeders that sold puppies to Canadian pet stores shipped puppies under conditions that exposed them to disease and kept them in transit for more than thirty-six hours, which the government regarded as cruel. "[The new regulations] will reduce the number of [Canadian] families that are traumatized by purchasing imported dogs that die or suffer from disease," officials of Agriculture Canada explained.[49]

But U.S. breeders and kennel owners objected, arguing that the regulations would increase puppy prices and reduce pet ownership in Canada. So they asked the U.S. government to sue Canada because, they said, the regulations were a nontariff trade barrier that violated the U.S.–Canada Free Trade Agreement.

Although the dispute over the puppy trade was a minor affair, it illustrates how regulations designed to protect consumers, and in this case, animals, were attacked under new free trade agreements as obstacles to trade. According to economists, free trade agreements are supposed to *benefit* consumers. But the new FTAs often disadvantage consumers. Environmental and consumer advocates have argued that provisions in new free trade agreements have been used to challenge or modify regulations imposed by the Convention on the International Trade in Endangered Species, the Montreal Protocol, which limits the production of ozone-depleting chemicals, recycling laws, and the U.S. Marine Mammal Protection Act (MMPA). On June 25, 1991, Mexico sued the United States in GATT after U.S. officials blocked the import of Mexican tuna because Mexican fishermen caught tuna using methods that resulted in the death of dolphins, marine mammals protected under provisions of the MMPA.[50] The GATT arbitration panel assigned to hear the dispute ruled for Mexico, arguing that member countries could not discriminate against goods produced in ways they viewed as "unacceptable." This meant that Canada could not restrict the import of puppies raised in a manner Canadians regarded as "inhumane," the United States could not restrict the import of goods manufactured by prisoners (as many goods are in China), of goods manufactured by dictatorships that suppress human rights (as in Burma), of goods made by children (as they are in many parts of the world), or of goods made by workers who are denied the right to organize unions (as they are in many countries). Critics of FTAs argued that rulings like that in the Mexican tuna case opened the door to challenges against a host of regulations, even if these regulations are designed to protect consumers, workers, or the environment.[51]

After the WTO ruled that the United States could not restrict shrimp imports from countries that did not protect sea turtles from becoming trapped in the nets of shrimp boats, the *New York Times* observed, "the decision . . . was the latest sign that when free trade conflicts with environmental protection, the international trade body is unlikely to swerve from its central mission of promoting trade."[52]

Of course, free trade agreements did not eliminate all regulations that affected trade, in part because government regulations that affect trade are considered under free trade agreements on a case-by-case basis. This takes time, and arbitration panels, which are made up of trade experts, do not always agree on the interpretation and application of provision in free trade agreements.

Where regulations are seen as necessary to protect the safety and integrity of trade, FTAs assign authority to regulate trade to international agencies like Codex Alimentarius, which sets standards and regulates trade in food. These scientific agencies are responsible for creating uniform regulations that apply around the world. But the effort to create uniform global standards has led to a third problem: uniform standards often resulted in regulations with *lower* standards.

Codex, for example, set standards for the amount of pesticide residues allowed in imported fruits and vegetables. But these levels were lower than standards set by the U.S. Environmental Protection Agency (EPA). Codex regulations, for example, allowed banana producers to export fruit containing fifty times as much residual DDT, a pesticide banned in the United States since 1970, as the U.S. EPA permitted.[53] The EPA accepted only about 20 percent of Codex standards for residual pesticides, rejecting the majority because they are too low.[54] Because Codex assumed authority for setting global food regulations, existing standards of food safety could be lowered significantly in many countries. In 1999, for example, the WTO ruled that Japan's health-related, pesticide residue standards violated trade rules because Japan's standards were higher than those established by Codex.[55] This did not mean, of course, that American or Japanese consumers were forced to consume fruits with high levels of pesticide residues. But it meant that they had to learn more about the fruit they purchased and exercise greater caution because they could not rely on government agencies to intervene on their behalf at the border. And their ability to make this determination became more difficult because many companies have asked that government labeling requirements—that products containing pesticides or genetically modified organisms (GMOs) or hormones be labeled on products sold so that consumers have the information they need to make intelligent choices—be ruled a nontariff barrier to trade and prohibited under the WTO. The WTO's ruling that the European ban on beef grown with hormones, its ruling that Guatemala could not restrict the advertising claims on Gerber's infant formula bottles, have made it increasingly difficult for governments to require labels that guarantee consumer choice.[56]

Of course, Codex did not always set lower standards. Indeed, for many countries, adoption of Codex standards might actually raise their standards. Sometimes, Codex agreed to higher standards. And sometimes Codex sets absurd standards. For a time Codex ruled that "milk" was a product *only* of cows. This meant that producers who made dairy products from goats or, in India, from buffalo could not describe their main ingredient as "milk." After vociferous objections from dairy producers in poor countries, Codex amended its ruling.

But whether it sets high or low standards, environmental and consumer groups argued that Codex should not be given authority to set uniform standards for the world because it preempted the ability of local, state, and national governments, which are composed of elected representatives, to set standards acceptable to the communities they represent. As a result, critics of the WTO have argued that standard-setting agencies like Codex violate the sovereign authority of elected, representative governments.

Extending Patent Protection

Although Hollywood was unable to eliminate restrictions on its film exports in the WTO, it was able to obtain expanded patent protection for its films, songs, and merchandise. The WTO and other free trade agreements extended patent, trademark, and copyright protection around the world and granted protection for longer periods of time. These measures were of great interest not only to Hollywood but also to pharmaceutical, chemical, and agricultural companies who argued that their inventions or "intellectual property rights" were being pirated or used without their authorization by competitors in other countries. But the extension of protection for inventions promoted monopoly and raised the cost of food and drugs in other countries.

In the United States, patents, trademarks, and copyrights have long been used to give inventors of technologies, drugs, brand names, songs, and books a monopoly over the use of that invention for a given period of time, seventeen years for a patent approved by the U.S. government. Because they were government-granted monopolies, patent law did *not* promote competition or trade in goods or ideas. Instead it *restricted* them.

> As its name suggests, intellectual property "protection" is a surprising issue for the GATT [because] . . . the GATT's mission has always been to prevent, or at least circumscribe, countries' efforts to "protect" their domestic industries. Now, [in the case of patents] the GATT is being called upon to *extend* protection, not restrict it . . . the goal of Uruguay Round negotiations in restricting this free flow may be viewed as perverse.[57]

The first problem with the restriction of patent protection and monopoly was that it strengthened the technological advantages of countries in the North, which have the educational systems and research infrastructures—skilled engineers and scientists, government-funded research universities, and programs such as NASA and the National Academy of Sciences—necessary for invention in the modern world. As a result, inventors in the North own the bulk of the world's patented inventions. According to one study, "Only one percent of the patents are owned by third world nationals. Of the 3.5 million patents in existence worldwide in the 1970s, only about 200,000 were granted to developing countries. Most of these third world patents, some 84 percent, were owned by transnational corporations from the richest five countries."[58]

Critics have also noted that research has been increasingly conducted in the North by private firms not public institutions and that when private firms obtain patents, they are less likely to share them with other researchers.[59] As a result, "patent restrictions are choking the free exchange of seeds and technology that nourished the public system," a system that made possible important scientific advancements in the past.[60] Moreover, private research is driven by profit, not public interest, so critics worry that research in important but unprofitable areas will be neglected in the future.

A second problem was that patent protection led to higher prices for consumers. (Generally, free trade agreements were supposed to *lower* consumer prices.) Many countries that provided patent protection did so for short periods of time. Canada, for example, protected drug patents for only seven to ten years, about half the duration of U.S. patents. According to the U.S. General Accounting Office, Canada's shorter-term patent laws kept drug prices there 32 percent lower than drug prices in the United States.[61] Many countries also prevented patents from being awarded for some technologies, or required patent holders to license their products at a low cost. In India, for example, "patents cannot be given for a method of agriculture or horticulture" or for medical processes that "render [humans, plants, or animals] free of disease."[62] Both Canada and India required foreign drug companies to license their products at a low cost so that medicine could be made more cheaply available to consumers. Oxfam's Kevin Watkins argued, "Compulsory licensing is widely used in India and other developing countries in order to limit the abuse of monopoly power conferred by patents."[63]

In India and Brazil, for instance, local drug companies made copies of anti-AIDS and other lifesaving drugs and sold them for a fraction of the price set by the pharmaceutical companies that held the patents. For example, a drug company in India sold amoxicillin tablets for five cents, while the patent holder sold it for twenty-one cents; it offered albuterol for one dollar, compared to $26.77 from the patent holder.[64] In very poor countries like India, cheaper drugs have meant that many lives were saved. For a young child, cheap amoxicillan can mean the difference between life and death. But the United States has led the attack on copycat drugs in poor countries, demanding that they change their patent laws and enforce patents obtained in other countries. This had led to a bitter dispute, and poor countries have charged the United States with indifference to the pain and suffering of sick people in the South.[65] After the September 11 airplane and anthrax attacks in the United States, the U.S. government's position changed.[66] Officials demanded that the makers of Cipro (a drug used to treat anthrax) surrender its patent and allow others to make and sell it at a low cost to people exposed to the deadly bacteria.[67] As a result, U.S. trade officials have eased their blanket opposition to this same practice in poor countries.

A third problem was that inventors in the North patented goods or ideas taken initially from others. On March 3, 1993, two hundred thousand Indian farmers rallied in Delhi to protest GATT proposals to extend patent protection to seed and agricultural chemical companies.[68] They regarded this as a problem because it meant that seed companies could demand a royalty for the use of patented seeds and demand that farmers pay royalties on seeds saved from the previous harvest. Under the new rules, "a farmer purchasing [patented] seed would have the right to grow the seed but not the right to make seed," argued Indian economist Vandana Shiva.[69]

Seed companies argue that they need patent protection to protect costly inventions. "Even though it has been a tradition in most countries that a farmer can save from his own crop, it is under [current] circumstances not equitable that farmers can use this [patented] seed and grow a commercial crop out of it without payment of royalty [to its inventors]," argued Hans Leenders, secretary general of the International Association of Plant Breeders for the Protection of Plant Varieties.[70]

The irony of this position was that much of the raw material for new drugs, seeds, and chemicals originally came from rain forests and the farms and gardens of poor people in the South. Some of this material—wild and cultivated varieties of plants, grains, and vegetables—was gathered by scientists from the North who did not pay for cuttings and specimens. Shiva notes that a variety of Turkish barley was donated to U.S. farmers to combat a yellow dwarf virus, saving U.S. farmers $150 million a year in crop losses, and "a wild tomato variety taken from Peru in 1962 has contributed $8 million a year to the American tomato processing industry by increasing the content of soluble solids."[71] "Baseball" tomatoes, which can be harvested by machine and are sold in U.S. supermarkets, are the result of cross-breeding tomato varieties taken from Latin American countries during the 1950s and 1960s. "Yet none of these benefits have been shared with Peru, the original source of the genetic material," notes Shiva.[72] According to some estimates, "wild varieties contributed $340 million per year between 1976 and 1980 to the U.S. farm economy," and the "total contribution of wild germplasm to the U.S. economy has been $66 billion."[73]

Farmers and government officials in India were outraged in 1997 when the U.S. government issued a patent for basmati rice—an important and highly valuable rice that originated in India—to Ricetec, a Texas company. "The battle against Ricetec is just the beginning of India's battle against bio-piracy and theft of indigenous plant wealth," Shiva argued.[74]

So, having taken genetic material from sources in the South, processed it, and patented this process or invention, scientists in the North then sold it back to people who initially supplied the material and demanded royalties from them.

Much the same is true of ideas. Most of Disney's major cartoon productions were based on fables and folklore originally told by people in other countries. *The Little Mermaid* had Danish origins, *Beauty and the Beast* and *Cinderella* were told in France and Italy, and *Aladdin* was a story that originated in the Middle East. But by copyrighting its own particular version (in words, music, and images), Disney then sold these stories to people around the world and denied others the right to use them.

GENERAL PROBLEMS

New free trade agreements contained provisions that affected subsidies, export restrictions and import quotas, taxes and regulations on imported goods, and patents on inventions. While they provided some benefits, they also contributed to a variety of problems. In addition to the problems associated with specific provisions, the new free trade agreements also contributed to three general problems.

In the abstract, free trade agreements were designed to open doors so that businesses could participate and compete with each other in markets around the world. Consumers benefited from this because increased competition, and the decline of burdensome government taxes and regulation, permitted businesses to specialize and deliver their goods at the lowest possible price. But in many cases, free trade agreements opened markets *not* to competition between businesses, but to monopoly because they facilitated the entry of large-scale transnational corporations. According to the World Bank, "transnational corporations control 70 percent of world trade. In 1990, the world's largest 350 TNCs accounted for almost 40 percent of world merchandise trade, which then totaled $3.485 trillion. The top 500 TNCs control two-thirds of world trade."[75]

As a result, large TNCs captured most of the economic benefits provided by free trade agreements. When NAFTA cut tariffs, U.S. corporations operating in Canada and Mexico received tax cuts that were unavailable to firms based only in the United States. Because three to six TNCs control 85 to 90 percent of world wheat, corn, coffee, cotton, and tobacco exports, 90 percent of forest product exports, and 90 to 95 percent of iron ore exports, the reduction of import and export restrictions provided immediate benefits to a small number of large firms.[76]

The problem was that where a small number of large firms controlled world trade in a given industry, free trade agreements lead *not* to greater competition and lower prices, which is what economists expected them to do. They lead instead to monopoly and higher prices. If free trade agreements included antitrust or antimonopoly provisions of the kind embodied in U.S. antitrust law, they would stimulate competition and lower prices. The Sherman Antitrust Act of 1890, for example, prohibited companies from engaging in practices that unfairly restrain trade, reduce competition, or raise prices.[77] In a sense, U.S. *antitrust* law has long been used as an important way to promote *"free trade,"* at least within the United States. But the new free trade agreements do *not* include antitrust provisions. When U.S. officials initiated new free trade agreements in the mid-1980s, they did not propose that antitrust provisions be included in negotiations. Instead, they insisted that patent *monopoly* law be extended.

Indeed, many government officials have argued that U.S. antitrust laws should be eliminated. In 1989, Vice President Dan Quayle argued, "To make America more competitive, we are . . . going to have to reexamine our anti-trust laws, many of which are anachronistic in the age of global competition."[78] More recently, Lester Thurow, an adviser to President Clinton, said that antitrust laws were "out of date. Big companies do sometimes crush small companies, but better that small American companies be crushed by big American companies than that they be crushed by big foreign companies."[79]

As a consequence, the new free trade agreements contained no antitrust provisions, measures that might be used to prevent "big foreign companies" from crushing small companies in the United States or elsewhere, or from using their economic power unfairly to restrain international trade. The new free trade agreements sometimes prohibit governments from restraining trade, but they do nothing to prevent private companies from acting in ways that unfairly reduce competition and raise prices. Under these circumstances, where large TNCs control much of the world's trade, and much of this trade is within firms located in different countries, free trade agreements have not always delivered the goods—greater competition and lower consumer prices—that their proponents expected.

A second general problem is that the creation of *regional* free trade agreements discriminated against countries that did not belong to regional trade blocs, a development that ran counter to the idea that free trade agreements should end trade discrimination.

One of the central, original provisions in GATT was that its trade rules should *apply equally to all* of a country's trading partners. So if the United States imposed a tariff on goods from one country, it had to tax equally the same goods from other countries. Article XXIV permitted the creation of regional trade arrangements so long as they did not raise trade barriers with countries that did not belong. But this rule has not been closely observed, and a number of regional trade groups have emerged over the years that created "free trade" among a particular group of countries but discriminated against countries outside this group. The European Union (EU) is the most prominent such group or "trade bloc," as they are sometimes called, but there are other smaller ones in Asia, Africa, and Latin America.[80] The adoption of a U.S.–Canada FTA and then NAFTA created another large and powerful trade bloc. Countries that belong to the WTO, but not to the EU or NAFTA, have complained with justification that these regional FTAs discriminate against them.

Newly democratic countries in Eastern Europe complained that the EU raised new trade barriers to them even as it negotiated a reduction of trade barriers in the WTO. "The process of liberalization and the opening of [EU] markets to us is going slowly," complained Andrzej Arendarski, Poland's minister for trade and foreign economic relations. "It is our intention to press our partners [in the EU] to change their attitudes."[81] But the EU has been reluctant to do so, putting import restrictions and tariffs on as much as one-half of the goods imported from Eastern European countries.[82] These restrictions made it difficult to export goods and use export earnings to pay back loans from EU countries.

Countries in Latin America also complained that NAFTA excludes them from the U.S. market. When they negotiated NAFTA, U.S. officials promised to extend it to other Latin American countries, first Chile and then eventually all of Latin America. But a recent U.S. government report found that "Mexico is reportedly *not* interested in allowing other countries in the region into an arrangement that offers considerable benefits, which were achieved because of its relationship to the United States."[83] Governments in Latin America, but also in Asia, complained that NAFTA discriminated against them because the United States granted preferential trading status to members of the WTO and then granted even greater trade preferences to its partners in NAFTA. As one economist warned, new trade blocs may "set a dangerous precedent for further special deals, fragmentation of the trading system, and damage to the interests of non-participants."[84]

A third problem was that while free trade agreements increased the volume of trade, the economic benefits associated with expanding trade opportunities were not equally shared.

Indeed, economists and government officials *expected* this to happen. As Robert Gilpin explains:

> It is important to stress what liberal [free trade] theory does *not* assert. Liberals do not argue that everyone will necessarily gain from trade. . . . Rather [they] assert that there are potential gains. . . . Furthermore, liberal theory does not argue that everyone will gain equally. . . . Instead, it maintains that everyone will gain in absolute terms, although some will gain relatively more. . . . The argument for free trade is based not on grounds of equity and equal distribution but on increased efficiency and the maximization of world wealth.[85]

"Our trade policy is guided by a simple credo," Mickey Kantor, the U.S. trade representative in the Clinton administration, observed at the conclusion of the

GATT negotiations. "We want to expand *opportunities* for the global economy."[86] But it is important to note that the goal of U.S. officials was expanded opportunities. They did not argue that the benefits of expanded opportunities would be widely shared.

In this regard, it is noteworthy that the volume of world trade has increased ten times since GATT was formed in 1947. But the economic benefits associated with this dramatic increase in trade—an increase made possible in part by a general reduction of tariffs—has not been widely shared. As we have seen, the gap between rich and poor countries has grown in this period, *despite* the expansion of trade. According to Tim Lang and Colin Hines, "Developing nations' share of global wealth fell from 22 percent to 18 percent between 1980 and 1988."[87] Although trade may not alone have caused the gap between rich and poor countries to grow—falling commodity prices, indebtedness, and inflation probably played bigger roles in this period—expanded trade has *not* provided substantial benefits either. During the postwar period, most of the world's trade has been conducted among countries in the North. There is little evidence to suggest that new free trade agreements have substantially changed this. As a 2001 CIA report concluded, "Globalization will not lift all boats."[88]

WINNERS AND LOSERS

The free trade agreements adopted in the mid-1990s promoted a "globalization" of trade, lowering tariffs and removing many of the obstacles and barriers to trade around the world. Although proponents have claimed that trade globalization has been a great success and critics have argued that it has proved a failure, it has in fact produced both winners and losers. It is difficult to draw up a comprehensive balance sheet because free trade agreements were complex sets of rules, because they were implemented slowly, piecemeal, on a case-by-case basis, and because they combined with other ongoing economic developments in different parts of the world. But despite these difficulties, some patterns have become evident. A brief examination of developments in the United States, Canada, and Mexico can be used to illustrate some of the diverse consequences associated with the adoption of the U.S.–Canada Free Trade Agreement and then NAFTA in the early and mid-1990s. Then we will turn to some of the general developments associated with GATT and the WTO in the late 1990s.

NAFTA

When Congress debated NAFTA, critics like Ross Perot argued that it would hurt the United States and benefit Canada and Mexico, particularly Mexico. But that proved not to be the case. And the consequences of NAFTA were more complicated than either proponents or critics predicted. Generally speaking,

NAFTA produced modest economic gains (along with some losses) in the United States, but resulted in major economic losses and political difficulties for governments in both Canada and Mexico, which in turn created problems for the United States that officials here did not anticipate.

United States

When NAFTA was adopted, trade barriers fell, and U.S. exports to Canada and Mexico increased, providing some new jobs. However the gains were modest. A 1997 congressional report found that NAFTA "has made a modest positive contribution to the U.S. economy in terms of net exports," a development that created between 90,000 and 160,000 new jobs in the United States.[89] But U.S. workers also lost jobs, particularly in the textile industry. In 1994, NAFTA's first year, the textile and apparel industry lost 141,000 jobs, largely as a result of competition from Mexico.[90] NAFTA's net job impact may have been small, but U.S. job losses were felt primarily by women because the textile and apparel industries relied heavily on female workers (86 percent of sewing machine operators are women).[91]

Canada

The impact of the U.S.–Canada FTA and then NAFTA on Canada was more dramatic. In the first three years after the U.S.–Canada agreement, the Canadian economy lost 510,000 jobs.[92] Job loss was keenly felt in Canada because it has a far smaller population than the United States (it has about as many people as California). Consumers in Canada began buying more goods from the United States, reducing Canada's trade surplus and forcing a devaluation of the Canadian dollar. As a result of these economic woes, Prime Minister Brian Mulroney, who had sponsored and signed the two trade agreements, saw his popularity plummet. In the 1993 elections, his Progressive Conservative party, which had controlled 153 seats in Parliament, lost every seat but two, a collapse even more dramatic than the losses experienced by communist parties in the Soviet Union and Eastern Europe.

Mexico

In Mexico, falling tariffs implemented by NAFTA triggered a buying binge by consumers, which created a $23 billion trade deficit in 1994. The government then devalued the peso to increase the cost of imports and slow consumer purchases of foreign goods. But this made foreign investors lose confidence in the economy, and they withdrew large sums of capital. This further lowered the value of the peso and threatened the government with financial ruin. Economic crisis was averted only when the U.S. government intervened, providing $50 billion to bail out the Mexican government. This development was not anticipated by U.S. policymakers who sponsored and passed NAFTA. While falling tariffs helped increase U.S. exports to Mexico, they also triggered a crisis that required massive U.S. financial intervention.

This was not all. The Mexican government also raised interest rates to restore foreign investor confidence and persuade them to purchase bonds, which the government needed to survive. But higher interest rates caused a recession and increased debt payments for workers who had borrowed money (many of them had borrowed to purchase imported goods), forcing many into bankruptcy.

Of course, NAFTA provided some benefits. Export industries, particularly textile and apparel firms, grew during the mid-1990s. Employment in the maquiladoras doubled from 600,000 to 1.2 million between 1994 and 2000, providing many jobs for women.[93] But these apparent gains were reversed in 2001, as the new WTO began to make itself felt. Businesses in Mexico's maquiladoras began moving to other WTO member countries, where labor was cheaper, and Mexico lost two hundred thousand jobs in 2001 alone.[94] Moreover, rising employment in Mexican maquiladoras did not offset the massive job losses in other domestic Mexican industries, which had been exposed by NAFTA for the first time to competition with U.S. firms.

Ongoing economic problems in Mexico also had important political consequences. Zapatista guerillas launched a rebellion in 1994 against the PRI government, which had ruled Mexico since the 1930s. During the late 1990s, opposition parties began winning local elections against PRI candidates and, in 2000, opposition leader Vincente Fox captured the presidency. Although many regard these as positive political developments, it is nonetheless ironic that the PRI, which sponsored and signed NAFTA, did not benefit politically from its implementation. Like the Progressive Conservatives in Canada, the PRI's difficulties can be largely attributed to the economic problems associated with NAFTA.

It bears noting that these economic and political difficulties were not anticipated or appreciated by the political parties and policymakers that had sponsored NAFTA in the United States, Canada, and Mexico.

GATT and the WTO

Taking a wider look, what can be said about the globalization of trade associated with GATT and the WTO?

In general, the globalization of trade has been good for large, export manufacturing and service industries in the North. Aircraft, auto, computer, and entertainment industries based in Western Europe, the United States, and Japan have benefited from the WTO, largely because they have been able to capture markets from businesses that had long been protected by governments in Africa,

Asia, Eastern Europe, Latin America, and the Soviet Union. But large industries in the North have not all benefited. In the United States, for example, globalization has been extremely bad for the steel industry and the male workers employed in it, and for the textile-apparel industry and the female workers employed in it.

But while trade globalization has benefited some industries in the United States, it has *not* significantly improved the U.S. trade deficit. Recall that one of the primary objectives for U.S. policymakers in the 1980s was to use FTAs to expand U.S. exports and reduce the trade deficit. But since NAFTA and then the WTO were adopted, the U.S. trade deficit has grown substantially, from about $125 billion in the late 1980s to about $350 billion in the early 2000s. The overall trade benefits expected by U.S. trade negotiators did not materialize. Nor have the benefits of the WTO materialized for other groups in the North and South.

North

In the North, trade globalization has adversely affected industries that service domestic economies and hurt small businesses, particularly small shopkeepers in Japan and Western Europe, who have been exposed to increasing competition from large retail chain stores, supermarkets, and franchises. The reduction of subsidies and tariffs has also undermined many small farmers, rice farmers in Japan and farmers in the heavily subsidied countries of Western Europe: Ireland, Greece, Portugal, Spain, and the United Kingdom. It has had less of an impact on small farmers in less subsidized countries: France and the Netherlands. It has even been good for some farmers. French wine makers have generally benefited from trade globalization, and they campaigned for passage of GATT. This put them at odds with French wheat farmers and other small farmers across Western Europe, who mounted protests against the WTO and the globalization, or "MacDonaldization," of food as they call it.[95]

South

In the South, few benefits have been associated with trade globalization. In principle, free trade agreements should have assisted *export* industries. Indeed, those have been the principle beneficiaries of FTAs in the North. But in the South, export industries have not been greatly assisted by trade globalization; indeed they have frequently been substantially undermined by it. As we have seen (chapter 6), the prices that commodity producers in the South have received for their goods have declined substantially in recent years. WTO rules have made it even more difficult, even illegal, for raw material producers in the South to cooperate, organize cartels, restrict supplies, or raise prices. Meanwhile, the reduction of tariff barriers has exposed domestic manufacturing industries to withering competition from TNCs based in the North. And in many countries, binge-buying consumers who want to purchase goods imported from the North have contributed to trade imbalances, currency devaluations, rising interest rates, and recession, as they did in Mexico.

Of course, export industries in some countries have benefited from trade globalization: wine makers in Chile and New Zealand, apparel and toy manufacturers in China and other low-wage countries in the South, and export manufacturing industries in the free trade maquiladoras around the world. But positive benefits in these industries have not compensated for falling commodity prices, the collapse of domestic manufacturing industries, or the economic problems associated with trade deficits, currency devaluations, rising interest rates, and recession. In short, the benefits expected from trade globalization have not materialized in the South. As trade economist Clyde Prestowitz, Jr., admitted in 2001, "What is happening now is a recognition that the global marketplace, left to itself, is not going to automatically produce wealth and prosperity in less-developed countries unless there is rule-making and new structures that reduce the potential for destructiveness."[96]

Gender and FTAs

The gender implications of FTAs depend on the gender characteristics of the labor force in different industries, which vary by region. This makes it difficult to make general characterizations of the impact of FTAs on gender. Still, it is possible to make some observations.

In the North, export manufacturing and service industries that benefit from FTAs (aircraft, auto, computer, entertainment) are dominated by men, while some industries adversely affected by FTAs largely employ men (steel), and others rely on women (textiles and apparel).

In the South, export manufacturing industries based in the maquiladoras, which have gained from FTAs, employ women, while domestic industries that have found it difficult to compete employed men. So the gender consequences of FTAs in the North and South are asymmetrical: good for men, bad for women in the North; bad for men, good for women in the South.

The gender impact also frequently varies within the same industry. FTAs have benefited firms growing bananas on large plantations in Central America, where men predominate, and hurt farmers growing bananas on a small scale in the Caribbean, where women make up a large proportion of the workforce. In many countries, small businesses have been adversely affected by FTAs and the chain stores that have followed in their wake. In some of these countries, men are the primary shopkeepers; in others, women run the business. But in most settings these businesses are run by families, by women and men, assisted by children and relatives. Much the same is true for small farms. As a result, it is important to recognize that the gender consequences of FTAs are complex, diverse, and vary considerably in different settings.

Protest

Given the fact that trade globalization produced losers in the North and the South, for a wide variety of different social groups, both rural farmers and urban shopkeepers, women textile workers and male steel workers, and consumers and environmentalists, it should not be surprising that representatives of these groups organized against trade globalization and the WTO. During the late 1990s they mounted large demonstrations and protests at the WTO's meetings in Seattle (1999) and Genoa (2001).[97]

One remarkable feature of these anti-WTO demonstrations is that they brought together groups that had *not* cooperated in the past: environmentalists, labor unions, small farmers, feminists, consumer and religious groups, and entrepreneurs from both the North and the South. Although it is too early to assess what impact they will have on the trade globalization process, it is already evident that they have blocked consideration of new free trade negotiations and slowed the implementation of existing FTAs.[98] It is also apparent that trade globalization has contributed to the globalization of movements opposed to trade globalization.

NOTES

1. Tim Lang and Colin Hines, *The New Protectionism* (New York: New Press, 1993), 26.

2. Environmental News Network, *GATT: The Environment and the Third World, A Resource Guide* (Berkeley, Calif.: Environmental News Network, 1992), section 3, 3.

3. William P. Avery, ed., *World Agriculture and the GATT* (Boulder, Colo.: Rienner, 1993), 1.

4. Peter Passell, "Regional Trade Makes Global Deals Go Round," *New York Times*, December 19, 1993.

5. Kevin Watkins, "GATT and the Third World," *Race and Class* 34, no. 1 (1992): 36.

6. Joel Davidow, "The Relationship between Anti-Trust and Trade Laws in the United States," *The World Economy* 14, no. 1 (1991): 47; Chakravarthi Raghavan, *Recolonization: GATT, the Uruguay Round and the Third World* (Penang, Malaysia: Third World Network, 1990), 73. In 1999, a WTO panel ruled that Section 301 did not violate trade law. The European Union, Japan, and a number of other countries argued that the use of Section 301 by the United States violated WTO provisions. Joseph Kahn, "U.S. Wins Round in Trade War with Europe," *New York Times*, December 23, 1999.

7. Robert L. Paarlberg, "Why Agriculture Blocked the Uruguay Round: Evolving Strategies in a Two-Level Game," in *World Agriculture and the GATT*, 32.

8. Theodore H. Cohn, "The Changing Role of the United States in the Global Agricultural Trade Regime," in *World Agriculture and the GATT*, 31.

9. Avery, *World Agriculture and the GATT*, 1.

10. Robert Gilpin, *The Political Economy of International Relations* (Princeton, N.J.: Princeton University Press, 1987), 195.

11. Environmental News Network, *GATT*, section 1, 2.

12. Stephanie Strom, "As Japan Deregulates, Quality-of-Life Laments," *New York Times*, August 8, 2000.

13. "New Trends to Agriculture Exports Seen under Guise of Food Safety," *Inside U.S. Trade*, Special Report, March 16, 1990, S-8.

14. Environmental News Network, *GATT*, section 5, 1.

15. W. John. Moore, "Stopping the States," *National Journal*, July 21, 1990, 1758.

16. "The New Age of Trade" [advertisement], *New York Times*, April 15, 1994.

17. Noam Chomsky, "Notes on NAFTA: The Master of Mankind," *The Nation*, March 29, 1993, 412.

18. Keith Bradsher, "Asians and Latins Object to GATT Deals," *New York Times*, December 8, 1993; Lang and Hines, *The New Protectionism*, 50.

19. Alan Riding, "Seven Years of Struggle Ends as 109 Nations Sign Trade Accord," *New York Times*, April 16, 1991.

20. Keith Bradsher, "US and Europe Clear the Way for a World Accord on Trade, Setting Aside Major Disputes," *New York Times*, December 15, 1993.

21. [Advertisement], *New York Times*, April 15, 1994.

22. Anthony DePalma, "NAFTA's Powerful Little Secret," *New York Times*, March 11, 2001.

23. DePalma, "NAFTA's Powerful Little Secret."

24. Frank James Tester, "Free Trading the Environment," in *The Free Trade Deal*, ed. Duncan Camerin (Toronto: Lorimer, 1988), 207.

25. DePalma, "NAFTA's Powerful Little Secret."

26. Jeanne J. Grimmet, *Environmental Regulation and the GATT* (Washington, D.C.: Congressional Research Service, 1991), 38.

27. Susan Ferriss, "NAFTA Coming into Focus," *San Francisco Examiner*, June 19, 1994.

28. Edmund G. Brown, "Race to the Bottom," *San Jose Mercury News*, September 15, 1992.

29. Tester, "Free Trading the Environment," 204–13; Steven Shrybman, "The Environmental Costs of Free Trade," *Multinational Monitor*, March 1990, 20.

30. Charles Arden-Clarke, "Conservation and Sustainable Management of Tropical Forests: The Role of ITTO and GATT" (Gland, Switzerland: World Conservation Center, 1990), 6, 9.

31. Roger Cohen, "A Realignment Made Reluctantly," *New York Times*, December 15, 1993.

32. Andrew Pollack, "For Rice Lobby, the Bowl Dries Up," *New York Times*, December 13, 1993.

33. Pollack, "For Rice Lobby, the Bowl Dries Up."

34. Bradsher, "US and Europe Clear the Way"; Bernard Weintraub, "Clinton Spared Blame by Hollywood Officials," *New York Times*, December 16, 1993.

35. Cohen, "A Realignment Made Reluctantly."

36. Bernard Weintraub, "Directors Fight for GATT's Final Cut and Print," *New York Times*, December 12, 1993.

37. Meera Mitra, "A Question of Indianness amid Western Influence," *World Paper* (March 1992): 11.

38. Philip Shenon, "Giant U.S. Film Studios Overwhelm Indonesia's," *New York Times*, October 29, 1992.

39. Alexander Cockburn, "In Bed with America," *American Film* (November–December 1991): 42.

40. Elizabeth Kolbert, "Canadians Act to Restrict Violence on TV," *New York Times*, January 11, 1994; Roger Cohen, "France and Spain Are Adopting Quotas on U.S. Arts Imports," *New York Times*, December 22, 1993.

41. Weintraub, "Directors Fight for GATT's Final Cut and Print."

42. Weintraub, "Directors Fight for GATT's Final Cut and Print."

43. Peter Morici, "Grasping the Benefits of NAFTA," *Current History*, 92 (1993): 51; Bruce W. Wilkerson, "Trade Liberalization, the Market Ideology, and Morality: Have We a Sustainable System?" in *The Political Economy of North American Free Trade*, eds. Ricardo Grinspun and Maxwell A. Cameron (New York: St. Martin's, 1993), 35.

44. Sidney Weintraub, "Free Trade in North America: Has Its Time Come?" *The World Economy* 14, no. 1 (1991): 59.

45. Personal interview, March 5, 1993.

46. G. Perry, *Trade Liberalization and Export Promotion* (Washington, D.C.: World Bank, 1982), 136.

47. Celia W. Dugger, "Market Economics," *New York Times*, June 14, 2000.

48. Dugger, "Market Economics."

49. Clyde H. Farnsworth, "Next Trade War Target May Be Dogs," *New York Times*, December 2, 1992.

50. David Phillips, "Dolphins and GATT," in *The Case against Free Trade: GATT, NAFTA and the Globalization of Corporate Power* (San Francisco: Earth Island, 1993), 135.

51. Lang and Hines, *The New Protectionism*, 65–66, 68.

52. John H. Cushman, "Trade Group Strikes Blow at U.S. Environmental Law," *New York Times*, April 7, 1998.

53. Mark Ritchie, "GATT, Agriculture and the Environment," *The Ecologist* 20, no. 6 (1990): 216.

54. Maury E. Bredahl and Kenneth W. Forsythe, "Harmonizing Phyto-Sanitary and Sanitary Regulations," *The World Economy* 12, no. 2 (1989): 196–97.

55. Debi Barker and Jerry Mander, *Invisible Government: The WTO: Global Government for the New Millennium?* (San Francisco: International Forum on Globalization, 1999), 27.

56. Barker and Mander, *Invisible Government*, 35; Edmund L. Andrews, "Europe Refuses to Drop Ban on U.S. Beef," *New York Times*, March 14, 1998; Edmund L. Andrews, "Europe's Banning of Treated Beef Is Ruled Illegal," *New York Times*, May 9, 1997.

57. Alan V. Deardorff, "Should Patent Protection Be Extended to All Developing Countries?" *The World Economy* 13, no. 4 (1990): 498.

58. "Of Minds and Markets: Intellectual Property Rights and the Poor," *GATT Briefing* 2 (July: European Network on Agriculture and Development, 1990), 2.

59. Andrew Pollack, "The Green Revolution Yields to the Bottom Line," *New York Times*, May 15, 2001.

60. Pollack, "The Green Revolution Yields."

61. Freudenheim, Milt. "For Canada, Free Trade Accord Includes Higher Prices for Drugs," *New York Times*, November 16, 1992.

62. Vandana Shiva, "Biodiversity and Intellectual Property Rights," in *The Case against Free Trade*, 112.

63. Kevin Watkins, "GATT and the Third World: Fixing the Rules," *Race and Class* 34, no. 1 (1992): 38.

64. Donald G. McNeil, Jr., "Selling Cheap 'Generic' Drugs, India's Copycats Irk Industry," *New York Times*, December 1, 2000.

65. Joseph Kahn, "Trade Deal Near for Broad Access to Cut-Rate Drugs," *New York Times*, November 13, 2001.

66. Kahn, "Trade Deal Near."

67. Elizabeth Olson, "Drug Issue Casts a Shadow on Trade Talks," *New York Times*, November 2, 2001.

68. Shiva, "Biodiversity and Intellectual Property Rights," 55.

69. Vandana Shiva, "The Crisis of Diversity," *Third World Resurgence* 13 (1991): 11.

70. Vandana Shiva, "The Seed and the Earth: Biotechnology and the Colonisation of Regeneration," in Vandana Shiva, *Close to Home: Women Reconnect Ecology, Health and Development Worldwide* (Philadelphia: New Society, 1994), 135.

71. Shiva, "Biodiversity and Intellectual Property Rights," 119.

72. Watkins, "GATT and the Third World," 37–38.

73. Shiva, "Biodiversity and Intellectual Property Rights," 119.

74. Saritha Rai, "India-U.S. Fight on Basmati Rice Is Mostly Settled," *New York Times*, August 25, 2001.

75. Lang and Hines, *The New Protectionism*, 34.

76. Michael Barrat Brown, *Fair Trade: Reform and Realities in the International Trading System* (London: Zed, 1993), 51.

77. Davidow, "The Relationship between Anti-Trust and Trade Laws," 39.

78. Davidow, "The Relationship between Anti-Trust and Trade Laws," 38.

79. David Morris, "Free Trade: The Great Destroyer," in *Case against Free Trade*, 140.

80. Lang and Hines, *The New Protectionism*, 43–44.

81. Richard W. Stevenson, "Europe Says Barriers to Trade Hurt Its Economies," *New York Times*, March 1, 1994.

82. Stevenson, "Europe Says Barriers to Trade Hurt Its Economies."

83. Keith Bradsher, "U.S. Memo Says Mexico May Bar NAFTA Growth," *New York Times*, March 1, 1994.

84. Jeffrey J. Schott, "Trading Blocs and the World Trading System," *The World Economy* 14, no. 1 (1991): 3.

85. Gilpin, *The Political Economy of International Relations*, 179.

86. [Advertisement], *New York Times*, April 15, 1994.

87. Lang and Hines, *The New Protectionism*, 8, 113, 161.

88. Elaine Sciolino, "2015 Outlook: Enough Food, Scarce Water, Porous Borders," *New York Times*, December 18, 2000.

89. Richard W. Stevenson, "U.S. to Report to Congress NAFTA Benefits Modest," *New York Times*, July 11, 1997.

90. John Holusha, "Squeezing the Textile Workers," *New York Times*, February 21, 1996.

91. Holusha, "Squeezing the Textile Workers."

92. Bruce Campbell, "Restructuring the Economy: Canada Into the Free Trade Era," in *The Political Economy of North American Free Trade*, 100; Louis Uchitelle, "NAFTA and Jobs: In a Numbers War, No One Can Count," *New York Times*, November 14, 1993.

93. Ginger Thompson, "Fallout of U.S. Recession Drifts South Into Mexico," *New York Times*, December 26, 2001.

94. Thompson, "Fallout of U.S. Recession."

95. Alix Christie, "Trade Talks Are Tearing France," *San Francisco Chronicle*, November 28, 1993.

96. Louis Uchitelle, "Globalization Marches On, as U.S. Eases Up on the Reins," *New York Times*, December 17, 2001.

97. David Moberg, "Seattle Showdown: Citizens Stand Up to the WTO," *In These Times*, November 28, 1999.

98. Joseph Kahn, "A Trade Agenda Tempts Murphy's Law," *New York Times*, November 9, 2001.

10

The Emergence of a Global Environmental Movement

During the last thirty years, a global environmental movement has emerged. This movement is not organized under a single institutional umbrella but consists of scores of large, national environmental organizations and thousands of small, local grassroots groups. These groups work on diverse issues—global warming, acid rain, ozone depletion, free trade, population growth, deforestation, whaling, animal rights, nuclear power, nuclear weapons, air and water pollution, toxic waste, land use, recycling, food and hunger, global financial institutions, environmental education, genetic engineering, and many more—that have grown in number and scope over time. But the globalization of the environmental movement has had its ups and downs, successes and failures. An examination of the environmental movement in the United States, and its relation to environmental movements around the world, illustrates the globalization process.

During the 1970s, the environmental movement that emerged in the United States made remarkable political gains. It persuaded the U.S. government to pass twenty-three important new laws and create a new Environmental Protection Agency (EPA) and Council on Environmental Quality to administer and monitor new legislation.[1] The movement persuaded the Nixon administration to ban DDT and adopt population control, then the most important issue for environmentalists, as part of its foreign policy.[2] In 1969, President Richard Nixon announced that the government would "give population [control] and family planning a high priority," called on other governments to take "prompt action" to slow population growth, and later lobbied the United Nations to convene its first World Population Conference in Bucharest, Romania, in 1974.[3]

Outside Washington, the movement raised public awareness and convinced many Americans to take environmental issues seriously. By 1990, 75 percent of

Americans identified themselves as "environmentalists," and 45 percent believed that "protecting the environment is so important that requirements and standards cannot be too high and continuing environmental improvement must be made regardless of cost."[4] The movement urged consumers to adopt new habits, and they did. The number of Americans who recycled grew from 33 percent in 1972 to 80 percent in 1990, and a majority of Americans claimed to have "made changes in [their] day-to-day behavior because of concern about the environment."[5] As Americans became more aware of environmental issues, they joined new and old environmental organizations and donated time and money to their cause. Membership in the major organizations grew from 819,000 in 1969 to two million in 1983, and then to three million by 1990, and the collective income of the major groups grew to $217.3 million in 1990.[6]

Given the movement's rapid, remarkable, and numerous achievements in the 1970s, many observers agreed with the sociologist Robert Nisbet, who in 1982 argued, "It is entirely possible that when the history of the twentieth century is finally written, the single most important social movement of the period will be judged to be environmentalism."[7] But Nisbet's assessment was premature.[8] After Ronald Reagan took office in 1981, the U.S. movement was unable to maintain its forward momentum. It was unable to pass new laws or defend earlier legislation and its political progress stalled. After 1990, as the movement's political weakness became apparent, public support for environmental organizations waned and membership plummeted, creating a crisis for many groups. Greenpeace alone lost more than one million donors between 1990 and 1994.[9] The movement's political impasse and organizational crisis then generated an acrimonious debate about its social character and political future.

Given these developments, it is important first to explain how the U.S. environmental movement successfully changed state policy, raised public consciousness, increased its domestic organizational strength, and spread its ideas to some other countries around the world in the 1970s. It will then be possible to explain why the political fortunes of the environmental movement in the United States and in other countries changed during the 1980s and 1990s.

U.S. MOVEMENT SUCCESS IN THE 1970s

The achievements of the U.S. environmental movement in the 1970s were made possible by four important social, economic, political, and theoretical developments. First, the *union* of diverse social groups in the late 1960s and early 1970s created a widely based social movement that could successfully promote change.

The environmental movement has often been described as consisting of two parts: "conservationist" and "environmentalist."[10] The "conservation" movement, which included nineteenth-century groups such as the Audubon Society and

Sierra Club, was joined in the late 1960s and early 1970s by new "environmental" groups such as the Environmental Defense Fund, Natural Resources Defense Council, Environmental Action, Friends of the Earth, and Greenpeace.[11]

These two currents had different social origins and philosophical orientations. The conservation movement can be traced back to the mid-nineteenth century, when movements in the United States and Great Britain organized to protect animals, women, children, slaves, and sailors from flogging and corporal punishment.[12] These assorted movements assumed responsibility for protecting domesticated animals (principally draught horses), women, children, slaves, and mariners because these groups had no legal standing—they were treated as chattel—and could not effectively "protect" themselves.[13] Because abused groups had new legal standing, nineteenth-century movements assumed a "custodial" role on their behalf, acting like "guardians" of "minors."[14] In the same spirit, subsequent conservation groups moved to "protect" birds (the Audubon Society), game animals, and wild lands (the Sierra Club). The self-appointed guardians of wildlife and wild lands sometimes differed over the extent and kind of protection they might extend—-John Muir favored the "preservation" of land in its wild state, while Gifford Pinchot advocated the "conservation" and use of wild lands—but they shared a custodial approach. And it was not until the early 1970s that a series of U.S. Supreme Court decisions gave conservationists the full legal standing they needed to act effectively as custodians, to exercise what they called "stewardship."[15] These rulings made it possible for conservationists to litigate on behalf of their wards, an important tactic for the U.S. movement in the 1970s.

By contrast, the new environmentalists that emerged in the late 1960s did not see themselves as guardians. They worried instead about how environmental problems affected their own lives, and they insisted on protecting human "rights," such as the right to clean water and clean air. Unlike conservationists, who had adopted an "altruistic" orientation, environmentalists advanced a more "self-interested" perspective, a philosophical approach in keeping with the spirit of the 1960s. These different approaches to the natural world were usually associated with different socioeconomic circumstances. In the 1960s, for instance, conservation groups were typically supported by elderly, upper-class Republicans, a legacy of the conservationist traditions established by Theodore Roosevelt and other progressive Republicans during the early twentieth century. By contrast, the environmental groups of the 1960s typically drew supporters from young, middle-class Democrats, whose interest in the environment grew out of a concern for civil rights and participation in the student, antiwar, and women's movements.[16]

Conservationists and Environmentalists Unite

Many writers have described the environmental movement as a union of conservationists and environmentalists. But few have explained why this union was forged at a time when age, gender, political, and class divides were sharply felt. During the tumultuous Sixties, different generations, genders, and classes fought bitterly over music, drugs, politics, fashion, civil rights, and the war in Vietnam. Under these circumstances, one might have expected the young, Democratic environmentalists to reject an alliance with elderly, Republican conservationists.[17] But conservationist and environmentalist groups did not fight; they made common cause instead. They did so because they shared important experiences, common values, and mutual goals, which helped them bridge other differences.

The postwar baby boom gave both young and old a firsthand experience with rapid population growth and the problems of scarcity associated with it.[18] Paul Ehrlich's argument that population growth was an environmental and social problem found widespread support among both old and young, helping bridge the generation gap that otherwise loomed large in this period. Mutual agreement on the need for population control, reproductive rights, family planning, birth control, and abortion (environmental groups like Zero Population Growth filed *amicus* briefs in *Roe v. Wade*, arguing for a woman's right to chose) drew women into the movement and bridged the gender gap, which was then dividing other contemporary movements.[19] Moreover, the spread of secondary education, which enabled wealthy conservationists *and* middle-class students to attend college and meet as intellectual equals, helped bridge class divides. These class divides had loomed large before World War II, when college education was restricted to the children of wealthy parents.

Conservationists and environmentalist also shared mutual political goals. Elder Republicans and young Democrats recognized that political success might be possible if they worked together, not separately.[20] Their common desire for change helped them put aside the ideological differences associated with their separate party identifications—Republican conservationist and Democratic environmentalist—and fashion a bipartisan approach to the state, which in this period was divided between a Republican executive and a Democratic Congress.[21] As a result, the older conservation movement could supply experience and money to the younger environmental movement, and gain new members, youthful enthusiasm, and wider political support in return.[22] These developments made it possible for different social groups, with different political ideologies, to unite in a movement that reached across age, gender, class, and political divides.[23]

Inflation and Scarcity

A second development that assisted the environmental movement was economic. During the 1970s, rising inflation provided a *material* basis for environmental concerns and contributed to the movement's early political success. In 1972, President Nixon imposed wage and price controls to curb inflation, then increasing at about 4 percent annually (see chapter 4).[24] His efforts failed because the OPEC oil embargo and Soviet grain shortages increased prices dramatically and accelerated inflation into double-digit annual rates after 1973. Higher energy, food, and commodity prices made these natural resources "scarce" for people living in the United States. Increasingly scarcity made credible the environmental movement's economic argument that energy, food, and natural resources were diminishing and that there were real "limits to growth." As one environmental writer argued, "The inevitability of resource scarcity is [now] a staple in modern environmental thought. Thanks to OPEC it is fair to say that these ideas are not much more widely appreciated by the public than they were in the early 1970s."[25]

Under conditions of apparent "scarcity," consumers began recycling, using renewable energy sources, and practicing conservation, which reduced energy demand for the first time in the postwar period. By making goods scarce, the rising prices associated with inflation corroborated the environmental movement's economic arguments and contributed to its political success in this period.

Republican Environmentalism

A third development that assisted the environmental movement was political support from what now seems an unlikely source: President Nixon and Republicans in the House and Senate. These environmental Republicans played a crucial role in the environmental movement's political success. Some movement historians have discounted Nixon's role, arguing that he initiated, supported, and signed environmental legislation only because he was cynical, opportunistic, or simply indifferent to these issues.[26] They argue that Nixon supported environmental legislation to "steal" the increasingly popular issue from Democratic senator Edmund Muskie, who had emerged in 1970 as Nixon's most likely challenger for the presidency.[27] But this misrepresents Nixon's motives and minimizes his role, which was rather more substantial than many historians admit.

Nixon's initiatives—creating the EPA by executive order, establishing the Council on Environmental Quality, banning DDT, adopting population control as a domestic and foreign policy, and signing numerous environmental bills—have often been depicted as an attempt to "steal" the environmental issue from Muskie and the Democrats. But instead of trying to steal the issue from Muskie, Nixon was actually trying to prevent Muskie from "stealing" this issue from the Republicans, who had long supported "conservation" and population control. The Republican Party's interest in conservation dated back to Theodore Roosevelt. Interest in this issue by the Democrats was much more recent. So Nixon wanted to prevent a repeat of 1960, when his Democratic opponent, John Kennedy, had "stolen" the civil rights issue from Republicans. Nixon acted in 1970 to ensure that Muskie would not likewise steal environmental issues from the

Republican party in the upcoming elections.[28] Nixon himself maintained that he belonged to a Republican conservationist tradition stretching back to Roosevelt. As Nixon argued in 1970, a few months before Earth Day:

> At the turn of the century, our chief environmental concern was to conserve what we had—and out of this concern grew the often embattled but always determined "conservation" movement. Today, conservation is as important as ever—but it is no longer enough to conserve what we have; we must also restore what we have lost. We must go beyond conservation to embrace restoration.[29]

This speech was remarkable because it was made in advance of Earth Day, when widespread public support for environmental issues first because apparent, and because his call not just for conservation but for "restoration" was a more radical statement than most contemporary conservationists were then willing to make. Nixon also supported population control, which was then the main objective of the fledgling environmental movements. Nixon's enthusiasm for population control grew out his close association with the Rockefeller family. In 1952, John D. Rockefeller III had organized the Population Council to promote population control and he helped persuade Nixon of its merits.[30] As president, Nixon initiated domestic family planning programs, made population control a feature of U.S. foreign policy, and, at the first UN Conference on Population, "put forward a forceful policy agenda urging global action to reduce high fertility, including demographic targets" for every country.[31] Nixon's support for population control, then a central tenant of the new environmental movement, contrasted sharply with that of many Democratic politicians, who drew support from working-class Catholic constituencies opposed to family planning, birth control, and abortion.

Although Nixon's presidency was ruined by scandal, corruption, dishonesty, and the abuse of power, it was also characterized by bold initiatives: breaking up the international monetary system, imposing government controls on wages and prices to control inflation, opening diplomatic relations with China, launching affirmative action, and initiating a war on drugs that emphasized treatment not punishment. In this context, Nixon's environmental initiatives were serious attempts to grapple with important problems, and these initiatives often anticipated or exceeded the demands of movements activists and their congressional allies.[32] Although historians now are reluctant to recognize Nixon as the most "environmental" president since Theodore Roosevelt, the fact remains that many of the movement's most important political gains came during his presidency.

But while the movement's work with Nixon and its bipartisan efforts in Congress produced major *domestic* gains, the movement's close association with U.S. foreign policy—particularly policies supporting population control—antagonized people in the South and prevented, for a decade, the spread of environmental ideas in many countries around the world.

Antienvironmentalism around the World

Environmental movement ideas and organizations did not spread to poor countries or communist countries during the 1970s for different reasons. First, many people around the world were antagonized by the environmental movement's close association with the U.S. state, which they regarded as imperialist, and by U.S. population control efforts. They were particularly troubled by the fact that the Nixon administration increased spending on the U.S. Agency for International Development's population control programs while cutting its funding for overseas health care. They were angered by administration efforts to tie food aid to a country's population control efforts, and, after 1974, its decision to reduce food aid as prices rose (see chapter 7). In this case, U.S. policymakers used Ehrlich's concept of "triage" (withholding food aid from countries like India that were deemed incapable of becoming self-sufficient in food) as their rationale for changed food aid and population control policies.[33]

Second, global inflation had a different economic meaning in the South. For producers of energy, food, and natural resources, the rising prices associated with inflation brought "plenty" not scarcity. Rising prices in the 1970s generally increased incomes in the South, and the transfer of wealth from the United States and Western Europe to OPEC countries (the result of higher oil prices) created surpluses that were used to finance economic development throughout the South (see chapter 5). The new terms of trade fueled an optimism that population growth and economic development might go hand in hand. As a result of these developments, environmental movement arguments that population control was needed and that that development would eventually encounter "limits to growth" were not welcomed by people in the South. U.S. environmental groups managed to organize a few sister groups in Malaysia and Sri Lanka, largely as a result of efforts by Friends of the Earth (FOE). But because dictators ruled many states in Africa, Asia, Eastern Europe, Latin America, the Middle East, and the Soviet Union, dissident environmental groups found it difficult to organize or raise environmental issues effectively.[34] India was perhaps the exception during this period. Indira Gandhi's coercive population control policies, large-scale development projects, and emergency political rule antagonized many local groups, giving rise to widespread environmental activism that drew effectively on grassroots and democratic political traditions in India.[35]

Environmentalism in Western Europe

But while the views of U.S. environmental groups were not welcome in the South during the 1970s, their ideas and organizations did spread across much of Western Europe. The environmental movement in Europe grew in part because U.S.-based movements—particularly FOE and Greenpeace—organized effectively there, transferring money, ideas, and tactics to sister orga-

as in Europe.[36] The UN Conference on the Human Environment, which met in Stockholm in 1972, and the UN World Population Conference, which met in Bucharest in 1974, played important roles by calling European attention to environmental issues (the 1992 UN Conference on the Environment in Rio would later call attention to environmental issues in the South).[37]

Unlike the U.S. movement, European environmentalism was not a union of "conservationist" and "environmental" movements, largely because conservationist organizations outside of the United Kingdom were rare.[38] Instead, most environmental groups in Europe united people from political, New Left organizations and relatively *a*political, countercultural groups.[39] Participants of New Left organizations started "Green" political parties in Europe during the 1970s, while participants in the counterculture organized less political, "lifestyle" environmental groups.[40] For example, Brice LaLond, a leader of FOE in France and later an environmental minister with the Mitterand government, once described French environmentalism as an "epicurian ecology—the ecology of enjoying life, having animals, drinking and loving and talking, getting cheese and dessert and a little bit more, as we say."[41] His views were representative of countercultural environmentalism. New Left and countercultural groups in Europe were joined in the 1970s by their common experience with inflation and scarcity and by their opposition to nuclear power and weapons. For example, all of the Friends of the Earth sister organizations in Europe campaigned against nuclear power in the 1970s and against nuclear weapons in the 1980s.[42] As Green Party representatives from West Germany explained in 1983, the Green Party coalition, which brought together remnants of the New Left and Counterculture, was "sewn together with a hot needle," the hot needle being nuclear power and nuclear weapons.[43]

Although environmental movements emerged in Western Europe during the 1970s, they did not flourish in Japan. In 1990, for example, Greenpeace counted only three hundred members in Japan, compared to more than two million in the United States and eighty thousand in the Netherlands.[44] Environmental issues did not enjoy widespread public support in Japan largely because the Japanese were greatly antagonized by the U.S. environmental movement's efforts to use the International Whaling Commission to curb Japanese whaling.[45] Anger about this issue in Japan made it extremely difficult to organize support for other environmental issues, much as anger about U.S. population control policies made it difficult to raise environmental issues in poor countries during this period.

Movement Theories

A fourth reason why the environmental movement made political gains during the 1970s was that it was assisted by an astute set of theories, or sets of expectations about the future. Because the expectations advanced in theories developed in the 1960s were apparently confirmed by events in the 1970s, they contributed to an effective movement politics.

Generally speaking, the major theories adopted by the environmental movement in the 1960s, 1970s, and 1980s were developed by authors of popular books—Rachel Carson's *Silent Spring*, Paul Ehrlich's *The Population Bomb*, Amory Lovins's *Non-Nuclear Futures*, Jonathan Schell's *The Fate of the Earth*, and Bill McKibben's *The End of Nature*—many of which first appeared excerpted in *The New Yorker*.[46] Although they addressed different topical problems—pesticides, population, nuclear power, nuclear war, and global warming—they shared a common purpose: to anticipate and avert some awful environmental problem. Carson set the tone in *Silent Spring*, which began with this warning from Albert Schwitzer: "Man has lost the capacity to foresee and forestall. He will end by destroying the Earth."[47]

Although many critics have commented on the movement's apocalyptic character, they have not explained why this should be a salient feature, not only for environmentalists but for religious fundamentalists in the same period.[48] The apocalyptic literature of millennial Christians during the postwar period runs parallel to that of environmentalists.[49] For example, Michael Barkan has argued that environmental and religious literatures are both

> conducted in the idioms of social and political criticism . . . [evoking] world destruction and transformation through ecological disaster, nuclear holocaust and technological breakdown. The curious result is that two quite different bodies of apocalyptic literature flourish simultaneously . . . they converge on the belief that the accepted texture of reality is about to undergo a staggering transformation, in which long-established institutions and ways of life will be destroyed.[50]

Doomsday theories have found receptive audiences in both secular and religious communities. But while doomsday theories have been used to mobilize both communities, the theories advanced by secular environmentalists were more readily tested by real-world developments.

During the 1960s, Carson, Ehrlich, and Lovins advanced theories that were adopted by the environmental movement or important groups in it. In *Silent Spring*, Carson expected three things to occur as a result of widespread pesticide use. First, she argued that pesticides would kill not only harmful insects but also "nontarget species" such as insect predators, birds, household pets, and humans. Second, she maintained that some insects would survive the chemical onslaught and then thrive, making pesticides increasingly ineffective as insect "resistance" grew stronger. Finally, she argued that poisons would spread in the environment and pose a growing threat to species at the top of food chains. Her expectations, which were based on a scientific literature then in its infancy, were subsequently confirmed by scientists. During the next two decades, scientists found that nontarget species were harmed, pesticide resistance increased, and poisons spread, posing problems for animals and humans.[51]

Carson's theoretical arguments provided a useful guide to grassroots antipesticide groups in the United States, many of them affiliated with the National Coalition against the Misuse of Pesticides (NCAMP). The 1981 publication of David Weir and Mark Shapiro's *Circle of Poison*, which found that DDT use continued in the periphery after it was banned in the United States, and that DDT-contaminated produce was frequently exported to the United States, led in 1982 to the formation of the Pesticide Action Network.[52] Grassroots groups, guided by Carson's theories and supported by a growing scientific literature, found that where pesticide use was controlled by local authorities—by city, county or state officials or by private utility companies, railroads or farmers— they could litigate, lobby, and protest successfully against pesticide use in the 1970s and 1980s.

In the *Population Bomb*, Ehrlich expected four things to occur as a result of rapid population growth. First, he argued that the population would outstrip the available food supply, leading to widespread hunger and famine in the mid-1970s. Second, he maintained that food shortages would lead to conflict and war. Third, he warned that a growing population would increase levels of pollution and waste. Finally, he argued that the growing population would rapidly deplete nonrenewable resources.[53] To forestall these developments, Ehrlich advocated aggressive population control measures and recommended that the concept of "triage" be used as a way to determine which countries should receive food aid and which should be denied assistance.[54]

Events in the 1970s seemed initially to confirm Ehrlich's theoretical expectations. The 1972 famine and war in Bangladesh, Soviet grain shortages, the energy crisis, and inflation-induced scarcity all suggested that population growth was related to hunger, war, pollution, and shortage.

In *Non-Nuclear Futures* and *Brittle Power*, Lovins advanced a simple expectation about nuclear power: that accidents would happen. He argued that complex technologies were accident-prone or "brittle." Lovins warned that the risks of failure were magnified when a complex, brittle technology was combined with extremely hazardous nuclear materials. He also noted that the nuclear power industry's efforts to reduce risk by adding safety features would be counterproductive because they would make the technology even more complex and therefore more prone to failure, and that redundant safety systems would greatly increase the cost of producing energy, making it uneconomical.

Lovins's expectations were made credible by a series of small-scale accidents and snafus that came to light as a result of diligent research by anti-nuclear activists and information provided by industry dissidents and whistle-blowers.[55] Lovins's theoretical expectations proved a useful guide to grassroots antinuclear groups across the country. These groups were successful for a variety of reasons. First, authority for nuclear power had been delegated by the U.S. government to public utilities and private businesses, which made them vulnerable to grassroots litigation, lobbying, and protest. Second, government laws about nuclear power were less stringent than those applying to nuclear weapons, so grassroots protestors could risk arrest for simple misdemeanors rather than serious felonies. This made grassroots protest easier. Third, the energy crisis and inflation slowed the demand for energy and increased the cost of nuclear power. Rising costs and the risks associated with nuclear power made it seem an increasingly poor investment for utilities and stockholders. This confirmed Lovins's argument that nuclear power was "uneconomical."[56] Finally, the partial meltdown at Three Mile Island in March 1979 (and later the meltdown at Chernobyl in the Soviet Union) provided proof that Lovins's theory was sound: major accidents *could* happen.

THE IMPASSE OF THE
ENVIRONMENTAL MOVEMENT

The environmental movement's political success did not long endure. Beginning in the 1980s, the movement reached a political impasse. It failed to pass new legislation or improve old legislation when it came up for renewal. Although membership and financial contributions increased during the 1980s, environmental organizations experienced sharp declines in the 1990s as the movement's political ineffectiveness became apparent. In 1994, *USA Today* reported that the ten largest environmental groups "were facing their worst financial and philosophical unrest ever, with membership down 6.5 percent and income flat since 1990."[57]

The movement's political impasse generated an acrimonious debate about its social character and political future. Some critics blamed the impasse on the movement's "elitist" and "upper middle class" social character, or on the "professionalization" of the major organizations.[58] They argued that these reformist, "eight-to-five" environmental organizations have sought political compromise and accommodation with the state, which has weakened the movement's ability to promote real change. And they charged that the big organizations have neglected the grassroots, where, they say, real political change was being made.[59] Other critics argued that grassroots groups have promoted an "eco-extremism" that has undermined the credibility of responsible or "progressive" environmental organizations, making it difficult to promote positive change.[60]

The movement's political practices also became the subject of acrimonious debate. Some critics argued that lobbying was more effective than direct action at the grassroots, while others defended direct action and argued that lobbying was a sterile form of politics. Some observers argued that the movement devoted too much attention to insignificant issues (recycling was widely cited as a well-meaning but insignificant practice), which deflected attention from really serious issues like global warming.[61] Although most critics agreed that attention should be paid to the serious problems and that the movement risked "courting irrelevance" if it did not, they could not agree which issues were really serious or identify how they might be collectively addressed.[62] These debates grew out of a frustration with the movement's political failures and generally reflected the political differences of the movement's two important social constituencies: conservationist and environmentalist. But I do not want to arbitrate these debates and assess their merits. Instead, I think it important to analyze how political, economic, theoretical, and social developments in the 1980s and 1990s changed the movement's political fortunes in the United States and around the world.

Republican Antienvironmentalism

After 1980, a number of important political developments contributed to the movement's political difficulties. When Ronald Reagan became president in 1981, his administration cut budgets for environmental programs and policies, eliminated regulations designed to protect the environment, refused to enforce environmental legislation, transferred twenty million acres of public land to private owners, and appointed hundreds of conservative judges to the federal bench.[63] In effect, the Reagan administration abandoned the proenvironmental policies of its *Republican* predecessors: Nixon, Ford, and, of course, Roosevelt. As Interior Secretary James Watt told Sierra Club president Michael McClosky, "We're going to get things fixed here, and you guys are never going to get it unfixed when you get [back] in."[64]

Not only did Reagan evict the environmental movement from positions of power in government, he also drove congressional conservationists from the Republican Party. Support for environmental legislation within the Republican Party declined sharply during the 1980s, as the party denied its own political traditions and purged conservationists from its ranks.[65] These two developments destroyed the bipartisan basis for environmental legislation on Capitol Hill, which had been so effective in the 1970s. It simultaneously drove the environmental movement, both conservationist and environmentalist, into the Democratic Party.

Initially, Reagan's antienvironmental onslaught, which McClosky said "stunned the movement," helped environmental groups mobilize.[66] Leaders of the major environmental groups agreed to collaborate with each other through the Group of 10 (an informal conclave of environmental leaders based in Washington, D.C.), organized a petition drive to oust Secretary Watt, and created Political Action Committees to contest the Republicans in the 1984 elections.[67] During the 1984 election, groups such as the Sierra Club and Friends of the Earth for the first time endorsed a presidential candidate: the Democrats' Walter Mondale.[68]

But by abandoning its bipartisan political approach and joining the Democratic Party, the environmental movement tied its political fortunes to a party whose presidential candidates were crushed in general elections by Reagan in

1994 and then by George W. Bush in 1998. As a result, the movement became associated in the public mind as just another "special interest" group within the Democratic Party, while the party's political defeats crippled the movement's ability to lobby Congress effectively. The growth, meanwhile, of antienvironmental grassroots groups in the Wise Use movement, which served as Republican auxiliaries (alongside the religious right) outside the Washington Beltway, created a constituency that could counter the environmental movement's pressure on local, state, and federal representatives. These antienvironmental grassroots groups litigated effectively against environmental laws in the increasingly conservative courts.[69]

Grassroots Success

Although the environmental movement experienced a general setback in the 1980s, it nonetheless won some important battles. Antitoxics grassroots groups grew dramatically and enjoyed considerable political success in the 1980s despite, or rather *because* of, the Reagan administration's policies.

The antitoxics movement emerged in poor, minority, and working-class communities across the country after Love Canal in 1978.[70] Generally speaking, grassroots groups emerged in response to the discovery of chemical hazards in their community. The women who typically led them organized protests against landfills, dumps, incinerators, and pesticides in rural and urban settings.[71] By 1984, 600 groups participated in the Citizen's Clearing House for Hazardous Waste (CCHW), an umbrella organization that serviced many grassroots groups, and 4,687 groups participated in antioxics campaigns by 1988.[72] These groups successfully blocked the construction of nearly one hundred garbage incinerators, banned aerial pesticide spraying in many counties, forced companies to install pollution equipment, withdraw pesticides from the market and cleanup waste dumps, raised public awareness (most Americans listed hazardous waste as an environmental priority), and passed laws requiring states to ban or curb toxic chemical use.[73]

Why did antitoxics grassroots groups do well at a time when large, Washington-based environmental lobbies fared poorly? Antitoxics grassroots groups made political gains during the Reagan-Bush years for several reasons. First, grassroots groups were determined opponents of toxic chemicals. When chemical hazards were discovered in poor and minority communities, property values plummeted. Because poor and minority residents found it extremely difficult to flee the hazard, they fought tenaciously in defense of their homes and communities. Although these groups have often been criticized as NIMBY (Not in My Back Yard) movements, they should more accurately be described as NIABY (Not in Anyone's Back Yard) movements. I have coined this term because, as one antitoxics activist explained to me, "No one wants to send leukemia to another community. The American people just aren't that way."[74]

Second, their antitoxics group efforts were inadvertently assisted by Reagan administration policies. During the 1980s, the Reagan administration dismantled the EPA, thereby weakening its control over pesticide and toxic use policy. It also delegated considerable federal authority to state and local governments as part of its devolutionary "New Federalism," which was designed to reduce federal authority and promote state's rights.[75] The Reagan administration expected that weakened federal authority would make it easier for *industry* to operate without restraint. But grassroots groups found that dispersed local authority was more vulnerable to protest than centralized, federal authority and that organized protest could be effective in contests with local government and private industry. Moreover, the conservative, Reagan-appointed judiciary often sided with grassroots groups in court, ruling that local authorities had the authority to regulate pesticide and toxic chemical use. In 1984, for example, judges appointed by then-Governor Reagan to the California Supreme Court ruled that Mendicino County *could* regulate pesticide use, a decision that NCAMP spokesman Jay Feldman said was "extremely important" because it meant "that local communities have the power to protect themselves from the effect of pesticides."[76]

After conservative courts made a number of rulings that favored grassroots groups across the country, the Reagan administration took a new tack. It recognized that the devolution of federal authority could strengthen environmental groups, so it tried to reassert federal authority and centralize control over toxic chemical use in the EPA.[77] Initially, some of the major environmental groups welcomed the Reagan administration's efforts to *re*centralize authority for toxic substances and preempt local regulations that were tough on polluters. The large environmental groups supported this Reagan administration initiative because they wanted to restore the EPA to it previous stature. But Lois Gibbs's CCHW and local grassroots groups were able in 1986 to block the administration's proposal and persuade the major environmental groups to withdraw their ill-considered support after a furious campaign.[78] Because grassroots antitoxics groups were able to take advantage of the political and legal opportunities made available to them by the Reagan administration, they were able to make some important gains during the 1980s and 1990s.

Of course, when the Democrats recaptured the presidency in 1992, environmentalists expected their political fortunes to improve.[79] But while Clinton appointed some environmentalists to positions in the administration, the movement's support for the Democratic Party produced few tangible results.[80] The movement's difficulties continued because the Clinton administration, which focused on the economy, health care, and free trade agreements during its first two years, generally neglected environmental issues.[81] The movement's position within the Democratic Party made it hard for it to criticize the administration, and the movement was disarmed by the expectation that the administration could be counted on to take care of the environment. Much the same had happened after the Democrat Jerry Brown replaced Reagan as governor in California. As Sierra Club leader Carl Pope observed, "The [environmental] constituency lost its momentum. [Because the movement got] the subliminal message that 'some one else is taking care of things,' constituents stopped writing angry letters. . . . Two years after Brown was elected . . . he turned to his former campaign manager and asked, 'Are there any environmentalists left in California?'"[82] Environmentalists also found that other *Democrats* opposed pro-environmental policies and blocked environmental political appointments, making it difficult to make gains even though Democrats controlled the executive and the Congress.[83] Then, after Republicans took control of Congress in 1994, the brief prospect of political gains evaporated. As a result, the movement found that it was difficult to "unfix" what Secretary Watt and successive Republican administrations had previously "fixed."[84]

Economics and the Return of "Plenty"

Economic developments in the 1980s also undermined support for the environmental movement in the North, though they helped expand the movement in the South. In 1979, Paul Volcker and the Federal Reserve used high interest rates to curb inflation in the United States (see chapter 4). This policy reduced inflation in the United States, but it triggered a debt crisis for dictatorships that had borrowed heavily in the 1970s. The debt crisis of the 1980s contributed both to structural adjustment and to democratization.[85] Because indebted states increased their exports of energy, food, and natural resources to earn income that could be used to repay debt, commodity supplies increased and prices fell (see chapter 6).

In the United States, Western Europe, and Japan, lower inflation rates and falling commodity prices meant an end of "scarcity" and a return of "plenty." Under these conditions, U.S. industries and consumers abandoned "conservation" and embraced "consumption." As an editorial in *Not Man Apart* argued in 1983, "Lower oil prices may undo much of the progress that's been made toward developing alternative sources of power. No longer driven by necessity, the technological push toward [alternative] sources of energy will slow drastically."[86] That is exactly what happened during the late 1980s and 1990s. U.S. production of energy from solar, geothermal, wind, waste, wood, photovoltaic, and solar thermal sources fell by half between 1985 and 1995, undoing most of the gains made during the 1970s. Consumers purchased gas-guzzling trucks, jeeps, and minivans, which lowered the average fuel efficiency of the U.S. fleet, and energy consumption resumed its upward growth.[87] The return of "plenty" in the 1980s undermined environmental arguments about "scarcity" and deflected or deferred fears about the "limits to growth." Whereas economic developments (inflation) had contributed to environmental movement success in the 1970s, economic

developments (deflation) in the 1980s undermined public support for movement policies (limits to growth) and practices (conservation).

But while deflation undermined public support for the environmental movement in the United States, it contributed to the growth of the environmental
movement in the South. Debt crisis and austerity programs in the South accelerated the production of energy, food, and raw materials, resulting in the conversion of small-scale subsistence agriculture to export and feed crops and the
destruction of tropical forests (see chapter 7). As a result, the food and resources
that many people relied on for survival became more expensive, more "scarce."
Conditions of growing scarcity in the 1990s provided economic support for environmental arguments in the South, much as they had previously done in the
North.

During the 1970s, people in the North experienced global inflation as a period
of "scarcity," while people in the South experienced it as a period of relative
"plenty." Conversely, deflation in the 1980s meant the return of plenty in the
North, but the return of scarcity in the South. Yet people in both regions
responded in much the same way when confronted with similar economic conditions. Under conditions of scarcity, environmental movements grew in both
North (1970s) and South (1980s), while in times of plenty, environmental
movements in both the North (1980s) and South (1970s) fared poorly.

Political developments also contributed to the spread of environmental movements in the South. The democratization of states around the world made it
possible for environmental movements there to organize in relative safety for the
first time (see chapter 11). When environmental groups emerged in the South,
they received, for the first time, real support from well-established groups in
the North: Greenpeace, World Wildlife Fund, Pesticide Action Network, and
Rainforest Action Network.[88]

Relations between environmental groups in the North and in the South
improved dramatically in the 1990s, not only because environmental groups in
the North provided important technical assistance and real economic aid but
also because they had revised their policies toward environmental problems in
the South. They had abandoned their view that people in the South were
responsible for the all the problems associated with population growth, and they
recognized that industry and consumers in rich countries were responsible for
many environmental problems: the waste trade, global warming, debt crisis and
deforestation, and food exports and hunger. They learned to approach common
problems with a new awareness of their complexity.[89]

Greenpeace, for example, had long urged a complete moratorium on whaling
and an embargo on tuna caught using methods that killed dolphins. But it
revised its blanket opposition to these activities after it became apparent that a
whaling moratorium conflicted with the needs of indigenous, subsistence, Inuit
whalers in Alaska and that the tuna embargo undercut tuna fishers in Mexico,
who argued that a blanket embargo helped the U.S. tuna fleet monopolize the

industry.[90] As Greenpeace international director Matti Wuori explained, "We have made mistakes in the past. Some of the solutions we have advocated in the rich North simply don't work or are harmful when applied to other countries. . . . Our [tuna–dolphin] campaign had had discriminatory effects on the poorer parts of the Western Hemisphere."[91] A new appreciation of the global social consequences of environmental policy helped environmental groups in the North and South develop common agendas. As we have seen, the implementation of free trade agreements in the 1990s assisted this process and helped forge alliances between different groups in the North and South (see chapter 9).

Theoretical Failures

A third problem for the environmental movement in the 1980s and 1990s was that some of its theoretical expectations failed to materialize, undermining its legitimacy and damaging important political relations with key social constituencies. At the same time, some of its political tactics failed to produce the kind of results they had earlier achieved, largely because the movement failed to develop a useful theory of the state.

By the early 1980s, it became apparent that Ehrlich's theories about the consequences of rapid population growth were wholly inadequate and that events in the early 1970s had masked important social, economic, and demographic developments that prevented the Population Bomb from exploding. Ehrlich's basic theoretical expectations were wrong for five reasons: (1) the sexual revolution transformed gender relations and slowed birth rates; (2) the widespread adoption of Green Revolution agricultural technologies increased global per capita food production and raised per capita food production even in countries like India; (3) it became evident that war in Bangladesh, Ethiopia, and Somalia produced famine, not famine war; (4) scientists discovered that worrisome environmental problems such as global warming were more often a product of affluence and technology than a product of poverty and overpopulation; and (5) economic developments—debt crisis and technological innovation—made the supplies of many nonrenewable resources cheaper and more "plentiful" than they had been in the 1970s.

By the mid-1980s, the theoretical expectations outlined in the *Population Bomb* had been discredited. The collapse of this theory, which held a central place in the thinking of most environmental groups, had important political consequences because it removed a source of unity for different environmental constituencies. Population control groups declined—Zero Population Growth went out of business and some of its activists moved on to work on anti-immigration policy in the Federation for American Immigration Reform—and environmental groups dropped population as a political issue.[92] These developments broke the environmental movement's close association with the women's movement, just as the women's movement faced new battles over reproductive rights with the

Reagan administration and its auxiliaries on the religious right. Instead of joining this fight, the environmental movement sat on the sidelines in battles over abortion, a stance that caused a breech with the women's movement.[93] Likewise, the emphasis on anti-immigration reform by some former population control advocates antagonized minority groups in the United States and made it difficult for minority grassroots groups to collaborate with some of the large environmental groups like the Sierra Club, which for a time considered adopting anti-immigration policies as part of its agenda.

Tactical Problems

Tactics that had been successful in the 1970s often failed to work in the 1980s. For example, when the nuclear power industry declined in the early 1980s, many antinuclear power groups joined with peace groups to create a movement against nuclear weapons and the arms race.[94] But grassroots activism on the Nuclear Weapons Freeze Campaign failed to accomplish the kind of political success that anti–nuclear power activists had earlier achieved, and they won only a nonbinding resolution endorsing the Freeze in the House.

The effort to use grassroots tactics that had been effective against nuclear *power* were largely ineffective when used against nuclear *weapons*. They were inappropriate because authority over nuclear weapons was not dispersed or delegated to local authority, which might be vulnerable to grassroots protest, but were instead centralized in the federal government and defended by the military-industrial complex. Not only was authority over nuclear weapons policy extremely centralized, but the rules of political engagement were different. Information about nuclear *weapons* was subject to stringent secrecy laws and even minor protest actions could be treated as serious felonies, not as simple misdemeanors. As a result, the risks associated with nonviolent direct action were considerably higher in protests against nuclear weapons than they were in actions against nuclear power. The Freeze campaign never appreciated these differences, though they did try to "centralize" the movement by merging with SANE and moving their headquarters from St. Louis to Washington, D.C.[95] Then, when Reagan and Gorbachev signed a modest arms control treaty in 1987, SANE–Freeze quickly collapsed and the movement dispersed.[96]

The failure of grassroots antinuclear activism in the United States and in Western Europe demonstrated the movement's inability to theorize adequately its relation with the state.[97] There have been several obstacles to useful theorizing. One problem was that a singular relation to the state can have both beneficial and negative consequences. The movement's close association with the U.S. state in the 1970s helped it pass important domestic legislation. But the movement's close association with Nixon's population control policies harmed its relations with movements and the South. Conversely, when the movement was denied access to the U.S. state, it was unable to pass domestic legislation, but it was able to improve its relations with movements in the South.

A second problem was that movement groups often had very different relations with the state. Greenpeace, for example, conducted three important campaigns in the late 1980s, each with a different relation to the U.S. state. The marine mammals and Antarctica campaigns worked closely and cooperatively with the U.S. Commerce Department, which for a variety of reasons supported the antiwhaling moratorium in the International Whaling Commission and supported efforts to protect Antarctica. By contrast, the Greenpeace antitoxics campaign, which worked closely with grassroots antitoxic groups around the country, had an adversarial relation with the EPA. Meanwhile, the organization's nuclear-free seas campaign had an extremely hostile relation with the U.S. Navy, which became acute after Navy warships rammed the *M.V. Greenpeace* during a protest against a Trident missile test in international waters. Because Greenpeace and other environmental organizations had *different* relations with the state, which varied from one issue to the next, it was difficult for movement leaders to develop a comprehensive theory of the state, a theory that could guide its multiple and complex relations to state power.

A third problem was that the movement's relation to the state varied over time. As we have seen, a strategy that proved effective in one period sometimes proved ineffective in another, depending on how the state organized power and delegated its authority. Generally, grassroots tactics were effective when state power had been devolved or assigned to local authorities, hence the success of grassroots civil rights, antinuclear power, and antitoxics campaigns. But grassroots were generally ineffective when state power was centrally held—hence the failure of grassroots antiwar and antinuclear weapons campaigns. This also held true in Western Europe, where grassroots antinuclear power and antinuclear weapons campaigns both failed, largely because authority over nuclear *power* and nuclear *weapons* were *both* centrally held in Western European states. The movement's inability to theorize multiple, complex, and historically contingent relations to state power has meant that it has been difficult to find a way out of its current political impasse.

Gender and the Environmental Movement

The environmental movement has encouraged active participation by women and men throughout its history. Indeed, it is one of the few social movements with substantial participation by both. But its politics also reflect a gender-based division of labor. The large, centralized, lobby-oriented groups based in Washington, D.C., are typically led by men. The diverse, local, grassroots groups that favor direct action campaigns against nuclear and other toxic materials are generally organized and led by women, many of them minorities. To a large extent, the ongoing debate over the merits of a lobby-based or direct-action-based politics reflects the different orientations and political strategies of men and women in the movement.

Of course, women in grassroots, direct action groups have been successful at a time when male-identified centralized groups have been relatively ineffective, though the latter control most of the economic resources available to the movement and generally define its main issues and political agenda. This has been an ongoing source of frustration for women in grassroots groups.

There is another gender-based divide within the movement. Women activists have developed ecofeminist theories and have embraced or advanced a spiritual approach to environmental politics. These ecofeminists often draw on pagan, Native American, New Age, and Eastern religious traditions that emphasize a close association between women and nature (Mother Earth). According to movement historian Barbara Epstein, many of the women who participated in grassroots protests against nuclear power and new weapons adopted ecofeminist, pagan, and other spiritual orientations.[98]

By contrast, the men who organize and lead large environmental organizations tend to take a secular, scientific approach to environmental problems. These gender-based divisions of labor, and the philosophical orientations often associated with them, have made it difficult for environmental groups to identify common issues, develop collective strategies, and make common cause in recent years.

Despite these ongoing difficulties, the environmental movement has not collapsed; it has not experienced the kind of organizational failure that visited its contemporaries: the New Left, civil rights, and peace movements. The environmental movement has not collapsed for a variety of reasons. First, it has deep organizational roots. Many conservationist groups are now more than one hundred years old. Second, the movement has become socially diverse. While it initially drew from the wealthy and upper-middle classes, it has been joined in recent years by working and poor people, many of them from Hispanic and African-American minorities. So it now includes upper-class groups such as the Nature Conservancy but also poor, minority groups such as the Mothers of East L.A. Antitoxics campaigns have been responsible for bringing minorities into the movement in recent years. Third, the movement is fairly decentralized, consisting of a large number of separate organizations. The environmental movement never created a central organization like Students for a Democratic Society or the National Organization for Women. This organizational diversity has been a strength, not a weakness, during a time of crisis and change. Fourth, the movement has recruited new social groups, including poor and minority groups, and maintained high levels of public consciousness largely because it has made environmental education an integral part of elementary, high school, and college curriculums.[99] One of the most important and unheralded developments in recent years has been the adoption of environmental science curricula in public schools across the country. Ongoing instruction about environmental issues has encouraged the spread of environmental ideas and kept public support for the environment high, even though the movement has made few political gains.

In global terms, the environmental movement will likely grow for two reasons. First, conditions of scarcity, perhaps best represented by falling commodity prices, will persist. Poor economic conditions have generally made it possible for environmental groups to make headway in the past. Second, democratization in countries around the world has made it easier for environmental groups to organization without fear of arrest or attack. It is to this latter development that we now turn: the democratization of dozens of countries around the world.

NOTES

1. Mark Dowie, *Losing Ground: American Environmentalism at the Close of the Twentieth Century* (Cambridge, Mass.: MIT Press, 1996), 33; James P. Lester, ed., *Environmental Politics and Policy: Theories and Evidence* (Durham, N.C.: Duke University Press, 1995), 3; Victor B. Scheffer, *The Shaping of Environmentalism in America* (Seattle: University of Washington Press, 1991), 143–44, 150–66.

2. Sherry Cable and Charles Cable, *Environmental Problems: Grassroots Solutions: The Politics of Grassroots Environmental Conflict* (New York: St. Martin's, 1995), xvii–xxii.

3. Bonnie Mass, *Population Target: The Political Economy of Population Control in Latin America* (Toronto: Women's Press, 1976), 63.

4. Riley E. Dunlap and Angela G. Mertig, "The Evolution of the U.S. Environmental Movement from 1970 to 1990: An Overview," in *American Environmentalism: The U.S. Environmental Movement, 1970–1990*, eds. Riley E. Dunlap and Angela G. Mertig (Philadelphia: Taylor & Francis, 1992), 2. Polls show that concern for the environment increased dramatically for a few years after Earth Day. Dowie, *Losing Ground*, 4; Sheldon Kamieniecki, "Political Parties and Environmental Policy," in *Environmental Politics and Policy*, 162; Riley E. Dunlap, "Trends in Public Opinion toward Environmental Issues, 1965–1990," in *American Environmentalism*, 113; Dunlap, "Public Opinion," in *Environmental Politics and Policy*, 99.

5. Dunlap, "Public Opinion," 101–2.

6. Andrew Szasz, *EcoPopulism: Toxic Waste and the Movement for Environmental Justice* (Minneapolis: University of Minnesota Press, 1994), 72; Robert Cameron Mitchell, Angela G. Mertig, and Riley E. Dunlap, "Twenty Years of Environmental Mobilization: Trends among National Environmental Organizations," in *American Environmentalism*, 13, 15, 18; Robert Cameron Mitchell, "From Conservation to Environmental Movement: The Development of the Modern Environmental Lobbies," in *Government and Environmental Politics: Essays on Historical Developments since World War Two*, ed. Michael J. Lacy (Washington, D.C.: Woodrow Wilson Center Press, 1991), 96; Helen M. Ingram, David H. Colnic, and Dean E. Mann, "Interest Groups and Environmental Policy," in *Environmental Politics and Policy*, 122; Mitchell et al., "Twenty Years of Environmental Mobilization," 13, 18.

7. Russell J. Dalton, *The Green Rainbow: Environmental Groups in Western Europe* (New Haven, Conn.: Yale University Press, 1994), 243.

8. One is reminded of Henry Kissinger's conversation with Mao Tse-tung. Kissinger asked Mao what he though had been the results of the French Revolution. Mao replied, "It's too early to tell." Philip Shabecoff, *A New Name for Peace: International Environmentalism, Sustainable Development and Democracy* (Hanover, N.H.: University Press of New England, 1996), 171.

9. "Blues for Most Green," *Greenview* 4, no. 119 (October 19, 1994). Greenpeace lost more than one million donors between 1990 and 1994. "Environmental Movement Fights for Lost Momentum," *Oakland Tribune*, September 22, 1994; Dowie, *Losing Ground*, 41, 46, 70, 175, 193–94.

10. Mitchell, "From Conservation to Environmental Movement"; W. Douglas Constain and James P. Lester, "The Evolution of Environmentalism," in *Environmental Politics and Policy*, 26.

11. Allan Schnaiberg and Kenneth Alan Gould, *Environment and Security: The Enduring Conflict* (New York: St. Martin's, 1994), 148–49; John McCormick, *Reclaiming Paradise: The Global Environmental Movement* (Bloomington: Indiana University Press, 1989), 15; Mertig and Riley call EDF "the first of a new breed of national environmental organizations," Dowie, *Losing Ground*, 23.

12. Glenn notes that "transatlantic protests against corporal punishment occurred concurrently with Anglo-American campaigns against slavery, capital punishment, dueling, war, and cruelty to animals." Myra C. Glenn, "The Naval Reform Campaign against Flogging: A Case Study in Changing Attitudes toward Corporal Punishment, 1830–1850," *American Quarterly* 35, no. 4 (Fall 1983): 409.

13. Glenn, "The Naval Reform Campaign"; McCormick, *Reclaiming Paradise*, 4–5. At first, they were particularly concerned with the flogging of horses, children, slaves, and sailors. Later they became concerned about more general cruelties.

14. Glenn, "The Naval Reform Campaign," 413.

15. Richard N. L. Andrews, "Class Politics or Democratic Reform: Environmentalism and American Political Institutions," in *Natural Resources Journal* 20, no. 2 (April 1980), 227, 231; Mitchell, "From Conservation to Environmental Movement," 101–2; Tom Turner, *Wild by Law: The Sierra Club Legal Defense Fund and the Places It Has Saved* (San Francisco: Sierra Club Legal Defense Fund and Sierra Club Books, 1990), 16–21.

16. Scheffer, *The Shaping of Environmentalism in America*, 6–7; Lester W. Milbrath, *Environmentalists: Vanguard for a New Society* (Albany: State University New York Press, 1984), 75–76.

17. Massimo Teodori, *The New Left: A Documentary History* (New York: Bobbs-Merrill, 1969), 2–54, 163–239; Todd Gitlin, *The Sixties: Years of Hope, Days of Rage* (New York: Bantam, 1987), 45–80.

18. For the young, the baby boom meant huge, impersonal universities; for the old, it meant the spread of suburban housing developments and freeways across the landscape.

19. Kristin Luker, *Abortion and the Politics of Motherhood* (Berkeley: University of California Press, 1984), 142–43.

20. Andrews, "Class Politics or Democratic Reform," 239.

21. Michael McClosky, "Twenty Years of Change in the Environmental Movement: An Insider's View," in *American Environmentalism*, 78; Laura Pulido, *Environmentalism and Economic Justice: Two Chicano Struggles in the Southwest* (Tucson: University of Arizona Press, 1996), 24.

22. The "old money" supplied by the Ford Foundation played an important role in knitting the two groups together. Mitchell, "From Conservation to Environmental Movement"; Ingram et al., "Interest Groups and Environmental Policy," 118.

23. Scheffer, *The Shaping of Environmentalism in America*, 6–7; Andrews, "Class Politics or Democratic Reform," 222–24; Schnaiberg and Gould, *Environment and Security*, 150; W. Douglas Constan and James P. Lester, "Introduction," in *Environmental Politics and Policy*, 26; Dunlap and Mertig, "The Evolution of the U.S. Environmental Movement from 1970 to 1990," 5; Frederick H. Buttel and Oscar W. Larson III, "Whither Environmentalism? The Future Political Path of the Environmental Movement," in *Natural Resources Journal* 20, no. 2 (April 1980): 326.

24. "Transcript of President's Address on Moves to Deal with Economic Problems," *New York Times*, August 16, 1971;

25. Mitchell, "From Conservation to Environmental Movement," 218. Other writers argued that resource scarcity "might actually be turned into a grand opportunity to build a more humane post-industrial society." Buttel and Larson, "Whither Environmentalism?" 344. But James O'Connor differed, arguing that "ecological economists unwittingly strengthened the hands of the neo-classical economists' claim that consumption was too high by pointing to shortages of natural resources and dangerous levels of pollution." James O'Connor, *The Meaning of Crisis: A Theoretical Introduction* (Oxford: Blackwell, 1987), 33–34.

26. A common perspective was advanced by Denis Hayes, who argued, "I suspect that politicians and businessmen who are jumping on the environmental bandwagon don't have the slightest idea what they are getting into." Jim Schwab, *Deeper Shades of Green: The Rise of Blue-Collar and Minority Environmentalism in America* (San Francisco: Sierra Club Books, 1994), 11.

27. John DeWitt, *Civic Environmentalism: Alternatives to Regulation in States and Communities* (Washington, D.C.: Congressional Quarterly Press, 1994), 23–24; Dunlap, "Trends in Public Opinion," 91–92; James Rathlesberger, *Nixon and the Environment: The Politics of Devastation* (New York: Village Voice Books, 1972), viii.

28. Taylor Branch, *Parting the Waters: America in the King Years, 1954–63* (New York: Simon & Schuster, 1988), 305–8, 321–23, 341–42, 348–75.

29. Richard M. Nixon, "Environmental Quality," in *Politics, Policy and Natural Resources*, ed. Dennis L. Thompson (New York: Free Press, 1972), 167. This, incidentally, is a theme that David Brower recently revived, arguing not only for conservation but also "restoration."

30. Mass, *Population Target*, 37; Michael S. Teitelbawm, "The Population Threat," *Foreign Affairs* (Winter 1992/93): 66; Carl Pope, "Population," in *Nixon and the Environment*, 170.

31. Pope, "Population," 163–79; Teitelbawm, "The Population Threat," 67.

32. DeWitt, *Civic Environmentalism*, 24; Rathlesberger, *Nixon and the Environment*, xii–ix.

33. Paul Ehrlich, *The Population Bomb* (New York: Ballantine, 1968), 159–61; Asoka Bandarage, "A New Malthusianism," *Peace Review* 6, no. 3 (Fall 1994): 294; Mass, *Population Target*, 48, 50–58, 138.

34. Ziauddin Sardar, "Malaysia Silences FOE and Other Groups," *Not Man Apart* (June 1981): 6.

35. Richard P. Tucker, "India Gets Serious about Conservation," *Not Man Apart* (May 1981): 10–11.

36. International environmental groups with roots in the United States became among the largest environmental groups in many European countries. Brendan Prendiville, *Environmental Politics in France* (Boulder, Colo.: Westview, 1994): 7, 86; Matthew Nemiroff Lyons, *The "Grassroots" Network: Radical Nonviolence in the Federal Republic of Germany, 1972–1985* (Ithaca, N.Y.: Center for International Studies, Cornell University, 1988), 26; Dalton, *The Green Rainbow*, 41, 54, 58, 89–90, 95; Joni Seager, *Earth Follies: Coming to Feminist Terms with the Global Environmental Crisis* (New York: Routledge, 1993), 177.

37. Lynton K. Caldwell, "Globalizing Environmentalism: Threshold of a New Phase in International Relations," in *American Environmentalism*, 64; Lyons, *The "Grassroots" Network*, 21.

38. Prendiville, *Environmental Politics in France*, 106.

39. Dalton, *The Green Rainbow*, 64; Prendiville, *Environmental Politics in France*, 106; Lyons, *The "Grassroots" Network*, 17.

40. Jacqueline Vaugh Switzer, *Environmental Politics: Domestic and Global Dimensions* (New York: St. Martin's, 1994), 37.

41. Gale Warner and David Kreger, "Friends All over Europe," *Not Man Apart* (February–March 1984): 17. LaLond would later join the Mitterand government as minister of the environment in 1988. Dalton, *The Green Rainbow*, 216.

42. Warner and Kreger, "Friends All over Europe," passim.

43. Robert Schaeffer, "Green Pitch for Peace," *Not Man Apart* (November 1983): 12.

44. Switzer, *Environmental Politics*, 42. The U.S. environmental movement's criticism of the French nuclear weapons testing program in the Pacific antagonized the French and undermined public support for environmental issues in France. Dalton, *The Green Rainbow*, 90.

45. Switzer, *Environmental Politics*, 42.

46. *Silent Spring, The Fate of the Earth*, and *The End of Nature* all appeared first in the *New Yorker*. Its role as the unofficial theoretical journal of the environmental movement has been unappreciated.

47. Shirley A. Brigges, "Silent Spring: The View from 1990," *The Ecologist* 20, no. 2 (March–April 1990).

48. Keith Schneider, "For the Environment, Compassion Fatigue," *New York Times*, November 6, 1994; Theodore Rozak, "Green Guilt and Ecological Overload," *New York Times*, June 9, 1992.

49. Hal Lindsay's fundamentalist tome *The Late Great Planet Earth*, which appeared in 1970, sold nine million copies by 1978. Paul Boyer, *When Time Shall Be No More: Prophecy Belief in Modern American Culture* (Cambridge, Mass.: Belknap, 1992), 5.

50. Boyer, *When Time Shall Be No More*, 336.

51. Health officials estimate that 750,000 people are annually poisoned by pesticides around the world, and as many as 14,000 die. Constance Matthiessen, "The Day the Poison Stopped Working," *Mother Jones* (March–April 1992); Robert Schaeffer, "Bhopal Spurs Pesticide Reform Movement," *Not Man Apart* (July–August 1985): 11.

52. Schaeffer, "Bhopal Spurs," 10.

53. Ehrlich, *The Population Bomb*, passim.

54. Ehrlich, *The Population Bomb*, 159.

55. See Jim Harding's "Nuclear Blowdown" in *Not Man Apart*.

56. Komanoff Energy Associates, *Fiscal Fission: The Economic Failure of Nuclear Power* (n.p.: Komanoff Energy Associates, December 1992); Schwab, *Deeper Shades of Green*, 221.

57. Keith Schneider, "Big Environment Hits a Recession," *New York Times*, January 1, 1995.

58. Schneider, "Big Environment Hits a Recession"; Pulido, *Environmentalism and Economic Justice*, 23; Mark E. Rushefsky, "Elites and Environmental Policy," in *Environmental Politics and Policy*, 280; Bill Duvall, "Deep Ecology and Radical Environmentalism," in *American Environmentalism*, 55; Seager, *Earth Follies*, 185–86, 191–93; Karl Grossman, "The People of Color Environmental Summit," in *Unequal Protection: Environmental Justice and Communities of Color*, ed. Robert D. Bullard (San Francisco: Sierra Club Books, 1994), 291; William Tucker, *Progress and Privilege: America in the Age of Environmentalism* (Garden City, N.Y.: Anchor Press, 1982, pp. 25, 34, 80; P. J. O'Rourke, "The Greenhouse Affect," in *The Rolling Stone Environmental Reader*, ed. Jann S. Wenner (Washington, D.C.: Island, 1992), 22; Dowie, *Losing Ground*, xi–xii, 146–47, 205–6.

59. Bill Duvall, "The Deep Ecology Movement," *Natural Resources Journal* 20, no. 2 (April 1980): 303, 319–20; Bill Duvall and George Sessions, *Deep Ecology* (Salt Lake City: Gibbs M. Smith, 1985), 3; Ben Bloch and Harold Lyons, *Apocalypse Not: Science, Economics and Environmentalism* (Washington, D.C.: Cato Institute, 1993), 7; Martin W. Lewis, *Green Delusions: An Environmentalist Critique of Radical Environmentalism* (Durham, N.C.: Duke University Press, 1992), 7–8.

60. Lewis, *Green Delusions*, 1–2.

61. Robert M. Lilienfeld and William L. Rathje, "Six Enviro-Myths," *New York Times*, January 21, 1993; Gregg Easterbrook, "Everything You Know about the Environment Is Wrong," *New Republic*, April 30, 1990; William K. Stevens, "What Really Threatens the Environment?" *New York Times*, January 21, 1993; Wallace Kaufman, *No Turning Back: Dismantling the Fantasies of Environmental Thinking* (New York: Basic Books, 1994), 5, 7; Schnaiberg and Gould, *Environment and Security*, v; John Tierney, "Recycling Is Garbage," *New York Times Magazine*, June 30, 1996; Duvall, "The Deep Ecology Movement," 299; Duvall, "Deep Ecology and Radical Environmentalism," 51–52.

62. Schnaiberg and Gould, *Environment and Security*, 161; Dowie, *Losing Ground*, 1, 144; Schwab, *Deeper Shades of Green*, 417–18; Duvall and Sessions, *Deep Ecology*, ix.

63. David Kreger and Gale Warner, "The Reagan Presidency," *Not Man Apart* (September 1984): 1–16; Scheffer, *The Shaping of Environmentalism in America*, 18; DeWitt, *Civic Environmentalism*, 53; Dowie, *Losing Ground*, 92; Walter A. Resenbaum, "The Bureaucracy and Environmental Policy," in *Environmental Politics and Policy*, 224; Keith Schneider, "Thwarted Environmentalists Find U.S. Courts Are Citadels No More," *New York Times*, March 22, 1992; Dowie, *Losing Ground*, 79–80.

64. Kreger and Warner, "The Reagan Presidency," 10.

65. Kamieniecki, "Political Parties and Environmental Policy," 156.

66. McClosky, "Twenty Years of Change in the Environmental Movement," 81.

67. Dowie, *Losing Ground*, 68–69; McClosky, "Twenty Years of Change in the Environmental Movement," 82.

68. Ingram et al., "Interest Groups and Environmental Policy," 134–35.

69. Schneider, "Thwarted Environmentalists."

70. Judy Christrup and Robert Schaeffer, "Not In Anyone's Backyard," *Greenpeace* (January–February 1990); Robert D. Bullard, *Dumping in Dixie: Race, Class, and Environmental Quality* (Boulder, Colo.: Westview, 1994), passim; Dowie, *Losing Ground*.

71. Seager, *Earth Follies*, 269–70, 275; Szasz, *EcoPopulism*, 70; Bullard, *Dumping in Dixie*, 100.

72. Szasz, *EcoPopulism*, 72.

73. Christrup and Schaeffer, "Not In Anyone's Backyard"; Nicholas Greudenberg and Carol Steinsapir, "Not in Our Backyards: The Grassroots Environmental Movement," in *American Environmentalism*, 33–34.

74. Christrup and Schaeffer, "Not In Anyone's Backyard," 18; Bullard, *Dumping in Dixie*, 6.

75. Margaret Kriz, "Ahead of the Feds," *National Journal*, December 9, 1989, 2991; James P. Lester, "Federalism and State Environmental Policy," in *Environmental Politics and Policy,* 41–42.

76. Robert Schaeffer, "California Upholds Aerial Spraying Ban," *Not Man Apart*, September 1984, 5.

77. Schneider, "Thwarted Environmentalist"; Philip Shabecoff, "The Environment as a Local Jurisdiction," *New York Times*, January 22, 1989.

78. Dowie, *Losing Ground*, 136.

79. Frederick H. Buttle, "Rethinking International Environmental Policy in the Late Twentieth Century," in *Environmental Justice: Issues, Policies and Solutions,* ed. Bunyan Bryant (Washington, D.C.: Island, 1995), 187.

80. Harold Gilliam, "Does Anyone Care about the Environment Anymore?" *San Francisco Chronicle*, March 5, 1995; Dowie, *Losing Ground*, 119, 179.

81. Kreger and Warner, "The Reagan Presidency," 10; The debate over free trade also split the movement. Dowie, *Losing Ground*, 188; Robert Schaeffer, "Free Trade Agreements: Their Impact on Agriculture and the Environment," in *Food and Agrarian Orders in the World-Economy*, ed. Philip McMichael (Westport, Conn.: Praeger, 1995), 270.

82. Robert Schaeffer, "Green Envy," *Not Man Apart* (September 1984): 11; Schneider, "Big Environment Hits a Recession." It was also the case that foundations withdrew their support for environmental issues and began funding other, more "pressing" issues. Dowie, *Losing Ground*, 176.

83. Dowie, *Losing Ground*, 182, 184, 186.

84. Kreger and Warner, "The Reagan Presidency," 10.

85. Robert K. Schaeffer, *Power to the People: Democratization around the World* (Boulder, Colo.: Westview, 1997), chapters 5 and 6.

86. Sandra Kaiser, "Cheap Oil: Such a Bargain?" *Not Man Apart* (April 1983): 2.

87. Agis Salpukas, "Green Power Wanes, but Not at the Grassroots," *New York Times*, March 9, 1997.

88. Schaeffer, "Free Trade Agreements," 10–11; Wapner, 1996, 82–96.

89. Wapner, 104–6, 109, 129, 138–39, 152–53.

90. Alessandro Bonanno and Douglas Constance, "The Global Agri-Food Sector and the Case of the Tuna Industry: Global Regulation and Perspective for Development," *International Journal of Sociology of Agriculture and Food* 4 (1994): 118–34; Joel Bleifuss,

"The Great Dolphin Divide," *In These Times*, August 5, 1996, 12–13; Bob Ostertag, "Greenpeace Takes Over the World," *Mother Jones* (March–April 1991).

91. Mark Waller, "Behind New Leader, Greenpeace Reexamines Itself," *In These Times*, February 12–18, 1992, 6.

92. Susan Ferriss, "FAIR: Mounting Campaign to Keep Immigrants Out," *San Francisco Examiner*, December 12, 1993; Dowie, *Losing Ground*, 160, 163–65.

93. Seager, *Earth Follies*, 217–18.

94. Robert Schaeffer, "Anti-Nuclear Families," *Nuclear Times* (January–February 1989); David Lewis, "Tough Choices for the Freeze," *Not Man Apart* (October 1984); Steve Wheeler, "Support Builds for a Nuclear Freeze," *Not Man Apart* (May 1982).

95. Lewis, "Tough Choices for the Freeze," 8.

96. See *Nuclear Times*, 1985–1987.

97. Prendiville, *Environmental Politics in France*; Lyons, *The "Grassroots" Network*.

98. Schaeffer, "Anti-Nuclear Families," 104. See Betty H. Zisk, *The Politics of Transformation: Local Activism in the Peace and Environmental Movements* (Westport, Conn.: Praeger, 1992).

99. Dunlap, "Public Opinion," 97; Dowie, *Losing Ground*, 32.

11

Dictatorship and Democracy

In late 1989, communist dictatorships in seven Eastern European countries suddenly fell, most of them peacefully, and civilian democrats assumed power for the first time in more than forty years. The simultaneous collapse of seven communist dictatorships, capped by the dramatic opening and then destruction of the Berlin Wall, the most visible symbol of dictatorship in one-party states, was the high-water mark of contemporary democratization. But democratization in Poland, East Germany, Czechoslovakia, Hungary, Bulgaria, Romania, and Albania was not the first or the last episode of democratization in recent years. Events in Eastern Europe were only one act in a global drama spanning the past twenty years, a process that first toppled "capitalist" dictatorships in southern Europe, Latin America, and East Asia, then destroyed communist regimes in Eastern Europe and the Soviet Union, and, finally, brought an end to whites-only rule in South Africa.[1]

The rise of democracy in at least thirty countries around the world since 1974 was not only welcome but remarkable for two reasons.[2] First, democratization or the transfer of political power from dictators or one-party regimes to civilian democrats occurred *peacefully*. With the exception of some violence in Romania and considerable violence in South Africa, the transfer of power was achieved without bloodshed. Second, dictators themselves often initiated the process, taking steps that made possible open elections and a return to civilian authority. Few analysts or dissident movements opposed to dictatorship expected dictators to propose dramatic reforms or to surrender power without a fight. But many of them did just that, opening negotiations with their opponents, quitting their offices, and retiring from public life. Of course, dissident movements and popular protests played an important role in some countries, particularly in South Korea, Poland, and South Africa. But in most cases, mass movements organized protests only after dictators initiated reform. Democratization might therefore be described as a "devolutionary" process because the transfer of political power was peacefully achieved and because it did not result in the kind of violent "revo-lutionary" change associated with the American, French, or Bolshevik Revolu-tions.

Contemporary democratization occurred in great regional waves, moving westward around the world. It began in southern Europe in the mid-1970s, then moved west across the Atlantic to Latin America. The dictatorships in major Latin American countries began folding in the mid-1980s, and most of the remaining dictatorships disappeared by the end of the decade. In the late 1980s, several countries in East Asia democratized, followed in 1989 by the collapse of communist regimes in Eastern Europe. A few years later, the Soviet Union democratized and dissolved into separate republics, as did Yugoslavia and Czechoslovakia. Then South Africa abandoned apartheid, adopted majority rule, and, in 1994, inaugurated a black president.

In each of these geographic regions, democratization had rather different *causes*. For example, the debt crisis contributed to democratization in most Latin American countries, while in East Asia it was rapid economic growth that helped trigger democratization. Economic stagnation was a primary cause of democratization in the Soviet Union and Eastern Europe, while trade sanctions, embargo, and divestment played a major role in South Africa. In these different regions, economic crises of one sort or another, compounded by problems asso-ciated with military defeat, the illness or death of an aging dictator, popular uprising, or changed superpower policy, forced dictators to surrender power.

Although democratization had very different causes in each region, its politi-cal and economic *consequences* were everywhere much the same. In political terms, democratizing countries drafted new constitutions, held elections, and allowed numerous and diverse political parties to participate. In economic terms, most democratizing countries opened their economies to foreign invest-ment and trade, sold state-owned assets and industries to private investors and entrepreneurs, processes associated with "globalization," and reduced military spending.

Of course, people in many countries expected democratic politics and eco-nomic policies to solve the problems that first confronted dictators and helped force them from power. Unfortunately, civilian democrats in many countries have been unable to solve their country's economic problems. Where demo-cratic politics have been corrupted or new economic policies have failed, new dictators have threatened a return to power.

To understand the prospects of democratizing states, we will look first at the problems that led to the collapse of capitalist dictatorships and communist regimes in different regions during the past twenty years. Then we will examine the common political and economic strategies adopted by most civilian demo-crats after they assumed power. In this context we will discuss the problems and prospects of democratizing states around the world.

SOUTHERN EUROPE: FALLING BEHIND

Although fascist dictatorships in Italy and Germany were crushed by Allied forces during World War II, dictatorships in Portugal and Spain survived the war, largely because they stayed neutral in the conflict. In Portugal, António de Oliveira Salazar, a former economics professor, assumed power in 1930; in Spain, General Francisco Franco defeated republican forces during a bitter civil war and became dictator in 1939. The Iberian dictatorships, which would survive until the early 1970s, were joined by Greece in 1967, when a military coup established a dictatorship on the Ionian peninsula.

By Western European standards, Portugal, Spain, and Greece were poor countries. After World War II, dictatorship in Portugal and Spain, and civilian and later military government in Greece, made some economic gains, but their improvements in per capita incomes and literacy were based on relatively weak economies. Because none of them had substantial industries that could compete in overseas markets, they all imported more than they exported and posted trade deficits for every year between 1946 and 1974. As the Turkish economist Caglar Keyder noted, "None of the southern European countries (except Spain in 1951 and [again] in 1960) ran a commodity surplus in all the years between 1946 and 1974. This is to say that none of [them] ever reached a point when their economies generated sufficient exports to pay for their imports."[3]

Most economies and the dictators who run them cannot long survive persistent trade deficits of this sort. But Iberian and Ionian dictatorships were able to make up for their industrial deficiencies and grow somewhat during this period (Spain more than Portugal or Greece) because they exported *workers*, not industrial goods, imported free-spending Western European tourists, and received significant infusions of cash from external sources.[4] As Raymond Carr and Juan Aizpura note, "The economy was refueled from abroad: by tourist earnings, by the remittances of emigres working abroad, and by foreign loans. Only these invisible earnings and loans made it possible to realize . . . plans for rapid growth without running up against the balance of payments problems that bring growth to a grinding halt in most poor economies."[5]

After World War II, Western European countries, with the assistance of the U.S. Marshall Plan, recovered and began to grow. They soon experienced labor shortages, in part because the war had killed or crippled many potential workers. So they began hiring workers from Europe's periphery, particularly from Spain, Portugal, southern Italy, Greece, and Turkey. Workers in those countries, particularly in rural areas, were eager to seek work abroad because they faced poverty and unemployment at home. During the 1960s, nearly one million Portuguese workers left the country to work in France and West Germany, and in the early 1970s, one hundred thousand were emigrating annually.[6] In Spain, half a million workers had left the province of Andalusia during the 1950s. This emigration emptied rural villages. The Castilian novelist Miguel Dlibes wrote of one village:

"Cartiguera is a dying village, in agony. Its winding streets, invaded by weeds and nettles, without a dog's bark or a child's laugh to break the silence, enclosed pathetic gravity, the lugubrious air of the cemetery."[7]

But while this was a difficult and sometimes painful process, it greatly reduced domestic unemployment, providing a safety valve for dictatorships, and helped boost their economies because emigrants sent "remittances" or money they earned abroad back to families who stayed behind. In Spain, for example, emigrants' remittances made up about one-half of the annual trade deficit in the 1960s.[8]

While they exported workers, governments in Spain, Portugal, and Greece also imported tourists and spent much of their budgets to build the hotels, resorts, and infrastructure needed to develop this industry. For example, the number of tourists visiting Spain exceeded the number of people living in Spain by 1973.[9] These tourists spent money and created jobs, which also helped what the economist Paul Samuelson called "market fascism" in Spain to survive.[10]

All three countries also received large infusions of economic aid from external sources. Although the United States had fought to destroy dictatorships in Europe during World War II, it provided financial aid to Iberian dictatorships after the war in return for the establishment of U.S. military bases there in the 1950s, and it provided economic and military assistance to Greece, a country bordering communist dictatorships in Eastern Europe.[11] Portugal also relied on another source of external wealth during the postwar period: its colonies in Africa. Portugal derived considerable income from its exploitation of Mozambique, Angola, and Guinea-Bissau. The Salazar dictatorship refused to relinquish its colonies, despite armed rebellion by independence movements and the withdrawal of other European states from Africa during the period of decolonization in the 1950s and 1960s.

Buoyed by income from emigrant workers, tourists, and superpower aid, the dictatorships in Portugal, Spain, and later Greece managed to keep their economies afloat during the 1950s and 1960s. Of the three, Spain was the most successful, recording rapid rates of growth, which some economists then described as a "miracle." But much of Spain's postwar growth simply recovered economic ground lost during the Depression, Civil War, and World War II.[12] By the end of the 1960s, it was clear that despite some modest gains, the rest of Western Europe was leaving these countries behind economically. In the 1970s, conditions that had made possible modest economic growth changed, confronting dictatorships with serious economic crises.

The crisis began when the United States devalued the dollar in 1971, making the value of Portuguese, Spanish, and Greek currencies rise. This made it more difficult for them to export goods, and it increased their already large trade deficits. This problem was compounded by rising oil prices. When OPEC countries cut oil supplies and raised prices following the 1973 Yom Kippur War, the economic crisis deepened. Portugal was particularly hard hit because OPEC countries refused to sell oil to the dictatorship, now headed by Marcello Caetano, because it had allowed U.S. forces to use Portuguese bases to assist the Israeli war effort.[13]

The oil crisis of 1973–1974 raised the cost of oil for countries with little oil of their own and increased their trade deficits. It also triggered a global recession. In response, Western European countries laid off immigrant workers and sent them home. This led to rising domestic unemployment and discontent and greatly reduced the money received from emigrant workers' earnings, which *further* increased trade deficits. And during the recession, fewer European families vacationed abroad, reducing tourist receipts.[14]

Of the three, the Portuguese dictatorship found itself in the most difficult straits. This was because its decade-long wars to prevent the independence of its Africa colonies had drained its treasury. "By 1974, a population of less than 9 million was sustaining a 200,000-man army in Africa and spending over 45 percent of its annual budget on the military," notes Kenneth Maxwell.[15] "The burdens of the African campaigns on a small, poor nation with limited resources and retarded economic and social infrastructures proved unsustainable."[16] With tongue in cheek, *The Economist* then described Portugal as "Africa's only colony in Europe."[17]

The economic crisis triggered by new conditions in the 1970s was compounded in Portugal, Spain, and Greece by military and political problems. For Portugal, massive military spending on wars in Africa did not help the military defeat armed independence movements. In 1973, António de Spínola, a leading Portuguese general, published a book arguing for a political solution. His book, *Portugal and the Future*, convinced many, particularly in the military, that Portuguese defeat was imminent.[18] Military officers who were radicalized by their experience in Africa then organized the Armed Forces Movement (AFM), which sought to overthrow the Caetano dictatorship, democratize the political system, and end Portugal's anticolonial wars in Africa. On April 25, 1974, AFM units in Portugal overthrew the Caetano regime.

Military defeat also played an important role a few months later in Greece. To deflect growing discontent at home, the "Colonels," as the Greek military dictatorship was known, supported a coup in Cyprus during the summer of 1974. The coup was led by Greek-speaking Cypriots who wanted to overthrow the government of Archbishop Makarios III so that the Mediterranean island could then be "united" with Greece.[19] But the coup prompted fighting between the island's Greek- and Turkish-speaking residents, a development that triggered an invasion of the island by Turkish forces and brought Greece and Turkey to the brink of war. Faced with humiliation in Cyprus and a potentially disastrous war with its more powerful neighbor, military leaders in Greece refused to wage war and demanded that the junta surrender power to a civilian government on July 24, 1974.[20]

In both Portugal and Greece, military defeat in wars abroad either turned ele-

ments of the military against the dictatorship (Portugal) or discredited it completely (Greece). Neither dictatorship could survive the loss of legitimacy
associated with military defeat.

In Spain, the economic crisis triggered by dollar devaluation and OPEC
embargo was compounded not by military defeat but by a crisis of succession.
Born in 1892, Franco was eighty-three in 1974. Increasing age and bouts of illness had forced him to designate King Juan Carlos as his successor in 1969. In
the years before his death, Franco tried to create political institutions that would
survive him. (This was also a problem in Portugal, where Salazar appointed Caetano as his successor in 1968, shortly before he died.) But dictators have found
it difficult to transfer power to successors without interruption, largely because
dictatorship requires aggregating, not delegating power. So when Franco died in
November 1975, Juan Carlos appointed a prime minister who began to disman-
tle the political institutions of the dictatorship and move the country toward
civilian, democratic government, a protracted process that took three more
years. Elites in Spain moved toward democracy because they wanted to join the
Spanish economy with the rest of Western Europe. But the European Community would not let Spain share the substantial economic benefits of EC membership so long as it remained under fascist rule. So by abandoning dictatorship,
elites hoped to join the EC, which would help Spain overcome both the immediate economic crisis and chronic economic backwardness and promote new economic development. Franco's death gave them the political opportunity to
pursue a democratization policy that many regarded as an economic necessity.[21]

Spanish elites who pressed for democratization (called *aperturistas*) and those
arguing for continued dictatorship (*immobilistas*) were also mindful of the social
and political turmoil prompted by the coup and collapse of the Caetano regime
in neighboring Portugal, a revolution that brought to power communists and
then socialists. They were also aware of the trials and convictions of military
leaders and torturers in Greece following democratization there. For Spanish
elites, a carefully managed devolution of power from Francoist dictatorship to
civilian democracy seemed a good alternative to events in either Portugal or
Greece.

In all three countries, political intermediaries played important roles in the
devolution of power. In Portugal, a movement of Marxist military officers served
as intermediaries; in Greece, the military president and a former prime minister
living in exile in Paris managed the government before full-scale elections were
held; in Spain, a king and his technocratic allies in government oversaw the
devolutionary process.[22] All of them made democratization and entry into the
European Community their primary political and economic objective.[23] When
elections were held, socialist governments assumed power in all three countries,
a development that would have been unimaginable in the early 1970s, because
socialist and communist parties were banned or severely restricted by dictatorships in all three countries.[24] All three soon joined the European Community—

Greece in 1981, Spain and Portugal in 1986—a development that proved to be a great boon to their economic fortunes in the 1980s.

The transition to democracy on the Iberian peninsula did not go unnoticed in Latin American dictatorships, where most countries were once colonies of Portugal and Spain. In 1978, seventeen of the twenty Latin American countries were governed by military or "authoritarian" governments, according to political scientist Robert Pastor.[25] Unlike dictators in Portugal and Spain, most Latin American dictators would survive the 1970s. But the debt crisis that emerged in the early 1980s would create problems that would sweep most of them from power and establish democratic civilian governments by the end of the decade. By 1990, "17 of the 20 countries and over 90 percent of its population [could be] said to live under democratic governments," Pastor observed. "More of Latin America is now democratic . . . than at any time in the previous 160-year period of the continent [since] the struggle for separation from Spain and . . . Portugal."[26]

LATIN AMERICA: DEBT AND DEVOLUTION

Most Latin American dictatorships had come to power in the 1950s and 1960s, though a few, like Chile's General Augusto Pinochet Ugarte, seized power in the 1970s. Modest economic growth throughout the 1960s provided economic credibility to dictators and the bureaucracies associated with them. The alliance between military rulers and bureaucratic elites formed the social basis of what political scientists called "bureaucratic authoritarian regimes" in the region.

The 1973 oil crisis and the recession associated with it created many of the same economic problems for Latin American dictatorships that it did for regimes in southern Europe. It increased the cost of imported oil and food, which raised prices and contributed to inflation, and created trade deficits, which weakened their currencies. But while it created immediate problems for some Latin American countries, the oil crisis also presented dictatorships with an opportunity. Rising oil prices were good for oil-producing countries (which in Latin America included Mexico and Venezuela) and new revenues from higher oil prices found their way into financial pools that were then made available to dictatorships by lenders in the North. Because Latin American dictators had access to low-cost credit through private U.S. banks and international lending agencies, they could borrow money to cover trade deficits and invest in their economies. By borrowing money, dictators were able to create jobs, build dams and roads, increase exports, raise military spending, cover budget deficits, and create the kind of economic growth that enhanced their legitimacy. Dictators across the continent borrowed about $350 billion between 1970 and 1983, funds that helped them achieve rapid rates of economic growth. The Brazilian dictatorship, which borrowed the largest amount, also recorded the highest rates of growth, a development that many economists described as a "miracle." Dictators then pointed to this miraculous economic development, in much the same way that Benito Mussolini had boasted of having made Italy's trains run on time, as proof of their competence.

Massive borrowing enabled Latin American countries to avert the problems that undermined southern European dictatorships in the early 1970s. But having used borrowed money to address their economic problems in the 1970s, Latin American dictatorships created economies that were vulnerable to changed conditions in the 1980s. This vulnerability increased when northern lenders insisted in the late 1970s that loans be tied to floating, not fixed, interest rates, rates that subsequently rose dramatically.

Economic conditions changed when the U.S. Federal Reserve raised interest rates to fight inflation in 1979 and 1980 (see chapter 4). Because most of their loans were tied to U.S. interest rates, dictators had to make higher interest payments on money they had borrowed in the 1970s. Moreover, high U.S. interest rates attracted Latin American investors, who withdrew their money from domestic bank accounts and invested in U.S. government securities. This capital flight from Latin America made it more difficult for countries to purchase imports and repay debt. It also eroded the tax base, depriving Latin American dictatorships of money at a time when they needed it most.

While higher interest rates increased costs, falling commodity prices reduced the income of Latin American countries (see chapter 6). The prices Latin American countries could get for their beef, food, timber, minerals, or oil began to fall after 1980 for two reasons. First, borrowed money had been used by dictatorships and private industry to increase their production of exports, and increased production glutted markets. Second, high U.S. interest rates triggered a recession in the United States and around the world, which reduced the demand for goods produced in Latin America and other Third World countries. Rising supplies and falling demand led to falling prices. This meant that Latin American dictatorships were earning less while being asked by lenders to pay more.

By 1982, when Mexico announced that it could no longer make payments on its $90 billion foreign debt, most of the Latin American dictatorships faced a serious economic crisis. One World Bank official described Argentina's economy, then saddled with $40 billion in foreign debts, as a "financial Hiroshima."[27]

Although the debt crisis undermined the economic legitimacy of dictators throughout Latin America, the crisis did not alone lead to the collapse of dictatorship. But economic crisis was compounded by political disaster in Argentina, and events there soon led to the collapse of the regime, a development that helped trigger democratization elsewhere.

On April 2, 1982, Argentine troops crossed three hundred miles of South Atlantic Ocean and landed in Port Stanley, the capital of an island group the British call the Falklands and the Argentines call the Malvinas.[28] General Leopoldo Galtieri and the rest of Argentina's military junta apparently believed that the British would surrender the islands without a fight and that capture of the islands would bolster domestic support for the regime. Instead, the invasion triggered a ruinous war with the United Kingdom, which destroyed the regime's credibility at home.

Within days of the invasion, a British fleet had shipped south, to land troops on the islands on May 21. They quickly defeated Argentina's ill-equipped army, a force cut off from Argentina by the British navy, and forced its surrender on June 14.

As it turned out, the war in the Falklands/Malvinas was for Argentina's dictatorship what war in Cyprus was for the Greek junta: a humiliating defeat that forced them both from power. In Argentina, power was first assumed by another military government. But deteriorating economic and political conditions soon forced this government to call elections and they transferred power to a civilian government the following year.

The collapse of dictatorship in Argentina, a large and relatively wealthy country in Latin American terms, reverberated across the continent. Dictators in other countries recognized that they shared many of the same economic problems. They also noted that U.S. policy toward dictatorship had undergone an important shift.

For many years, U.S. officials permitted, condoned or even encouraged dictatorship throughout much of Latin America. The United States had long provided food aid and military assistance to dictators. But during the Falklands war, U.S. officials did not support or defend the Argentine dictatorship. In fact, in a phone call with Galtieri just one day before the Argentines seized the islands, President Reagan told him, "I do not want to fail to emphasize pointedly that the relationship between our two countries will suffer seriously."[29] Galtieri evidently expected the United States to ignore the conflict, and the junta even suggested to the United States and other Latin American governments that they were obligated to come to Argentina's "defense" under the mutual security provisions of the 1947 Rio Treaty. They were greatly disappointed when they received no diplomatic assistance from the United States or other dictatorships, and they felt betrayed after they learned that the U.S. government had provided important military assistance to the United Kingdom during the war. Dictators across the continent regarded these developments as an indication that U.S. policy had shifted and that they could not longer count on U.S. support in the event of a crisis.

In Brazil, the debt had grown from $12.6 billion to $90 billion between 1973 and 1982, inflation had soared into quadruple digits, and the economy had become, from the government's perspective, unmanageable. For more than a decade, the dictatorship had said it was moving toward eventual democratization, but it moved at a glacial pace. Economic crisis and changed political conditions sped up the process after the collapse of the dictatorship in neighboring

Argentina in 1983 and in Uruguay in 1984. Brazil's dictators returned power to civilian authority in 1985.

Events then shifted to the Philippines, a country that more closely resembles Latin American countries in political and economic terms than its Asian neighbors. Like many Latin American countries, the Philippines were colonized and catholicized by Spain, then brought into the U.S. sphere of influence during the Spanish-American War. In 1972, President Ferdinand Marcos declared martial law and assumed dictatorial powers. Like the Latin American dictatorships, the Marcos regime borrowed heavily in the 1970s, the country's foreign debt growing to $26 billion by 1985, an amount equal to the country's annual gross national product (GNP).[30] For the Marcos regime, profound economic crisis was joined by political turmoil when government soldiers assassinated opposition leader Benigno Aquino in 1983. His murder triggered widespread protest and massive capital flight, leading to a moratorium on debt payments and a real decline in the economy.[31] During 1984 and 1985, the economy registered "negative growth," shrinking by nearly 9 percent in those two years.[32] Faced with deteriorating economic and political conditions, Marcos suddenly called a presidential election for early 1986, an election he expected to win over the disorganized opposition.[33] But opposition candidate Cory Aquino, widow of the slain Benigno Aquino, won despite massive election fraud. When Marcos refused to surrender power, civilians and some army units took to the streets, while U.S. officials invited Marcos to find exile in Hawaii. Foreign pull and domestic shove soon forced Marcos from office and into exile in 1986.

In Argentina, Brazil, and the Philippines and throughout Latin America, dictatorships confronted debt-related economic crisis. Because First World lenders insisted that dictators institute "austerity" programs to ensure repayment of debt, dictators found themselves in the difficult position of introducing extremely unpopular economic policies. To make these policies succeed, dictators needed the acquiescence or cooperation of other social groups, particularly wealthy elites and middle classes. But these groups demanded that they obtain political power and a return to democracy if they were to assume responsibility for managing the economic crisis. Under the circumstances, the dictatorships could not easily refuse. Moreover, they recognized that U.S. support for dictatorship had eroded and they worried about the alternatives to a managed or controlled democratization process. They feared popular revolts of the kind that had emerged in Portugal and later threatened in the Philippines. They also worried about events in Greece, where dictators and torturers were tried and jailed for their criminal conduct in office. Many dictators had reason to fear the Greek example. In Argentina, the military had waged a "dirty war" against civilian dissidents during the 1970s and 1980s, kidnapping, torturing, jailing, and murdering its opponents. As one army general explained, "We are going to kill 50,000 people: 25,000 subversives, 20,000 sympathizers, and we will make 5,000 mistakes."[34]

Many officials in dictatorial regimes had also illegally profited from office, siphoning off borrowed public money into private bank accounts. When civilian government returned in Argentina, many people demanded that officials in the dictatorship be tried and punished for economic and political crimes. Military officials lobbied desperately to prevent this action, while army units staged mutinies and attempted coups to discourage the civilian government from prosecuting those responsible for the dirty wars.

Throughout Latin America, the generals concluded that a "managed" devolution of power would be preferable to the alternatives. So they devised constitutions that would transfer power while retaining some prerogatives and protections from legal proceedings after they surrendered power. As a result, dictators in Argentina, Uruguay, Brazil, Peru, Ecuador, El Salvador, Panama, Honduras, Bolivia, and Paraguay transferred power, returned to the barracks, or retired from public life.[35] In 1990, even General Pinochet returned power to civilian government in Chile.

EAST ASIA: GROWING PAINS

In 1950, South Korea was the economic equal of Kenya or Nigeria, while Taiwan was comparable to Egypt. But during the next thirty years, the economies of South Korea and Taiwan grew by leaps and bounds. Between 1962 and 1980, South Korea's GNP increased 452 percent, growing from $12.7 billion to $57.4 billion, a development that distanced it from most other poor countries. By 1983, *The Economist* noted, the 18 million people in Taiwan exported more goods than 130 million Brazilians or 75 million Mexicans.[36]

Economic growth in South Korea and Taiwan, which was the envy of poor countries everywhere, was made possible by three important developments. First, both South Korea and Taiwan had been colonized by Japan at the beginning of the century. Japanese colonial administrators developed important economic infrastructures and tied the colonial economies to Japan. Close economic relations survived the war, and when Japan began its remarkable economic ascent, it pulled them along. It is important to note, however, that Japanese economic growth always exceeded that of its former colonies, which meant that their rise, while significant, was not as spectacular as that of Japan.[37]

Second, after the Korean War began in 1950, South Korea and Taiwan received substantial economic and military benefits from the United States, largely because U.S. policymakers regarded them as front-line states in the battle against communism. To shore up Chiang Kai-shek's one-party dictatorship in Taiwan and the military governments that ruled South Korea after 1962, the U.S. government provided $5.6 billion in economic and military aid to Taiwan and $13 billion to South Korea between 1945 and 1978. U.S. aid to Korea was greater than aid to all of Africa ($6.89 billion) and India ($9.6 billion) and nearly as much as to all of Latin America ($14.8 billion) in the same period.[38] The United States also opened its markets to importers from Korea and Taiwan, giving them preferential trading privileges enjoyed by few other countries, while allowing them to erect formidable trade barriers against U.S. imports so they could protect and nurture domestic industry.

Third, the dictatorships in South Korea and Taiwan instituted land reform, thereby creating an urban workforce that could work in their growing export industries. They banned labor unions and strikes to keep wages low, a policy designed to give their export industries a competitive advantage in U.S. and world markets. They also used high tariff barriers to protect domestic industry from foreign competition and fostered the growth of large, export-oriented monopoly firms, what the Koreans call *chaebols* and the Taiwanese call *caifa*, to create businesses that could compete with large transnational firms in Japan and the United States.[39]

These three developments—Japanese colonialism before 1945, U.S. assistance after 1945, and domestic economic policy that capitalized on economic opportunities—enabled the South Korean and Taiwanese economies to grow rapidly, providing considerable economic legitimacy for the dictators that directed them. But changing economic and political conditions in the 1970s and 1980s caught South Korea and Taiwan in an economic squeeze that made it increasingly difficult for the dictatorships to maintain rapid rates of growth.

For Taiwan, problems began in 1972, when President Nixon suddenly recognized communist China and cut off much of U.S. economic, military, and diplomatic aid to the nationalist government. Although these developments shocked the dictatorship, which viewed changed U.S. policy as a betrayal (much as dictators in Greece, Argentina, and the Philippines viewed other U.S. policies), the U.S. government did not curtail Taiwan's trading privileges, so it could still export goods to the United States.

Then, in the early 1980s, both South Korea and Taiwan began to experience growing competition from other Asian countries—China, Thailand, and Indonesia—that adopted their "model" of economic growth and developed export industries that relied on workers who were paid even lower wages. Workers received $643 a month in Taiwan and $610 in South Korea in 1988; workers received $209 in Indonesia, $132 in Thailand, and $129 in Malaysia.[40] Lower wages enabled businesses in other Asian countries to manufacture goods at prices that undercut firms in South Korea and Taiwan.

While new Asian competitors pushed from below, the United States began to push from above. Because East Asian countries were so successful at selling their goods in U.S. markets, while blocking the sale of U.S. goods in their countries, the United States began running large trade deficits with South Korea, Taiwan, and, most important, Japan. Persistent trade deficits strained U.S. support for East Asian dictatorships. To reduce its trade deficits with Asian countries and improve its competitiveness in overseas markets, the U.S. government in 1985 devalued the dollar (see chapter 3). This forced up the value of the South Korean currency by 30 percent. "We can absorb wage increases," a South Korean executive explained, "but we can't take any more [currency] appreciation."[41]

In 1987, U.S. officials also began restricting its preferential trading relations with East Asian countries, making it more difficult and more expensive for them to sell goods in U.S. markets.[42] U.S. officials also demanded that East Asian countries lower their trade barriers so that U.S. firms could sell more goods there, using bilateral and multilateral trade talks to press their case (see chapter 9).[43]

At the same time, domestic social groups began pressing for change. Rapid urbanization had moved many people off the land and into the cities, but housing shortages and real estate speculation had pushed up housing costs for workers and the middle class. In Taipei, land was more expensive than in Manhattan, but workers earned only half as much as their counterparts in New York City.[44] Workers grew weary of working long hours with little pay—South Koreans worked 54.3 hours a week on average.[45] Although the economy grew and per capita income increased, this did not mean that wages also increased. The dictatorships restrained wage increases and kept them from growing as fast as the economy. Workers who labored hard for their country became increasingly unhappy about their inability to share in its rewards. As a result, legal and illegal labor disputes rose sharply in the mid-1980s. In South Korea, for example, the number of disputes rose from 276 in 1986 to 3,749 in 1987, a thirteenfold increase.[46] Legal and illegal strike activity forced up wages, despite the dictatorships' determined efforts to arrest labor leaders and curb wage increases, and this made South Korean goods more expensive and less competitive on world markets. Moreover, industrial workers, and increasingly, middle-class workers, joined student demonstrators in demanding an end to dictatorship and a return to democracy. Although the dictatorship had been able to contain and isolate student radicals for some years, it became more difficult to do so when economic demands echoed political demands and workers and white-collar employees joined student protests.

For South Korea and Taiwan, economic success invited lower-wage Asian countries to emulate them, invited retaliation by the United States, and triggered domestic protest against them.

In Taiwan, these economic problems were compounded by a succession crisis. The Republic of China was created in 1948 when nationalist armies under General Chiang Kai-shek fled from the Chinese mainland after being defeated by communist armies and took refuge on Taiwan, creating a dictatorship that ran the country under martial law for the next thirty-nine years. When Chiang Kai-shek died in 1975, power invested in the one-party regime passed to his son, Chiang Ching-kuo. By the time he inherited his father's power, Chiang Ching-kuo was sixty-five, already an old man. Near the end of his life, in 1986, he

,egan casting around for a successor. Chiang began to consider reforms that could eventually transform Taiwan into a multiparty democracy and finally lifted martial law in 1987. When he died in 1988, power passed to Lee Teng-hui, who, like Juan Carlos in Spain, initiated a leisurely reform process that eventually led to open elections in 1992.[47]

In both South Korea and Taiwan, dictatorships closely observed the hapless demise of the Marcos dictatorship in 1986. Although the Philippines was more like Latin American countries in economic and political terms, it was an Asian society in geographic terms. And its proximity to South Korea and Taiwan made dictators fear the spread of Corazon Aquino's "People Power" to restive populations in their own countries.

By 1986–1987, as economic growth slowed from double-digit to single-digit rates, the dictatorships in South Korea and Taiwan became extremely anxious about economic and political developments. Cho Soon, South Korea's minister of economic planning, warned that without economic reform, "Our country will collapse like some of the Latin American countries," such as Argentina.[48] Military leaders such as Roh Tae Woo concluded that greater democratic participation was necessary if the country was to move ahead economically. During the late 1980s, military regimes in South Korea and Taiwan came to view democratization as a way to share power with the middle class, create a multiparty system dominated by a center-right party as a way to restore the government's legitimacy, deflect popular protest, and get the economy moving again.

In South Korea, it was Roh Tae Woo who initiated reform in 1987, arguing that "this country should develop a more mature democracy," transforming himself from military leader to presidential candidate.[49] After he won election in 1987 as president when dissident leaders split the opposition vote, he took steps that resulted in the 1992 election of dissident civilian Kim Young-sam. "Now we have finally created a truly civilian-led government in our country," Kim said after the vote.[50]

In 1992, Thailand joined South Korea and Taiwan when the military government stepped down and transferred power to civilians. Like them, Thailand experienced many of the problems associated with rapid growth. When government troops massacred student and middle-class demonstrators demanding political reform in May 1992, the military regime was discredited. Acting as an intermediary, King Bhumibol Adulyadei then assumed the role that Juan Carlos had played in Spain and managed a transfer of power to civilian government by September.[51]

During the late 1980s, communist dictatorships in China and Vietnam also initiated some economic and political reforms to address the economic problems that confronted them. The aging political leadership of communist parties in China and Vietnam faced the problem of choosing more youthful political successors, a problem shared by rulers in Taiwan. In 1989, students and workers in Beijing occupied Tiananmen Square and demanded political reform, much as demonstrators in Seoul had been doing for some years. It appeared, during the spring of 1989, that these developments in China might lead to democratization there, just as it was then doing in South Korea and Taiwan. But the massacre of protesters camped in Tiananmen Square and the arrest of dissidents throughout the country aborted reforms that seemed in the offing. Events in China did not lead to the collapse of dictatorship. Nor did the Vietnamese regime devolve power, though it, too, was experiencing a deep economic crisis.

Communist regimes in East Asia did not democratize as capitalist dictatorships in southern Europe, Latin America, and East Asia did or as communist dictatorships in Eastern Europe and the Soviet Union subsequently would. They did, however, reform their economies and adopt many of the same economic policies that civilian democrats deployed in many democratizing states, an approach that in China has been called "market Leninism."[52] Communist regimes in Asia survived, at least for the present, because they possessed considerable political legitimacy derived from having fought and won wars against colonial powers and domestic rivals. The Chinese communists fought the Japanese in China, U.S. and UN forces in Korea, and nationalist rivals during a long civil war. The Vietnamese communists had fought for independence against France, Japan, and the United States, and they defeated the South Vietnamese regime in 1975 after U.S. troops withdrew. Their ability to defeat formidable opponents, and their programs designed to improve conditions for the rural population, gave them a reservoir of support they could draw on during the economic and political crises of the 1980s. (Fidel Castro's communist regime in Cuba survives for many of the same reasons.) By contrast, communist dictatorships in Eastern Europe (with the exception of Yugoslavia), assumed power not as a result of their own efforts but because they were installed by the Soviet Union and backed by the Red Army. By the 1980s, dictators in Eastern Europe and the Soviet Union had long since exhausted the patience of domestic populations. So when crisis struck, they found themselves isolated and vulnerable.

THE SOVIET UNION AND EASTERN EUROPE: DECLINE AND DEMOCRATIZATION

Democratization in the Soviet Union and Eastern Europe was a product of economic crisis originating in the Soviet Union. This crisis was rooted in the stagnation of collectivized agriculture and the heavy burden of military spending in the postwar period. "By the beginning of the 1980s," Soviet leader Mikhail Gorbachev observed, "the [Soviet Union] found itself in a state of severe crisis which has embraced all spheres of life."[53]

During the 1920s and 1930s, the Soviet dictatorship under Joseph Stalin forced small and medium-sized farmers to join large-scale, state-owned collectives. By increasing farm size and mechanizing agriculture under state authority, the government hoped to increase agricultural output and use much of the wealth it produced to finance industrial development. But collectivization was an extremely disruptive process. The regime killed farmers who opposed these measures or sent them to Siberia, and agricultural output faltered, contributing to famine in some regions.

After World War II, agriculture revived and the large-scale collective farms increased production, for a time. But because the communist regime continued siphoning off agricultural resources to finance industrial growth and, during the cold war, the military, there was little investment in agriculture and few incentives for farmers to increase yields or produce more food. Crop yields in the Soviet Union were only about half those obtained in the United States.[54] These problems reached crisis proportions in the mid-1970s, when Soviet grain harvests failed, a development that sent world grain prices soaring (see chapters 4 and 7). Because farm production failed to keep pace with the growing Soviet demand for food, the Soviet Union had to import more food. The cost of food imports doubled from $5.1 billion to $10.2 billion between 1974 and 1978, a development that increased the Soviet trade deficit.[55] And because farmers in the 1970s and 1980s began selling a growing share of their crops through unofficial black markets that offered higher prices, less food was available in state stores. Consumers found it difficult to obtain food using ration coupons, though they could purchase higher-priced food on black markets.[56] The result was long lines, frayed tempers, and considerable resentment.

The Soviet regime might have invested more heavily in agriculture if it had not been preoccupied with military spending. But during the cold war, the Soviets spent heavily to develop and maintain its new status as a military and political superpower. According to military analyst Ruth Sivard, the Soviets spent $4.6 trillion between 1960 and 1987, or between 12 and 15 percent of its annual GNP, on the military.[57] Other economists argued that the Soviets spent even more, as much as 20 to 28 percent of GNP.[58] (By comparison, the United States spent only 6 to 8 percent of its GNP on the military during the cold war.)

Massive military spending enabled the Soviet regime to expand its political influence, maintain an occupying army in Eastern Europe, assist socialist movements and communist governments abroad, and obtain substantial income from arms sales to other countries—$64 billion worth of arms between 1973 and 1981.[59] But it did not provide substantial economic benefits in Soviet Union or secure military advantages abroad.

Domestically, heavy military spending absorbed scarce supplies of capital, skilled labor, and natural resources, diverting resources from other sectors of the economy, particularly from agriculture and consumer industries. As a result, it retarded economic growth and contributed to stagnation and decline.[60] The Soviet invasion of Afghanistan in 1979 greatly increased military spending and stimulated an arms race with the United States in the early 1980s, a development that further increased military spending. Gorbachev later said that increased military during the Afghan war and the arms race of the 1980s had "exhausted our economy."[61]

It also became apparent in the 1980s that massive military spending had not enabled the Soviets to produce weapons that could compete with U.S. and Western European arms on battlefields in Afghanistan and the Middle East. In 1982, for example, during an air battle over Lebanon, Israeli pilots flying U.S. and French jets "shot down 80 Soviet-made planes [flown by Syrians] while losing none of their own."[62] This kind of lopsided battlefield performance was dramatically underscored during the 1991 Persian Gulf War, when the U.S.-led coalition crushed Iraqi forces, which were supplied with Soviet arms, destroying four thousand Soviet-built tanks in the process. The failure of Soviet weaponry in battlefield competition led Soviet military planners to conclude that the entire Soviet military model was "obsolete."[63] Soviet marshal Dmitry Yazov admitted, "What happened in Kuwait necessitates a review of our attitude toward the [Soviet Union's] entire defense system."[64]

Soviet economic problems worsened after 1985. Falling world oil prices reduced income from oil exports, one of the country's major sources of foreign currency, and increased its trade deficit. To cover the trade deficit so that it could import the food and technology it needed from the West, the Soviets began borrowing heavily. The Soviet debt to Western European governments and banks nearly quadrupled between 1984 and 1989, growing "from $10.2 billion at the end of 1984 to $37.3 billion at the end of 1989."[65] And the regime's attempts to stimulate the stagnating economy led to growing budget deficits. "In 1981–85, the budget deficit only averaged 18 billion rubles per year, [but] in 1986–89, it averaged 67 billion rubles," a more than threefold increase.[66]

The Soviet *economic* crisis was compounded by two *political* crises. First, the communist regime faced not one but three crises of succession between 1982 and 1985. When Leonid Brezhnev died suddenly after reviewing the annual parade celebrating the anniversary of the Bolshevik Revolution on November 10, 1982, a political battle to chose his successor ensued. Brezhnev's chosen successor, Konstantin Chernenko, was passed over and Yuri Andropov selected as the new Soviet leader. But Andropov died after a long illness on February 9, 1984. A second succession crisis then ensued. Andropov's choice, Mikhail Gorbachev, who represented the young, reform-minded wing of the Communist Party, was passed over and Brezhnev's old protégé, Chernenko, was chosen instead. But he died a year later, on March 10, 1985, and Gorbachev, then fifty-four, assumed power.[67]

Second, by the time the protracted succession crisis had been sorted out, it had become evident that the Soviet Union faced military defeat in Afghanistan. The looming defeat by anticommunist mujahadeen rebels supplied with U.S. arms undermined the legitimacy of a regime that relied on its military standing as a political cornerstone, much as military defeats undermined the legitimacy of dictatorships in Portugal, Greece, and Argentina.

After he assumed power in 1985, Gorbachev took steps to address the economic crisis. By reducing military spending, transferring these resources to other sectors of the economy, and allowing some privatization of state-owned farms and industry to give farmers and workers incentives to increase the quantity and quality of food and consumer goods, Gorbachev hoped to jump-start the languishing economy. But dramatic economic restructuring, called *perestroika*, antagonized the military and the Communist Party bureaucracy that directed agriculture and industry. To overcome opposition within the Communist Party and push ahead with economic reform, Gorbachev needed to develop a wider social constituency that could provide political support for reform outside the party. So Gorbachev promoted political reform and limited democratization, what he called *glasnost* (openness), as a way to rally wider popular support for perestroika, demilitarization, and reform. As Gorbachev explained, democratization was "a guarantee against the repetition of past errors, and consequently a guarantee that the restructuring process is irreversible." There was no choice, he said; it was "either democracy or social inertia and conservatism."[68]

Because reduced military spending was a central part of perestroika, Gorbachev devoted considerable attention to Soviet military and foreign policy. He withdrew the Soviet army from Afghanistan, stopped aid to the communist regime in Ethiopia, and initiated arms control agreements with the United States and its NATO allies in Western Europe. The 1987 Intermediate-Range Nuclear Forces Treaty, which removed intermediate-range nuclear missiles from Europe, was the first arms control agreement to reduce the size of superpower arsenals. Gorbachev also initiated talks that led to a reduction of conventional troops in Europe. He pursued détente with China and sought an end to the long cold war with the United States. And he renounced long-standing Soviet claims that it had a right to use military force in Eastern Europe to support communist dictatorships there, a "right" that the Soviets exercised in East Germany in 1953, in Hungary in 1956, and in Czechoslovakia in 1968.

By renouncing the right to intervene in Eastern Europe, Gorbachev undercut client dictatorship that had first been installed by the Soviets in the late 1940s. At a press conference on October 25, 1989, Foreign Minister Gennady Gerasimov was asked whether the Soviet Union still adhered to the Brezhnev Doctrine, which was used to justify Soviet intervention in Eastern Europe. He said it did not. Instead, he said, new Soviet policy would be called the "Sinatra Doctrine," because the American singer Frank Sinatra "had a song, 'I did it my way.' So every country decides in its own way which [economic and political] road to take."[69] The Soviet adoption of a new foreign policy toward Eastern Europe fatally weakened communist dictatorships and fueled the rise of dissident opposition movements in Poland, East Germany, Hungary, Czechoslovakia, Romania, Bulgaria, and Albania. By the end of 1989, just two months after Gerasimov's press conference, communist dictatorships in all these countries had been swept from power. Some tried to initiate and manage a devolution of power to dissident democrats so that they could retain some power. But an economic crisis rooted in stagnation and debt (recall that Eastern European countries were the first casualties of the debt crisis in the early 1980s) left them without any economic credibility, while the new Soviet policy deprived them of any remaining political legitimacy or military power.

Because they possessed a very narrow social base, with little economic credibility or political legitimacy, communist dictatorships in Eastern Europe collapsed like a house of cards at the first appearance of organized dissent or concerted civic action. In East Germany, it was the flood of migrants from East Germany to Hungary and then to West Germany that brought down the dictatorship, while in Poland it was an organized labor movement. In Hungary and Czechoslovakia, newly organized dissident movements negotiated an end to dictatorship. In Romania, street demonstrations and mob action brought a bloody end to the brutal regime of Nicolae Ceaucescu.

The dramatic events of 1989 had important consequences for the Soviet Union. The collapse of communism in Eastern Europe, the emergence of protest movements in some Soviet republics, and the extension of reforms in response to a deepening economic crisis led in August 1992 to a coup by hard-liners in the military and Communist Party who were determined to restore one-party dictatorship. But whereas Chinese hard-liners had been able to crush dissent and maintain dictatorship, Soviet hard-liners found few allies. Instead, people in Moscow and important elements of the army rallied to Russian president Boris Yeltsin, forcing the coup to collapse. These developments led, by the end of 1992, to democratization but also to the division of the Soviet Union into fifteen independent countries.

SOUTH AFRICA: EMBARGO, DEFEAT, AND DEMOCRATIZATION

On February 2, 1990, South Africa's President Frederik W. de Klerk told the country's whites-only parliament that he was legalizing the outlawed African National Congress (ANC) and other black political organizations and would soon release ANC leader Nelson Mandela, who had been imprisoned for twenty-seven years. Although he told one Western diplomat, "Don't expect me to negotiate myself out of power," de Klerk did just that.[70] One year later, he introduced changes that removed "the remnants of racially discriminatory legislation which have become known as the cornerstones of apartheid," and he began a process of negotiation and constitutional reform that would lead in April 1993 to elections that swept Mandela to power as the country's first black president. When Mandela was inaugurated on May 10, 1994, joyous black crowds chanted in Xhosa, "Amandla! Ngawethu!" (Power! It is ours!)[71]

De Klerk initiated the devolution of power in response to a worsening economic and political crisis in South Africa. During the 1950s and 1960s, "the apartheid system probably aided economic growth in South Africa" because it locked in low wages for black South African workers.[72] But by the late 1960s, "this position began to change" because low wages discouraged businesses from spending money to introduce new technology that would increase productivity and make South African goods more competitive on world markets, so economic growth began to slow.[73]

In 1976, South African police killed numerous black demonstrators protesting apartheid in Soweto, an action that triggered a wave of protests and strikes that continued during the 1970s and 1980s. During the second half of the 1980s, "5,000 people died and more than 30,000 were jailed without charge."[74] Black protests called international attention to and condemnation of apartheid. Spurred by protests in South Africa and in Western countries, companies and countries began to withdraw investment from South Africa, levy economy sanctions, and eventually reduce much of their trade with South Africa. By the end of the 1980s, sanctions and disinvestment had brought the South African economy to a standstill. Economists estimated that in 1989, that average income had fallen 15 percent from 1980 and that economic sanctions were costing the economy $2 billion a year.[75]

While the economy stagnated, military spending grew, both because the government was waging an internal war against domestic black protesters and because it deployed troops to fight a communist guerrilla movement in Namibia and intervened in neighboring Angola to overthrow the communist government there. These costly external wars led in 1988 to the South African army's defeat by Angolan and Cuban troops at the battle of Cuito Cuanavale in 1988. As Kevin Danaher and Medea Benjamin noted, "The defeat forced the South Africans to sign a peace treaty [with Angola] on December 22, 1988, requiring them to withdraw from Angola [after a thirteen-year occupation] and a phase-out of their decades-long control of Namibia."[76]

When de Klerk became president on August 15, 1989, after the illness and resignation of hard-line President P. W. Botha, known by associates as the "Old Crocodile," he confronted a worsening economic, military, and political crisis. During the next six months, he came to view an end to apartheid as the key to ending the crisis. By ending apartheid, de Klerk hoped that domestic turmoil would wane, military expenditures could be reduced, and foreign investors and Western governments could be persuaded to end economic sanctions and reinvest in the economy. (As in southern Europe, improved economic relations depended on ending dictatorship.) The collapse of communism during the six months between his appointment as president and his dramatic February 2 speech made de Klerk's decision easier, he said, "because it created a scenario where the communist threat . . . lost its sting."[77]

By initiating a devolution of power, de Klerk sought to manage events so that the white minority could reserve their economic power and retain some political power in a postapartheid state. And democratization in South Africa has encouraged democratization in other African countries. About half of the continent's forty-eight countries have since held multiparty elections, though this process has had, as yet, only limited results.[78]

DEMOCRACY AND DEVELOPMENT

Contemporary democratization is largely a product of economic crisis. The problems associated with different kinds of economic crises were compounded by political problems related to the death or illness of dictators, defeat in war, and public protest by dissident groups. Faced with difficult economic and political problems, dictators and one-party regimes realized they needed to take drastic steps to resolve their problems. But to be successful, radical economic and political reform needed broad public support. And other social groups refused to accept responsibility for solving economic problems they did not create unless they could obtain real political power. As Walden Bello and Stephanie Rosenfeld have written, "Economic policies that are not supported by a rough consensus forced by democratic means are likely to founder over the long run. Democracy, one might say, has become a factor of production."[79]

Under these circumstances, dictators devolved power to civilian democrats, trying to manage the process so that they could retain some residual political power and possibly protect themselves from prosecution for economic crimes (corruption) or violations of human rights (illegal arrests, torture, murder of dissidents). As we have seen, the devolution of power was abrupt in some places and protracted in others, and dictators had only limited success in managing the democratization process.

Once they assumed political power, civilian democrats had to address difficult economic problems. Although the origin and character of economic crises differed from one region to the next, and from one country to the next within these regions, civilian democrats everywhere adopted a common economic approach that they hoped would solve their separate problems. In nearly all democratizing states, civilian democrats have (1) opened their economies to foreign investment and trade, (2) sold off or privatized state-owned public assets and industries, and (3) cut military spending. This common set of economic policies, which are associated with economic globalization generally, has produced some economic benefits in some democratizing states. But they have also created economic, social, and political problems of their own.

Opening the Economy

Around the world, civilian democrats have reduced tariff barriers, opened their economy to foreign investors, and lifted currency exchange restrictions. Lower tariff barriers are designed to make imported goods more readily available to domestic consumers who have long craved many goods from other countries, and force domestic industries to lower their prices and improve the quality of their goods, or go out of business. Foreign competition and the threat of bankruptcy are supposed to shake up domestic industries that have grown inefficient and wasteful as a result of government protection under dictatorship. By opening the economy to foreign investment, governments hoped that foreign companies would inject new money, management skills, and technology into the economy, thereby providing jobs in industries that can compete on world markets. By lifting currency restrictions, government economists expected world currency markets to appraise their currency and set exchange rates at realistic levels. As a result, the currencies of most democratizing states were devalued, which made their goods cheaper and easier to sell abroad, a development that helped them increase their exports and reduce their trade deficits. These three measures were designed to achieve what the Brazilians called a "competitive integration" with the world economy.[80]

The problem for many countries, however, was that when tariff barriers were lowered, domestic consumers bought expensive imported goods: Nike shoes, Levi's jeans, foreign cars. This orgy of consumer spending on imports created trade deficits, which forced down the value of their currency (see chapter 3). And while a devalued currency should have made their goods easier to sell on overseas markets and improved their trade balance, their goods were often regarded as shoddy by consumers elsewhere. The result was that they found it difficult to sell their goods at *any* price. Foreign investors did open some new factories and purchased some government-owned industries at bargain basement prices (currency devaluations made businesses cheaper for foreign buyers). But the large-scale investment that many governments expected did not materialize, largely because global economic activity has been slow and there is excess capacity in many industries, and partly because investors are waiting to see whether governments can control inflation and create a favorable business climate and strong consumer market before risking substantial sums of money. Meanwhile, the widespread sale of public assets and industries has glutted investment markets, which has slowed sales and lowered prices.

Selling Off State Assets

Civilian democrats around the world have sold public assets that had previously been controlled by dictators, bureaucrats, and their friends and families, an economic system that Peruvian economist Hernando de Soto has described as "buddy-buddy" or "crony capitalism."[81] Civilian democrats hoped that the sale of public assets would raise money that could be used to repay debts, reduce government budget deficits, and cut the cost of subsidizing inefficient industries. The sale of public assets was also supposed to provide new economic opportunities for domestic investors, who were expected to emerge as a new class of energetic entrepreneurs.

As a result, the sale of national banks, airlines, telephone companies, shipping lines, cement factories, port facilities, and land has been widespread. In Eastern Europe, assets worth more than $100 billion have been offered for sale.[82] In Brazil, the sale of ninety-two parastatal firms and a port authority by the end of 1992 had been valued at $62 billion.[83]

Privatization has been less extensive in East Asia, though South Korea sold off seven firms in 1990, because both South Korea and Taiwan have few public assets compared with countries in southern Europe, Latin America, or Eastern Europe and because the state supports large *private* monopolies, chaebols, which they were unwilling to break up.

The problem with this strategy was that few domestic investors could afford to purchase large companies, while currency devaluations made them cheaper, in real terms, for foreign investors. Foreign firms have snapped up the best offerings at bargain prices, but they have not been interested in purchasing poor-quality companies. The worldwide sale of so many properties has glutted investment markets. With airline companies battling each other for scarce travelers in the North, the last thing they needed to do was to purchase the Argentine airline fleet. In Eastern Europe, Poland has managed to sell only a fraction of the firms it offered for sale, and Germany has sold only a fraction of the eight thousand or so former East German state firms.[84] In Czechoslovakia, and in many former Soviet republics, the governments abandoned plans to sell most of their assets on the open market and instead gave or sold vouchers to residents who used them to buy shares in privatized firms. The idea was to sell the firms to domestic buyers and then use the money raised to introduce technology, improve productivity, and increase competitiveness. But this approach has not always worked out. After a Czech government effort to sell some large businesses failed miserably, the prime minister defended his government from criticism, arguing, "We are not a banana Republic."[85] It is not clear that experiments of this sort will provide sufficient capital, that the money collected from small investors will flow to the right firms, that these firms will use the money wisely, or that newly privatized firms will be able to compete effectively against well-established, large-scale firms from Western Europe, North America, or East Asia. So far, the attrition rate of recently privatized firms has been high, and business failures have contributed to rising unemployment in many democratizing states.

Demilitarizing the Economy

Demilitarization has been most dramatic in Eastern Europe and the Soviet Union. Under Gorbachev, the Soviet Union began withdrawing troops from Afghanistan and Eastern Europe and cut military spending and troop levels. This made possible the devolution of power to democrats in Eastern Europe,

who promptly slashed military spending, cut troop levels, disbanded party militias, and withdrew from the Warsaw Pact, causing its demise in 1991.[86]

After the 1992 coup failed and the Soviet Union democratized and divided,
military spending fell in most of the former republics. The decline was dramatic.
In 1987, the Soviet Union had 3.9 million troops under arms and spent $356
billion on defense. In 1994, the Russian government (the largest of the former
Soviet republics) had 2.1 million troops under arms and spent only $29 billion
on defense.[87]

In Latin America, successive Argentine presidents have cut military spending
in half, scaled back the draft, and cut the army to one-half its Falklands/Malvi-
nas size.[88] Armies across the continent have been scaled back. Julio María San-
guinetti, who became Uruguay's president in 1985, described the changed
political atmosphere: "If you get a group of Latin American politicians together
in a room and ask, 'Who wants to be foreign minister?' everyone will wave his
or her hand in the air. But if you ask, 'Who wants to be defense minister?' everyone stares at the floor."[89]

East Asian states have been the exception to this general rule. After Tiananmen Square, the Chinese increased military spending, so Taiwan and South
Korea did too. South Korea increased its military spending both because its dis-
agreements with North Korea remain unresolved and because the United States
cut back its military spending on the peninsula, which forced the South Korean
government to assume a greater share of defense costs.

Although military spending in East Asia has increased somewhat, the general
trend is to demilitarize, and world military expenditures are down 14 percent
from 1987 levels.[90]

Governments have demilitarized for a variety of economic reasons. Most governments believe that heavy military spending did little to contribute to economic growth and may even have put their economies at a disadvantage in global
competition with states that devoted a smaller percentage of the GNP to military expenditures, like Germany and Japan. In a study on the relation between
military spending and economic growth, A. F. Mullins found that "in general,
those states that did best in GNP growth . . . paid less attention to military capability than others. This relation . . . holds right across the range from poor states
to rich states and from weak states to powerful. Those that did poorly in GNP
growth . . . paid more attention to military capability."[91]

CONTINUING ECONOMIC
CRISIS AND DEMOCRACY

During the 1970s and 1980s, economic crises of different sorts created problems that contributed to the collapse of dictatorships around the world. The
civilian democrats who assumed power then attempted to solve their separate

crises by opening their economies, selling off state assets, and reducing military spending. Some have had more success than others, but difficult economic problems remain for most countries.

In Spain, for example, the economy boomed during much of the 1980s, largely because membership in the European Community (now the European Union) provided real benefits. But growth slowed dramatically in the 1990s and unemployment grew to a staggering 21.5 percent in 1993, the highest in the EU and twice the average of other EU countries.[92] The problem was that despite improved economic performance, Spanish industry was still not competitive with other European heavyweights. "We were seduced into believing we were in the major league," explained Spanish business consultant Jaime Mariategui. "But when you are racing a Spanish SEAT [a car made in Spain] against a Mercedes, eventually you [must] face reality."[93] Pointing to the anemic 1 percent growth in 1992 and 1993, as well as to the collapse of Spain's stock market, journalist Roger Cohn observed, "The danger seems real that Spain, having made a great leap, could slip back."[94] A spokesman for a large Spanish firm complained, "Europe means progress, but right here progress means unemployment, and I don't know if that is acceptable."[95]

In Latin America, many new democracies have also recorded impressive economic growth in recent years, but the number of people in poverty has nonetheless increased. "The resumption of economic growth has been bought at a very high social price, which includes poverty, increased unemployment and income inequality, and this is leading to social problems," observed Louis Emerij, an economist at the Inter-American Development Bank in 1994.[96] By the end of the decade, 192 million people or 37 percent of the population will live in poverty. "Growth has really been on only one end of the spectrum, the wealthy. The rich are getting richer and the poor are getting poorer. And this will generate social conflict," argued UN official Peter Jensen.[97]

In 1992 a Harvard University study found that "the vast majority of people in Eastern Europe live in economic conditions demonstrably worse than those under the inefficiencies of central planning."[98] In the former Soviet Union, a deepening economic crisis has actually lowered the life expectancy of adult men and led to a decrease in the population, a development that British demographer David Coleman described as "an incredibly clear picture of a society in crisis. A decline in life expectancy this dramatic has never happened in the postwar period. . . . It shows the malaise of society, the lack of public health awareness and the fatigue associated with people who have to fight a pitched battle their whole lives just to survive."[99]

Under these circumstances, it should not be surprising that in a 1994 opinion poll, two-thirds of Russians believed that things were "better" under communism than they are "now."[100] In Eastern Europe, substantial minorities, and sometimes majorities, agreed.[101]

Gender and Democratization

In gender terms, dictatorships were male-dominated political institutions. No postwar dictatorship anywhere was led by a woman. In capitalist dictatorships, this gendered, patriarchal form of government generally provided some jobs in the military and bureaucracy to some men, but disadvantaged women, who were expected to stay at home and raise children. In communist regimes, by contrast, this gendered form of government provided these benefits to men but also extended them to women. So in Eastern Europe and the Soviet Union, many women found work in manufacturing and service industries, in professions, and in government, though they were never assigned top positions in any field. When dictatorships fell, men and women were able to create democratic political institutions that were more open to women and men outside the elites who had controlled patriarchal dictatorships. So now, women more often run for office. In a few cases, women even assumed power as president—for example, Corazon Aquino in the Philippines and Violeta Chamorro in Nicaragua.

In economic terms, democratization has had important, though varied, gender consequences. Where democratic governments opened their economies to foreign trade and sold public assets, as they did almost everywhere, many of the domestic manufacturing industries were ruined. In Southern Europe, Latin America, East Asia, and South Africa, deindustrialization typically resulted in job loss for men, as we have already seen (see chapter 6). Where commodity prices fell, men and women were adversely affected, depending on the gender character of the labor force in agriculture, mining, and natural resource industries (see chapter 6). Where governments demilitarized and reduced the size of standing armies, men lost jobs because few women (even in communist countries) served as soldiers in the military.

But while deindustrialization led to job loss for men in many countries, it led to disproportionate job loss for women in Eastern Europe and the Soviet Union. A 1999 UN study found that women lost jobs more often than men. "In the transition to a market economy," the UN observed, "the status of women is eroding further.[102]

The scale of deindustrialization in Russia has been enormous. Economists estimate that its GNP has declined 45 percent since the fall of communism in 1992.[103] Nearly 40 percent of the population in the former Soviet Union now lives in poverty.[104] These economic developments have had important consequences for women. As the Russian economy contracted, the government lost tax revenue and was unable to provide many services or pay salaries or pensions. This latter development hurt older women, who typically survive their male spouse. It also affected younger women. "With political collapse and economic uncertainty [in the former Soviet Union and in Eastern Europe], many women stopped having children or decided to delay motherhood," a UN study found in 2000. "People have been impoverished and decided that having kids at a time of poverty and misery is not the right thing to do, so they cut back. This is family downsizing . . . a rational economic behavior in some ways."[105] As a result, birthrates have fallen sharply. At current rates, demographers expect the population to shrink by as much as fifty-seven million in Russia during the next fifty years.[106]

A Temporary Crisis?

Of course, economists and policymakers who defend the economic policies of democratizing states have argued that contemporary problems are the product of *previous* economic policy—the residual effects of discredited dictators—or that they are *temporary* problems associated with a difficult "transition" process. That may be. But many people in these countries nonetheless associate these problems with the democrats who recently assumed power. And unless democratic governments speedily solve some economic problems, public disenchantment may grow.

In some countries, continuing economic crisis, which differs in important ways from the crises that preceded the fall of dictatorship, has created political problems for democratic governments, and dictatorship again threatens. In some Eastern European and former Soviet states, former communists have returned to power in recent elections, ousting the democrats who took power after communism collapsed. Just as the current economic crisis differs from the one that preceded the collapse of dictatorship, the advocates of a new kind of authoritarianism differ from their dictatorial predecessors. In Brazil, for example, Congressman Jai Bolsonaro argued, "Real democracy is food on the table, the ability to plan your life, the ability to walk on the street without getting mugged." He has said, "I am in favor of dictatorship" because "we will never resolve serious national problems with this irresponsible democracy."[107]

Economic crisis, it seems, can create serious problems for dictators and democrats alike. Although dictatorship has collapsed in countries around the world during the past twenty years, many economic and political problems remain. Unless democratic governments can solve some of these problems and make some demonstrable economic progress, the threat of dictatorship, in some form, will remain.

Another problem has been associated with democratization. When some countries democratized, they also divided into separate states. The Soviet Union divided into fifteen states, Czechoslovakia into two states, and Yugoslavia into five and perhaps more. In the case of Yugoslavia, division has been a tumultuous process, leading to war and ongoing conflict in the region. It is to these developments that we now turn.

NOTES

1. Robert Schaeffer, "Democratic Devolutions: East Asian Democratization in Comparative Perspective," in *Pacific-Asia and the Future of the World-System*, ed. Ravi

Palat (Westport, Conn.: Greenwood, 1993); Robert Schaeffer, *Power to the People: Democratization Around the World* (Boulder, Colo.: Westview, 1997).

2. Samuel P. Huntington, "Democracy's Third Wave," in *The Global Resurgence of Democracy*, eds. Larry Diamond and Marc F. Plattner (Baltimore: Johns Hopkins University Press, 1993), 3.

3. Caglar Keydar, "The American Recovery of Southern Europe: Aid and Hegemony," in *Semiperipheral Development: The Politics of Southern Europe in the Twentieth Century*, ed. Giovanni Arrighi (Beverly Hills, Calif.: Sage, 1985), 141–42.

4. Giovanni Arrighi, "Fascism to Democratic Socialism: Logic and Limits of a Transition," in *Semiperipheral Development*, 265; Giovanni Arrighi, "World Income Inequalities and the Future of Socialism," *New Left Review* 189 (September–October 1991): 47; Keydar, "The American Recovery of Southern Europe," 145.

5. Raymond Carr and Juan Pablo Fusi Aizpurua, *Spain: Dictatorship to Democracy* (London: Allen & Unwin, 1979), 57.

6. Kenneth Maxwell, "The Emergence of Portuguese Democracy," in *From Dictatorship to Democracy: Coping with the Legacies of Authoritarianism and Totalitarianism*, ed. John H. Herz (Westport, Conn.: Greenwood, 1982), 233.

7. Carr and Aizpurua, *Spain*, 68, 67.

8. Eric N. Baklanoff, "Spain's Emergence as a Middle Industrial Power: The Basis and Structure of Spanish-Latin American Economic Relations," in *The Iberian-Latin American Connection: Implications for U.S. Foreign Policy*, ed. Howard J. Wiarda (Boulder, Colo.: Westview, 1986), 139; John Logan, "Democracy from Above: Limits to Change in Southern Europe," in *Semiperipheral Development*, 164.

9. Edward Malefakis, "Spain and Its Francoist Heritage," in *From Dictatorship to Democracy*, 218.

10. Arrighi, "Fascism to Democratic Socialism," 265.

11. Logan, "Democracy from Above," 163.

12. Arrighi, "World Income Inequalities," 47.

13. Maxwell, "The Emergence of Portuguese Democracy," 235.

14. Baklanoff, "Spain's Emergence as a Middle Industrial Power," 140.

15. Maxwell, "The Emergence of Portuguese Democracy," 235.

16. Maxwell, "The Emergence of Portuguese Democracy," 235.

17. Maxwell, "The Emergence of Portuguese Democracy," 235.

18. Rodney J. Morrison, *Portugal: Revolutionary Change in an Open Economy* (Boston: Auburn House, 1981), 2; Logan, "Democracy from Above," 158.

19. Logan, "Democracy from Above," 270.

20. Harry J. Psomiades, "Greece: From the Colonels' Rule to Democracy," in *From Dictatorship to Democracy*, 253.

21. Malefakis, "Spain and Its Francoist Heritage," 220.

22. Psomiades, "Greece," 258.

23. Michael Harsgor, *Portugal in Revolution*. (Washington, D.C.: Center for Strategic and International Studies; Beverly Hills: Sage, 1976), 28; Logan, "Democracy from Above," 166, 168.

24. Maxwell, "The Emergence of Portuguese Democracy," 238.

25. Robert A. Pastor, *Democracy in the Americas: Stopping the Pendulum* (New York: Holmes & Meier, 1989), xi.

26. Pastor, *Democracy in the Americas*, ix.

27. William C. Smith, *Authoritarianism and the Crisis of the Argentine Political Economy* (Stanford, Calif.: Stanford University Press, 1989), 249.

28. Gary W. Wynia, *Argentina: Illusions and Realities* (New York: Holmes & Meier, 1986), 3.

29. Wynia, *Argentina*, 15.

30. Belina A. Aquino, "The Philippines: End of an Era," *Current History* (April 1986): 158.

31. John Bresnan, *Crisis in the Philippines: The Marcos Era and Beyond* (Princeton, N.J.: Princeton University Press, 1986), 145.

32. Aquino, "The Philippines," 158.

33. Bresnan, *Crisis in the Philippines*, 142.

34. Smith, *Authoritarianism*, 232.

35. Jonathan Hartlyn and Samuel A. Morley, *Latin American Political Economy: Financial Crisis and Political Change* (Boulder, Colo.: Westview, 1986), 1.

36. Chalmers Johnson, "Political Institutions and Economic Performance: The Government–Business Relation in Japan, South Korea and Taiwan," in *The Political Economy of the New Asian Industrialism*, ed. Frederic C. Deyo (Ithaca, N.Y.: Cornell University Press, 1987), 136.

37. Bruce Cumings, "The Origins and Development of the Northeast Asian Political Economy: Industrial Sectors, Product Cycles and Political Consequences," in *The Political Economy of the New Asian Industrialism*.

38. Cumings, "The Origins and Development," 67; Hagen Koo, "The Interplay of State, Social Class, and World System in East Asian Development: The Cases of South Korea and Taiwan," in *The Political Economy of the New Asian Industrialism*, 167; Walden Bello and Stephanie Rosenfeld, *Dragons in Distress: Asia's Miracle Economies in Crisis* (San Francisco: Food First Books, 1990), 4.

39. Johnson, "Political Institutions and Economic Performance," 147.

40. Bello and Rosenfeld, *Dragons in Distress*, 15.

41. Bello and Rosenfeld, *Dragons in Distress*, 9.

42. Bello and Rosenfeld, *Dragons in Distress*, 9.

43. John F. Cooper, "Taiwan: A Nation in Transition," *Current History* (April 1989): 174.

44. Cooper, "Taiwan."

45. Frank Gibney, *Korea's Quiet Revolution: From Garrison State to Democracy* (New York: Walker, 1992), 83.

46. Bello and Rosenfeld, *Dragons in Distress*, 43.

47. Cooper, *Taiwan*, 176.

48. Bello and Rosenfeld, *Dragons in Distress*, 21.

49. Clyde Haberman, "Korean Declares 'Sweeping' Change Is the 'Only' Way," *New York Times*, July 5, 1987.

50. David E. Sanger, "Korea's Pick: A Pragmatist," *New York Times*, December 20, 1992.

51. Joseph J. Wright, Jr., "Thailand's Return to Democracy," *Current History* (December 1992): 421–23.

52. Nicholas D. Kristof, "China Sees 'Market-Leninism' as Way to Future," *New York Times*, September 6, 1993.

53. Marshall I. Goldman, "The Future of Soviet Economic Reform," *Current History* (October 1989): 329.

54. Edward C. Cook, "Agriculture's Role in the Soviet Economic Crisis," in *The Disintegration of the Soviet Economic System*, eds. Michael Ellman and Vladimir Kontorovich (London: Routledge, 1992), 199, 200.

55. Michael Ellman, "Money in the 1980s: From Disequilibrium to Collapse," in *The Disintegration of the Soviet Economic System*, 196.

56. Ellman and Kontorovich, *The Disintegration of the Soviet Economic System*, 1; Cook, "Agriculture's Role in the Soviet Economic Crisis," 210.

57. Ruth Sivard, *World Military Expenditures, 1987–88* (Washington, D.C.: World Priorities, 1987), 5, 54–55; Bomnath Sen, "The Economics of Conversion: Transforming Swords to Plowshares," in *Economic Reform in Eastern Europe*, ed. Graham Bird (Brookfield, Vt.: Elgar, 1992), 21.

58. David F. Epstein, "The Economic Cost of Soviet Security and Empire," in *The Impoverished Superpower*, ed. Henry S. Rowen and Charles Wolf, Jr. (San Francisco: Institute for Contemporary Studies, 1990), 153.

59. Alan Smith, *Russia and the World Economy: Problems of Integration* (London: Routledge, 1993), 74, 88–89; Michael T. Klare, *American Arms Supermarket* (Austin: University of Texas Press, 1984), 312.

60. David Gold, "Conversion and Industrial Policy," in *Economic Conversion,* ed. Suzanne Gordon and Dave McFadden (Cambridge, Mass.: Ballinger, 1984), 195.

61. Serge Schememann, "The Sun Has Trouble Setting on the Soviet Empire," *New York Times*, March 10, 1991.

62. Mark Kramer, "Soviet Military Policy," *Current History*, October 1989, p. 351.

63. James Blitz, "Gloom for the Russians in Gulf Weapons Toll," *Sunday Times* (London), March 3, 1991.

64. Blitz, "Gloom for the Russians."

65. Smith, *Russia and the World Economy*, 158.

66. Ellman and Kontorovich, *The Disintegration of the Soviet Economic System*, 25, 114.

67. Stephen White, *After Gorbachev* (Cambridge: Cambridge University Press, 1993), 1–8.

68. Grigorii Khanin, "Economic Growth in the 1980s," in *The Disintegration of the Soviet Economic System*, 29.

69. Ralf Dahrendorf, *Reflections on the Revolution in Europe* (New York: Times Books, 1990), 16.

70. Allister Sparks, "Letter from South Africa: The Secret Revolution," *The New Yorker*, April 11, 1994, 59.

71. Christopher S. Wren, "Mandela, Freed, Urges Step-Up in Pressure to End White Rule," *New York Times*, February 12, 1991.

72. T. C. Moll, "'Probably the Best Lager in the World': The Record and Prospects of the South African Economy," in *Can South Africa Survive? Five Minutes to Midnight*, ed. John D. Brewer (New York: St. Martin's, 1989), 153.

73. Moll, "'Probably the Best Lager in the World,'" 153, 144.

74. Pauline H. Baker, "South Africa on the Move," *Current History* (May 1990): 197.

75. "How Do South Africa Sanctions Work?" *The Economist*, October 14, 1989, p. 45. Baker, "South Africa on the Move," 200.

76. Kevin Danaher and Medea Benjamin, "Great White Hope de Klerk Brings *Glasnost* to Pretoria," *In These Times*, February 7–13, 1990, 10.

77. Baker, "South Africa on the Move," 197.

78. John Darnton, "Africa Tries Democracy, Finding Hope and Peril," *New York Times*, June 21, 1994.

79. Walden Bello and Stephanie Rosenfeld, "Dragons in Distress," *World Policy Journal* 7, no. 3 (1990): 460.

80. Riordan Roett, "Brazil's Transition to Democracy," *Current History* (March 1989): 149.

81. James Brooke, "Peru Rises Up against Red Tape's 400-Year Rule," *New York Times*, August 8, 1989.

82. Steven Greenhouse, "East Europe's Sale of the Century," *New York Times*, May 22, 1990.

83. Eul-Soo Pang and Laura Jarnagin, "Brazil's Catatonic Lambada," *Current History* (February 1991): 75.

84. Stephen Engleberg, "First Sale of State Holdings a Disappointment in Poland," *New York Times*, January 13, 1991; Ferdinand Protzman, "Privatization Is Floundering in East Germany," *New York Times*, March 12, 1991; Peter S. Green, "Bonanza or Bust? Czech Sale of Privatized Assets Fizzles," *New York Times*, December 18, 2001.

85. Peter Passell, "A Capitalist Free-for-All in Czechoslovakia," *New York Times*, April 12, 1992.

86. Daniel N. Nelson, "What End of Warsaw Pact Means," *San Francisco Chronicle*, April 24, 1991.

87. "The World's Shrinking Armies," *New York Times*, May 30, 1994.

88. "The World's Shrinking Armies"; Gary W. Wynia, "Argentina's Economic Reform," *Current History* (February 1991): 59–60.

89. James Brooke, "Latin Armies Are Looking for Work," *New York Times*, March 24, 1991.

90. "The World's Shrinking Armies."

91. A. F. Mullins, Jr., *Born Arming: Development and Military Power in New States* (Stanford, Calif.: Stanford University Press, 1987), 103.

92. Craig R. Whitney, "Western Europe's Dreams Turning Into Nightmares," *New York Times*, August 8, 1993.

93. Roger Cohen, "Spain's Progress Turns to Pain," *New York Times*, November 17, 1992.

94. Cohen, "Spain's Progress Turns to Pain."

95. Cohen, "Spain's Progress Turns to Pain."

96. Nathaniel C. Nash, "Latin American Speedup Leaves Poor in the Dust," *New York Times*, September 7, 1994.

97. Nash, "Latin American Speedup."

98. Silvia Brucan, "Shock Therapy Mauls Those Who Unleashed It in Eastern Europe," *World Paper* (June 1994): 3.

99. Michael Specter, "Climb in Russia's Death Rate Sets Off Population Implosion," *New York Times*, March 6, 1994.

100. Michael Burawoy, "Reply," *Contemporary Sociology* 23 (January 1994): 166.

101. Burawoy, "Reply."

102. Lenore B. Goldman, "To Act without 'Isms': Women in East Central Europe and Russia," in *The Gendered New World Order: Militarism, Development, and the Environment*, ed. Jennifer Turpin and Lois Ann Lorentzen (London: Routledge, 1996), 41.

103. Alan B. Krueger, "Economic Scene: Legal Reform Is What the Old Soviet Bloc Needs to Put It on the Path to Growth," *New York Times*, March 29, 2001.

104. "Study Finds Poverty Deepening in Former Communist Countries," *New York Times*, October 12, 2000.

105. Steven Erlanger, "Birthrate Dips in Ex-Communist Countries," *New York Times*, May 4, 2000.

106. Erlanger, "Birthrate Dips."

107. James Brooke, "A Soldier Turned Politician Wants to Give Brazil Back to Army Rule," *New York Times*, July 25, 1993.

12

Division and War in Yugoslavia

B etween 1974 and 1994, economic and political crises forced dictators to surrender power in more than thirty countries around the world.[1] These economic crises had different regional origins: oil embargo in Southern Europe, debt in Latin America, slowed growth in East Asia, stagnation in the Soviet Union and Eastern Europe, and trade embargo in South Africa (see chapter 11). For most dictators, capitalist and communist alike, economic crisis was compounded by the political turmoil associated with the death of a dictator, defeat in war, popular protest, withdrawal of superpower support, or electoral defeat. When economic and political crises joined, dictators transferred power to civilian successors, who then rewrote constitutions, held multi-party elections, restored civil society, and moved to address the economic problems that precipitated crisis. Remarkably, the dramatic political and economic change that accompanied democratization was, for the most part, peacefully accomplished.

Like many other states in recent years, Yugoslavia also democratized, meaning that political power was extended to people who had not previously participated in political decision making. But even though political power was more widely shared, it was simultaneously narrowed because Yugoslavia also divided during this process, and the political powers of the unitary state (Yugoslavia) were redistributed between successor republics (Slovenia, Croatia, Bosnia-Herzegovina, Macedonia, and Serbia, which kept the name "Yugoslavia"). Some of these independent republics (Slovenia) were more "democratic" than others (Croatia, Serbia). In Yugoslavia, democratization did not necessarily result in "democracy," with fully functioning constitutional institutions, a free media, an independent judiciary, and a vigorous civil society. But whatever its limits, the partial and sometimes halting democratization of parts of Yugoslavia during the 1990s occurred for many of the same reasons that it did elsewhere: economic and political crisis combined to create political change. Unlike that in most other states, however, democratization in Yugoslavia was *also* accompanied by division, which was uncommon, *and* by war, which was rare. From a global comparative perspective, events in Yugoslavia illustrate both the exception (division and war) and the rule (democratization).

Many scholars have argued that Yugoslavia was exceptional because indigenous ethnic conflict was too strong and foreign diplomacy too weak to ensure peaceful conformity with democratizing norms.[2] I take a different view, arguing, first, that Yugoslavia, like other states, democratized in response to common economic and political problems and, second, that the unconventional results of democratization were largely a product of the communist regime's postwar principles and practices, which facilitated division and legitimized war. Although the multisided conflicts that erupted in the 1990s took an ethnic-religious form, they did not *begin* as ethnic conflict. Instead, they grew out of conflicts between factions of the communist party that struggled for power after Tito died. (Joseph Broz Tito, a communist guerilla leader against the Nazis during World War II, established a communist regime after the war and ran it until his death in 1980.) To explain why democratization in Yugoslavia was accompanied by division and war, it is necessary to examine economic, political, and military developments since 1941, using comparisons with other states to bring the common and exceptional character of Yugoslavia into relief.

ECONOMIC DEVELOPMENT
AND DIFFERENTIATION

Although Yugoslavia's postwar economic policies are regarded as unique among socialist countries, they were actually quite similar to those of other states in southern Europe. In economic terms, the policies adopted by Tito's communist regime closely resembled those adopted by fascist regimes in Spain, Portugal, and Greece between 1945 and 1974 and those adopted by military dictatorships in Latin America and communist regimes in Eastern Europe after 1974.

Throughout the postwar period, Yugoslavia, like Iberian and Ionian states, ran persistent trade deficits because its export industries were too weak to pay for the imports the country needed.[3] Trade deficits are typically a problem because they deplete monetary reserves, force currency devaluations, reduce imports, and slow the industries that rely on imports. This was a particular problem for southern European countries whose industries needed imported energy to survive. Without some way to pay for imports, southern European states would have been unable to recover from civil war or wartime destruction and spur economic growth, which would have undermined their political authority.[4] As it happened, they were all able to mitigate their persistent trade deficits because they received large infusions of U.S. economic and military aid in the 1940s and 1950s, and then they adopted policies that produced income from the import of tourists and the export of domestic workers in the 1960s.

In the late 1940s, U.S. and European aid enabled Yugoslavia to close trade deficits and promote economic growth. U.S. officials were at first unwilling to provide aid either to fascist dictatorship in Spain or to the communist dictatorship in Yugoslavia after the war. But as U.S.-Soviet conflict sharpened, U.S. officials reconsidered and began providing aid to dictatorships on its side of the cold war divide.[5] After Yugoslavia broke with the Soviet Union in 1948, the U.S. government released frozen Yugoslav assets, including $47 million in gold, and later provided Tito's regime with loans, grants, and military aid in concert with aid from the World Bank and U.S. allies in Western Europe.[6] Between 1951 and 1960, "the United States extended to Yugoslavia $2.7 billion worth of military and economic assistance on a non-repayable basis," somewhat more than it provided to regimes in Spain, Portugal, and Greece in the same period.[7] This influx of foreign aid promoted double-digit economic growth in Yugoslavia, as it did in Iberia and Ionia, during the 1950s.[8] Economic recovery and growth was also assisted by the normalization of Yugoslavia's trade relations with the Soviet Union and Eastern Europe after Khrushchev repaired Soviet relations with Tito in 1955.[9]

But generous U.S. aid did not continue into the 1960s. As cold war tensions eased in the late 1950s, the United States discontinued military aid to Yugoslavia and reduced financial aid, as it did in Spain and Greece, and balance of payment difficulties reemerged as a problem.[10] As it happened, communist and capitalist regimes in Yugoslavia, Spain, Portugal, and Greece all discovered they could solve their problems by exporting workers and importing tourists. Income from the remittances of southern European workers employed in Western Europe, and money from Western European workers who spent their savings on holidays in southern Europe, provided regimes with the hard currency they needed to promote economic growth and create domestic jobs. Earnings from émigré workers and vacationing tourists "made it possible [for these countries] to realize . . . rapid growth without running up against the balance of payments problems that bring growth to a grinding halt in most poor countries."[11]

While this economic strategy was called different things— "market fascism" in Spain, and "market socialism" in Yugoslavia—it was in fact a common economic policy.[12] It was pursued with varying degrees of success by regimes in all four countries because they possessed a plentiful supply of workers, recently released from agriculture, and an abundant supply of sunny beaches, which they could mine for the tourist trade. By the early 1970s, Spain, Portugal, Yugoslavia, and Greece each had nearly one million workers employed in Western Europe, and they returned nearly $1 billion in remittances annually.[13] This income provided hard currency for the government and income for worker households, which used money from relatives to build houses and start businesses, thereby promoting local development.[14]

Although southern European states exported workers at about the same rate, which provided comparable remittance income, they were not equally successful at importing tourists. Spain far outpaced the others. The number of tourists visiting Spain increased from half a million in 1950 to thirty-four million in 1973—more people visited Spain than lived in Spain—and tourist receipts contributed $3.3 billion to the economy in 1971.[15] In Yugoslavia, by contrast, the number of tourists grew from forty-one thousand in 1950 to six million in 1973, and they poured about $470 million into the economy.[16] Yugoslavia also relied more on Eastern European tourists, who spent less and paid in soft currencies.[17] In Yugoslavia, as in Spain, the regime assisted tourism by devaluing its currency (the dinar) by half in 1965, making Yugoslavia a cheap vacation destination for tourists.[18]

This development strategy had important economic consequences in Yugoslavia. The government lifted the labor controls common in other communist states and allowed workers and businesses to keep some hard currency earnings, which they could use for savings, consumption, and investment.[19] By giving workers and businesses considerable control over economic decisions and by promoting self-management in state-controlled firms, the government provided incentives that helped increase productivity and promote development. As a result, Yugoslavia, like Spain, Portugal, and Greece, recorded rapid rates of growth in the 1960s and early 1970s.[20]

In 1973–1974, global economic developments brought an end to development based on the export and import of workers. Rising world food and energy prices triggered a recession in Western Europe, bringing an end to the decades-long economic boom (see chapter 2). Faced with rising domestic unemployment, West Germany and other worker-importing states began returning workers to southern Europe, and as many as one-third of Yugoslav workers returned in the next decade, reducing remittance income and increasing domestic unemployment.[21] Moreover, because recession, rising inflation, and unemployment in Western Europe reduced incomes generally, fewer Western European workers vacationed in southern Europe, thereby reducing tourist receipts in Yugoslavia.

This shared economic crisis was joined in Portugal, Greece, and Spain by political crises. In Portugal, military defeat in its African colonies triggered a military revolt; in Greece, military defeat in Cyprus led to mutiny and the dissolution of the junta; in Spain, the death of Franco (and assassination of his political heir, Admiral Carrero Blanco) created a succession crisis. Simultaneous economic and political crises proved fatal for regimes in these countries, but not in Yugoslavia. There the regime survived because Tito remained in power and used his considerable personal authority to deflect potential political crises.[22] It survived also because the regime, like capitalist dictatorships throughout Latin America and communist regimes in Eastern Europe, borrowed heavily to replace lost revenue and finance continued development.[23] Yugoslavia's debt doubled between 1971 and 1975, from $2.7 billion to $5.8 billion, and then rocketed to $20.5 billion by 1981.[24] Indebted development in Yugoslavia deferred incipient crisis and promoted economic growth in the 1970s, as it did elsewhere. But economic crisis returned in 1979, when the United States raised interest rates (see chapter 4). This measure increased borrower interest payments because loans had been tied to floating rates, and it reduced borrower incomes because high interest rates also triggered a recession, which lowered demand for their goods.[25] The onset of renewed economic crisis in 1979–1980 was then joined in Yugoslavia by the political crisis that ensued after Tito's death in 1980.

During the 1980s, lenders forced dictators in Latin America, Eastern Europe, and post-Tito Yugoslavia to make strenuous efforts to repay their debts (see chapter 5). In Yugoslavia, as elsewhere, this meant devaluing the currency to increase exports, reducing imports, and creating trade surpluses to provide the hard currency they needed to repay debt. It also meant curbing government spending—eliminating jobs and cutting food, transportation, and energy subsidies—and raising taxes to create budget surpluses that could be used to repay debt.[26] In Yugoslavia, "structural adjustment" resulted in widespread shortages of imported goods and energy, recession, rising unemployment, falling real wages and declining rates of growth.[27] Between 1985 and 1988, per capita GNP had declined from U.S. $3,000 to $2,400, and in 1991 the World Bank predicted that Yugoslavia would not regain 1989 income levels for more than a decade.[28]

In many countries, the debt crisis was a collective evil, joining different social groups in a common misery. Economic crisis typically joined them against a common political foe: the regimes whose heavy borrowing had made them vulnerable to global economic change. But in Yugoslavia, the debt crisis produced *different* results. Growing economic misery drove people in *opposite* political directions.

The response to the debt crisis in Yugoslavia was different because the regime's postwar development policies had divided Yugoslavia economically. At the beginning of the postwar period, economic development in Yugoslavia was unevenly distributed. But the regime's adoption of a worker-export, tourist-import development strategy in the 1960s exacerbated economic differences. Because most of the workers who migrated to Western Europe were from Slovenia and Croatia, the money they remitted provided hard currency and economic benefits to households and businesses in *these* regions.[29] And because Slovenia, Croatia, and the Dalmatian coast were the primary destinations for tourists, workers and businesses there were the principal beneficiaries of the tourist trade and the hard-currency earnings associated with it. There was also a synergy between the two: worker remittances helped finance private tourist industry businesses for households in these regions.

Of course, the government recognized that its development strategy contributed to uneven development. So it used various mechanisms and institutions—hard-currency regulations, the development fund—to redistribute the income, hard currency and wealth earned in the prosperous republics to the poorer republics: Bosnia, Serbia, and Macedonia.[30] But the economic gap between rich and poor republics widened nonetheless.[31] Other economic developments also contributed to economic differentiation. Currency devaluations—rapid ones in 1965 and 1981–1983, and a slow one between 1975 and 1981—were generally good for the prosperous republics but bad for the poor ones. Meanwhile, ongoing inflation, which was bad for everyone, was generally worse for people in the poor republics.[32]

As a result of the regime's domestic economic policies, the gap between prosperous (Croatia and Slovenia) and poor republics (Bosnia, Macedonia, and Serbia) grew wider during the postwar period, particularly after 1965.[33] The prosperous republics had higher incomes and lower unemployment than the poor ones: "In 1947 the per capita social product in Slovenia was 2.4 times higher than in Kosovo, while in 1974 it was over 6 times higher."[34] Put another way, "the gross social product per capita of the Republic of Slovenia . . . roughly approximates that of central Italy, while [that] of the autonomous province of Kosovo is comparable to that of Congo (Brazzaville), Ghana, or Liberia."[35]

In the 1980s, the political response to the debt crisis varied by region. People in the prosperous republics wanted to keep what they earned from remittances and tourism and use these resources to weather the crisis. They *resisted* redistributive policies that siphoned off their income to the poorer republics.[36] They saw economic advantage in political *separatism*.[37] As one Croatian hotelier explained, "The best thing is for us to live together with the Serbs, but with separate governments and separate accounting books. If the books could be kept separate, then I think we would get along."[38] Meanwhile, people in the poorer republics wanted to *keep* redistributive policies and institutions intact so they could use the resources provided by the central government to weather the storm.[39] They saw economic advantage in political *unionism*. As a result, leaders in the prosperous republics began refusing to share their wealth; leaders in the poor republics began demanding that wealth be redistributed.[40] Because Communist Party leaders in different republics each saw economic advantage in different political solutions, economic crisis contributed to political crisis.

Like its postwar development policy, the regime's postwar political policies also contributed to conflict after Tito died.

REPUBLICAN POLITICS

During the postwar period, the regime adopted foreign and domestic principles and policies that facilitated a struggle for power between Communist Party factions based in the republics after Tito died. These policies grew out of Tito's attempt to address foreign and domestic problems.

Tito's communist regime came to power after the war largely as a result of its own efforts. In this regard, it was different from communist regimes in Eastern Europe, which were installed by the Soviets, but similar to communists who achieved postwar independence on their own initiative in China and in Vietnam. The determination of communist leaders in Yugoslavia (Tito) and China (Mao) to act independently brought them into conflict with the Soviet Union, which wanted to subordinate them to Soviet diplomacy.[41] Stalin's determination to crush Yugoslav insubordination prompted him to break with Tito in 1948, forcing Tito to reassert Yugoslav "nationalism" as his regime's defense against domestic and foreign "internationalists [Stalinists]."[42]

To prevent Yugoslavia from being isolated, a position that would make it vulnerable to his domestic competitors and foreign opponents, Tito purged the communist party in Yugoslavia of domestic rivals, requested U.S. economic and military aid, and then joined with leaders of postcolonial states that were, like Yugoslavia, seeking to maintain an independent foreign policy as cold war spheres hardened around them. Tito's decision to join with India and Egypt to promote "nonalignment" was an important initiative because it provided a collective defense against superpower intervention and gave them, and later others, the opportunity to fashion independent foreign policies. Tito, India's Pandit Nehru, and Egypt's Gamal Nasser made an unlikely trio, given the fact that they arrived at a common destination—nonalignment—from different directions. Yugoslavia had broken away from the Soviet sphere (*de*aligned); Egypt had broken away from the U.S. sphere and joined the Soviet sphere (*re*aligned); and India had refused to join either sphere (*non*aligned).[43] Although they came from different directions, they could agree on the need for two principles: self-determination and nonalignment. They supported self-determination, by which they meant the right of nations to secede from colonial empires, because they believed that a growing of independent states would help safeguard their own independence.[44] And they supported nonalignment to prevent newly independent, postcolonial states from being forcibly incorporated into superpower spheres of influence.[45] "There is no justification at all for the view that small nations must jump into the mouth of this [Soviet] or that [U.S.] shark," one Yugoslav official explained.[46]

By developing foreign policies that promoted self-determination, Tito's regime would later help legitimize domestic demands for self-determination. This was reinforced by domestic policies that legitimized secession and delegated considerable political power to Yugoslavia's constituent republics.

The devolution of central political authority took place in stages, and for different reasons, during the postwar period. The adoption of constitutional provisions granting the right of self-determination and of secession by constituent republics was consistent with prewar, Communist Party programs and modeled after Soviet constitutional provisions.[47] The Soviet Union, Czechoslovakia, and Yugoslavia all had federal constitutions that allowed constituent republics the right to self-determination. Communist leaders did not expect the republics to exercise this right but gave it to them as a matter of principle. Of course, when communist parties fell, leaders of republics in all three countries exercised their constitutional rights and demanded states of their own. So democratization in all three states was also accompanied by division. Constitutional provisions adopted by communist regimes played an important role in these developments.

After Yugoslavia broke with the Soviet Union in 1948, Tito devolved considerable economic and political power to the republics in the 1950s and 1060s. He evidently did so for several reasons. First, he wanted to distinguish the Yugoslav "model" from other centralist, Soviet models, which enhanced the regime's international credibility with other nationalist movements. Second, he wanted to prevent a resurgence of "Serbian hegemony," which he saw as a defect of the royalist state before the war. Third, he wanted to prevent rivals such as Djilas and Rankovic from using central institutions to mount a challenge to his authority. And finally, he wanted to promote the regime's developmentalist strategy, which was regionally based.[48] The constitutional revisions of 1971 and 1974, which devolved even power to the constituent republics, were introduced in response to try to meet Croatian demands in 1970–1971 for greater autonomy and to create institutions that could survive Tito's death.[49] Because he had worked assiduously throughout the postwar period to prevent the emergence of political rivals, Tito could designate no heir. As an alternative, he divided his legacy among multiple estates.[50]

During the postwar period, Tito developed a foreign policy that cherished independence, promoted self-determination, and advance nonalignment. He simultaneously adopted domestic political policies that legitimized secession, promoted regional autarky, and provided for the creation of relatively autonomous political institutions in the constituent republics. While the economy was growing and Tito was still alive, these ideas and institutions functioned well, providing an alternative model of socialist economic and political development that contrasted sharply with Soviet and Chinese centralist models. But when debt crisis struck and Tito died, the conditions that made this model function disappeared.

After Tito's death, a succession crisis ensued. As we have seen, this was a common problem in regimes where dictators died: China, South Korea, North Korea, Taiwan, and the Soviet Union. But the succession crisis in Yugoslavia most closely resembled the crisis that followed Brezhnev's death in 1982, mainly because in both Yugoslavia and the Soviet Union, potential successors representing factions of the communist party used their political bases in the constituent republics to struggle for power.[51] In both cases, communists or former communists used the regime's political values (self-determination) and constitutional principles (the right of secession) to legitimize their demands for separate political authority. They used political institutions in the republics to establish alternative political authority, capitalized on their opposition to central government austerity programs to organize political support, and made ethnonational appeals to construct a "popular front" or multiclass alliance that could contest for power on their own terms. In the Soviet Union and in Yugoslavia, the political struggle in the republics was initiated by factions of the *Communist* Party, though some noncommunist dissident groups effectively participated in some republics (Slovenia and Croatia; Lithuania). So in both countries, roads to independence in separate states were paved by central government policies.

In Yugoslavia, the contest between Tito's successors within the communist party became a struggle between successors in constituent republics, as factions abandoned Communist Party labels and affiliations identified with the center and created "nationalist" parties based on ethnic-religious identities in the republics.[52] The creation of national and ethnic identities by communist party factions began in Serbia, where Sloboban Milosevic used nationalist-ethnic appeals to bid for power within the Serbian League of Communists and then demanded that Serbia obtain a greater share of power in the post-Tito state. But this antagonized factions based in other republics. So they began demanding greater political and economic autonomy on behalf of ethnic groups in different republics.[53] As a result of their separate efforts, Yugoslavia democratized and also divided. Because the regime's ideas and institutions facilitated power struggles between communist party factions based in the republics, the struggle for secession ended in the division of power. Ironically, factions in the 1980s-1990s inadvertently realized the Communist Party program of the late 1920s, when the party supported the right of self-determination for constituent nations and advocated the dissolution of the royalist state.[54] "Long live independent Croatia, Macedonia, Montenegro, Bosnia, Vjvodina and Serbia," the Communist Party proclaimed in the 1920s.[55] With minor changes, this slogan essentially became the program adopted by Communist Party factions in the 1980s and 1990s.

SETTING THE STAGE FOR WAR

In Yugoslavia, the economic and political crises of the 1980s led to democratization and division in the 1990s, as it did in the Soviet Union and Czechoslovakia. But why, in Yugoslavia, did it also lead to war? Democratization and division in Yugoslavia resulted in war for several reasons. First, the regime's celebration of civil war in the 1940s legitimized violence. Second, Tito's military policy, which grew out of the regime's wartime experience in the 1940s, made it possible for individuals and republics to wage civil and uncivil war. Third, the central government's popularity and the army's military strength made it possible for these institutions to fight rather than surrender quietly, as they did across most of Eastern Europe during this period.

Political scientists have often said that war contributes to state building. This was certainly true in Yugoslavia. The communist party's successful partisan war against Axis invaders and its civil war against domestic fascist and royalist opponents during World War II enabled it to win state power and establish a socialist state.[56] It wartime efforts enabled Tito and the communist party to defeat domestic opponents, win both U.S. and Soviet support, establish an independent communist state, survive a break with the Soviet Union (the party's war record enabled it to garner widespread public support in its confrontation with the Soviet Union and also deter Soviet invasion after the break), and establish the regime as a credible independent force in international diplomacy.[57] The party's military effort during the war contributed directly to its postwar success. So it is not surprising that the regime celebrated partisan civil war— memorializing it as a heroic, purposeful activity—despite the fact that communist guerillas had waged a ruthless partisan war and, at war's end, mercilessly slaughtered disarmed opponents.[58]

But the regime's celebration and memorialization of partisan civil war created two problems. First, it antagonized groups who were defeated in war (particularly in Croatia), cultivating bitterness among people who continued to reside in postwar Yugoslavia. Second, and perhaps more important, it sanctioned state violence and legitimized the kinds of violence associated with brutal partisan war. Sociologists have found that when states legitimize *official* violence, they often encourage *private*, unofficial violence. For example, in their study on the relation between war and homicide, sociologists Dane Archer and Rosemary Gartner found that homicide rates *increased* in states that waged war, particularly in victorious states that sustained heavy combat losses.[59] They explained this phenomenon by arguing "that wars do tend to legitimate the general use of violence in domestic society" because they teach "the unmistakable moral lesson that homicide is an acceptable, even praiseworthy, means to certain ends . . . [a] lesson [that] will not be lost on at least some of the citizens in a warring nation."[60] They noted that murder rates *rarely* rose in countries defeated in war, arguing that because civilians in these countries viewed war as senseless, not purposeful, public defeat effectively discouraged private acts of violence.[61] By analogy, the Yugoslav regime's decades-long memorialization of its brutal partisan war may have effectively legitimized civil war as a means of settling disputes in the 1990s.

Of course, other regimes also celebrated formative civil wars. In Spain, Franco long memorialized the Spanish Civil War. But when Spain democratized after Franco's death, civil war did not reignite, though Spanish elites were extremely worried that it might. The threat of renewed civil war became a kind of "virtual reality" for Spanish participants in the democratization process.[62] But while civil war did not recur in Spain, it did erupt in Yugoslavia. The comparison is instructive because in both Spain and Yugoslavia, civil wars during the 1930s and 1940s joined fascists, royalists, and republicans in brutal, multisided wars for state power.

But democratization was not accompanied by civil war in Spain, as it was in Yugoslavia, in part because Franco's portrayal of civil war as heroic and purposeful had, over time, been discredited by its association with fascism. This was not the case for the victors in Yugoslavia, who did not have their victory impugned by others. Instead, their success was acclaimed by others because communists in Yugoslavia had fought to defeat fascist invaders. Postwar attitudes helped *de*legitimize civil war in Spain but *legitimize* it in Yugoslavia. Moreover, Tito's successors helped rationalize civil war. Franjo Tudjman's efforts to rehabilitate Croatian fascists (Ustashe) effectively legitimated civil war for ethnic groups that had been "defeated" during World War II.[63] By trying to get rid of the "Ustashe complex," Tudjman legitimized civil war as a purposeful activity for Croats, much as Tito's regime had already done for non-Croatian populations. Slobodan Milosevic, meanwhile, took steps to legitimize violence for Serbs, arguing that "nobody is going to beat these people [Serbs]."[64]

Tito's regime not only legitimized civil war, it adopted policies that *prepared* people to wage war. In the late 1950s, the regime adopted partisan war, what it called "General People's Defense," as an important part of its military strategy. The government took steps to conscript, train, and arm civilians for service not only in the regular army but also in territorial defense forces based in the republics and in local militias, which were expected to wage guerrilla war against foreign invaders.[65] The regime first adopted and later extended these practices for several reasons. First, the regime had used partisan war as an effective weapon against fascist invasion during World War II, so it seemed a promising strategy. Second, it feared an invasion by the Soviet Union. Successive Soviet invasions of Hungary (1956), Czechoslovakia (1968), and Afghanistan (1979) reinforced its fears of Soviet invasion. Military leaders in Yugoslavia recognized that the Yugoslav army could not alone withstand a massive and sudden assault by Soviet forces and thought that an armed nation, guerilla approach to defense might have more success against invading armies.[66] So the regime distributed military weapons and communication equipment widely, creating a well-trained and heavily armed militias across the country.[67] As Adam Roberts predicted in 1986, "the Yugoslav defense system rests on fragile social and political foundations. If those foundations fail, the idea of General People's Defense might be quickly forgotten; or, worse, it might be perversely misused for civil war."[68] As it happened, the regime's military policies prepared militias, based in different republics, to wage war on their own initiative.

Still, civil war might not have erupted had the army decided not engage militias in the republics and forcibly contest the division of power. After all, the Soviet military decided, during an attempted coup against Gorbachev, *not* to contest the dissolution of the Soviet state or initiate a civil war (though localized civil wars did erupt in a few successor states: Armenia, Azerbaijan, Georgia, and Chechnya, which was part of Russia). The Yugoslav army might have retired after its initial forays were rebuffed by militias in Slovenia and Croatia. Why did the central government, which was based in Belgrade under Milosevic's authority, and the army together wage war to contest the dissolution of the Yugoslav state? They did because the regime's residual popularity and the army's military strength made it possible for them to fight rather than surrender quietly, as they did in most of Eastern Europe.

Most of the communist parties in Eastern Europe had been installed by the Soviet Union. If their leaders did not serve the Soviet Union, they were replaced, sometimes by force. This made them deeply unpopular with domestic populations. When crisis struck, regimes could rely on only a narrow base of domestic support, and on the Soviet army, which was based in their countries. But when Gorbachev withdrew Soviet military support, dictators faced the crisis alone, and the appearance of even small opposition movements were sufficiently strong to force them from power.

In Yugoslavia, by contrast, the regime had defeated foreign invaders and domestic opponents, coming to power without Soviet assistance. It had developed an independent foreign policy. And it had promoted domestic economic development that provided real, though unequal, benefits to its citizenry. When crisis struck, Tito's successors in Belgrade could count on a considerable reservoir of domestic political support, particularly in Serbia, the largest of the five republics. In comparative terms, the regime in Yugoslavia closely resembled communist regimes in China, Vietnam, and Cuba, where dictators had defeated domestic opponents and foreign foes, and developed foreign and domestic policies that won the support of important sections of the population, particularly the large rural peasantry. When economic crisis struck, these regimes survived, while neighboring dictatorships did not, largely because they could draw on substantial domestic support and, in the last resort, count on the army.[69]

In Yugoslavia, central authority remained fairly strong, largely because it enjoyed considerable popular support, and much of the army remained loyal, largely because its leadership consisted of pro–central government Serbs.[70] Moreover, the army itself enjoyed considerable prestige, having served with distinction as part of UN peacekeeping forces around the world.[71] Unlike the Soviet army, which had been defeated in Afghanistan, the Yugoslav army's credibility and willingness to fight had not been undermined by defeat. Moreover, because the Belgrade–Milosevic regime and the army could claim to defend minority interests outside the boundaries of the residual Yugoslav state—Serbs living in Croatia and Bosnia—they could legitimize their aggressive efforts to prevent Communist Party factions from seceding and establishing separate states in the republics.[72] Political popularity and military strength, two legacies of Tito's postwar policies, stiffened the central government's determination to fight. As in China, the central government in Yugoslavia was strong enough to resist. But unlike China, it was not strong enough to win outright. Milosevic and the army could not reassert central authority throughout Yugoslavia because support for the regime was more narrowly based in geographic and ethnic terms than it was in China, it could count only on Serbian, Montenegrin, and Serb minority populations in some other republics. Moreover, because the opponents of central government were better organized and more heavily armed than they were in China, and these opponents could count on financial and political support from émigré communities, particularly from Croatian ones in Germany and the United States, and from foreign states, first Germany and later the United States.[73] These developments legitimized violence and prepared people to wage uncivil war. When economic and political crises joined, they did just that.

The argument here is that the regime's economic policies resulted in uneven development and promoted opposing political responses to the economic crisis of the 1980s. The devolution of central power to political institutions in the republics gave Tito's successors the means to struggle for power on their own terms, while the regime's celebration of partisan war and its adoption as military doctrine legitimized and prepared factions to wage civil war. Moreover, the regime's foreign and domestic policies gave it a strength that few other dictatorships possessed, giving Tito's successors in Belgrade the determination and ability to resist the division and dissolution of their authority. As a result of these developments, civil wars erupted across the region during the 1990s.

UNCIVIL WARS

Division in Yugoslavia was accompanied by a series of civil, or rather *un*civil, wars. To understand the course of different wars and appreciate their consequences for people in the region, it is useful to conceptualize them as consisting of five successive, related "rounds." Each of these rounds were identified, more or less, with ethnic conflicts in different regions: round 1 in Slovenia, round 2 in Croatia, round 3 in Bosnia-Herzegovina, round 4 in Kosovo, and round 5 in Macedonia.

Round 1: Slovenia

In 1991, war briefly erupted between the central government of Yugoslavia, based in Belgrade, and the breakaway republic of Slovenia. The central government was controlled by Slobodan Milosevic, leader of the Communist Party faction based in Serbia. He used government troops under his control to try to prevent leaders in Slovenia from declaring their independence and withdrawing from Yugoslavia. Militias in Slovenia mobilized to fight Yugoslav army detachments and forced them to withdraw after brief fighting. The ten-day war in June resulted in the death of forty-six soldiers from both sides, a number that would seem miniscule in the wars that soon followed.[74]

Slovenia was fortunate that the war was brief. It was also fortunate in other respects. The government, which had come to power in multiparty democratic elections, was able to secure international recognition for an independent Slovenia and establish amicable relations with its neighbors. European and Austrian firms invested in the economy and helped boost incomes and living standards, in what was already the most prosperous republic in Yugoslavia. Unlike other breakaway republics, there were no large, non-Slovenian minorities who objected to the creation of an independent Slovenia, and the Slovene majority proved relatively tolerant of German-speaking, Italian-speaking, and Croatian minorities.[75]

Round 2: Croatia

In the summer of 1991, war broke out in Croatia. The fighting pitted the breakaway Croatian government led by Franjo Tudjman against the large Serb minority living in Croatia, which was supported by Yugoslav army forces and the Milosevic government in Belgrade. The Croatian government was determined to withdraw from Yugoslavia and create an independent state for the Croat-Catholic majority. It was also determined not to let the Serbian-Orthodox minority play an important role in shaping the new state, arguing that the benefits of citizenship should be reserved for Croats not Serbs.[76] The Serb minority boycotted the referendum on independence and, after it passed, announced that they would secede from secessionist Croatia and form a Serb state of their own.

Because the Croatian government defined the new republic in ethnic terms and used elections to consolidate political power for the ethnic majority, and the Serb minority mobilized ethnic identities to contest electoral results, the conflict rapidly assumed a violent *ethnic* character. Serbian militias and Yugoslav army units in Croatia attacked government forces and Croatian civilians in the regions, attempting to drive them out of the area so they could create ethnically homogeneous enclaves in eastern Croatia and the western, Krajina region. The massacre, rape, and destruction associated with "ethnic cleansing" as it came to be called, prompted retaliation in kind by the Croatian government, so the conflict deepened and intensified. Serb forces pushed government forces and civilians out of most of eastern Croatia and much of the Krajina during the next two years of heavy fighting. Thousands of soldiers and civilians were killed and wounded, and hundreds of thousands were displaced as refugees by the fighting.[77]

The fighting paused for several years as war shifted into Bosnia, but resumed in Croatia in 1996, when Croatian central government forces, with some U.S. military assistance and encouragement, assaulted minority Serb enclaves in the Krajina region.[78] The Croatian government reasserted its control in many areas, driving hundreds of thousands of Serbs out of Croatian and into Serbia and Serb-controlled Bosnia.[79]

The outbreak of war in Croatia decisively shaped its political and economic institutions. Although Tudjman came to power in multiparty elections, he assumed dictatorial control of the government and media, and used control of key economic sectors and foreign aid to benefit an elite group of political supporters and enrich his own family.[80] The economy sagged and foreign debt sky-rocketed during the 1990s, leaving the country independent but impoverished.

Round 3: Bosnia

In 1992, a multi-sided war broke out in Bosnia. The war, which continued until a peace agreement was reached in 1995, joined three different ethnic groups in a brutal struggle. Initially, the war pitted the Bosnian government, which represented the Muslim population (43 percent of residents) in the breakaway republic, against the Croatian–Bosnian minority (17 percent) supported by Tudjman's Croatian government, *and* the Serbian-Bosnian minority (31 percent) supported by Milosevic's Serbian government in Belgrade.[81] For a time, minority Croatian and Serbian forces battled to divide Bosnia between them. But in 1994, Croatian–Bosnian forces joined in a tenuous alliance with the Bosnian Muslim government against the Serbs and their allies.[82]

Fighting erupted in early 1992 after the Bosnian government held a referendum on independence. Croat and Serb minorities boycotted the election and announced they would secede from the secessionist state.[83] Again, Serb militias supported by regular army units from Yugoslavia made extensive gains, driving Bosnian soldiers and civilians from Serb territory in a brutal campaign of ethnic cleansing, and laid siege to Sarajevo, the Bosnian capital. Croatian militias, meanwhile, consolidated their control of Croatian enclaves, using similar tactics.

Appalled by ethnic cleansing and the siege of Sarajevo, the international community imposed economic sanctions against the Serbian government in Belgrade, sent UN peacekeeping forces to protect some Bosnian enclaves and monitor local cease-fires, and began providing some economic and diplomatic assistance to the Bosnian government.[84] Muslim soldiers recruited from Iran and other Muslim countries traveled to Bosnia to join the fighting on the Bosnian government's behalf.[85] But international efforts did little to stop the fighting, which resulted in tens of thousands of deaths, the rape of thousands of women, and the forcible relocation of hundreds of thousands more.

In 1995, events persuaded the UN and NATO to take more serious measures. After Serb forces shelled civilians at a market in Sarajevo, and then massacred more than seven thousand unarmed Muslim men from the town of Srebrenica, NATO forces began bombing Serb positions to lift the siege of Sarajevo, expand the territories under the control of the Bosnian government and their Croatian–Bosnian allies, and force the Bosnian Serbs and their Yugoslav allies to the bargaining table.[86] NATO's military campaign brought a halt to the fighting in October 1995 and the opening of negotiations in Dayton, Ohio, one month later.[87]

At Dayton, the various parties agreed to create a "unified" Bosnia composed of two parts: the Federation of Bosnia and Herzegovina (a Muslim and Croat political unit) and the Republika Srpska (a Serb political unit). The central government assumed responsibility for foreign and economic policy, but the two units would govern regions under their control. NATO, meanwhile, agreed to provide thousands of peacekeeping forces (U.S., British, and French forces took charge of security in different regions) and ensure adherence to the peace accord by all parties.[88] The NATO-appointed "high representative" was assigned ultimate authority, as a "friendly arbitrator" under the accord.[89] As High Representative Carlos Westendorp explained, "I will put an end to all that endless decision making. . . . If the parties do not agree, I will tell them, no problem. I will make the decision for them. . . . And if they systematically block Dayton, I will ask those who are not cooperating to resign."[90]

While the Dayton accords brought an end to the fighting, it also led to the creation of two parastates whose leaders do little to cooperate on economic, political, or social problems. Although each zone conducts multiparty elections, the victors have, for the most part, been ethnic nationalists. Most of the money earmarked for reconstruction has gone to the Bosnian government, widening an economic divide between Bosnian- and Serb-controlled regions. Few refugees have returned to homes in regions controlled by different ethnic groups, and resettlement has been difficult. If NATO troops are withdrawn and foreign economic aid reduced, most observers expect that fighting among the three groups will resume and that the country will be more rigorously partitioned.

Round 4: Kosovo

In Kosovo, conflict grew slowly before erupting in large-scale violence in 1997–1998, which triggered NATO intervention and a wider war in 1999.

In Kosovo, a province of Serbia, the Albanian Muslim majority (80 percent) possessed considerable autonomy until 1987, when the Milosevic government in Serbia stripped the province of its autonomous status, dismissed many Muslims from government jobs, and reasserted Serb control of the region.[91] A nonviolent movement of Albanian Muslims in Kosovo (Kosovars) organized to protest Serb policies in 1992, and the Kosovo Liberation Army (KLA) was created in 1996 to contest Serb authority by force. But the KLA remained small and ineffective until 1997, when events in Albania contributed to the escalation of conflict in Kosovo and, later, to the outbreak of war in Macedonia.

Albania, a small country adjacent to Kosovo, was run by a communist dictatorship until it collapsed in 1992. Like Kosovo, most of its inhabitants are Albanian-speaking Muslims. And like Kosovo, it is extremely poor. In the 1990s, the Albanian economy functioned only because workers who fled the country after the collapse of communism sent money home.[92] Then in 1997, things took a disastrous turn for the worse. People began investing their savings in "pyramid" or "Ponzi" schemes. "Strictly defined, a pyramid scheme is an enterprise that rewards initial investors or customers with the money paid in by later customers. A true pyramid scheme is like a chain letter, with no product or service being sold," one observer explained.[93] Lured by extravagant promises of quick wealth from promoters, Albanians invested $1 billion in these schemes and then lost everything when these house-of-card investments collapsed.[94] Distraught investors then rioted across the country, looting banks and raiding government armories, seizing weapons, ammunition, and even tanks. As a result, more than six hundred thousand military weapons fell into civilian hands.[95] Albanians then began supplying these weapons to the KLA in Kosovo and, later, to Albanian Muslims in Macedonia.

With weapons provided by supporters in Albania, the KLA began waging an escalating guerilla war against Serb forces in Kosovo. In early 1998, Serb units mounted an intensive counterinsurgency campaign, which led to more serious fighting across the province.[96] Worried that the growing conflict would lead to ethnic cleansing and the forcible eviction of Kosovars by the Serbs, the United States and NATO threatened to bomb Serb forces unless they withdrew from the fighting and negotiated a peace agreement with the KLA. At the February 1999 negotiations in Rambouillet, France, the various parties agreed that Serbia would withdraw most of its forces from Kosovo but retain formal authority over the province; the KLA would disarm and put aside its demand for independence for three years, when a referendum would be held to determine Kosovo's permanent political status.[97] But fighting soon resumed, the conflict intensified, and people began fleeing the province into neighboring states, creating a serious refugee crisis for neighboring governments and international authorities. To stop the fighting, return the 685,000 refugees who fled abroad, and enforce the Rambouillet agreement, NATO forces began bombing Serb forces in Kosovo *and* military–government targets in Belgrade and across Serbia on March 24, 1999. The bombing campaign continued until early June, when Milosevic's government in Serbia agreed to withdraw its forces from Kosovo and permit NATO and also Russian forces to occupy the province. Although NATO forces were supposed to keep the peace, they did not prevent the KLA and its supporters from attacking the Serb minority in Kosovo, which triggered the exodus of 150,000 Serbs and Montenegrins from Kosovo, as well as thousands of Gypsies who had become the target of Kosovar resentment.[98] The KLA did not disarm but instead used its new authority to extract taxes from returning refugees, traffic in drugs and women (see chapter 6), in 1996 and supply men and arms to the Albanian Muslim minority in Macedonia, a development that contributed to conflict there.[99]

Round 5: Macedonia

In February 2001, war erupted in Macedonia, a breakaway republic that had long escaped the violence associated with the division of Yugoslavia during the 1990s.[100] A decade earlier, in 1991, Macedonia had established a democratic and independent government without violence. The new government had some difficulty establishing diplomatic relations with other countries because Greek officials objected to its name and its flag. Officials also had trouble improving the economy, which suffered from neighboring wars and trade disruption. During the 1990s, the government, which represented the Macedonian majority, maintained decent relations with the Albanian Muslim minority (22 to 31 percent of the population). But relations were not without complaint. Some Albanian Muslim political parties demanded Albanian language instruction in the schools and greater access to university education.[101] Then relations between majority and minority took a turn for the worse as a result of developments in Albania and Kosovo.

With arms from Albania and with soldiers supplied by the KLA in Kosovo, some Albanian Muslims in Macedonia organized the National Liberation Army (NLA) and, in 2001, began a guerilla war against the Macedonian government.[102] The NLA demanded the creation of a separate state, the "Ilirida Republic," much as minorities in Kosovo, Bosnia, and Croatia had done.[103] The KLA's seven thousand well-armed soldiers were able to make considerable headway against the Macedonian government, even threatening the capital of Skopje. It is difficult to say how much support the NLA had among Albanian Muslims in Macedonia, but the Macedonian government's military response to the insurgency no doubt antagonized many Albanian Muslims and increased support for the NLA.

In August 2001, after six months of escalating fighting, NATO leaders brokered an agreement between the government and the NLA. The government agreed to grant amnesty to rebel fighters and provide wider rights to the minority, changing the constitution to make Albanians a "constituent nation" rather than a simple "nationality."[104] For its part, the NLA agreed to disarm. Both sides agreed to return displaced refugees to their homes. In addition, NATO promised to provide a small number of troops to police the agreement reached in Ohrid.[105] But it is unclear whether the NLA will actually disarm or refugees return to their homes in areas dominated by different ethnic groups. As in Croatia, Bosnia, and Kosovo, the agreement reached in Macedonia bought a halt to the fighting, but did not altogether prevent it from erupting again in the future.

THE CONSEQUENCES OF DIVISION, SUBDIVISION, AND WAR

The toll associated with successive rounds of war in Yugoslavia has been enormous. Between 200,000 and 300,000 people died as a result of conflict in the 1990s, and 2.7 million people were displaced and fled as refugees.[106] Central governments elected by ethnic majorities in separated republics discriminated against ethnic minorities, who responded with violence and demanded states of their own, where they might govern without consideration for any ethnic minorities who might remain. Parties to the conflict have redrawn the political map and then insisted it be redrawn again to accommodate the territorial demands of different ethnic groups. Economies have collapsed, burdened by war and the disruption of trade. Conflict invited foreign military intervention. U.S., NATO, UN, and Russian forces have conducted bombing campaigns and peace keeping operations, and now occupy two regions (Bosnia and Kosovo) in number, at considerable expense.

To some extent, these developments were *predictable*. When other countries have been partitioned during the postwar period, and political power divided between competing ethnic or political groups (as occurred in Korea, China, Vietnam, India, Pakistan, Palestine, Cyprus, and Germany), several common problems emerged.[107] First, partition triggered massive migrations across newly created borders, a kind of ethnic/political "cleansing" on a large scale. But while many fled, many people did not move to their "assigned" states and remained in place. Second, governments of divided states typically discriminated against residual minority populations. Ill treatment antagonized these minority groups and their supporters in neighboring states. Third, governments disputed the boundaries of territories assigned to them as a result of partition, leading to territorial disputes and to conflicts over the sovereignty of sibling states. These problems often led to conflict within or between divided states: war in Korea, Vietnam, Cyprus; conflicts between China and Taiwan; repeated wars between India and Pakistan and between Israel and its neighbors; and a long cold war between East and West Germany. These conflicts in turn often triggered superpower military intervention and sometimes threatened wider, even nuclear wars.

As might be expected, these same problems emerged as Yugoslavia divided. Yugoslavia's division into multiple republics was associated with massive migrations, discrimination against minorities by majorities, disputes over territory and the sovereignty of independent states, and intervention by foreign powers. But while these developments were familiar and might have been expected given the history of partition elsewhere, events in Yugoslavia also took new, unexpected turns. One distinctive feature of conflict was that it was expressed not only in *ethnic* terms but also in *gender* terms.

Gender and War in Yugoslavia

During the ethnic cleansing campaigns in Croatia, Bosnia, and Kosovo, the males of target ethnicities were frequently murdered in groups; the females raped, often repeatedly, then released. More than seven thousand Muslim males were murdered by Serb forces in Srebreneca, and twenty thousand to thirty thousand Bosnian Muslim women were raped by Serb and Croat soldiers in the Bosnian enclaves they controlled.[108] Many of these women subsequently gave birth to children fathered by rapist soldiers. These women and their children were often shunned by their own ethnic community, an outcome evidently intended by the rapists. The gender-specific violence deployed in this conflict was a new development in divided-state wars, and it led to international recognition of rape not only as a criminal act but also as a war crime.

Another gender characteristic of the conflict was that men with guns made war. Few women participated in the fighting. And in the chaotic conditions associated with the breakdown of government, men with guns were able to levy taxes and steal goods from unarmed civilians, particularly from women. These wars created a climate extremely inhospitable to women.

Division and Democratization

Yugoslavia was unusual in other respects. When Yugoslavia divided in 1991, it split into five or more parts, not just two, as was common in most other divided states.[109] Moreover, the states that emerged from the breakup of communist Yugoslavia took different political forms, some more democratic than others. In Slovenia and Macedonia, multiparty elections immediately led to the creation of democratic, noncommunist governments. But in Croatia and Serbia, multiparty elections led to the election of authoritarian leaders—Tudjman in Croatia and Milosevic in Serbia—who used the democratic electoral process to consolidate ethnic majority rule and denigrate ethnic minorities. These "discriminatory democracies," or "elected dictatorships," as they might be called, defined "democracy" in narrow ethnic terms. They insisted that majority rule meant the suppression of minority rights and the expulsion of ethnic minorities if necessary. Their ethnic, authoritarian politics fueled conflict in their own countries and in neighboring republics for many years. Fortunately, the departure of both men facilitated a second phase of more meaningful democratization in Croatia and in Serbia.

In 1999, Tudjman died of cancer after ten years in power. The political party that he had established and that had supported him in office lost the elections held after his death. This led to a more democratic, less confrontational government, one more interested in repairing the economic and social damage of war than in fueling the fires of conflict.[110] Tudjman's death probably prevented him from being indicted as a war criminal.

Then in 2000, Milosevic was ousted from power after losing an election to Vojislav Kostunica, the leader of a coalition of opposition groups. Milosevic had survived repeated efforts to dislodge him because he retained political support from poor rural voters, controlled the armed forces, and faced a divide opposition.[111] But military setbacks in Croatia and Bosian, military defeat by NATO forces during the Kosovo war, foreign economic sanctions, deteriorating economic conditions, and the unification of opposition groups behind a young leader uncompromised by corruption or war crimes finally took its toll on Milosevic. After he left office, he was arrested and deported to the Hague for trial as a war criminal. In his absence, Kostunica has worked to repair the country's economy and diplomatic relations and make Serbia a "normal, boring state."[112]

In a sense, Croatia and Serbia have democratized twice: the first time as part of a transition from a communist dictatorship to a discriminatory, authoritarian democracy, and then, after Tudjman's death and Milosevic's fall, they were transformed into more "normal," multiparty democracies, albeit ones burdened by economic collapse and a decade of war.

Political developments in Bosnia and Kosovo were more complex. Conflict in Bosnia led to the creation of several ethnic parastates administered, for now, by NATO officials with the support of three NATO armies. This hybrid political entity cannot be characterized as generally democratic, though separate ethnic communities vote regularly for ethnic nationalist leaders in multiparty elections. Without any real mechanism to integrate these ethnic parastates, political divisions may harden and NATO may eventually consider partition, or the subdivision of divided Bosnia, as a solution that would enable it to withdraw.

NATO intervention in Kosovo also created an ethnic parastate, administered by NATO forces occupying the province. U.S. and NATO officials promised to use a referendum to determine its final political status. If it is held, the referendum will likely result in a vote for independence, which would subdivide Serbia. The irony is that NATO would then be in the position of supporting the secession of Kosovo. This would bring to power an ethnic authoritarian government led by the KLA, which has expelled resident Serbs and supported ethnic secessionists in Macedonia. Of course, NATO support for an independent Kosovo led by the KLA would greatly antagonize the Serbian government, which recently ousted Milosevic and democratized, and also antagonize the democratic government in Macedonia, where KLA support for Albanian Muslim separatists has led to war. As a result of recent developments, NATO may find itself allied with ethnic, authoritarian separatists against democratic governments in the region.

The problem is that the subdivision of either Bosnia or Serbia will likely result in conflict, just as the earlier division of Yugoslavia resulted in a series of wars across the region. Although no wars are now raging (as of this writing), it is difficult to imagine that another round of war is no longer possible.

NOTES

1. See Robert Schaeffer, *Power to the People: Democratization around the World* (Boulder, Colo.: Westview, 1997).

2. Lenard J. Cohen, "The Disintegration of Yugoslavia," *Current History* (November 1992): 370, 373. If one argues, as many do, that ethnic antagonisms were the root cause of democratization, division, and war, then one will hold Tito's regime as largely blameless for events that occurred. From this perspective, Tito tried for many years to contain

simmering conflict, but he failed in the end because ethnic identities were too strong and secular identities too weak to prevent conflict from erupting. But I think this treatment is unwarranted. First, it fails to treat the regime as a dictatorship, perhaps more moderate and popular than most, but a dictatorship nonetheless. Second, it minimizes the regime's role in the contemporary crisis. Finally, because cause (ethnic conflict) and consequence (ethnic conflict) are the same, the one begins and ends in the same place, treating the intervening history as irrelevant.

3. Caglar Keyder, "The American Recovery of Southern Europe: Aid and Hegemony," in *Semiperipheral Development: The Role of Southern Europe in the 20th Century,* ed. Giovanni Arrighi (Beverly Hills: Sage, 1985), 141–42; David A. Dyker, *Yugoslavia: Socialism, Development and Debt* (London: Routledge, 1990), 94; William Zimmerman, *Open Borders, Nonalignment, and the Political Evolution of Yugoslavia* (Princeton, N.J.: Princeton University Press, 1987), 115.

4. Ljubomir Madzar, "The Economy of Yugoslavia: Structure, Growth Record and Institutional Framework," in *Yugoslavia in Transition: Choices and Constraints,* ed. John B. Allcock, John J Horton, and Marko Milivojevic (New York: Berg, 1992), 76.

5. Beatrice Heuser, *Western "Containment" Policies in the Cold War: The Yugoslav Case, 1948–53* (London: Routledge, 1989).

6. Zimmerman, *Open Borders,* 18, 22–23; Duncan Wilson, *Tito's Yugoslavia* (Cambridge: Cambridge University Press, 1979), 68, 75; T. E. Vadney, *The World since 1945* (London: Penguin, 1992), 53–54.

7. Dijana Plestina, "From 'Democratic Centralism' to Decentralized Democracy? Trials and Tribulations of Yugoslavia's Development," in *Yugoslavia in Transition,* 132, 133; Dimitrije Djordjevic, "The Yugoslav Phenomenon," in *The Columbia History of Eastern Europe in the Twentieth Century,* ed. Joseph Held (New York: Columbia University Press), 334–35; Constantine Tsoucalas, *The Greek Tragedy* (Harmondsworth, England: Penguin, 1969), 67; Sheelagh Elwood, *Franco* (London: Longman, 1994), 151, 158, 163, 169; Kostis Papadantonakis, "Incorporation is Peripheralization: Contradictions of Southern Europe's Economic Development," in *Semiperipheral Development,* 93.

8. Plestina, "From 'Democratic Centralism' to Decentralized Democracy?" 132; Wilson, *Tito's Yugoslavia,* 125.

9. Wilson, *Tito's Yugoslavia,* 97.

10. Fred A. Singleton, *A Short History of the Yugoslav Peoples* (Cambridge: Cambridge University Press, 1985), 44. Poor harvests in 1960 and 1961 "necessitated food imports [and] placed additional strain on the balance of payments." Plestina, "From 'Democratic Centralism' to Decentralized Democracy?" 132, 133.

11. Raymond Carr and Juan Pablo Fusi Aizpurua, *Spain: Dictatorship to Democracy* (London: Allen & Unwin, 1979), 57; Keyder, "The American Recovery of Southern Europe," 135, 145.

12. Giovanni Arrighi, "Fascism to Democratic Socialism: Logic and Limits of a Transition," in *Semiperipheral Development,* 265, 268.

13. Spain and Yugoslavia each earned $1.4 billion from worker remittances in 1973; Greece and Portugal somewhat less. John Logan, "Democracy from Above: Limits to Change in Southern Europe," in *Semiperipheral Development,* 164; Salustiano del Campo, "Spain," in *International Labor Migration in Europe,* ed. Ronald E. Krane (New York: Praeger, 1979), 162; Rocha Triniadade and Maria Beatriz Rocha, "Portugal," in

International Labor Migration in Europe, 171; David D. Gregory and Cazorla J. Perez, "Intra-European Migration and Regional Development: Spain and Portugal," in *Guests Come to Stay: The Effects of European Labor Migration on Sending and Receiving Countries*, ed. Rosmarie Rogers (Boulder, Colo.: Westview, 1985), 237; George Yannopoulos, "Workers and Peasants under Military Dictatorship," in *Greece under Military Rule*, ed. Richard Clogg and George Yannopoulos (London: Secker & Warburg, 1972 121; Zimmerman, *Open Borders*, 114; Jasminka Udovicki, "Nationalism, Ethnic Conflict and Self-Determination in the Former Yugoslavia," in *The National Question: Nationalism, Ethnic Conflict and Self-Determination in the 20th Century*, ed. Berge Berberoglu (Philadelphia: Temple University Press, 1995), 292; Milan Mesic, "External Migration in the Context of the Post-War Development of Yugoslavia," in *Yugoslavia in Transition*, 180; Carl-Ulrik Schierup, *Migration, Socialism and the International Division of Labor: The Yugoslav Experience* (Aldershot, England: Avebury, 1990), 18, 77.

14. Udovicki, "Nationalism, Ethnic Conflict and Self-Determination," 292; Mesic, "External Migration," 180; Schierup, *Migration, Socialism and the International Division of Labor*, 18, 77.

15. Jaime Gama, "Foreign Policy," in *Portugal: Ancient Country, Young Democracy*, ed. Kenneth Maxwell and Michael H. Haltzel (Washington, D.C.: Woodrow Wilson Center Press, 1990), 97; Gregory and Perez, "Intra-European Migration and Regional Development," 236; Robert P. Clark, *The Basques: The Franco Years and Beyond* (Reno: University of Nevada Press, 1979), 211; Carr and Aizpurua, *Spain*, 57.

16. Wilson, *Tito's Yugoslavia*, 238–39.

17. Wilson, *Tito's Yugoslavia*, 232.

18. Alvaro Soto Carmona, "Long Cycle of Social Conflict in Spain (1868–1986)," *Review* 16, no. 2 (Spring 1993): 179; Ellwood, *Franco*, 180; Wilson, *Tito's Yugoslavia*, 156; Zimmerman, *Open Borders*, 78.

19. Dennison Rusinow, *The Yugoslav Experiment, 1848–1974* (London: Hurst, 1977), 207–8; Zimmerman, *Open Borders*, 76; Mesic, "External Migration," 178.

20. Laura D'Andrea Tyson, *The Yugoslav Economic System and Its Performance in the 1970s* (Berkeley, Calif.: Institute of International Studies, 1980), 33.

21. Schierup, *Migration, Socialism and the International Division of Labor*, 100–101; Tyson, *The Yugoslav Economic System*, 52; Zimmerman, *Open Borders*, 92; Plestina, "From 'Democratic Centralism' to Decentralized Democracy?" 146; Susan L. Woodward, *Balkan Tragedy: Chaos and Dissolution after the Cold War* (Washington, D.C.: Brookings Institution, 1995), 49.

22. See Schaeffer, *Power to the People*, chapter 4.

23. Tyson, *The Yugoslav Economic System*, 95.

24. Christopher Bennett, *Yugoslavia's Bloody Collapse: Causes, Course and Consequences* (New York: New York University Press, 1995), 69; Madzar, "The Economy of Yugoslavia," 84; Udovicki, "Nationalism, Ethnic Conflict and Self-Determination," 295.

25. Paul A. Volcker and Toyoo Gyohten, *Changing Fortunes: The World's Money and the Threat to American Leadership* (New York: Times Books, 1992), 115.

26. Woodward, *Balkan Tragedy*, 51; John Walton and David Seddon, *Free Markets and Food Riots: The Politics of Global Adjustment* (Oxford: Blackwell, 1994), 298–99.

27. David A. Dyker, *Yugoslavia: Socialism, Development and Debt* (London: Routledge, 1990), 131–32; Woodward, *Balkan Tragedy*, 52, 55, 82, 96; Walton and Seddon, *Free Markets and Food Riots*, 324.

28. Walton and Seddon, *Free Markets and Food Riots,* 321; Plestina, "From 'Democratic Centralism' to Decentralized Democracy?" 152.

29. Mesic, "External Migration," 185; Chris Martin and Laura D'Andrea Tyson, "Can Titoism Survive Tito? Economic Problems and Policy Choices Confronting Tito's Successors," in *Nationalism and Federalism in Yugoslavia, 1963–1983,* ed. Pedro Ramet (Bloomington: Indiana University Press, 1984), 197; Plestina, "From 'Democratic Centralism' to Decentralized Democracy?" 140.

30. Plestina, "From 'Democratic Centralism' to Decentralized Democracy?" 140, 144; Pedro Ramet, "Apocalypse Culture and Social Change in Yugoslavia," in *Nationalism and Federalism in Yugoslavia, 1963–1983,* 140.

31. John B. Allcock, "Tourism and the Private Sector," in *Yugoslavia in Transition,* 404.

32. Martin and Tyson, "Can Titoism Survive Tito?" 189; Dyker, *Yugoslavia,* 101; Tyson, *The Yugoslav Economic System,* 76.

33. Singleton, *A Short History of the Yugoslav Peoples,* 68.

34. Woodward, *Balkan Tragedy,* 293; Plestina, "From 'Democratic Centralism' to Decentralized Democracy?" 133–34; Schierup, *Migration, Socialism and the International Division of Labor,* 166, 168.

35. Zimmerman, *Open Borders,* 4.

36. Woodward, *Balkan Tragedy,* 73; Susan Bridge, "Some Causes of Political Change in Yugoslavia," in *Ethnic Conflict in the Western World,* ed. Milton Esman (Ithaca, N.Y.: Cornell University Press, 1975), 355.

37. Bogdan Denitch, *Ethnic Naturalism: The Tragic Death of Yugoslavia* (Minneapolis: University of Minnesota Press, 1994), 71; Woodward, *Balkan Tragedy,* 64.

38. Blaine Harden, "A Body Blow to Croatia's Tourist Industry," *San Francisco Chronicle,* June 17, 1991.

39. Bridge, "Some Causes of Political Change in Yugoslavia," 355.

40. Woodward, *Balkan Tragedy,* 69, 74, 115, 130.

41. Fernando Claudin, *The Communist Movement: From Comintern to Cominform* (Harmondsworth, England: Penguin, 1975), 487; Wilson, *Tito's Yugoslavia,* 50.

42. Zimmerman, *Open Borders,* 17.

43. Peter Willets, *The Non-Aligned Movement: The Origins of a Third World Alliance* (London: Pinter, 1978), 6, 7; Ali E. Hillal Dessouki, "Nasser and the Struggle for Independence," in *Suez 1956: The Crisis and Its Consequences,* ed. William Roger Louis and Roger Owen (Oxford: Clarendon, 1989), 33.

44. Robert Schaeffer, *Warpaths: The Politics of Partition* (New York: Hill & Wang, 1990); see chapter 4.

45. Schaeffer, *Power to the People;* see chapters 1–3.

46. Zimmerman, *Open Borders,* 21; Claudin, *The Communist Movement,* 488; Alvin Z. Rubinstein, *Yugoslavia and the Nonaligned World* (Princeton, N.J.: Princeton University Press, 1970), 24, 29, 77.

47. Aleksa Djilas, *The Contested Country: Yugoslav Unity and Communist Revolution, 1919–1953* (Cambridge, Mass.: Harvard University Press, 1991), 167, 168; Vojin Dimitrijevic, "The 1974 Constitution and Constitutional Process as a Factor in the Collapse of Yugoslavia," in *Yugoslavia the Former and Future: Reflections by Scholars from the Region,* eds. Payam Akhavan and Robert Howse (Washington, D.C.: Brookings Institution, 1995), 58.

48. Zimmerman, *Open Borders*, 28; Randy Hodson, Dusko Sekulic, and Garth Massey, "National Tolerance in the Former Yugoslavia," *American Journal of Sociology* 99, no. 6 (May 1994): 1539; Joel S. Migdal, *Strong Societies and Weak States: State Society Relations and State Capabilities in the Third World* (Princeton, N.J.: Princeton University Press, 1988), 215–24.

49. Hodson et al., "National Tolerance," 1540; Ramet, "Apocalypse Culture," 125; Udovicki, "Nationalism, Ethnic Conflict and Self-Determination," 291; Denitch, *Ethnic Nationalism*, 105; Dimitrijevic, "The 1974 Constitution," 71–72; George Schopflin, "Political Decay in One-Party Systems in Eastern Europe: Yugoslav Patterns," in *Nationalism and Federalism in Yugoslavia, 1963–1983*, 316; John Feffer, *Shock Waves: Eastern Europe after the Revolutions* (Boston: South End Press, 1992), 258–59.

50. "'Much has been written,' he said, [to the effect] that Yugoslavia will disintegrate when I go.' He conceded that his death 'could cause a very difficult crisis . . . because the question then would be pose who will take my place?' He concluded, therefore, that 'we have to carry out this reorganization precisely so that our Yugoslav socialist community would not come to such a crisis.'" Ramet, "Apocalypse Culture," 189; see also Zimmerman, *Open Borders*, 45.

51. Schaeffer, *Power to the People*; see chapters 8 and 9.

52. Djordjevic, "The Yugoslav Phenomenon," 338.

53. Bennett, *Yugoslavia's Bloody Collapse*, 117.

54. Djilas, *The Contested Country*, 56, 68, 70, 76, 78, 84, 86, 97; Djordjevic, "The Yugoslav Phenomenon," 321; Wilson, *Tito's Yugoslavia*, 15.

55. Djilas, *The Contested Country*, 88.

56. Denitch, *Ethnic Nationalism*, 34–35.

57. Wilson, *Tito's Yugoslavia*.

58. Robert Adams, *Nations in Arms: The Theory and Practice of Territorial Defense* (Houndmills, England: Macmillan, 1986), 140, 142; Denitch, *Ethnic Nationalism*, 31–33; Woodward, *Balkan Tragedy*, 1; Djordjevic, "The Yugoslav Phenomenon," 324.

59. Dane Archer and Rosemary Gartner, *Violence and Crime in Cross-National Perspective* (New Haven, Conn.: Yale University Press, 1984), 79, 86.

60. Archer and Gartner, *Violence and Crime*, 65, 66, 76, 92, 94–5.

61. Archer and Gartner, *Violence and Crime*, 86.

62. As Walter Lippmann observed long ago, "it is very clear that under certain conditions men respond as powerfully to fictions as they do to realities, and that in many cases they help to create the very fictions to which they respond. . . . Whatever we believe to be a true picture [of the outside world], we treat as if it were the environment itself." Walter Lippman, *Public Opinion* (New York: Free Press, 1922), 4. In this context, memorializing the civil war created a powerful contemporary political environment. It was a "fiction" because it combined real memory with worried imagination about the present. And elites responded to this fictional environment, which they helped create, as if it were real.

63. Udovicki, "Nationalism, Ethnic Conflict and Self-Determination," 299–300.

64. As Djilas observed, "The Second World War in not over, not here anyway." Michael Ignatieff, *Blood and Belonging: Journeys into the New Nationalism* (New York: Farrar, Straus & Giroux, 1993), 53.

65. Adam Roberts, *Nations in Arms*, 137, 154–55, 172–73; James Gow, *Legitimacy*

and the Military: The Yugoslav Crisis (London: Pinter, 1992), 44–46; Woodward, *Balkan Tragedy*, 26.

66. Roberts, *Nations in Arms*, 159, 161, 163–64; Zimmerman, *Open Borders*, 30.

67. Roberts, *Nations in Arms*, 180–81, 215–16.

68. Roberts, *Nations in Arms*, 217.

69. Schaeffer, *Power to the People*, passim.

70. Udovicki, "Nationalism, Ethnic Conflict and Self-Determination," 308.

71. Gow, *Legitimacy and the Military*, 56–57, 59, 72; Rubinstein, *Yugoslavia and the Nonaligned World*, 143.

72. Robin Alison Remington, "Political-Military Relations in Post-Tito Yugoslavia," in *Nationalism and Federalism in Yugoslavia, 1963–1983*, 57; Roberts, *Nations in Arms* 202.

73. Woodward, *Balkan Tragedy*, 137.

74. Metta Spencer, "What Happened in Yugoslavia?" in *The Lessons of Yugoslavia, Research on Russia and Eastern Europe, Volume 3*, ed. Metta Spencer (New York: Elsevier Science, 2000), 17.

75. Still, public opinion polls in the early 1990s found considerable anti-Semitism (20 percent of those polled expressed anti-Semitic views), despite the fact that only 36 Jews lived in the *entire* country, and half of young Slovenians favored "ethnic cleansing" as a way to create an ethnically homogeneous state. Sabrina P. Ramet, "The Slovenian Success Story," *Current History* (March 1998): 116–17.

76. Cohen, "The Disintegration of Yugoslavia," 372; Spencer, "What Happened in Yugoslavia?" 21.

77. Christopher Cviic, "Croatia's Violent Birth," *Current History* (November 1993): 370.

78. Spencer, "What Happened in Yugoslavia?" 25.

79. Drago Hedl, "Living in the Past: Franjo Tudjman's Croatia," *Current History* (March 2000): 106.

80. Hedl, "Living in the Past," 108.

81. Cohen, "The Disintegration of Yugoslavia," 374.

82. Hedl, "Living in the Past," 105; Sabrina P. Ramet, "The Bosnian War and the Diplomacy of Accommodation," *Current History* (November 1994): 384.

83. Ramet, "The Bosnian War," 381.

84. Cohen, "The Disintegration of Yugoslavia," 375.

85. Ramet, "The Bosnian War," 384.

86. Spencer, "What Happened in Yugoslavia?" 25–27; Lenard J. Cohen, "Bosnia and Herzegovina: Fragile Peace in a Segmented State," *Current History* (March 1996): 106–7.

87. Cohen, "Bosnia and Herzegovina," 107–8.

88. Cohen, "Bosnia and Herzegovina," 107–9; Susan L. Woodward, "Bosnia after Dayton: Year Two," *Current History* (March 1997): 98.

89. Lenard J. Cohen, "Whose Bosnia? The Politics of Nation Building," *Current History* (March 1998): 109–10.

90. Cohen, "Whose Bosnia?" 109–10.

91. Spencer, "What Happened in Yugoslavia?" 32.

92. Fabian Schmidt, "Upheaval in Albania," *Current History* (March 1998): 128.

93. Celestine Bohlen, "Albanian Parties Trade Charges in the Pyramid Scandal," *New York Times*, January 29, 1997.

94. Bohlen, "Albanian Parties Trade Charges."

95. Schmidt, "Upheaval in Albania," 129–30.

96. James Hooper, "Kosovo: America's Balkan Problem," *Current History* (March 2000): 160–61.

97. Hooper, "Kosovo," 161–62.

98. Lenard J. Cohen, "Kosovo: Nobody's Country," *Current History* (March 2000): 118–19.

99. Cohen, "Kosovo," 120–22.

100. Duncan Perry, "Macedonia: Melting Pot or Meltdown?" *Current History* (March 2001): 362.

101. Duncan Perry, "Destiny on Hold: Macedonia and the Dangers of Ethnic Discord," *Current History* (March 1998): 121–23; Perry, "Macedonia: Balkan Miracle or Balkan Disaster?" *Current History* (March 1996): 115.

102. Perry, "Macedonia," 362.

103. Perry, "Macedonia," 116.

104. Perry, "Destiny on Hold," 121.

105. Edward P. Joseph, "A Chance to Prevent the Partition of Macedonia," *New York Times*, August 31, 2001.

106. Ramet, "The Bosnian War," 385.

107. Schaeffer, *Warpaths*; Robert K. Schaeffer, *Severed States: Dilemmas of Democracy in a Divided World* (Lanham, Md.: Rowman & Littlefield, 1999).

108. Ramet, "The Bosnian War," 385.

109. In 1948, the United Nations divided Palestine into two parts, but only one state—Israel—came into being at that time. The state designed for Palestinians was abrogated during the fighting that accompanied partition.

110. Hedl, "Living in the Past," 104; Marina Ottaway and Gideon Maltz, "Croatia's Second Transition and the International Community," *Current History* (November 2001): 375.

111. Eric D. Gordy, "Why Milosevic Still?" *Current History* (March 2000): 99–100.

112. Eric D. Gordy, "Building a 'Normal, Boring' Country: Kostunica's Yugoslavia," *Current History* (March 2001): 110.

13

Mafias and the Global Drug Trade

I n 1970, President Nixon announced the government's War on Drugs, the first
of many contemporary antidrug campaigns. Since then, the U.S. government
has spent nearly $70 billion on law enforcement and drug treatment programs
and now budgets about $12 billion annually for antidrug campaigns.[1] But despite
massive government spending, heroin and cocaine supplies have grown, becoming cheaper, purer, and more readily available. And the violent foreign mafias
that control the global trade in these drugs have become rich and powerful.

The expansion of the global drug trade in recent years has increased the power
of foreign mafias, created social and environmental problems in countries where
drugs are produced and consumed, and contributed to widespread violence and
the spread of disease. To appreciate these developments, it is necessary first to
outline a brief history of the regional mafias that seized control of the global drug
trades in the 1970s, 1980s, and 1990s.

REGIONAL MAFIAS

The mafias that came to control the global drug trades in the 1970s, 1980s, and
1990s grew out of regional crime gangs that emerged in Europe, the Americas,
and Asia during the previous century. The Sicilian and Italian American mafias,
Chinese triads, Japanese *yakuza,* and Colombian *bandidos* had different organizational structures. But because they behaved in similar ways and engaged in
similar criminal activities—providing "protection," operating "vice industries,"
and trafficking in illegal drugs—they can collectively be described as mafias.

The term *mafia* first appeared in Sicily during the 1860s, when republican
revolutionaries successfully overthrew the island's Spanish monarchy and united
it with other states on the peninsula, resulting in the creation of modern Italy.[2]
Because the new Italian government did not exercise great power in Sicily after

the Spanish rulers had retired, government authority declined just as landlords and peasants were trying to redefine their economic and political relations. Peasants, for example, had only recently been released from feudal obligations to aristocratic landlords, but new market relations between landowners and a free peasantry had not yet been established. The political vacuum and economic uncertainty gave soldiers who had fought in the war of independence a chance to take matters into their own hands. They offered to guarantee the informal and contractual obligations made by members of competing social groups, using force if necessary. In the absence of central government authority or fully functioning markets, landlords, merchants, and peasants all feared that they would be cheated or preyed upon by others. To prevent this, they relied on a powerful third party to ensure that obligations were met and injustices punished. As one Sicilian more recently explained, "When the butcher comes to me to buy an animal, he knows that I want to cheat him. But I [also] know that he wants to cheat me. There we need, say [a third party] to make us agree. And we both pay [the third party] a percentage of the deal."[3]

By offering to "protect" each party from the other and to punish either party if they reneged on the agreement made, the third-party "mafioso" came to play an important and lucrative role in Sicilian society after independence. As anthropologist Diego Gambetta explained, "Protection . . . can play a crucial role as a lubricant of economic exchange. In every transaction in which at least one party does not trust the other to comply with the rules, protection becomes desirable, even if it is a poor and costly substitute for trust."[4]

In Sicilian society during the late nineteenth and early twentieth centuries, the self-appointed providers of protection and guardians of public order became known as mafioso. According to the sociologist Pino Arlacci, anyone in Sicily could become a mafioso or a man of honor: "Men of honor were made, not born, and the pursuit of honor was a free competition, open to all."[5] But the prize went most often to the man who could act with greater "cunning, courage and ferocity" than others, a man "strong enough to avenge himself for any insult to his person, or any extension of it, *and* to offer any such insult . . . to his enemies."[6]

According to the historian Eric Hobsbawm and Arlacchi, there was never a "single secret society," or a "secret, hierarchical and centralized criminal organization called the mafia, its members bound to one another by sinister and solemn oaths of mutual loyalty and assistance."[7] Instead, mafioso formed small local gangs, usually composed of five or six blood relatives, family members, and friends called *cosca* that operated independently.[8] Their sometimes-murderous competition was tempered by informal associations that could assign monopolies and arbitrate disputes among competing mafias. It is these informal groups that are described by journalists as "the mafia," but they are more like a trade association composed of affiliated competitors than a corporation made up of members organized into a single hierarchy.

At the turn of the twentieth century, some mafioso immigrated to the United

States along with the thousands of Sicilian peasants who could not find land or make a living on the island. In the United States, mafioso offered protection in immigrant urban communities, trying to broker relations among local government officials, employers, and immigrant communities. In contrast with Sicilian mafias, U.S. mafia families recruited or admitted members of other ethnic groups—Jewish and Irish mafioso participated in U.S. gangs. They were also larger in size, with some five thousand members in the United States and perhaps fifty thousand close associates.[9]

In other countries, mafialike groups also emerged: triads in China, yakuza in Japan during the nineteenth century, bandidos in Colombia during the 1950s, and *mafiyas* in the former Soviet Union in the 1990s.

In nineteenth-century China, young single men who could not rely on their families or communities to support them formed what anthropologists called "fictive kinship" in "mutual-aid societies." Young men who joined these societies pledged to protect each other from feudal landlords, unscrupulous merchants, corrupt officials, predatory warlords, and the Manchu dynasty.[10] They frequently organized in secret to shield members from the state, which viewed them as a threat to its power and made membership in secret societies illegal. As a Chinese proverb explained, "Armies protect the emperor, secret societies protect the people."[11]

Like their Sicilian counterparts, "the line between protection and predation was always thin [in Chinese society]," and secret societies often turned to "thievery, extortion, and the control of . . . gambling, robbery and prostitution enterprises in China and in Chinese overseas communities."[12] Also like Sicilian mafias, they had a political dimension. Early Chinese secret societies or triads tried to overthrow the alien Manchu rulers, much as Sicilian mafias were originally rebels against Spanish Bourbon rule.[13] Indeed, triads first came to prominence during their role in the Taiping Rebellion (1851–1864), at about the same time that mafias emerged during the rebellion in Sicily and the unification of Italy (1860–1861).[14] After the Taiping Rebellion failed, many politically minded "Triad members became involved in . . . piracy and smuggling [and] some fled to America, where they established branches of the Triad Society known as the Chee kung Tong."[15] So, like their Sicilian counterparts, Chinese gangsters joined the migration to the United States and organized criminal enterprises in immigrant communities, the "Chinatowns" of San Francisco, Los Angeles, and New York City.

In China, triads became prominent in Shanghai, which became a notorious center of opium use and prostitution after the Chinese monarchy was overthrown in 1911.[16] After World War II, triads fled China when the communists took power and established a new base in Hong Kong, then a British colony.

The arrival of numerous triads in postwar Hong Kong initially led to a fierce, murderous competition among triad groups for control of criminal activity in the city. In 1955, the 14K Triad, the largest group, attempted to amalgamate the colony's three hundred thousand triad members into a single criminal syndicate.[17] They nearly succeeded. In 1956, however, the triad joined a popular demonstration against continued British rule in the colony, evidently hoping that the revolt would result in independence for the colony and even greater power for the triad. But the British crushed the revolt and deported much of the 14K leadership. This led to renewed competition among Hong Kong triads, but also to the creation of new triads by gangsters deported to Taiwan.[18]

Postwar triads based in Hong Kong and Taiwan differ in some important respects from Sicilian and Italian American mafias. While Italian and American mafia groups are usually composed of family members and friends of the same ethnic groups, members of Chinese triads are not related by blood but are joined in fictive kinships, in which people adopt one another as brothers and embrace the gang as their family. Because they are based on fictive rather than real kinships, triads can admit more members and grow larger than blood-related mafia groups. So, for example, the 14K Triad has some twenty-four thousand members, and the Wo group has twenty-nine thousand.[19] Compare this with Italian American mafia families in the United States, which only have between fifty and two hundred members.[20]

Like Chinese triads, the yakuza in Japan are large criminal gangs based on fictive kinships. They also first emerged in the mid-nineteenth century, when Japan, like China and Sicily, was undergoing rapid political and economic change.

After 1854, when U.S. naval forces under Commodore Matthew C. Perry forced Japan to trade with the world, Japan's central government—the Tokugawa shogunate—collapsed. The demise of the shogunate and the subsequent installation of the Meiji government in 1868 led to the end of feudalism, the rapid development of industry, and a quick migration of rural peasants to the cities. Under these conditions, masterless samurai who had become gamblers (*bakuto*) and street peddlers (*tekiya*) began to provide "protection" to peasants who had seen old feudal obligations disappear and new, market-based contractual relations arise. In Japan, this development led, as it did in Sicily during the same period, to considerable mistrust and uncertainty.[21] The individuals and groups who enforced "obligations" in a situation where government laws and market relations were not fully functioning took the name *yakuza* from a traditional card game, in which the combination of 8 (*ya*), 9 (*ku*), and 3 (*sa*) was the worst possible hand.[22]

Yakuza in Japan were joined by a common ideology of *giri*, an obligation to show gratitude but also the duty to exact revenge, and *ninjo*, the obligation to be generous and compassionate for the weak and disadvantaged.[23] The ability to practice both giri and ninjo enabled yakuza to claim a role in Japanese society as "protectors," people able to guarantee obligations between parties who could not trust each other and punish those who reneged on their duties. Like "men of honor" in Sicily, yakuza took great pride in the social role. They demonstrated this by covering their bodies with distinctive tattoos, an extremely painful process that served as a test of endurance and courage, and by using kitchen knives or small swords to sever parts of their fingers (*yubitsume*) to demonstrate the sincerity of an apology for failing to fulfill their own obligations to others, usually duty to their gang.[24]

Yakuza gangs first became prominent in the 1920s. They grew from small local gangs to large national gangs during the U.S. occupation of Japan after World War II. By 1978, the Yamaguchi-gumi, the largest yakuza gang, counted 10,382 members and police estimated that there were 108,266 yakuza in Japan.[25] Unlike their triad and mafia counterparts, the yakuza play a very public role in society. Yakuza members sport lapel badges indicating their membership and rank in particular gangs, operate local storefront offices that display their gang emblems, and publish newspapers: the Yamaguchi-gumi "publishes the monthly *Yamaguchi-Gumi Jiho* and sends it to all gang members."[26] They do this in part because Japanese society is more tolerant of their role and because yakuza operate many legitimate businesses alongside their illegal enterprises. Although the yakuza have historically trafficked in methamphetamine or "speed," they did not trade in heroin, largely because there is little demand for it in Japan (drug users prefer speed to heroin or cocaine).

The Colombian cartels that came to control the cocaine trade in the 1970s and 1980s first arose during the 1950s. The assassination of leftist leader Jorge Eliécer Gaitán in 1948 led to a decade of fighting, martial law, civil war, and widespread political corruption. During this period, known in Colombia as *la violencía*, in which some two hundred thousand people were killed, groups of smugglers, bandits, and gunmen emerged. Although the fighting eventually ended and a functioning government was reestablished, many of these groups of armed men remained, engaging in criminal enterprises rather than conducting political warfare. "At the beginning of the 1970s," Arlacchi argues, "many members of this outlaw army became involved in international cocaine and marijuana smuggling, often meeting the needs of the Colombian mafia families."[27] These origins suggest many similarities with other mafialike groups around the world: the emergence of armed men who take charge of local affairs at a time when government authority is weak and normal economic relations are disrupted.

The Russian mafiyas have emerged in the same kind of setting, where government authority was weak and new economic relations were uncertain and problematic. They have grown strong in Russia but have not, as yet, emerged as a powerful *global* mafia.

There are important differences among the mafias, triads, yakuza, bandidos, and mafiyas that emerged in different parts of the world. They emerged at different times: Sicilian mafias, Chinese triads and Japanese yakuza in the mid-nineteenth century, Italian American mafias in the 1920s, Colombian bandidos in the 1950s, and Russian mafiyas in the 1990s. Some of these mafias were based on blood relations and family members, which kept them relatively small

(Sicilian, Italian American, and Colombian mafias), while Asian gangs were based on fictive kinships, which enabled them to become quite large.[28] But despite different social origins and organizational orientations, criminal groups in different regions behaved in much the same way, acting with both courtesy and cunning, demonstrating both compassion and revenge, and displaying great energy.

> These people have amazing vitality. They never stand still, they're never idle. One moment they are busy over some deal, later on they're having lunch with friends, then they are working on some other business affair, then they visit one of their lovers. Then some "situation" comes up which they have to "control." . . . They are always on the move, traveling from place to place in their cars. . . . Then it's off to the bar, to talk. They go see some relatives and discuss business again. . . . Lots of them are polygamous, they have several families and lots of children. They eat, they drink, they have a good time, they kill. The whole thing's done with feverish intensity: never an empty space, never a slack moment.[29]

More important, the different gangs engaged in common criminal activities, what might be called the "protection" and "vice industries."

When they first emerged, regional mafias provided "protection," acting to guarantee and enforce "obligations" between parties who could not trust one another because government laws and market relations were weak, ineffective, or incomplete. Members of ethnic communities—landowners, small businesses, peddlers, vendors, and shopkeepers—willingly or unwillingly paid mafias to provide protection and mediate relations among different groups. Although protection activities provided their initial source of income, mafias soon turned to vice industries—gambling, prostitution, and drugs—to generate income.

In illegal vice markets, demand is relatively "inelastic." This means that consumer demand remains high even if prices rise. (In legal markets, where need and compulsion are *less* strongly felt, consumer demand usually falls when prices rise, a relation that economists describe as "elastic.") Mafias typically seek out activities where consumers are compulsive, where goods and services are illegal, because profits are higher than those obtained in legal and competitive markets. By using violence or the threat of violence, mafias can discourage competition in these industries and obtain monopoly power, which enables them to reap even higher profits.

In the United States, for example, mafia families or firms have long controlled the major vice industries. In major U.S. cities, mafias operated numbers lotteries, off-track betting on horse races, and backroom casinos, and they loaned money at high interest rates to gamblers and operators of these enterprises, a practice known as "loansharking." Before state governments started their own lotteries, poor and working people wagered small amounts of money on a combination of three numbers (1 to 999). Numbers runners collected bets, and mafia firms paid winners in the daily lottery. To guarantee fairness, the winning number was selected from an external source that could generate random numbers—for example, the last three digits of the closing figures for the New York Stock Exchange.[30] Naturally, mafia firms collected more money in bets than they paid out in prizes, though this operation required considerable capital in the event that large amounts had been placed on winning numbers. Mafia entrepreneurs and bookies also collected bets on horse races, an illegal form of gambling because state laws required that bets could only be made at the racetrack. Because many poor or working people could not attend the races, mafia firms collected their wagers and paid off winners. For gamblers who preferred games of chance, mafias operated backroom casinos, complete with roulette wheels and tables for blackjack, poker, or craps.

Of course, people who gambled needed money to wager, and people who operated gambling businesses—often as a concession awarded by mafias to non-mafia members (there were too many outlets for mafioso to staff directly)—needed capital to set up shop and pay out prizes. Because it was difficult for many people to borrow money from a bank for illegal purposes, mafias loaned money to gamblers and gaming operators at high interest rates, typically at 150 percent interest per year, but ranging as high as 1,000 percent per year.[31] Loan sharks also made loans to owners of small businesses or to people who could not obtain unsecured loans from banks. In Japan, for example, where it was extremely difficult for small businesses and consumers to obtain credit—before 1983, *legal* interest rates for consumer loans were as high as 110 percent annually—yakuza firms played a major role as creditors in Japan's forty-two thousand loansharking firms.[32]

In addition to gambling, mafia firms controlled prostitution and the trade in hard-core pornographic goods. Although mafias sometimes owned and operated brothels, prostitution was typically operated by others—brothel madams and streetwalker pimps—who ran their businesses as concessions and paid a percentage of their earnings to mafias for protection. For many years, the pornographic industry in the United States—the manufacture of hard-porn books, magazines, and films—was directly controlled by mafia firms. In Asia, triads and yakuza organized the sex tourist industries in the Philippines, Taiwan, and Thailand and supplied women to work in brothels, a practice called "trafficking in women" (see chapter 6).[33]

Finally, U.S. mafias have long trafficked in illegal drugs, alcohol in the 1920s and early 1930s, and heroin "as early as 1935," according to Gambetta.[34] Triads in China trafficked in opium during the nineteenth century and then heroin after it was first synthesized in 1898. In Japan, the use of opiates is uncommon, but the use of speed became common during World War II when it was discovered that the drug could keep weary soldiers awake.[35] After the war, the yakuza monopolized the illegal trade in amphetamines. Bandidos in Colombia began trafficking in marijuana during the 1960s and then cocaine in the 1970s. But while illegal drug trades provided an important source of revenue for some mafias prior to 1970s, most mafias around the world relied on protection and other vice industries to provide the bulk of their income. Income from illegal drugs remained relatively unimportant until recently because the demand for drugs was small, steady, and geographically confined. In the United States, heroin use was confined to large cities, located mostly on the East Coast and centered in New York City. The triads supplied the heroin market in Hong Kong, where the addict population was quite large, but not markets outside the colony. The yakuza dominated amphetamine markets in Japan, but there was little international trade in this drug. Colombian bandidos smuggled marijuana to U.S. markets, but cocaine use was confined primarily to consumers in the Andean region—in the 1960s it was too expensive for most consumers outside the region.

But the local character of regional mafias changed dramatically in the 1970s. The booming trade in illegal drugs after 1970 transformed regional mafias, turning them into global gangs.

GROWING DRUG SUPPLIES, RISING DEMAND

In 1970, in the War on Drugs, Nixon consolidated federal drug control efforts, increased their budgets, expanded drug treatment programs, which promoted the use of methadone as an alternative to heroin, persuaded the governments of Turkey and Mexico to eradicate illegal opium fields in their countries, and passed laws that made it easier to prosecute mafias and protect witnesses from mob retribution.[36] Nixon's war on illegal drugs was a response to mounting supplies of and to increased use of marijuana, heroin, and psychoactive drugs like LSD. Cocaine was also popular, but it was not yet widely used in 1970. Heroin was the chief target of Nixon's drug war because the number of heroin users had grown from perhaps fifty thousand in 1960 to five hundred thousand in 1970, a tenfold increase.[37] The number of heroin addicts remained steady for five years and then dropped sharply to perhaps two hundred thousand addicts at the end of the 1970s. Heroin use increased slowly in the 1980s, reaching five hundred thousand again in 1985, and then grew to seven hundred thousand by the end of the decade. During the 1990s, heroin use increased dramatically again, growing to between 1 million and 1.5 million users by 1995. The recent influx of cheap, pure, smokable heroin from the Golden Triangle may increase heroin use again, much as the advent of cheap, smokable "crack" dramatically increased cocaine use in the mid-1980s.

To understand these developments, it is necessary to look first at the rising supply of illegal drugs, focusing on heroin and cocaine, and then at the growing demand for illegal drugs in the United States.

Drug Supplies

Prior to 1970, most of the world's opium was grown in the Golden Crescent (Turkey, Iran, Afghanistan, Pakistan, and India). Some opium was also grown in the Golden Triangle (Burma, Laos, and Thailand), with a small amount harvested in Mexico.

Opium, the raw material for refined heroin, is grown in rugged and remote areas, where governments exercise little legal authority, either by fiercely independent mountain farmers (in the Golden Crescent and in Mexico) or by local warlords (in the Golden Triangle). In the Golden Triangle, nationalist Chinese army groups took refuge in Burma during the Chinese Civil War and raised opium to finance their remnant military forces.[38]

Coca leaf, the raw material for refined cocaine, is grown in the White Mountains (Peru, Bolivia, and Colombia). Independent peasant farmers grow about 90 percent of the world coca crop in just one country: Peru.

The opium and coca grown in all three regions are refined, processed, and transported to global drug markets by mafias. Historically, opium from the Golden Crescent has been controlled by Sicilian, French, and Italian American mafias; opium from the Golden Triangle has been dominated by Chinese triads based in Hong Kong and Taiwan; and, more recently, coca from the White Mountains has been refined and transported by Colombian bandidos who, during the 1970s, organized the cartels based in Medellin and Cali.

It is important to note that mafias do not grow the raw materials or sell the refined drugs on the street. Instead, they monopolize the refining and transport sectors, what might be called the manufacturing and wholesale business. They let independent peasants or local warlords produce the raw material and then let local street gangs retail the drugs, both fiercely competitive sectors where the risk of discovery and arrest are high. Mafias thus concentrate on the *most profitable* and *least risky* part of the business.

According to *The Economist*, farmers in Peru grow coca leaf, which sells for $2.10 per kilogram; local entrepreneurs then treat it with chemicals to produce a crude paste, which they can sell to the cartels for $875 per kilo. The cartels then refine it into a base and then into pure cocaine, which in 1980 sold for $60,000 per kilo and in 1990 for $10,000.[39] The cocaine is then sold to street-level retailers, usually gangs, who dilute or "cut" the cocaine, which they sold for $150,000 per kilo in 1980 and about $90,000 per kilo in 1990.[40]

The process of growing, refining, transporting, and selling heroin is almost identical.[41] Farmers make substantial profits, much more than can be made growing any other crop. If they process opium or coca leaf crudely, they can increase their investment 400 percent. Mafias that refine and transport the drugs can realize profits of 6,000 percent at 1980 prices, perhaps only 1,200 percent at 1990 prices, while street gang retailers mark up their goods between 100 and 800 percent. Although everyone earns substantial profits from the drug trade, mafia firms make the greatest gains, while taking the smallest risks.[42]

When we examine the supply of illegal drugs since World War II, three important developments stand out. First, the global supplies of opium-heroin and coca-cocaine have grown dramatically. In 1950, about five hundred tons of heroin were produced, most of it from the Golden Crescent. In 1970, about one thousand tons were produced, much of the increase coming from the Golden Triangle. Global heroin production remained fairly steady during the 1970s, then increased again during the 1980s, so that more than 3,500 tons were produced in 1990, a more than threefold increase, due primarily to increased production in the Golden Triangle. Between 1950 and 1990, world heroin production increased *seven*fold.[43]

Accurate estimates of illegal cocaine production prior to 1980 are difficult to obtain, but in 1980, some 220,000 acres of coca leaf were grown, producing 40 to 48 tons of cocaine. In 1989, 520,000 acres of coca were grown and between 350 to 400 tons of cocaine were produced, a *ten*fold increase.[44]

Second, the center of cultivation shifted from the Golden Crescent to the Golden Triangle during the 1970s and 1980s, a development that greatly affected the mafia refiners connected to opium growers in each region.

In 1970, Turkey was the world's largest opium producer, growing as much as 80 percent of the world total.[45] But President Nixon persuaded the Turkish government to launch a successful poppy eradication campaign that effectively ended Turkey's role as the world's premier supplier. Nixon also persuaded India and Mexico to do the same, though Mexico was then only a minor producer.[46] As a result, opium cultivation shifted to other regions in the Golden Crescent, with Afghanistan becoming a major producer along with Iran and Pakistan during the 1970s. But during the 1980s, a number of developments would shift the center of opium cultivation east to the Golden Triangle.

In 1979, the Islamic Revolution in Iran led to the overthrow of Shah Reza Pahlavi's government. The new Muslim government banned opium production and heroin use. In the same year, the Soviet Union invaded Afghanistan to support the communist government there. Revolution curtailed opium production in Iran and invasion curtailed it somewhat in Afghanistan, though mujahadeen rebels fighting the Soviet invaders allowed farmers to continue growing opium in regions under their control so that the proceeds of opium sales could be used to finance arms purchases and assist the war effort. During the 1980s, the number of domestic drug users in Afghanistan, Iran, and Pakistan grew dramatically. In Pakistan, there are now 1.5 million heroin users and another 2 million hashish and opium addicts.[47] Domestic heroin users are now consuming more opium than Pakistan produces. There are 1.2 million heroin addicts in Iran and 1 million more casual users, nearly 5 percent of the population.[48] Because domestic consumption has increased, these countries no longer export heroin.[49]

With opium producers in the Golden Crescent facing these difficulties, Golden Triangle producers stepped into the breech. Opium production and heroin processing in the Golden Triangle had increased dramatically in the 1960s and early 1970s, principally to supply a growing population of user-addicts in Vietnam: U.S. soldiers fighting in the war and Vietnamese civilians. But by 1975, U.S. troops had been withdrawn, and the communist government that came to power banned the import and use of opium and heroin. This meant that opium growers and heroin refiners had surplus supplies—as much as 50 percent of their supply was available for export. So they turned their attention to U.S. drug markets. In 1980, only 5 percent of the heroin sold in New York City originated in the Golden Triangle. But by 1990, triad importers of Golden Triangle heroin had captured 90 percent of the market in New York City, home to two hundred thousand addicts.[50]

Farmers in Afghanistan continued to grow opium in the 1990s. Then in 2000, the Taliban government banned opium production, which rapidly decreased from 4,4042 tons to only 81.6 tons.[51] But when the Taliban government fell, a result of U.S. bombing and ground attacks by the Northern Alliance in 2001, opium production resumed.[52] The new Northern Alliance government had long supported opium production in areas under its control, and farmers began planting opium because it was one of the few crops that could earn money in the war-torn economy.[53] One Afghan farmer earned $13,000 for his 2.5 acres of opium in 2000, "allowing him to feed 15 people in his extended family and buy two new oxen to plow his fields. If he had planted wheat and vegetables, he might have made $100."[54] Much of the opium produced in Afghanistan is exported to Iran and Pakistan and, increasingly, to Russia, where the mafiya distribute it.

Third, rising drug supplies led to falling street prices and increasing purity, which made it economical to develop cheap kinds of drugs that can expand consumer demand in new ways. This process occurred first with cocaine, more recently with heroin.

During the 1980s, world cocaine supplies grew rapidly, from 40 to 48 tons in 1980 to 350 to 400 tons in 1989. As supplies grew, the price dropped and the purity increased. Cocaine sold on the street increased from about 12 percent pure in 1980 to 60 to 80 percent in 1989. By 1985, it became economical to process cocaine one step further, creating a smokable, crystalline form of cocaine called "crack."[55]

The widespread availability of inexpensive crack opened new consumer markets and stimulated demand for the drug, particularly in low-income neighborhoods where cocaine had been prohibitively expensive. Because smokable crack is psychologically more addictive than powdered cocaine, and because it is cheap—"a single dose might cost only $10 or $15"—mafias were assured of steady repeat sales among relatively poor consumers.[56] Since 1985, the number of cocaine users has nearly quadrupled, from 500,000 to 1.8 million.[57]

While the demand for cocaine and then crack equaled and then surpassed that of heroin in the mid-1980s, the demand for heroin rose again in the 1990s, largely as a result of similar developments.

During the 1980s and early 1990s, heroin production increased dramatically, particularly in the Golden Triangle, where supplies increased from about 1,000 tons in 1980 to between 2,400 and 3,950 tons in 1990. Mounting global heroin supplies led to falling prices and increased purity of drugs sold on the street. By 1991, the street price of a single dose of heroin had dropped from $10 to $3. "They're lowering the price of a single dose and over time more people are going to get hooked," said Richard Calkins, a drug abuse official at the Michigan Department of Health.[58] In 1979, for example, the heroin packets sold to user-addicts contained only 3.6 percent heroin. the rest consisted of additives. But by 1990, the purity had increased to 40 to 60 percent, and by 1994 it had increased to nearly 90 percent.[59] Lower prices and increasing purity made it possible to introduce and sell a new, smokable form of heroin. (In the nineteenth century, people smoked raw *opium*, not processed *heroin*.) "Heroin is not only cheaper than it once was, it's cleaner, purer," said Joseph H. Califano, director of the Center for Addicts and Substance Abusers at Columbia University. "And too many young people think they can snort it and they won't get hooked."[60]

Like crack, smokable heroin may stimulate consumer demand and open new markets for the drug. Unlike crack, smokable heroin is *less* addictive than heroin that is injected. Because it can be consumed without using needles, it reduces the risk of contracting AIDS and other diseases such as hepatitis.[61] Because it is perceived as less addictive and safer, smokable heroin may become popular among populations that had previously shunned or avoided the drug. "When a drug like heroin becomes more available and more potent, you attract the swing market of 'garbage heads' who take whatever drugs they can find until they get hooked on something," observed Pete Pinto.[62]

Some evidence indicates that this has already occurred. The number of people treated in hospital emergency rooms for heroin use has tripled from 10,561 visits in 1985 to 30,800 visits in 1993.[63] Based on evidence that the heroin addict population numbered half a million in 1985 and that ten thousand users sought emergency room treatment, the increase in hospital admissions would indicate that the user population had grown to as many as 1.5 million by 1993. But because the purity of the drug also increased in this period, the growing number of hospital admissions may be due to the fact that users more frequently took overdoses with increasingly "rich" heroin. If that is the case, the number of heroin users may not be as large as emergency admissions would suggest, perhaps only one million addicts.[64] Still, the fact that heroin supplies are growing, prices are falling, purity is increasing, and demand is growing for smokable heroin suggests that the demand for heroin is likely to increase rapidly in coming years.

Consumer Demand

Although consumer demand for illegal drugs is extremely hard to measure with certainty, it is clear that drug use in the United States and other countries has fluctuated during this century. In the United States, where some attempt has been made to estimate demand, the use of illegal drugs generally *declined* during the first half of the century and *rose* during the second half.

In 1900, when heroin could be purchased legally, there were perhaps two hundred fifty thousand heroin user-addicts in the United States.[65] Government restrictions, which were followed by the prohibition of heroin and cocaine sales in the 1920s (and marijuana in the 1930s), and drug treatment programs effectively reduced the supply and increased the price of these drugs. So the addict population steadily declined during the 1920s and 1930s. Heroin use nearly vanished in the 1940s when the war prevented drug supplies from reaching consumers, resulting in what some writers describe as a "drug famine" in the United States and Europe.[66]

It is not entirely clear why drug use declined so dramatically during these decades. However, the rising cost of heroin and cocaine, along with falling incomes for most people during the Depression and the availability of treatment programs, may have discouraged users from seeking these drugs and forced them to consume cheaper drugs such as alcohol and tobacco.

After World War II, heroin once again became available, and the number of heroin users grew to perhaps twenty thousand in 1950 and then to fifty thousand in 1960. In the next decade, the number of heroin users grew by leaps and bounds, to about 250,000 in 1970 and 500,000 by 1975, a tenfold increase.[67]

The number of users actually fell by more than half during the late 1970s, from 500,000 to about 200,000 between 1976 and 1979.[68] This sharp decline, what some experts have called a "heroin drought," was probably a result of two developments. First, successful opium eradication campaigns in Turkey, India, and Mexico reduced supplies from traditional sources and increased the price of heroin in the United States. Second, it fell because addicts made use of widely available federal drug treatment programs and heroin substitutes, particularly methadone.[69]

But the number of heroin users began to climb again in the 1980s, returning to the 1975 level of 500,000 by 1985, and then continued to grow to 700,000 in 1990 and perhaps as many as 1.5 million by 1994.

Just as it is not clear why heroin use *declined* between 1900 and 1945, it is not clear why demand for the drug *increased* after the war. Nor is it clear why it increased so dramatically in the United States and not in other first world countries. As sociologist Elliott Curry notes:

> Most Americans do not realize how atypical we are . . . that the United States leads the world in drug abuse. . . . More people died in 1989 of the effects of cocaine abuse alone in Los Angeles than died of all drug-related causes in Holland, with 15 times the population. . . . The American drug problem continues to tower above those of the rest of the industrial world, and it does so despite an extraordinary experiment in punitive control.[70]

The demand for heroin and other drugs may have grown in the postwar period because consumption is *more* sensitive to the supply-price-purity of drugs than previously thought. Many analysts assume that heroin is extremely addictive, so they argue that the demand for the drug is "inelastic" or *un*responsive to changes in availability, price, or purity. But heroin may *not* be as addictive as many people have assumed. In 1988, U.S. Surgeon General C. Everett Koop said that nicotine was as addictive as heroin.[71] The National Institute of Drug Abuse reported that nicotine is "as addictive as heroin and 5 to 10 times more potent than cocaine or morphine in producing effects on mood or behavior."[72] This point is interesting because many tobacco smokers quit even though nicotine is an addictive drug. This suggests that heroin users may be able to quit more easily than many analysts have previously assumed. For example, among patients who were given heroin/morphine to treat painful illnesses, only a small percentage of them became addicted, and researchers reported that "there is a growing literature showing that [narcotics] can be used by patients for a long time, with few side effects, and that addiction and abuse are not a problem."[73]

If heroin use is both less addictive and more sensitive to supply-price-purity than many analysts have long assumed, then demand for the drug may have increased dramatically during the postwar period because heroin supplies have increased and prices have fallen. The big increase in demand for heroin, during the 1960s and again during the 1980s, came at times when heroin supplies increased rapidly, tripling in the 1960s and nearly quadrupling in the 1980s. The demand for heroin actually fell during the late 1970s, when the availability of heroin from traditional sources in Turkey and Mexico declined. Much the same was true of cocaine. Cocaine use expanded dramatically as the supply of the drug increased and prices fell during the 1980s. This suggests that the demand for drugs in the United States expanded in large part *because* heroin and cocaine became cheaper and more widely available. These drugs became more plentiful because drug producers and mafia refiners increased supplies and made determined efforts to sell their drugs in U.S. markets, where they could get higher prices than they could by selling drugs to relatively poor domestic consumers in the Golden Crescent, Golden Triangle, and White Mountains. Their efforts to produce, refine, and transport drugs to U.S. markets may explain why drug use is more widespread in the United States than in other first world countries. Mafias may have flooded the U.S. market to increase demand among consumers able to pay relatively high prices. They can and do sell drugs to poor domestic consumers, but the price they can get is lower than what even poor U.S. consumers can pay.

While a comprehensive explanation of the changing relation between the supply of and demand for illegal drugs is difficult to make, there is no doubt that both drug supplies and drug use have increased. And these developments had important consequences for countries where drugs are produced, for mafias that refine and transport drugs, and for countries were drugs are consumed.

SOCIAL CONSEQUENCES OF THE DRUG TRADE

The emergence of a global drug trade has created a variety of social problems for different groups in different settings. In drug-producing countries, opium and coca production has led to rising domestic drug use, environmental destruction, widespread corruption, and outright civil war between governments and mafias. For mafias that refine and trade drugs, the rise of Golden Triangle heroin controlled by Chinese triads and of White Mountain cocaine by Colombian cartels has contributed to the decline of the Italian American mafia, which had been weakened by changing government policies and new social developments in the 1970s and 1980s. Moreover, widespread drug use in countries such as the United States has led to the spread of crime and disease, murderous competition among street gangs for control of the retail trade, and rising economic costs associated with prosecuting and imprisoning drug users and dealers.

In drug-producing regions, the cultivation and processing of opium and coca have created three kinds of problems. First, the increasing availability of drugs in raw, semiprocessed, and refined forms has stimulated consumption by domestic users and spread AIDS. Although people in the Golden Crescent and Golden Triangle have long used opium, and peasants in the White Mountains have long chewed coca leaf, the number of users consuming semiprocessed drugs like *basuco* (a smokable cocaine paste) has grown substantially in recent years.[74] Heroin use has grown significantly in Thailand and even in China along the Myanmar border, where heroin use for many years had disappeared.[75] The U.S. State Department reported in 1985 that "40,000 to 50,000 Bolivians, 150,000 Peruvians, and more than 600,000 Colombians have 'serious' addiction problems."[76] Heroin use among young people in Russia has triggered the onset of an AIDS epidemic, as it has in Thailand.[77]

Second, the cultivation of drugs in some settings has contributed to environmental destruction. In Peru, for example, coca cultivation is centered in the upper Huallaga River valley, a mountainous rain forest region. Growers there have cleared 1.7 million acres of fragile rain forests for the crop, which is hard on the soil and contributes to soil erosion.[78] Farmers dump the chemical used to process coca leaf into coca paste into the valley's rivers. A Peruvian forest engineer estimated in 1987 that coca growers annually dump "15 million gallons of kerosene, 8 million gallons of sulphuric acid, 1.6 million gallons of acetone, 1.6 million gallons of the solvent toluene, 16,000 tons of lime and 3,200 tons of carbide" into the watershed.[79]

Drug-producing countries have also experienced a third problem: corruption, conflict, and civil war. These problems have been most evident in Colombia. After Colombia's president Virgilio Barco Vargas moved to seize mafioso property and permit the extradition of Colombian cartel leaders to the United States for trial, the mafias based in Medellin declared war on the government on August 25, 1989: "We declare absolute and total war on the government, on the industrial and political oligarchy, on the journalists that have attacked and ravaged us, on the judges that have sold out to the government, on the extraditing magistrates, on the presidents of the unions and all those who persecuted and attacked us."[80] The "Extraditables," led by drug lord Pablo Escobar, warned the government that the cartel would "not respect the families of those who have not respected our families."[81]

Prior to 1989, Colombian cartels had assassinated ministers of justices, police chiefs, attorney generals, political candidates, union organizers, and political leaders. Nearly three thousand died in cartel-directed violence in 1988 alone.[82] But their declaration of war in 1989 escalated the conflict between mafias and government officials and led to mafia kidnappings and assassinations of journalists and others. After twenty-two journalists were assassinated, many newspapers shut their offices and reporters fled into exile.[83] Escobar offered bounties for the murder of policemen, and three hundred policemen were subsequently killed.[84]

Although the government managed to trap and kill Escobar on a rooftop in December 1993, the mafias remained intact under new leadership, based now in Cali. The cartel forced the government to retreat from its promise to extradite mafioso to the United States, which had been their chief demand at the outset of the conflict.[85]

For mafias that refine and trade in drugs, the emergence of the Golden Triangle and the White Mountains as centers of global drug production has had important consequences, particularly in the United States. As the center of opium production shifted from the Golden Crescent to the Golden Triangle in the 1980s, and as the White Mountains became the center of coca production, the triad and cartel mafias that refined and transported heroin and cocaine from these two regions prospered. Meanwhile, the Sicilian and Italian American mafias that traded heroin from the Golden Crescent suffered. The decline of the Golden Crescent contributed to the decline of the U.S.-based mafia, which had been weakened by as series of other legal and social developments in the 1970s and 1980s. By 1990, the Italian American mafia based in the United States had been eclipsed by foreign triads and cartels.

The decline of domestic U.S. mafias can be attributed to three legal, social, and economic developments in the 1970s and 1080s.

First, state governments and private entrepreneurs began taking over the vice industries, which had long been the domestic mafia's main source of revenue. Recall that mafias relied on income from the gambling and sex industries. But in 1964, New Hampshire opened the country's first state-run lottery. Since then, states have legalized many forms of gambling to raise revenues without raising taxes. By 1992, thirty-seven states ran lotteries, which displaced the old, mafia-run numbers lotteries. Many states now permit casino gambling, and Indian tribes operate casinos on reservations in states that do not otherwise permit them. Several states operate off-track betting parlors for racing fans: New York went into the bookmaking business in 1971.[86]

As a result of the widespread *legalization* of gambling, a development that began slowly in the 1970s and accelerated in the 1980s, "gambling is now squarely in the American mainstream," said gambling industry consultant Eugene Christiansen.[87] "When the British legalized casinos in 1968, the purpose was to control organized crime," argued Jerome Skolnick.[88] In the United States the purpose was to raise revenue, but the result was much the same. In 1992, Americans wagered $329.9 billion, and state and local governments collected $29.9 billion in revenues, three times as much as they had in 1982, a figure "more than six times what people spent on movie tickets."[89]

With the growing public enthusiasm for legal and state-run gambling, interest in illegal mafia-run gambling has waned, and numbers lotteries, bookies, and backroom casinos have virtually disappeared.

Just as state governments and private corporations took over the gaming sector of the vice industry, *private* entrepreneurs have taken over much of the sex industry. During the 1970s, when the Supreme Court eased obscenity laws and state and local governments decriminalized some sexual acts between consenting adults, private entrepreneurs began producing sexually oriented magazines, books, and increasingly, videotapes that consumers could purchase and watch at home.[90] Independent female sex workers abandoned pimps and mafia-run brothels and began providing sexual services to consumers directly through underground newspapers and advertisements in the Yellow Pages. Sex workers even organized prostitutes' unions such as COYOTE (Cast Off Your Old, Tired Ethics) that lobbied for decriminalization and greater legal protection for sex industry workers.[91] The rise of widespread pornography on the internet and independent female sex workers eroded the role previously played by madams, pimps, and mafias, a development that greatly reduced mafia income from the sex industry.

Second, while legalization and decriminalization of traditional vice industries eroded the mafia's income base, the federal government adopted laws and programs that helped it prosecute mafias successfully. The cornerstone of the government's antimafia policy was the passage in 1970 of the Racketeer-Influenced and Corrupt Organizations Act (RICO). This law allowed federal attorneys to prosecute criminal organizations (not just individuals) and seize money, businesses, and property acquired through criminal activity.[92]

The government also began a witness protection program designed to protect informants and witnesses from mafia retribution. It took some years before attorneys were able to make use of RICO, but in the 1980s, aggressive federal attorneys like Rudolph Giuliani (later mayor of New York) used the statute to prosecute New York mafia families successfully.[93] Aggressive application of the law, and timely defections by key mafioso who agreed to become witnesses against other mafiosi, enabled federal prosecutors to convict dozens of leading mafiosi in the "Mob Commission," "Pizza Connection," and "Gambino Crime Family" trials. These prosecutions effectively decapitated U.S. mafia firms. As Guiliani claimed in 1987, "I do not believe that the Mafia, or La Cosa Nostra, will be an organization that means anything to anyone a decade from now . . . it is something that will be part of our history."[94]

By 1992, police investigators in Los Angeles described Italian American gangsters as the "Mickey Mouse Mafia," saying that the L.A. mob was so weak that "illegal book makers refuse to pay it for the right to operate."[95] In New Jersey, the head of the state police described local mafioso as the "Geritol Gang" because they had become so aged and ineffective.[96]

For the U.S. mafia, the problems associated with the transformation of the vice industries and aggressive government prosecution were compounded, in the 1980s, by a third problem: decreased heroin supplies from the Golden Crescent, a result of the 1979 revolution in Iran and the Soviet invasion of Afghanistan, had disrupted its traditional sources of opium. So while U.S. and Sicilian mafias scrambled for secure supplies, they faced increasing competition from triads selling heroin and cartels peddling cocaine in U.S. markets.

In this intermafia competition, foreign mafias possessed important advantages over domestic U.S. mafias. Foreign mafias were based close to drug supplies but far from U.S. government prosecutors. This meant they were better placed to obtain drugs and evade the law, particularly since government authority was weak in their host countries. They were also able to establish connections with young, aggressive street gangs based in U.S. immigrant communities: Vietnamese, Russian, Israeli, Jamaican, and Hispanic. When triads entered the New York heroin market in the 1980s, they used Chinese street gangs to retail the drug.[97] It was difficult for undercover New York City police to prosecute these organizations because few officers spoke Chinese dialects. So while foreign mafias could draw recruits from new immigrant communities, domestic mafias found it increasingly difficult to recruit from Italian neighborhoods, which were disappearing as a result of migration to the suburbs.[98]

These advantages, coupled with new, lower-priced drugs (a product of expanding drug cultivation), enabled foreign mafias to wrest control of lucrative U.S. drug markets from weakened domestic mafias. As the *New York Times* reported in 1991, "New York's five mafia families . . . have deteriorated in recent months to the point that three are virtually out of business and two are crumbling."[99] The state's task force on organized crime predicted that the families would be "reduced to the level of street gangs within a decade."[100]

Although no one bemoans the disappearance of domestic U.S. mafias, the rise of foreign mafias means that law enforcement efforts will be less effective in coming years than they were in the 1980s.

The growing consumption of illegal drugs has also contributed to three kinds of problems in the United States. First, illegal drug use contributes to crime and the spread of disease. Although the price of heroin and cocaine fell during the

1980s, they were still relatively expensive, which meant that many users and addicts committed crimes to raise money to purchase drugs. A 1972 Ford Foundation study found that prostitution provided 30.8 percent, shoplifting 22.6 percent and burglary 19 percent of the funds raised by heroin addicts to purchase drugs, though the author noted that male addicts often sold heroin to defray costs and female addicts relied most heavily on prostitution to earn the money they needed.[101] Another Ford Foundation study estimated that "up to 50 percent of property crimes in the major metropolitan areas with a serious heroin problem are committed by addicts."[102] As a result, rising drug use helped drive up crime rates in the past thirty years.

Heroin use also contributed to the spread of disease in the 1980s. Because some heroin addicts work as prostitutes and/or share the needles used to inject the drug, the AIDS virus spread rapidly among heroin users, prostitutes, and their customers during the 1980s. In New York City, 4 to 7 percent of intravenous drug users contract AIDS every year, which means that between forty thousand and seventy thousand contracted AIDS in the 1980s.[103]

Second, street gangs have engaged in a murderous competition for control of the retail drug trade. The violence grew dramatically during the late 1980s as street gangs vied for control of the newly opening crack trade. In Washington, D.C., more than 80 percent of all homicides in 1989 were drug related, and residents of that city were more likely to be killed than people living in Northern Ireland, the Punjab, Lebanon, or El Salvador, places where civil wars then raged.[104] Although drug-related violence abated somewhat in the 1990s, violence had become so common among street gangs that they referred to young street dealers as "Dixie Cups, because they are so disposable," said New York District Attorney Walter Arsenault.[105]

Third, the crime and violence associated with the consumption and the trade in illegal drugs has created a variety of problems for federal, state, and local government officials. As officials intensified antidrug campaigns, they passed stiffer laws that led to more arrests. Between 1980 and 1989, drug arrests increased 105 percent.[106] But drug-related arrests clogged the courts and prisons. In California, the prison population quintupled from "20,000 in 1979 to over 100,000 in early 1991—roughly the number behind bars in Great Britain and West Germany combined . . . [and] more men are now in prison for drug offenses than were behind bars for all [other] crimes in 1980."[107] By 1995, nearly 70 percent of federal inmates were drug offenders.[108]

Growing prison populations led to increased prison construction, an expensive undertaking. Federal spending on the drug war grew to $13 billion in 1993, and states spent an additional $18 billion on enforcement and $20 billion for new prisons.[109]

Gender, Mafia, Drugs, and Sex

Mafias the world over admit men but exclude women. Mafias might be regarded as radical or extremist patriarchies, because they are so gender-identified.

Because these male fraternities (there are no female, sorority counterparts) use violence to create and maintain vice and drug monopolies, women are greatly disadvantaged where mafias are strong. Historically, mafia patriarchies have developed and profited from pornography, the sex industry, and the trafficking in women (see chapter 6). Where men with guns organize violent criminal enterprises, women become extremely vulnerable to their depredations. As poor Peruvian coca farmers discovered, "Cocaine traffickers abused the young women, and prostitutes who came from far and wide broke up families.[110]

Drug use has rather different consequences for men and women. Male drug users typically turn to robbery, burglary, and shoplifting to earn the money they need to purchase drugs. Female drug users often turn to prostitution to earn money. As prostitutes, they are vulnerable to extortion by male pimps and pushers who seek to profit from *both* their addiction and their trade. Of course, female and male drug users risk contracting AIDS and other diseases, either from sharing needles or from having sex, and this can spread the disease to people, male and female, who do *not* themselves use drugs.

Of course, young men are also disadvantaged by participation in mafia industries. Young men who work in retail drug sales on the streets risk violent death at the hands of competitors. In the United States, the violent deaths of African American and Hispanic youth (the "Dixie Cups") increased male mortality rates significantly in the 1980s. And if young men in the retail drug trades do not die on the streets, they risk jail, where violent male fraternities are often organized by mafia-connected inmates.

ASSESSING THE WAR ON DRUGS

Frustrated by these developments, some government officials have argued that drug use should be decriminalized or legalized under controlled circumstances. In 1993, U.S. Surgeon General Joycelyn Elders recommended that the government should study the idea of legalizing drugs because, she said, "I do feel that we would markedly reduce our crime rate if drugs were legalized."[111] Some federal judges have also called for the legalization of marijuana, heroin, and crack cocaine, arguing that the war on illicit drugs was "bankrupt" and was overwhelming the courts and prison system.[112] But most U.S. government officials oppose legalization, a view that has wide public support. As an alternative, some officials have urged the expansion of drug treatment, methadone maintenance, and needle swap programs.[113]

Historically, a number of policies have been effective against *mafias*, though not necessarily against drug use. The legalization of alcohol greatly reduced the power of mafias who prospered from the illegal trade during Prohibition. The government's restrictions on machine gun ownership took the dangerous .45-caliber Browning submachine gun out of circulation for many years, until the advent of new small-caliber, assault-rifle technologies put dangerous weapons back into circulation. The takeover of the vice industries—gambling by state governments and private corporations, pornography and prostitution by independent entrepreneurs and female sex workers—reduced mafia income sources and decreased much of the violence and coercion associated with mafia-run enterprises. The adoption of RICO and witness protection programs proved to be effective legal tools against domestic mafia firms. Overseas, the opium eradication campaigns in Turkey and Mexico were relatively successful, though production shifted to other regions. Antidrug campaigns in some countries have sometimes been effective, though their success depended on fairly draconian measures by revolutionary governments and Muslim revolutions in Iran and Afghanistan, and communist governments in China, and Vietnam.

But while these measures have undermined mafias and reduced the crime and violence associated with mafias and the vice industry, they did not greatly reduce *drug use*. Indeed, alcohol consumption increased after Prohibition, though alcohol consumption is now lower on average than it was at the beginning of the century. Marijuana is a good example of how decriminalization curbed *mafia violence* but also *increased drug use*.

In the 1960s, most of the marijuana consumed in the United States was cultivated in Mexico, Colombia, Jamaica, and Thailand and imported by foreign mafias, principally Mexican. Unlike heroin or cocaine, marijuana was not processed by mafia importers. Indeed, marijuana sold on U.S. streets contained seeds and stems that had to be cleaned out by consumers. During the 1970s, U.S. consumers began cultivating and hybridizing marijuana using seeds obtained from foreign imports. Growers in northern California developed new, more potent hybrid varieties, called "sensimilla" because they were "without seeds," that quickly captured a growing share of the U.S. market.

The widespread cultivation of hybrid marijuana by independent U.S. growers and the sale of the drug through networks of small-scale dealers—a development made possible by the decriminalization of marijuana possession in many states during the 1970s—greatly reduced demand for foreign marijuana and diminished the role of mafias in the trade. Consequently, there is little of the violence associated with the cultivation, trade, and use of marijuana that is seen with other illegal drugs.

But while little violence is associated with the marijuana trade, there is extensive marijuana *use*. Marijuana consumption rose in the 1960s and 1970s, declined somewhat in the mid- to late 1980s, and then rose again in the 1990s.[114] Moreover, the marijuana consumed by smokers today is much more potent, and more expensive, than the cheap, weak imports consumed in the 1960s. According to one federal study, the amount of THC (tetrahydrocannabinol, the active ingredient in marijuana) in the average joint increased every year after 1973, from 0.2 percent in 1972 to 3.6 percent in 1988.[115] If a joint of marijuana had the potency of a can of beer in the 1960s, it had the potency of whisky today.

To a large extent, governments face two related problems. If they want to curb drug use by making it illegal, they create a role for mafia firms and contribute to crime and violence. If they want to curb the role of mafias and reduce the crime and violence associated with the illegal drug trade, they may contribute to increased drug use, though determined public education and drug treatment programs can sometimes reduce drug use over a long period of time.

Both strategies have important social costs. On the one hand, laws criminalizing drug use have led, in the 1970s and 1980s, to the emergence of powerful, violent, and wealthy global mafias. UN Secretary-General Boutros Boutros-Ghali warned in 1994:

> Organized crime has become a world phenomenon. In Europe, in Asia, in Africa and in America, the forces of darkness are at work and no society is spared. Transnational crime undermines the very foundations of the international democratic order. It poisons the business climate, corrupts political leaders and undermines human rights.[116]

On the other hand, the continued or increased use of powerful drugs would have important consequences for consumers and societies. Drug users risk death and disease, and addictions can adversely affect individual behavior. The cost of treating or addressing the medical and social consequences of individual addiction can be high, as society has discovered with widespread alcohol and tobacco use.

The problem for government officials in coming years is to address both problems simultaneously, keeping in mind that efforts to address one problem may contribute to the other.

NOTES

1. Joseph B. Treaster, "20 Years of War on Drugs, and No Victory Yet," *New York Times*, June 14, 1992.

2. Eric Hobsbawm, *Primitive Rebels: Studies in Archaic Forms of Social Movement in the 19th and 20th Centuries* (New York: Praeger, 1963), 36–37; Diego Gambetta, *The Sicilian Mafia: The Business of Private Protection* (Cambridge, Mass.: Harvard University Press, 1993), 136.

3. Gambetta, *The Sicilian Mafia*, 1.

4. Gambetta, *The Sicilian Mafia*, 2.

5. Pino Arlacci, *Mafia Business: The Mafia Ethic and the Spirit of Capitalism* (London: Verso, 1986), 9.

6. Arlacci, *Mafia Business*, 4, 3.

7. Hobsbawm, *Primitive Rebels*, 33; Arlacci, *Mafia Business*, 44.

8. Hobsbawm, *Primitive Rebels*, 33–34; Arlacci, *Mafia Business*, 44, 138.

9. Annelise G. Anderson, *The Business of Organized Crime: A Cosa Nostra Family* (Stanford, Calif.: Hoover Institution Press, 1979), 12; David H. Stark, "The Yakuza: Japanese Crime Incorporated," Ph.D. diss., University of Michigan (Ann Arbor: University Microfilms, 1981), 237.

10. David Ownby and Mary Somers, eds., *Secret Societies Reconsidered: Perspectives on the Social History of Modern South China and Southeast Asia* (Armonk, N.Y.: Sharpe, 1993), 4.

11. Gerald P. Posner, *Warlords of Crime: Chinese Secret Societies—The New Mafia* (New York: McGraw Hill, 1988), 31.

12. Dian Murray, "Migration, Protection and Racketeering: The Spread of the Tiandihui within China," in *Secret Societies Reconsidered*, 181; Fenton Bresler, *The Chinese Mafia* (New York: Stein & Day, 1981), 29.

13. Bresler, *The Chinese Mafia*, 27–28.

14. Bresler, *The Chinese Mafia*, 30.

15. Bresler, *The Chinese Mafia*, 30.

16. Posner, *Warlords of Crime*, 34.

17. Posner, *Warlords of Crime*, 40.

18. Posner, *Warlords of Crime*, 40–41.

19. David E. Kaplan and Alex Dubro, *Yakuza: The Explosive Account of Japan's Criminal Underworld* (Reading, Mass.: Addison-Wesley, 1986), 214.

20. Kaplan and Dubro, *Yakuza*, 141.

21. Kaplan and Dubro, *Yakuza*, 18.

22. Kaplan and Dubro, *Yakuza*, 24; Stark, "The Yakuza," 27.

23. Kaplan and Dubro, *Yakuza*, 28–29.

24. Stark, "The Yakuza," 110–11.

25. Stark, "The Yakuza," 35, 36.

26. Stark, "The Yakuza," 56, 232–33; Kaplan and Dubro, *Yakuza*, 6, 146.

27. Arlacci, *Mafia Business*, 222.

28. Arlacci, *Mafia Business*, 219.

29. Arlacci, *Mafia Business*, 131.

30. Arlacci, *Mafia Business*, 56.

31. Anderson, *The Business of Organized Crime*, 65.

32. Kaplan and Dubro, *Yakuza*, 167–68.

33. Kaplan and Dubro, *Yakuza*, 203.

34. Gambetta, *The Sicilian Mafia*, 234.

35. Posner, *Warlords of Crime*, 76.

36. Daniel Musto, *The American Disease: Origins of Narcotic Control* (Oxford: Oxford University Press, 1987), 254–58.

37. Musto, *The American Disease*, 254.

38. Keith B. Richburg, "From Fighting Mao to Tending Opium Gardens," *Washington Post*, June 13, 1988.

39. Peter Andreas and Coletta Youngers, "U.S. Drug Policy and the Andean Cocaine Industry," *World Policy Journal* (Summer 1989): 535; Mathea Falco, "Foreign Drugs, Foreign Wars," in "Political Pharmacology: Thinking about Drugs" (special issue), *Daedalus* 121, no. 3 (Summer 1992): 4.

40. "The Kickback from Cocaine," *The Economist*, July 21, 1990, 40; Falco, "Foreign Drugs, Foreign Wars," 8.

41. John F. Holahan, "The Economics of Heroin," in *Dealing with Drug Abuse: A Report to the Ford Foundation*, ed. Patricia Wald and Peter Hutt (New York: Praeger, 1972), 261, 270; Arlacci, *Mafia Business*, 194.

42. Holahan, "The Economics of Heroin," 272.

43. Posner, *Warlords of Crime*, 72, 74, 77, 26; Peter Lintner, "A Fix in the Making," *Far Eastern Economic Review*, June 28, 1990, 20; Elaine Sciolino, "U.S. Finds Output of Drugs in World Growing Slowly," *New York Times*, March 2, 1988; Elaine Sciolino, "World Drug Crop Up Sharply in 1989 Despite U.S. Effort," *New York Times*, March 2, 1990; Arlacci, *Mafia Business*, 187–88, 215–16; George Winslow, "Credibility a Casualty in the War on Drugs," *In These Times*, May 12–23, 1989, 19; Alfred W. McCoy, *The Politics of Heroin in Southeast Asia* (N.Y.: Harper and Row, 1972), 78, 1, 354; Holahan, "The Economics of Heroin," 259; Bresler, *The Chinese Mafia*, 2–3.

44. Gustavo A. Gorriti, "How to Fight the Drug War," *Atlantic Monthly* (July 1989): 70.

45. Holahan, "The Economics of Heroin," 256–57, 258, 262.

46. Holahan, "The Economics of Heroin," 265.

47. Barry Bearak, "Adding to Pakistan's Misery: Million-Plus Heroin Addicts," *New York Times*, April 19, 2000.

48. Neil Farquhar, "Iran Shifts War Against Drugs, Admitting It Has Huge Problem," *New York Times*, April 5, 1995.

49. Falco, "Foreign Drugs, Foreign Wars," 10; Sciolino, "U.S. Finds Output"; "The Quality of Mercy," *The Economist*, July 22, 1989, 48; Katayon Ghazi, "Drug Trafficking Is Thriving in Iran," *New York Times*, December 4, 1991.

50. Steven Erlanger, "Burma's Unrest and Weather Help Opium Flourish," *New York Times*, December 11, 1988.

51. Barbara Crossette, "Afghan Ban on Poppies Is Convulsing Opium Market," *New York Times*, June 13, 2001.

52. Tim Golden, "Afghan Ban on Growing Opium Is Unraveling," *New York Times*, October 22, 2001.

53. Barry Meier, "Most Afghan Opium Grown in Rebel-Controlled Areas," *New York Times*, October 5, 2001.

54. Tim Weiner, "With Taliban Gone, Opium Farmers Return to Their Only Cash Crop," *New York Times*, November 26, 2001.

55. Alan Riding, "Colombian Cocaine Dealers Tap European Market," *New York Times*, April 29, 1989; Musto, *The American Disease*, 274; Richard L. Berke, "After Studying for War on Drugs, Bennett Wants More Troops," *New York Times*, August 6, 1989.

56. Jerome H. Skolnick, "Rethinking the Drug Problem," in *Crisis in American Institutions*, ed. Jerome H. Skolnick and Elliott Currie (New York: HarperCollins, 1994), 444; Musto, *The American Disease*, 274.

57. Scott B. MacDonald, *Dancing on a Volcano: The Latin American Drug Trade* (New York: Praeger, 1988), 3; "Drugs: How to Beat Them," *The Economist*, August 12, 1989, 20.

58. Joseph B. Treaster, "A More Potent Heroin Makes a Comeback in a New, Needleless Form," *New York Times*, April 28, 1991.

59. Treaster, "A More Potent Heroin."

60. Evelyn Nieves, "Heroin, an Old Nemesis, Makes an Encore," *New York Times*, January 9, 2001.

61. Joseph B. Treaster,. "To Avoid AIDS, Users of Heroin Shift from Injecting It to Inhaling It," *New York Times*, November 17, 1991.

62. Treaster, "A More Potent Heroin."

63. Trip Gabriel, "Heroin Finds a New Market along Cutting Edge of Style," *New York Times*, May 8, 1994.

64. Nieves, "Heroin, an Old Nemesis."

65. Musto, *The American Disease*, 5.

66. McCoy, *The Politics of Heroin*, 87, 24, 6, 16.

67. Wald and Hutt, *Dealing with Drug Abuse*, 4.

68. Falco, "Foreign Drugs, Foreign Wars," 2.

69. Peter Reuter, "Can Domestic Sources Substitute for Imported Drugs?" in *Drug Policy in the Americas*, ed. Peter H. Smith (Boulder, Colo.: Westview, 1992), 168.

70. Elliott Currie, *Reckoning: Drugs, the Cities and the American Future* (New York: Hill & Wang, 1993), 10, 12, 33.

71. Melinda Henneberger, "'Pot' Surges Back, but It's, Like, a Whole New World," *New York Times*, February 6, 1994.

72. "Addiction by Design," *New York Times*, March 6, 1994.

73. Elisabeth Rosenthal, "Patients in Pain Find Relief, Not Addiction, in Narcotics," *New York Times*, March 28, 1992.

74. MacDonald, *Dancing on a Volcano*, 4.

75. Nicholas D. Kristof, "Heroin Use Spreads in China among the Curious or Bored," *New York Times*, March 20, 1991.

76. MacDonald, *Dancing on a Volcano*, 4.

77. Michael Wines, "Heroin Carries AIDS to a Region in Siberia," *New York Times*, April 24, 2000.

78. James Brooke, "Peruvian Farmers Razing Rainforest to Sow Drug Crops," *New York Times*, August 13, 1989.

79. Brooke, "Peruvian Farmers"; Peter Dale Scott and Jonathan Marshall, *Cocaine Politics: Drugs, Armies and the CIA in Central America* (Berkeley: University of California Press, 1991), 74; Elena Alvarez, "Coca Production in Peru," in *Drug Policy in the Americas*, 83.

80. Kristof, "Heroin Use Spreads."

81. James Brooke, "Drug Traffickers in Colombia Start a Counterattack," *New York Times*, August 25, 1989.

82. Andreas and Youngers, "U.S. Drug Policy," 538; James Brooke, "Drugs and Terror Linked in Colombia," *New York Times*, April 6, 1989; Alma Guillermoprieto, "Exit El Patron," *New Yorker*, October 25, 1993, 79.

83. James Brooke, "Colombian Kidnappings are Gagging the Press," *New York Times*, January 28, 1991; James Brooke, "Colombian Abductions a Sign of Continuing Drug War," *New York Times*, September 23, 1990.

84. James Brooke, "Vigilantes Cut Murder Rate in Colombian Cocaine Center," *New York Times*, February 15, 1992.

85. Smith, *Drug Policy in the Americas*, 1; Felipe E. MacGregor, *Coca and Cocaine: An Andean Perspective* (Westport, Conn.: Greenwood, 1993), 46; Steven Gutkin, "Colombia Called 'Narco-Democracy,'" *San Francisco Chronicle*, October 1, 1994.

86. John Tierney, "For New York City's OTB, a Sure Bet Ends Up a Loser," *New*

York Times, November 14, 1994; Francis X. Clines, "Gambling, Pariah No More, Is Booming across America," *New York Times*, December 5, 1993.

87. Tierney, "For New York City's OTB"; Clines, "Gambling."

88. Skolnick and Currie, *Crisis in American Institutions*, 442.

89. N. R. Kleinfield, "Legal Gambling Faces Higher Odds," *New York Times*, August 29, 1993.

90. Valerie Jenness, *Making It Work: The Prostitutes' Rights Movement in Perspective* (New York: Aldine de Gruyter, 1993), 24–25; Richard Sandza, "Going after a Porn Czar," *Newsweek*, August 8, 1988.

91. Jenness, *Making It Work*, 2–6, 18–19.

92. Holahan, "The Economics of Heroin," 182.

93. John H. Davis, *Mafia Dynasty: The Rise and Fall of the Gambino Crime Family* (New York: HarperCollins, 1993), 183.

94. Michael Oreskes, "Guiliani Says Mafia is Dying under Prosecution," *New York Times*, March 3, 1987; Ralph Blumenthal, "Verdict Is Termed a Blow to the Mafia," *New York Times*, November 20, 1986.

95. "Mafia Prosecutors Quitting as Strike Forces Disband," *New York Times*, January 4, 1990.

96. "Mafia Prosecutors Quitting."

97. John Kifner, "New Immigrant Wave from Asia Gives the Underworld New Faces," *New York Times*, January 5, 1991.

98. Arlacci, *Mafia Business*, 227.

99. "Mafia Prosecutors Quitting."

100. "Mafia Prosecutors Quitting."

101. Holahan, "The Economics of Heroin," 292, 289–90.

102. Wald and Hutt, *Dealing with Drug Abuse,* 6.

103. Felicia R. Lee, "Data Show Needle Exchange Curbs HIV among Addicts," *New York Times*, November 26, 1994.

104. Richard L. Berke, "Capitol Offers Unlimited Turf to Drug Dealers," *New York Times*, March 28, 1989; "Uncivil Wars," *The Economist*, October 7, 1989, 38.

105. "Ganging Up on the Gangs," *New Yorker*, October 10, 1994, 44.

106. Currie, *Reckoning*, 14–15; Jerri A. Husch, "Culture and U.S. Drug Policy: Toward a New Conceptual Framework," in *Daedalus* special issue, "Political Pharmacology: Thinking about Drugs," 268.

107. Currie, *Reckoning*, 16.

108. James M. Blansfield, "What Legalizing Drugs Would Mean," *New York Times*, December 28, 1993.

109. David Moberg, "Codependence," *In These Times*, December 27, 1993, 24.

110. Clifford Krauss, "Desperate Farmers Imperil Peru's Fight Against Coca," *New York Times,* February 23, 2001.

111. Stephen Labaton, "Surgeon General Suggests Study of Legalizing Drugs," *New York Times*, December 8, 1993.

112. Stephen Labaton, "Federal Judge Urges Legalization of Crack, Heroin and Other Drugs," *New York Times*, December 13, 1989; Jack B. Weinstein, "The War on Drugs Is Self-Defeating," *New York Times*, July 8, 1993.

113. Michael Massing, "Help Addicts? Sure. We Promise. Really!" *New York Times*,

October 22, 1993; Lawrence K. Altman, "U.S. to Ease Methadone Rules in Bid to Curb AIDS in Addicts," *New York Times*, March 3, 1989; Steven A. Holmes, "Treasury Imposes New Regulations on Some Shotguns," *New York Times*, March 1, 1994; Lee, "Data Show."

    114. Henneberger, "'Pot' Surges Back."

    115. Reuter, "Can Domestic Sources Substitute," 172–73.

    116. Rosenthal, "Patients in Pain."

Index

About the Author

For many years, **Robert Schaeffer** worked as a journalist and an editor for Friends of the Earth, *In These Times*, *Nuclear Times*, and *Greenpeace Magazine*. He is now professor of sociology at Kansas State University. He participates in Pugwash Conferences on Science and World Affairs, which in 1995 won the Nobel Peace Prize. He is the editor of *War in the World-System* (1990), author of *Power to the People: Democratization around the World* (1997) and *Severed States: Dilemmas of Democracy in a Divided World* (1999), and coauthor, with Torry Dickinson, of *Fast Forward: Work, Gender, and Protest in a Changing World* (2001).